Banking on the Body

Banking on the Body

THE MARKET IN BLOOD, MILK, AND SPERM
IN MODERN AMERICA

Kara W. Swanson

Harvard University Press

Cambridge, Massachusetts, and
London, England
2014

To Wati, my sine qua non

Contents

Banking on the Body

Banking for Love and for Money

The term "blood bank" is not a mere metaphor.

—Dr. Bernard Fantus, 1938

In 2008 Connie Culp became the first American woman to undergo a face transplant, receiving the mouth, nose, and cheeks of a dead woman. The victim of a shotgun blast fired by her husband, Culp had been severely disfigured, missing both her nose and the roof of her mouth. After the surgery, she could talk, smile, and smell again, in a dramatic transformation of both her appearance and her quality of life. Her transplant, and earlier face transplants performed in France and China, transformed not only the recipients but all human faces.[1] What the ancient Romans knew as "the reflection of the soul," the face is now a body product that can be harvested from one body for use by another.[2]

The novel conception of our faces as items to be passed along to new owners heightened the public interest in Culp's saga of recovery. This transformation of the face, however, is only a recent example of a process that has been occurring to our bodies for over a century. Since treating accident victims with skin grafts at the turn of the twentieth century, surgeons have sought new ways of healing the sick and injured by replacing ever more body parts. The body that supplied Culp's new face was also the source of body parts for more than fifty other strangers whose surgical repairs were considered so routine that they were not reported by the media.[3]

While Culp's new look was the result of a groundbreaking procedure at the frontiers of medicine, since the 1950s doctors have been successfully transplanting kidneys, hearts, lungs, and livers.[4] On the western frontier of the nineteenth-century United States, pioneers staked their claims to homesteads acre by acre, incorporating land long used by Native Americans into the Anglo-American system of property. On the medical frontier of the twentieth and twenty-first centuries, it is the human body that is the natural resource available for development part by part. Through medical efforts to heal the sick, the human body has become a source of property and value, as well as a source of hope to the dying and the disfigured. Over time this transformation of the body has come to be understood as a mixed blessing. Miraculous recoveries like Culp's are celebrated; the specter of body parts sold to the highest bidder is deplored.[5] Over a century after it first became a reality, property in the human body is a troubled concept in law and society.

A New Look at an Old Problem

In order to understand this troubled concept, this book looks beyond headline-making transplants to the taken-for-granted use of body products that permeates modern medicine and makes such medical experimentation possible. Although Culp did not learn the identity of her donor until over a year after the transplant, Culp's face was a gift from the family of Anna Kasper, who made the decision to donate body parts from their wife and mother to strangers.[6] The altruism of the Kasper family could benefit Connie Culp and fifty other patients who received parts of Anna's body only because doctors had access to blood banks.

In the twenty-first century, thousands of times each day, stored blood from one person is taken from a hospital bank and transfused into the veins of a stranger.[7] Organized inventories of renewable body products, usually called "banks," are ubiquitous and familiar. If we have not received blood as patients, we may have given it as donors, responding to the appeal of a bloodmobile arriving at our workplace or campus. While blood banks are the most common type of body bank, there are others. Each day, women and men wishing to be parents are looking through online sperm bank catalogues, picking out potential biological fathers for their hoped-for children. In neonatal intensive care units, fragile premature infants are fed with milk provided by women who will never see them, the milk supply organized by community milk banks. A century ago body banks were at the frontier of transforming the body into property in the United States, and it is through experience with the body bank that Americans came to understand property in the human body. By examining the history of the first body products to be banked—human milk, blood, and semen—this book explains how bodies came to be understood as sources of property and, in particular, the unexpected consequences of using the term *bank* to explain body property exchange, a term that has straitjacketed American thinking about body products and markets.

Despite triumphs such as Culp's smiling new face, not all stories of body products end happily. While banked blood is generally available in emergency rooms across the United States, each year thousands of Americans die waiting for a kidney transplant, with deeply disturbing race and class disparities in the allocation of these scarce body products.[8] In the United States federal law prohibits buying and selling many nonrenewable body products; they are property that can be given from one possessor to another for love but not for money. The National Organ Transplant Act, passed in 1984, makes it illegal to "acquire, receive, or otherwise transfer any human organ for valuable consideration for use in human transplantation."[9] Kasper's family could not receive any compensation for her body parts, even if they lacked the resources to bury their mother and wife or to pay her last medical bills. This prohibition is creating a growing imbalance between demand and supply, as organ procurement organizations cannot find sufficient donors for love nor money. Each year more people are added to the list of potential recipients waiting for organs than organs are made available for transplant.[10]

This same law has also stymied efforts to use innovative approaches to increase the number and racial diversity of bone marrow donors, because bone marrow is legally defined as an organ. Currently, while 75 percent of European Americans can find a bone marrow donor through the national donor registry, only 25 percent of African Americans can find a genetic match, and the odds lengthen for people of mixed racial heritage.[11] When moremarrowdonors .org, a nonprofit corporation, sought to offer $3,000 rewards to donors in the form of scholarships, housing allowances, and the ability to direct charitable donations, it filed a lawsuit seeking to overturn the legal ban on compensation, arguing that "kindness was not enough," as thousands of patients die each year, unable to receive a bone marrow donation.[12] The organization won a narrow victory without a legal ruling on their argument about the insufficiency of kindness to solve allocation inequities.[13]

In the realm of reproductive medicine, where since 1984 donor eggs have been used to create embryos through in vitro fertilization, the sale of eggs is permitted but controversial.[14] The American Society for Reproductive Medicine has asked its members to adhere to a voluntary cap on compensation to egg donors of $5,000, which has been challenged in court by donors who would prefer less love and more money and think that the market should determine the level of compensation they receive.[15]

In the early twenty-first century, in both law and society, Americans divide most body product exchanges into two categories: exchanges for love, that is, gifts, which we consider pure and good, and exchanges for money, that is, sales, which we consider tainted and bad. Whether the supplier is or can be paid is believed to matter in significant ways. As the founders of moremarrowdonors.org and many Americans in need of transplants have discovered, this sharp either/or division between gifts and sales, while easy to explain and easy to write into law, has painful consequences in lives lost and in injustice. Outlawing markets in greatly desired body parts, like kidneys, has not prevented international gray markets from filling the need, further exacerbating injustices. More poor people and socially disadvantaged people, including a disproportionate number of racial minorities, are suppliers, and more rich people are recipients. Refusing to acknowledge markets in body parts has not stopped market allocation of these medical therapeutics.[16]

In order to understand this harmful and limiting dichotomy in our thinking about body products, we need to return to the history of body banks. At the origins of the transformation of the body into a source of harvestable property, *bank* was chosen as a metaphor for understanding body product exchange. This term, borrowed from financial banking and redolent with implications of markets and cash flows, created the context in which Americans learned to think about body products and in which we developed our contemporary laws governing property in the human body. Understanding body products through the body bank has created unforeseen consequences that need to be addressed as we continue to rely on body products on the frontiers of medicine.

Body Banking

When and why did Americans start using the terms *bank* and *banking* to apply to human body parts, and how has the experience of body banking shaped our current legal and lay understanding of body products? The *when* is the simplest question to answer. In 1937 Dr. Bernard Fantus, working at Cook County Hospital in Chicago, borrowed the term *bank* from the world of finance to describe the organization of stored blood in his hospital, which he sought to manage like money in the bank. His term stuck, as doctors across the country quickly moved to set up their own blood banks and then began to use the term to describe the management of other body products. To understand why *bank* became the dominant metaphor for body part exchange and how this metaphor shaped legal and lay understanding, this history follows the first body products to be banked in an organized and widespread way, that is, blood, breast milk, and semen, from the nineteenth-century experiments that made such medical therapeutics possible to the twenty-first-century websites that facilitate body product exchanges.

Doctors are the main actors in this history because body products have been created and banked in order to solve medical problems. From their Progressive-era origins to the present, these products have been bought and sold for medical purposes. As one early twentieth-century doctor described banked human milk, body products are "therapeutic merchandise."[17] This history is thus a medical history, analyzing the decisions of individual doctors treating patients and the collective action of medical societies seeking to advance professional goals, as traced through the medical literature, popular press accounts, and, when possible, the papers and records of individual doctors, hospitals, and body banks. Each new body product depended, like Culp's face transplant, on doctors willing to push the boundaries on behalf of their patients. Body products are also the result of advances in technology and science. Medical use of body products depended both on the most sophisticated biochemical and genetic research of the day and on that now most mundane of technologies, refrigeration, as cold storage made body banks possible. Just as western land, once homesteaded, became real estate subject to legal rules, body products, once they were made into "therapeutic merchandise," entered the domain of law. This history also follows body products into courtrooms and legislatures, as this new form of property law was created. And, like all American histories, the history of body banking is a history of race, class, and gender. All participants in body banking relied upon their assumptions about power hierarchies in American society as they reinterpreted the profoundly intimate acts of nursing a baby, sharing blood, and making babies through the new experience of body product exchange.

The thread that links this century of history is the banking metaphor itself. The metaphor has been so powerful that it has persisted for generations of doctors and patients, and it has been generalized beyond the blood bank to encompass a broad range of body banks; besides sperm and milk, it has also been applied to bones and eggs. That power and persistence demonstrates that the body bank rapidly became "a metaphor we live by." The banking metaphor is powerful because it is not simply a "rhetorical flourish" but "a concept that governs our thought."[18] The banking metaphor has encouraged us to think of body products in terms of money and markets. This association was Fantus's original intention. He urged his fellow doctors to see his new "blood bank" as more than a "mere metaphor."[19] He wanted the doctors in his hospital to take his bank seriously and to appreciate that, "just as one cannot draw money from a bank unless one has deposited some," so too his blood preservation department, soon to be formally renamed, "cannot supply blood unless as much comes in as goes out."[20] Fantus was deliberately seeking to draw upon what doctors knew about banking money when in 1937 he used *bank* to describe a new way of thinking about the blood supply.

Financial banks have been around much longer than body banks, in fact, longer than the United States itself. In the United States financial banks are bedrock institutions of a capitalist economy, but Americans have long worried about them. From the First Bank of the United States, established in 1791, to the widespread bank failures of the Great Depression of the 1930s—Fantus's city of Chicago was particularly hard hit—to the Great Recession of the early twenty-first century, the role of banks has been continually controversial.[21] Fantus sought to set aside this legacy of controversy and focus on the experience of individual bank depositors in a functioning bank: they deposit money, which is used by the bank to provide benefits to others in the form of loans, and when depositors need money they can withdraw it, not the same dollar bills they deposited but an equivalent amount. The bank makes each dollar into an abstract concept, credits and debits that link the physical material deposited and withdrawn. This trans-

formation is what Fantus sought to accomplish with his blood bank, creating abstract, tradable value out of the disembodied fluid his fellow doctors
collected.

Like financial banks, however, body banks have generated controversy
since they were first created. Part of this controversy preceded the body
bank. Even before there were any institutions to manage body products,
there was public excitement and anxiety about the medical technique of
using a part of one person to treat another person. Despite the use of wet
nurses for centuries across many cultures, for example, nineteenth-century
American parents and doctors continually worried that breast milk might
transfer personal characteristics, including class, race, ethnicity, religion,
and personality, from nurse to baby.[22] As Americans learned to participate
in body banking, these worries about the source of body products have
sparked controversies along the fault lines of identity and difference that
permeate American society and culture, particularly race, gender, and sexual identity. The medical insistence that body products are of equal value
regardless of source—in legal terms, completely fungible—has been difficult to accept. These controversies have been serious and long-lasting, ranging from decades of arguments about segregating blood by race to criticism
of the federal ban on blood donation by homosexually active men and the
debate about capping compensation for the sale of eggs but not sperm.[23]

In addition to these deep-rooted worries about the use of body products
in medical treatment, the banking metaphor has created its own set of controversies, which are linked to contemporary debates and problems surrounding body products. Fantus had a particular vision of what he was
trying to accomplish with his adoption of the term *bank*. By treating blood
as money, he was trying to circumvent the need to pay money for blood.
His goal was to replace reliance on "professional donors," the common term
for paid blood sellers, with a communal system of blood as a shared resource among patients, in which all who used blood also provided blood,
continually replenishing the supply. Like his medical colleagues who had
worked to make disembodied blood into a life-saving therapeutic in the decades before he set up his blood bank, he was interested in this body product as a fungible commodity—that is, a standardized item that could be
bought and sold—but also as a commodity that was under complete medical control, available to serve the professional goal of healing the sick. Fantus was not interested in organizing a free market in blood or in making a

profit from blood banking. He was interested in increasing the access of poor patients to blood transfusion at a hospital operating on a shoestring budget as a municipal charity. At Cook County Hospital, where Fantus worked, professional blood donors were beyond the financial means of most patients and of the hospital itself. During the Great Depression, high rates of unemployment and poverty exacerbated the continual tension between the professional ethic to treat the ill and doctors' need to earn a living by collecting fees from those they treated. Fantus borrowed a term associated with capitalism and markets to subvert the market allocation of blood solely to those who could afford to pay. His initial success with creating a new way of organizing private property to serve a medically defined public goal encouraged others to copy him.

This initial success, however, went hand-in-hand with the controversial aspect of body banking, obvious at the outset and powerfully present today as policymakers around the world worry about whether blood, organs, and gametes should be bought and sold: the body bank implies an association between human bodies and money. This association threatens long-standing Western philosophical and religious traditions about the sacredness of the body and is particularly fraught in a country whose history is inextricably bound up with the institution of racialized human slavery.[24] Immediately, Fantus found himself subject to "severe" criticism for using a "commercial term" to describe his otherwise worthy project.[25] Although use of body banks has become routine and accepted, such criticism has never vanished. Our failure to resolve this concern is reflected in the way we talk about making "donations" to body banks, phrasing that emphasizes the difference between body banks and financial banks.

At the same time, the more doctors and laypersons have talked about body banks, making the bank a pervasive metaphor, the more the association between bodies and commerce has seemed natural. It has led medical professionals to claim that body products were simply market commodities, like automobiles and silver teaspoons, and, according to liberal economic theory, should be exchanged according to individual preferences expressed by decisions to buy and sell. It has led lawyers to argue that commercial law should apply to these products just as it does to cars and spoons. When Americans embraced a market view of body products in the decades after World War II, these logical consequences of extending the metaphor between financial banks and body banks conflicted both with the medical ethic of service and with deeply held lay notions that property sourced from human bodies should be treated in special ways. The result has been polarization of the controversy around the flashpoints of markets and sales: Should body products be nonmarket gifts of love or market commodities subject to sale? The characterization of gifts and sales as opposite and mutually exclusive exchanges is often summed up by the shorthand phrase the *gift/commodity dichotomy.*

Taking the banking metaphor seriously led the medical profession and, later, policymakers to lose sight of Fantus's original goal of harnessing the market to serve communal ends. Instead we have allowed ourselves to become trapped in a dichotomy that is neither accurate nor useful. It is an inaccurate description of the experience of body product exchange to separate "gifts" from "commodities" as distinct and opposite. Through analyzing the experiences of exchanging money and market goods, as well as the economic aspects of intimate, seemingly nonmarket relationships, such as between parent and child, sociologist Viviana Zelizer has shown that the idealized division of the world into market and nonmarket spheres does not exist in lived experience.[26] Others have used her insight to explore markets in body products in the late twentieth and early twenty-first centuries. Their research has underscored the often forgotten truth that money paid to suppliers does not cause body products to become diseased and has also uncovered how suppliers and recipients of body products such as eggs, sperm, blood, and organs create their own experiences of commodification and altruistic gifting. These experiences often do not correlate with the presence or absence of money but are strongly influenced by the institutions and rhetorical frames through which body products are exchanged.[27] History reveals that the insights of contemporary sociology apply to the experiences of Americans struggling through earlier attempts to explain body product exchange. The intermingling of cash payments for body products with social aspects of such exchanges, such as gratitude, civic engagement, and generosity, was not new at the turn of the twenty-first century. Since the body bank became a possibility, the meaning of body product exchange to those who have engaged in it has ranged from alienating or mundane to self-enhancing or profoundly meaningful, without correlating with whether the supplier is paid or whether the recipient is buying. Upon close inspection, the categories of gift and commodity throughout the history of body products have been neither distinct nor opposite.

The gift/commodity dichotomy, in addition to being inaccurate, is also not useful, because as we have relied on the bank to shape our public discussion of body products, we have allowed our discourse to become limited by the dichotomy. Not only has the dichotomy made it more difficult to appreciate the overlapping sale and gift aspects of many exchanges, but it also has assumed a complete separation of private interests, expressed through market preferences, from the public interest in a particular distribution of body products. If private and public interests are necessarily at odds, then if we believe that vital medical therapeutics should go to the most ill rather than to the most wealthy, it makes sense to forbid enticing organ donation by compensation. Such a prohibition is enshrined in the National Organ Transplant Act, which forbids moremarrowdonors.org from offering valuable compensation to desperately needed donors of non-European extraction. What the gift/commodity dichotomy conceptually excludes are the types of intermingling that moremarrowdonors.org was attempting to create—the ways private interests expressed through individual sales of body products as private property can coexist with and even promote various conceptions of the public interest in body product allocation. Moremarrowdonors.org, as a nonprofit organization, was not focused on maximizing the profit to individual donors from underrepresented groups through an open market; rather, by the use of a flat fee, it was attempting to recruit more donors so that all patients needing a bone marrow transplant had an equal chance of finding a compatible donor, regardless of wealth or genetic background. The means it sought to use relied on private incentives, but the goal was the same public goal that Fantus was working toward in 1937: increasing access to a life-saving therapeutic by those who, on average, are less socioeconomically advantaged.

The focus on a choice between love and money has allowed us to forget Fantus's original vision and the many ways throughout the history of body banking that doctors have harnessed private interests for what they have perceived to be the greater good. These include midcentury attempts to manage blood as a national public resource and the long history of the professional donor as a safe and lauded supplier, who might, like twenty-first-century egg donors, combine a frank interest in cash payment with an altruistic vision of helping others.[28] The consequences of this narrowing of the debate about body banks and body products have shaped not only medical practice but also the law, in the form of the National Organ Transplant Act and other regulations.

New Bodies and New Property

As they were adopting the bank as a way of explaining how their bodies could become a source of property, Americans were also creating the need for new legal ways of understanding body products. What we know about bodies and body products is not the same set of things that Americans knew one hundred years ago, or even fifty years ago. When we began to "bank" our bodies, we made a significant shift from earlier metaphors of the body. As human tissue became body products through the body bank, by implication, the supplying body was also transformed, becoming a manufactory. While understanding the body as a machine or factory is not new, in Western traditions of medicine and religion, the body was generally considered unitary and uniquely sacred rather than severable and the source of substances to be sold. Human hair was the exception that proved the rule, being readily severable without damage to bodily integrity, the story of Samson and Delilah aside.[29] Unlike hair, the body fluids of blood, milk, and semen were understood as constitutive of the self. They were the physical basis of kinship and identity, an understanding captured in phrases like *blood brothers* and *the blood royal*. They also were understood as different forms of the same substance. In male bodies, blood became semen, whereas in female bodies, blood became milk.[30] Keeping these fluids balanced within the body was part of managing the "humors," a basis for medical treatment that persisted well into the nineteenth century in the United States.[31] Harvesting such substances from one body in order to move them to another body was a radically new way of thinking about the body, healing, and medicine.

This shift was in part the result of new medical and scientific knowledge about the human body. Daring innovations and technical breakthroughs by scientists and doctors made it possible for body products to be taken from one living body and used to treat another. By the early twentieth century doctors were using disembodied human milk, blood, and semen as medical therapeutics. History reveals, though, that much of what we know today about bodies and body products was not the inevitable result of new technologies of extraction and storage, or even of the evolving biomedical conception of the body as a harvestable source of therapeutics. It was the result of the term *bank* itself and the association it created between body products and markets.

That knowledge has been embedded in the law of human-sourced property. In the past century a new American understanding of property in the human body has emerged, based on the body bank as the dominant way such property is created and managed. Before the body became bankable, to the extent that there was a law of human-sourced property, it was the law of slavery, which was abolished by the Thirteenth Amendment to the U.S. Constitution in 1865. Fitting body products into modern American law has involved similar tensions to fitting body products into medical practice. Should body products be treated by the law like cars and spoons or placed in a special category? What sort of property should body products be?

In American political philosophy, *property* is commonly used to define the boundary between public and private: property is the individually owned private realm that requires the apparatus of the state to protect it. The essence of property is usually described as the right to exclude others; the state protects private property from invasion or interference.[32] Most property is not only exclusive but is alienable; that is, it can be bought and sold and traded in markets. With the rise of industrial capitalism in the nineteenth century, a market-based understanding of property as commodity came to dominate American political and legal thought. Property was that which could be traded in markets, and the purpose of the state, made manifest through law, was to protect the freedom to exchange property, allowing individuals to express their preferences through the marketplace.[33]

The emergence of body banks and the new body products in the first decades of the twentieth century appeared to fit well within this model of market property, already established in the law. Body banks helped create body products and facilitate their exchange, just as financial banks facilitate the circulation of money, credit, and goods. If body products are market property, the only question seems to be whether body products should be freely alienable commodities or should be one of the rarer forms of commodities, capable of being traded in markets but limited by law to gift exchanges, as a form of inalienable property. Should we bank body products for love or for money? This question, however, was not relevant to the originators of body products. Rather it developed over time, as a result of the banking metaphor.

The medical professionals who were instrumental in creating body banks did not start from the question of gift or commodity. They started with their burning desire to improve medical care for their patients. As far as doctors were concerned, the key quality of body products was their availability when doctors, in their professional discretion, believed they should be used to treat a patient. Body products as private property stored in banks supported the efficient treatment of patients in ways impossible before body banks. This new property was not created to satisfy individual preferences or to amass profits but as "the private basis for the public good."[34] Body products thus began not as market property but as what property theorist Gregory Alexander calls "civic property."[35] The essence of civic property is its role linking private property and private interests to the polity as a whole, spanning the theoretical divide between private and public. Civic property requires "some prior normative vision of how society and the polity that governs it should be structured," defining the public good.[36] This understanding of property, prevalent in the colonial era and the early republic, has waned since the eighteenth century, as the United States increased in population and diversity and as a market view of property became dominant in law and society.[37]

In the development of body products as a form of civic property, the medical profession provided the normative vision. This vision, while it had implications for all of society and the polity, focused on the realm of medical care. For the pioneering Dr. Fantus and some who followed his example, the body bank was a means of harnessing private property to the public good of providing medical care to those who needed it. But once created, body products also were capable of being traded in markets—that is, acting as the more common market property. Fantus's banking metaphor invited what another property theorist, Margaret Radin, has called "market rhetoric," that is, talking about body products in market terms, as commodities that could and should be bought and sold.[38] Within a decade of the adoption of the banking metaphor, the United States had moved from the depths of the Great Depression to the hope of postwar prosperity, when market rhetoric had a different resonance.

During the Cold War era, the so-called blood bank battles raged. The battle lines were drawn between those espousing a civic property view of banked blood as a medically managed public resource and those arguing for a market property view, in which banked blood was used to confer a

private benefit on patients who received it, creating an individual obligation
to repay bank blood "loans." These battles were so heated because to treat
body products solely as market property was to use the market to allocate
medical treatment. Allocating medical care solely to those who can pay
rather than on the basis of need is an approach that is both common in
American history and thought and intensely controversial, as the desire of
the medical profession to earn a living from patient fees conflicts with the
professional ethic of treating all those who need care. The civic property
view of blood as a public resource was also controversial, smacking of "socialized medicine" at a time when the American medical profession was
resisting any single-payer health care system.[39] As the bank gained prominence as the way body product exchange was understood through the second half of the twentieth century, the market property view of body products came to dominate and the original civic property view was lost, leaving
the debate to center on the narrower, and harmfully limited, question of
gift or commodity, love or money.

By adopting the metaphor of the bank, a free market institution of capitalism, the doctors who established and promulgated these institutions created links between money, bodies, and markets. These links led to current
divisions between sales and gifts and the current problematic legal landscape in the United States for supplying and allocating body products. By
retracing the history of body banks, we gain tools for moving beyond the
gift/commodity debate to a more expansive view of body products focused
on ends rather than means, a view that has ramifications not only in American law and medicine but in all countries where body product exchanges
are taking place.

I

Bankable Bodies and the Professional Donor

A new calling has been evolved by modern medicine for healthy, full-blooded young men and women . . . the occupation of professional blood donor.

—*Hygeia*, 1930

In 1908 Dr. Fritz Talbot spent three days riding street cars around Boston in a discouraging search for a wet nurse. Talbot was a recent graduate of Harvard Medical School, anxious to establish himself as a pediatrician, a new medical specialty.[1] One of his patients, a newborn baby, was not getting enough milk from his mother. The best hope for this baby's survival was for his parents to hire a woman who would be willing to leave her own nursing baby and move into their home to feed their baby. Wet nursing was a long-established occupation, but finding a wet nurse in the early twentieth century was increasingly difficult.[2] Doctors such as Talbot assumed this wearisome task as they sought to use their medical expertise to manage infant feeding as the best way of decreasing infant mortality. Talbot became discouraged as he crisscrossed the city in a time-consuming search. Doctors and parents found that wet nurse candidates often exhibited distressing signs of slovenliness, alcohol use, immorality, and lack of appropriate deference to the doctor and to their would-be employers, not to mention a reluctance to abandon their own child to an uncertain fate.[3] After numerous disappointments in hunting down and interviewing such women, Talbot felt his time could be better spent.[4] In order to care for his youngest patients, he needed a much more reliable and accessible source of breast milk.

In that same year another young doctor went on a frantic search through the streets of New York City. His quest too was motivated by a newborn hovering near death. Dr. Adrian Lambert's daughter was four days old. She was feverish, steadily bleeding from her nose and umbilical cord stump, and becoming pale and lethargic. Her rare condition, *melaena neonatorum,* a poorly understood bleeding disorder, was often fatal.[5] Based on recently published results from an Ohio surgeon, Dr. George Crile, the desperate father decided that a blood transfusion might save his daughter's life. In 1907 Crile had described the amazing recoveries of patients he had treated using transfusion performed by vascular anastomosis. In this surgical operation, blood vessels from the supplier and the recipient were sutured together, uniting the circulatory systems to allow blood to pass from one to the other.[6] Crile, Lambert knew, had learned the technique of vascular anastomosis by observing Dr. Alexis Carrel. Carrel, a French émigré, did not treat patients but worked as a medical researcher at the Rockefeller Institute in New York City. He had perfected the delicate technique of anastomosis as part of transplant experiments in dogs.[7] Unlike Talbot, Lambert had no difficulty identifying a source for the body product he needed; both he and his brothers were ready to provide blood. What Lambert sought in his rush through the darkened streets of the city was the expertise to perform this risky and experimental procedure. If Carrel himself would operate on his daughter, perhaps she might live. In the early hours of the morning, he banged on Carrel's door and implored the researcher to transfuse his daughter. Carrel heeded the call and performed the emergency surgery, attaching father to daughter in an operation that Lambert believed saved the baby's life.[8]

Talbot and Lambert were two of the many doctors at the beginning of the twentieth century who were turning to healthy human bodies as a source of medical therapeutics. Their efforts succeeded in making the human body accessible and bankable. Patients dying of hemorrhage and babies suffering from inadequate nutrition were not new; the urgency of medical demand had long been apparent to doctors. What was new was the willingness of doctors to use other bodies as the source of cures for their desperate cases. Before there could be body banks, doctors needed both expertise in methods of harvesting body products and a cooperative source of supply.

The task of pediatricians seeking milk was easier than the task facing doctors fighting to save hemorrhaging patients. There was already an established, socially accepted method for providing nonmaternal milk to babies, the wet nurse. Talbot was able, therefore, to concentrate on the question of supply. His exasperating search led him to launch a two-pronged project to modernize wet nursing, using classic Progressive-era approaches. For the next three decades he worked to organize and rationalize the wet nurse and to transform the service of wet nursing into the job of producing bottles of breast milk. Breast milk in bottles offered significantly more medical control over when, how, and how much milk patients drank. Both aspects of his project, which was joined by doctors in cities across the United States, were designed to improve medical control over milk as a body product. Regimentation of the wet nurse herself was good, but transforming human milk into a commodity was better. Disembodied, milk could be standardized, anonymized, and controlled in ways that the producing women could never be. Doctors could replace intimate personal exchanges—putting a baby to the breast—with transactions between strangers who might never see or know each other. As a result of the efforts of Talbot and other pediatricians, human milk became the first body product to be institutionally organized in disembodied form.

Making blood into a body product was significantly trickier. The tale of Carrel's successful operation on Lambert's daughter has often been cited as the beginning of modern blood transfusion practice.[9] The event received considerable press coverage at the time, both because Carrel, who later won the Nobel Prize, was already famous and because of the novelty of considering human blood to be like human milk, that is, a life-giving substance that could be transferred from supplier to recipient.[10] The positive reports of Carrel's feat prompted many doctors to attempt what Crile described as dramatic "resurrections" from blood transfusion, but they found that the procedure was much more complicated than feeding human milk to an infant, posing many problems in both harvesting and infusing blood.[11] Only when doctors had mastered the technique of blood transfusion did the supply problem become pressing. While medical attempts to transfuse blood preceded Carrel's exploit by centuries, there was no historical precedent like the wet nurse to use as a starting point to develop a source of supply.[12] For both infant feeding and blood transfusion, the medical profession would come to rely on a new creature: the "professional donor."

Regulating the Wet Nurse

Talbot's search for a wet nurse was frustrating in part because lactating women were getting harder to find. During the same decades that pediatricians were seeking to supervise and control infant feeding, American women were abandoning breastfeeding in droves.[13] Just as Talbot found wet nursing irritatingly old-fashioned and out of place in modern medicine, American mothers since the late nineteenth century had been finding maternal nursing old-fashioned and out of step with their lives. Women of all socioeconomic strata sought the ability to move freely outside their homes, unhampered by breastfeeding duties, out of either the necessity to earn wages or the desire to participate in social and civic life. As a result, not only did fewer women want to nurse their own infants, but women who could afford wet nurses were increasingly unable to find them.[14]

To replace human milk, mothers chose different forms of what was called "artificial feeding," using cow's milk–based concoctions. They might add milk to pap, a mixture of flour or bread cooked in water, or to panada, flour or bread cooked in broth.[15] The emerging dairy industry made these homemade infant foods possible. Dairy companies were making fresh milk available in cities and also offering shelf-stable milk products, like condensed milk, evaporated milk, and powdered milk. Mothers mixed infant foods using these products. As the century advanced, they could also buy commercial additives advertised for use in artificial feeding, such as Horlick's Malted Milk and Nestlé's Infant Food, a more expensive alternative to homemade foods.[16]

Pediatricians were disturbed by the results of this maternal-led revolution in infant feeding. One told his colleagues in 1913 that any mother or doctor who relied on artificial feeding was operating under "a false sense of security," because "a full one-third of all infant deaths [were due] to unnecessary bottle-feeding."[17] The culprit was often identified as "summer sickness," also known as "cholera infantum," a diarrheal disease leading rapidly to dehydration and death that could be caused by using unrefrigerated cow's milk. In Boston by the late nineteenth century, three times as many children under the age of five years died in July and August as in any other month of the year.[18] This death toll was repeated in cities across the United States and continued into the twentieth century.[19] Faced with this level of mortality, pediatricians concluded that infant feeding choices should not be left to mothers. These pediatricians believed that motherhood, like medicine itself, should be based on science.

Not all doctors promoting "scientific motherhood" shared Talbot's preference for human milk.[20] Some doctors, accepting the reality that many women were relying on artificial feeding, joined "pure milk" campaigns focused on improving the safety of cow's milk by improving the supply chain from farmer to distributor to corner store to kitchen to baby. Public health officials inserted themselves into this chain by creating "depots" or "stations" where they received supplies of milk and provided them to the urban poor at a subsidized price.[21] In addition to supplies of subsidized milk for the poor, doctors created "certified milk." This cow's milk, supplied from inspected farms and certified by a medical board as clean and disease-free, was available at a high cost to those who could afford to pay. For the ultimate in scientific infant foods, the most privileged babies could get bottles of formulas mixed according to their doctor's orders from commercial milk laboratories, combining pure milk with the latest research into the appropriate ingredients in infant foods.[22]

These artificial feeding options not only supported maternal preferences to avoid breastfeeding but also offered doctors much more scope to prescribe precise feeding regimens. Using their medical expertise, doctors could dictate the ingredients, volume, and timing of each feeding. In 1908, the year Talbot was searching for a wet nurse, he might have considered prescribing Nestlé's Food to his patient, which was advertised to Boston doctors as a powdered additive "particularly well adapted to the needs of the nursling because it is based upon modern knowledge of the laws"—that is, the new scientific principles governing feeding.[23] In his search for a wet nurse, Talbot was rejecting the tantalizing promise of infant formulas and pure milk campaigns, convinced that despite the advantages of artificial foods, breast milk was a superior infant food, especially for sick infants.

Despite the enthusiasm of some doctors for artificial feeding, Talbot was not alone in his dedication to promoting breast milk for his patients. Dr.

Julius P. Sedgwick, chief of the Department of Pediatrics at the University of Minnesota School of Medicine, became chair of the American Pediatric Society in 1917. He used his chairman's address to advocate for breast milk as the optimal infant food and continued to publish articles on the importance of breastfeeding for all babies.[24] Breastfed babies tended to survive at higher rates as long as the cow's milk supplies remained unpasteurized. Pasteurization of milk was not required in Boston, for example, until 1921.[25] The medical preference for breastfed babies was expressed in public health campaigns promoting maternal nursing. One such campaign in Chicago in the 1910s aimed at immigrant mothers admonished, "Don't kill your baby!"[26] Middle-class mothers, as well as impoverished immigrants, were included in Sedgwick's efforts in Minnesota. One of his nurses involved in his house-to-house breastfeeding campaign in 1919 and 1920 described her work with young women "who, previous to their marriage, had had only such responsibilities as college and social life call for." To convince these women to breastfeed, she avoided "the word duty" as much as possible, but did "try to make them feel that maternal feeding is as much a part of motherhood as is pregnancy, and, as such, must be gone through with."[27]

Breast milk advocacy, however, mixed uneasily with the ideals of scientific motherhood, particularly the medical ideal that mothers would turn to doctors for detailed, specific advice about what to feed their babies. The same research into the "laws" behind infant formulas—the optimum ratios of fat, sugar, and protein—had revealed that mothers' milk varied in composition.[28] The amount consumed, whether from a wet nurse or the baby's own mother, was also an irritating unknown. Doctors tried to mitigate this uncertainty and rationalize nursing by prescribing rigid nursing intervals, strictly limiting the duration of nursing sessions, and ordering mothers to weigh their babies before and after nursing.[29] Breast milk content was the responsibility of the mother, who needed the appropriate regimen of rest, exercise, and diet and an elimination of the stresses and excitements of modern life in order to produce the precious fluid.[30]

Even middle-class mothers had difficulty fulfilling these obligations. Dr. L. Emmett Holt, a prominent New York City pediatrician and author of a popular advice book for parents, *The Care and Feeding of Infants,* estimated that only 25 percent of the well-to-do mothers of New York City could nurse as long as three months, even exercising their best efforts.[31] Not surprisingly, medical admonitions and a clock-based nursing schedule sometimes had the unintended effect of diminishing the mother's milk supply, leading to a diagnosis of agalactia or oligogalactia, the medical terms for failure or insufficiency of milk production, and to the need for a wet nurse.[32]

As Talbot knew from firsthand experience, the wet nurse was often a highly unsatisfactory source of nutrition, what another doctor later called "that necessary but often slatternly female."[33] She was most often an unwed mother or an otherwise desperate, impoverished immigrant woman and, in Boston, frequently Irish Catholic.[34] As both an immigrant and an unwed mother, she entered a middle-class household with two strikes against her: perceived as lacking in morals and in the sociocultural assumptions of her Anglo-Saxon, native-born, Protestant employers. Employers and doctors not only worried about the nutritional content of her milk but also feared the transmission of disease, such as syphilis, as well as undesirable ethnic traits, individual moral failings, or personality flaws.[35] The use of nonmaternal milk was thus a threat as well as a boon.

Talbot sought to maximize both the easy availability and the quality of wet nurses for his patients. To do so, he focused on disciplining the wet nurse, applying the Progressive values of expertise and efficiency to reform wet nursing in the same spirit that other pediatricians tackled the reform of the cow's milk supply chain and the formulation of artificial foods. If he must rely on these "slatternly women," he would remake them into more ideal milk-producing units.

By 1908 a plan to organize wet nurses had already been proposed by Talbot's Boston colleague Dr. Francis Denny. Denny was interested in having access to human milk as a therapeutic for adult patients, believing that the milk had immunological and bacteriolytic properties that might help in treating typhoid. In order to test this therapy, he had organized a human milk collection and distribution service. He employed a nurse who, like Talbot, visited "a large number of nursing mothers living in the tenement house districts," searching for those who had an overabundance of milk.[36] Denny inspected the candidates and their babies for general health. The nurse, Mrs. Henderson, then instructed the chosen milk sellers in the manual expression of milk and arranged for each seller to have a supply of sterile bottles and, at a time before mechanical refrigeration, access to some form of low-temperature storage for the bottled milk until Henderson came to collect it. The women were paid by the ounce. Denny concluded from these efforts that "drawn human milk can be easily obtained in considerable amounts" and suggested organizing a registry of wet nurses for this purpose.[37]

While Denny's use of breast milk to treat adults was not generally adopted, Talbot turned Denny's suggestion of a registry into reality, creating the Directory for Wet Nurses.[38] The Directory was simply an office maintaining a list of lactating women looking for employment, similar to other area registries maintained to match nurses with employers.[39] The Directory opened for business on February 1, 1910, charging a small fee to employers for its matching services.[40] Talbot described his service to the medical community in an article in the *Boston Medical and Surgical Journal* and advertised the Directory in both that periodical and in its successor, the *New England Journal of Medicine,* to encourage his fellow doctors both to recruit nurses from their obstetrical patients and to hire nurses from the list.[41] When Talbot found that women on the registry had difficulty supporting themselves while waiting to be hired—their suitability as wet nurses depended on their continuing to nurse their own infant, a hindrance to most types of employment—he established a house where up to eight women could live with their infants, funding it for several years out of his private income when the fees of the Directory proved insufficient to cover its cost.[42]

This home did much more than help these women keep body and soul together while waiting for employment. It served as a site of discipline where the diet, dress, and behavior of the future wet nurses could be monitored by the resident nurse.[43] The residents were forbidden to drink alcohol and were monitored for symptoms of diseases such as tuberculosis and syphilis.[44] They were taught "to be cleanly and how to take care of babies" and also how to do light housekeeping, which might provide a source of wages after their wet nursing days ended.[45] When doctors advised parents to hire a nurse from the Directory, they were recommending the services of a medically managed body. In 1913 the Directory placed forty-two wet nurses with employing families.[46] Talbot's Directory not only increased the efficiency of searching for wet nurses but also took the first steps toward standardization of human milk by creating some standards for the lactating body.

Recruiting and managing the supplying individual was to be an ongoing problem, not just for Talbot and his fellow pediatricians but for all doctors seeking to use a body product. Even when hired from Talbot's new organization, the wet nurse remained troublesome. Once she left the controlled environment of the home, the doctor's hold on her vanished. The

Directory therefore guaranteed the health of its nurses and the quality of their milk, but not their "character, habits, or dispositions."[47] And Directory wet nurses were a solution only for the private patients of Talbot and his colleagues—those who merited house calls and personal searches for wet nurses. Talbot, like other urban doctors, also treated charity patients at children's hospitals, infirmaries, and dispensaries.[48] Since the late nineteenth century these institutional settings had relied on resident wet nurses who would nurse multiple babies as needed, receiving room and board from the hospital and perhaps a payment related to the volume of milk produced.[49] As residents, the women could be monitored continually during the entire time of their lactation services, with strict control over their diet and behavior.

Talbot was familiar with the resident wet nurses at the Massachusetts Babies Hospital, where he first located his Directory office.[50] Now he strove to improve their management. Each new hire was inspected for "any acute or chronic infectious disease or any physical defect" and subjected to a "probation" period during which the woman and her baby settled into the hospital routine, which included training in the care of her own baby and light housekeeping duties. The women were kept to a schedule of sleep and meals from 6:30 A.M. to 9 P.M. that included a two-hour afternoon rest, three meals and two hearty snacks, and ice cream three times a week. If they were "troublesome," they were dismissed, but most stayed about six to eight months.[51] Other pediatricians were engaged in similar regulation of hospital wet nurses. Dr. Julian Hess in Chicago, for example, designed a special uniform for his hospital wet nurses and, like Talbot, prescribed a set diet.[52] To the extent possible, the disparate bodies were homogenized through diet, dress, and scheduled activities. The standardization of these bodies served to reduce any particularities that might be transmitted in the women's milk and to transform a job, wet nursing, which had provided significant discretion and control, into something more akin to clock-based factory labor.

No matter how efficiently managed, however, even resident wet nurses still posed one problem for the supervising physicians. The doctors could not easily detect the quantity and quality of milk a nursed baby received. A solution was to require the wet nurses to express their milk, allowing the medical staff to measure the milk before it was given to a baby. The milk could also be analyzed for fat, protein, and carbohydrate concentration. Dr.

Isaac Abt, another Chicago pediatrician concerned with hospital wet nurse management, designed an electric breast pump in the 1920s. He claimed his "human milking machine" improved milk production in both efficiency and volume.[53] The wet nurse's job thus became to produce like a dairy cow rather than to suckle an infant, and her production was measured not in cries quieted but in ounces per minute. Hospitals already had milk laboratories, where technicians prepared bottles of artificial foods by prescribed formulas. Now breast milk could also be processed in the laboratory and become a standardized, anonymous product, interchangeable with other bottles of milk. By separating lactating breast and recipient baby, the doctors were making human milk into a body product that could be managed more like other medicines they prescribed and making the wet nurse into a paid supplier.

Making Transfusion Simple

In making human milk into a medically useful body product, supplied by regulated bodies, Talbot and his colleagues were simply adjusting the time-worn role of the wet nurse. But the blood donor was something new—a healthy body bled for the benefit of another body through an invasive and potentially harmful procedure. The term *donor,* with its implications of gifting and sociability, was applied indiscriminately by the pioneering Ohio transfusionist Crile, used to describe involuntary suppliers (the dogs of his early experiments) as well as both paid and unpaid human suppliers.[54] Until well into the twentieth century, no one paid much attention to the blood donor. The focus was all on transfusion itself. After centuries of bloodletting as a medical therapy, getting blood out of a body was no challenge. Getting it into a patient was another matter. Despite the optimistic assessment of two New York doctors in 1908 that with the development of vascular anastomosis, blood transfusion was a procedure "of simplicity and of certain success," in subsequent years it proved continually tricky.[55] Into the 1930s clinicians fought to make blood flow from one person to another in ways that were controllable, beneficial to the patient, and safe for the donor.

While the success of the medical researcher Carrel in transfusing Lambert's infant daughter caused a "sensation" in popular and medical circles, the idea of blood transfusion as a medical treatment already had a long history by 1908, a history linked to the symbolic significance of blood. Early

transfusions were attempts to transfer desired characteristics from the supplier to the patient to heal body or spirit.[56] There is a possibly apocryphal
story that the dying Pope Innocent VIII was unsuccessfully treated by the
transfusion of blood from several young boys in 1492, in an attempt to re-
store his youthful vigor.[57] In 1667 natural philosophers in England affiliated
with the Royal Society tried transfusing sheep's blood into a young scholar
suffering from "warmness of the brain," who testified that he was much
improved by the procedure. That same year French experimenters eager to
outdo their English rivals treated three human patients and one healthy,
paid volunteer with transfusions of lamb's and calf's blood, intended to
calm. Some well-publicized successes were intermingled with notorious disasters. After his patient died following a third attempted transfusion of
calf's blood to treat mania, French physician Jean-Baptiste Denis was tried
for murder in 1668. Although he was eventually acquitted, both French
authorities and the pope banned transfusions, and the English experiments
also stopped.[58] During the eighteenth century blood transfusion was more
discussed in theory than attempted in practice.[59]

Those who called a halt to the practice may have been responding both
to the perceived philosophical dangers of mingling blood and to the numerous practical problems.[60] The sheer physical difficulty of getting the
blood from one body to another was enormous, and the small amounts
actually transfused may have saved patients from the fatal effects of transfusion reactions, now known to occur in transspecies transfusions, due to
immunological incompatibilities unknown to the early modern experimenters. The clotting properties of blood upon exposure to the air rendered
any transfer nearly impossible, as clots clogged the intended conduit for the
blood. While doctors could never be sure how much blood was flowing into
the recipient, it was almost guaranteed that the supplier was losing significantly more blood than the recipient was gaining. The recipient sometimes
exhibited disturbing symptoms, such as fever, pain, and blood in the urine,
now understood to be a reaction to the transfusion of incompatible blood,
a possibility even when using a human donor.[61] When the patient died, it
was unclear whether death was caused by the underlying disease or as a result of the transfusion attempt.

In the first decades of the nineteenth century, however, a new generation
of practitioners revived the practice as a treatment for severe postpartum
hemorrhage, a condition so dire that dangerous therapies seemed worth the

risk. These obstetricians were watching previously healthy young women bleed to death and, unlike the early modern experimenters, were trying not to rebalance humors or transfer calming traits but simply to replace lost blood. The English doctor James Blundell made initial experiments with dogs, bleeding them and then reviving them by transfusion, and then tried transfusion from husband to wife to save his moribund patients.[62] Blundell, and doctors who enthusiastically tried his approach, published their results in the British medical literature beginning in 1818.[63] In his obstetrical textbook, published in both England and the United States in 1834, Blundell offered diagrams and descriptions of the instruments he used to persuade blood to flow from supplier to recipient.[64] He viewed the technique as warranted only in "desperate" cases where the woman "is sinking gradually into the grave."[65] His reports stimulated efforts in the United States, where a few isolated practitioners experimented with the technique.[66] An article in *Harper's Weekly* in 1874 introduced the new therapy to the educated American lay public. The article described in detail a transfusion of one ounce of human blood into a young Frenchwoman in Paris and reported that a transfusion had been performed recently in New York.[67]

Doctors continued to find desperately ill patients whom they hoped might be aided by the technique. In 1884 Dr. William Halsted, a surgeon working in New York, reported on his success using transfusion to treat patients suffering from severe carbon monoxide poisoning, either from coal gas or the new illuminating light gas. Because he was using what he called "refusion," that is, transfusion of his patient's own blood, today called autologous transfusion, he unknowingly avoided the immune problems that cause transfusion reactions. He was able to report several instances in which the infusion of the patient's own blood, somewhat reoxygenated from its time outside the body, restored life to nearly comatose poisoning victims.[68]

Following Blundell and Halsted, turn-of-the-century clinicians focused on using human blood for transfusions and sought better ways to move blood from one body to another, trying to get the blood into the recipient. The Parisian transfusion described in *Harper's Weekly* relied on two techniques to diminish the risk of blood clotting. The doctor used tepid water to maintain the warmth of the blood during the brief period of time it was between bodies and used a gold cannula (tube) to transfuse the blood into the patient, believing that gold provided a less hospitable environment for blood clots.[69] When Lambert dragged Carrel to his daughter's bedside in

1908, he was seeking Carrel's expertise in performing what Crile called "direct transfusion," developed to avoid the clotting problem. Vascular anastomosis, the technique Crile had learned from Carrel, eliminated the clotting problem by keeping the blood always within a body, as the circulatory systems of supplier and recipient were joined. It replaced the two steps of collection and transfusion with a single step. It was so successful that Crile nearly killed his first human donor—so much blood flowed to the recipient that the donor collapsed.[70] Some years later a novice at the technique killed his recipient when too much blood flowed too quickly into her body.[71] Not only did anastomosis thus create new problems, but it also required incredible technical skill, a challenge akin to sewing together two wet matchsticks. To aid in joining blood vessel to blood vessel, doctors experimented with using a variety of valves and tubes rather than sutures, none of which found universal acceptance as an adequate solution.[72]

With these challenges to performing successful transfusions, American doctors paid scant attention to new scientific investigations of blood. While Carrel and Crile were perfecting vascular anastomosis, the scientist Karl Landsteiner, working in Vienna, was applying Mendelian genetics and biochemistry to the constituent elements of blood.[73] In a series of papers published between 1900 and 1903, Landsteiner explained that not only was cross-species transfusion dangerous because it caused agglutination (clumping) of the blood cells, the cause of the disturbing reactions to some transfusions, but that some human-to-human transfusions could also cause agglutination.[74] Landsteiner identified chemical differences in human blood that were inherited in Mendelian ways, creating categories which he called "blood groups." The four most common of these groups were later called O, A, B, and AB.[75] Bloods from different groups were incompatible; when they came into contact, the seemingly identical fluids would not mix into a homogeneous fluid but clump in life-threatening ways. Blood groups redefined what it meant to be a "blood relative," sometimes sorting parent and child or brother and sister into different groups, while categorizing blood from a complete stranger as compatible, even a stranger of a different race or ethnic background. Throughout the twentieth century, American scientists would continue to identify additional minor blood groups and to use blood groups to explore their understanding of race.[76] Blood groups, also called blood types, proved that blood was both variable and peculiarly universal. While blood differed from person to person, blood from a stranger could be scientifically indistinguishable from one's own blood. The tension between folk beliefs about the particularity of blood and its role in creating family ties and scientific beliefs about blood types would continually affect how Americans thought about blood donors.

While Landsteiner's discoveries would earn him the Nobel Prize in 1930 and had obvious implications for the selection of blood donors, this scientific knowledge did not readily travel to the bedside. Neither Lambert nor Carrel stopped to think about blood groups when confronted with the need to transfuse Lambert's daughter in 1908. Crile himself rejected the idea that blood types had any clinical significance.[77] Dr. Reuben Ottenberg, a young pathologist at Mount Sinai Hospital in New York City, may have been the first American doctor to apply Landsteiner's discovery of blood groups to avoid transfusion reactions, by testing the blood of the intended patient and recipient before the procedure began.[78] But he found that he could not interest surgeons in the blood compatibility tests he offered to conduct. They felt no need for interference from "laboratory men," even men like Ottenberg who had medical degrees and were trained in surgery.[79] In fact most agreed with Crile that blood type incompatibility occurred in vitro, in the laboratory, but did not occur in vivo, in patients.[80] Landsteiner's discoveries were deemed irrelevant by the transfusion community.

As another young surgeon and blood transfusion enthusiast, Dr. Bertram Bernheim, remembered later in his popular book, *Adventure in Blood Transfusion,* surgeons in the 1910s were inclined to ignore the laboratory-based knowledge of blood because "the scientific had outstripped the practical, which is but another way of saying that men still were unable to make the actual blood transfer with any degree of constancy and certainty."[81] Because the amounts transfused were frequently small due to technical problems, reactions remained infrequent and less severe, and such reactions were only one of multiple difficulties that beset both practitioner and patient in this period. Laboratory men like Ottenberg also had a difficult time convincing surgeons like Bernheim to test the compatibility of their patients with intended donors because blood typing was a technically complex and lengthy procedure at this time, requiring expertise and several hours of waiting to see if there was a "match."[82] When the patient was sinking into her grave, doctors were disinclined to wait.

Despite the difficulties, and without the aid of blood typing, surgeons persisted, agreeing with Bernheim that, when it worked, blood transfusion was "the most powerful, the surest" aid to resuscitation "that had ever been placed at the disposal of the medical profession. Properly used, it could revive patients much more promptly—and sustain them longer and better. It made good [surgical] risks out of bad risks; it could and did sometimes make fair risks out of impossible ones."[83] Two innovations developed around 1913 helped to sustain medical enthusiasm for transfusion during its difficult early years. One crucial set of technical advances was a return in part to a style of transfusion used before vascular anastomosis, the use of syringes to withdraw and infuse blood, a technique used by the English obstetrician Blundell in the nineteenth century.[84] Following a protocol developed by a young American doctor impatient with direct transfusion, surgeons replaced the awkward tubes and valves with a set of fifteen syringes and a special set of needles.[85] The process was still complicated; in its recommended form, it involved four medical staff: one practitioner filling a syringe from the donor as another was injecting the previous syringe-full into the recipient, with the goal of having the blood outside the body for only seconds.[86] Having adopted this method in 1916, two physicians at Johns Hopkins Hospital in Baltimore enthused, "It is so easy and so simple . . . that it is almost an ideal method."[87] Having the blood outside the body for even this brief period greatly enhanced the ability of doctors to measure not only the volume withdrawn but also the volume transfused, increasing the safety and controllability of the procedure for both parties. Like expressed breast milk, blood was becoming a disembodied medical therapeutic, administered from the controlling hand of the doctor rather than from the living body of the supplier.

Taking the blood out of the body, though, returned practitioners to the constant fight against blood clots. While the syringe technique was much simpler than anastomosis when it worked, the less skillful found it impossible to prevent clots from blocking the needles.[88] Help came in the form of independent reports in the medical literature from Brussels, New York City, and Buenos Aires in 1914 and 1915, describing the successful use of sodium citrate solution to reduce clotting.[89] This was the second innovation that would allow transfusion to become a common medical procedure.

Sodium citrate had long been used by physiologists to keep blood from clotting in the laboratory; now clinicians were adapting its use to solve the clotting problem at the bedside. Blood mixed with sodium citrate remained fluid, easing its transfer into the recipient by syringe or tube, allowing the practitioner a moment's respite between the harvesting of the blood and its transfusion into the patient. In fact one of the pioneers of the technique stated that he had successfully transfused citrated blood stored from three to five days in an ice box.[90] From the perspective of thirty years later, Bernheim described this innovation as a miraculous advance: "it was almost as if the sun had been made to stand still" to be able to rely on disembodied blood remaining fluid during transfusion. The results were transformative. Transfusion became "available to every sick person in the world."[91]

Despite some hesitancy about using "citrated blood," the oft-predicted simplicity of transfusion had been finally actualized.[92] What had required all the skill of a renowned surgeon like Carrel became "a procedure of minor technical importance."[93] More doctors could safely perform more transfusions on more patients, particularly as doctors now admitted the usefulness of the "laboratory men" to make blood group analyses before performing transfusions.[94] With increased ease of transfusion, the demand for blood increased, as doctors experimented with transfusion as a treatment for a wide array of ailments beyond the life-threatening conditions that had motivated Blundell and Halsted in their early experiments. Through the 1910s eager practitioners tried blood transfusion as a therapy for a wide variety of ills: acute infectious diseases (typhoid, scarlet fever), blood disorders (pernicious anemia, leukemia, hemophilia), particular ailments of a body part (endocarditis, goiter), acute conditions (carbon monoxide poisoning, shock, hemorrhage), and long-term incurable diseases (tuberculosis, cirrhosis, cancer), as well as more general medical diagnoses, such as malnutrition, debility, and intoxication.[95] Disembodied blood had become an accepted medical therapeutic, which made the blood donor an increasing matter of medical interest.

Business for Mothers

While surgeons were optimizing the technique of blood transfusion through the 1910s and 1920s, Talbot and his pediatric colleagues continued to focus on creating a human milk supply. Just as indirect transfusion offered better medical control than direct transfusion, breast milk in bottles offered better control than feeding by suckling. The challenge of treating babies in a hospital unable to use resident wet nurses spurred Talbot to innovate further to replace the wet nurse with the milk seller.

The Boston Floating Hospital was the only ship-based civilian hospital in the United States.[96] Founded in 1894 by a local minister who sought to give poor women and infants access to cool and refreshing sea breezes in the heat of Boston summers, it was a seasonal facility, making day trips around Boston Harbor. At night its patients disembarked and returned home. While in its first summers the Floating Hospital made only a handful of trips, in 1906 it launched in its own specially designed hospital ship and began to travel more frequently.[97] Without overnight accommodations for wet nurses or patients, the hospital relied on its onboard milk laboratory to prepare a selection of artificial foods for its patients. One season it offered three different "strengths" of cow's milk, Horlick's Malted Milk, oatmeal water, rice water, "albumen water," Jacobi's mixture, "peptonized milk," and "dextrinized barley water." While the Floating Hospital had been involved in pure milk campaigns on behalf of its patients—for example, arranging for a milk station to make clean milk available to disembarking passengers for use during the night—it was while Talbot was on the visiting staff in 1910 that the Floating Hospital began purchasing breast milk from local mothers onshore for use by its patients.[98]

The hospital hired Mrs. Henderson, the nurse who had managed Denny's earlier human milk collections, to run its fledgling program. Several Floating Hospital physicians shared the work of inspecting prospective "wet-nurses," as the suppliers were called, and, in addition, the women were required to get written permission from their family doctors to sell their milk. As she had when she was collecting milk for Denny's adult typhoid patients, Mrs. Henderson provided "proper instruction about cleanliness," a daily sterile bottle, and daily collection and transport of the milk to the hospital, packed in ice. The mothers were paid 60 cents a quart, although Mrs. Henderson reported that some women refused payment, seeing their effort as repayment of the charity they themselves had received from the Boston medical community.[99] Her network of suppliers provided about four quarts of breast milk daily that summer.[100] Talbot reported that while there was never enough human milk for all the babies who might benefit from it, he believed it had been "life-saving for most of the babies who did receive it."[101]

While other institutions had previously dismissed such a system of separating breast and baby in space as "impossible," the idea, adapted from Denny and now proven on an institutional scale, quickly spread, both geographically and in its target patient population.[102] By 1915 Talbot's onshore Directory for Wet Nurses was offering bottled breast milk for purchase as well as wet nurses for hire. Parents could choose between hiring a Directory wet nurse to live in their home, at wages of $15 per week plus room and board, or paying $21 (later $30) per week to have the nurse remain at the Directory and express her milk exclusively for their child. A slightly cheaper option was simply buying bottled breast milk for 25 cents an ounce, to a maximum $4 per day, in that case getting milk produced by a variety of women resident at the Directory rather than from one dedicated nurse.[103] Parents liked getting rid of the troublesome wet nurse as much as doctors liked being able to prescribe breast milk by the ounce. By 1927 the Directory was renamed the Directory for Mother's Milk, having closed its residence and limiting itself to the collection and distribution of breast milk in bottles, produced by women in their own homes.[104] Allowing women to live at home, free from the scrutiny of the Directory nurse, broadened the pool of potential donors.

Talbot publicized these efforts in the medical literature, hailing "the present efficient delivery" of human milk as needed, in comparison with the "long delay and worry of twenty years ago."[105] Doctors in other cities adopted his idea, founding similar institutions to organize the collection of human milk as a medically controlled body product. Outside Boston the new institutions were usually "mothers' milk stations" or "mothers' milk bureaus," echoing the Progressive language of cow's milk stations and welfare bureaus. In New York City, Dr. B. Raymond Hoobler, who later moved to Detroit and worked with the mothers' milk bureau there, began a milk collection service at Bellevue Hospital in 1913, finding he could not recruit enough women willing to be resident wet nurses to provide milk for his hospital patients. The service later expanded to provide bottled milk more widely and was taken over by the urban philanthropy the Children's Welfare Federation.[106] By 1929 the Federation was supervising three mothers' milk stations where milk was collected to supply multiple New York City hospitals. Through these stations, the Welfare Federation collected over 2,500 quarts of breast milk per year.[107] In Detroit, as in Boston, a wet nurse directory established in 1914 quickly began to supply a mixture of wet nurses and bottled milk and by 1928 had changed its name to the Mothers' Milk Bureau, having placed only one wet nurse since 1926. The Detroit bureau distributed the 1,400 quarts it collected in 1927 by doctor's prescription to babies in private homes (purchased at 14 cents per ounce or given free of charge to charity cases) and to babies in the local children's hospital.[108] In 1929 at least twenty American cities had a mothers' milk station, buying and selling human milk.[109]

The stations combined medical discipline of the lactating body with medical control over the disembodied milk. They used procedures to standardize the milk itself into a fungible commodity and milk production into routinized paid labor. Without the space constraints of the Floating Hospital, these institutions preferred to buy milk from mothers who expressed on site, under the watchful eye of a nurse. The Detroit bureau allowed only "certain mothers" who had been proven "reliable" to express their milk at home and send it to the hospital—and paid them 2 cents less per ounce than mothers who expressed on site. The home-produced milk was pasteurized, while the on-site milk, left unpasteurized, was called "certified milk," a category borrowed from the dairy industry.[110] Other stations did not attempt to replicate certified milk and simply pasteurized all the milk as that procedure became more commonly used for cow's milk.[111]

Even though the milk was pasteurized, all the stations enforced strict hygienic procedures and monitored the mothers. Some stations offered a modicum of privacy in separate expression cubicles, but the producers remained "visible . . . to the matron who watches and advises during the progress of the milking."[112] In New York the mothers not only washed their hands with running water and soap, but the matron "cleanse[d] the mothers' nipples with boiled water and a cotton pledget, . . . the matron not permitting the mother to express milk from a nipple that has been touched by her clothing until again cleansed."[113] Eventually the New York station moved to transforming its donors from head to toe with "head caps," "freshly laundered gowns," and surgical masks over their nose and mouth.[114] In Kansas City the milk donor underwent a seven-step process to transform her body into an appropriate milk-dispensing device, including covering her entire head "with a triangular shaped cloth," having her hands scrubbed for ten minutes with a brush, permitting the cleansing of her breasts by the matron, and draping her body from the shoulders to the knees with a "special sheet" exposing only the nipples.[115] At Chicago's municipal mothers' milk station, the women, garbed in scarves, gowns, and masks, were examined by a male doctor and "scrubb[ed] within an inch of their lives," including scrubbing each breast three times with "green soap" and toweling dry with sterile towels handed to them "on sterilized metal tongs" by an attending nurse. Here they sat around a communal table to express into cups and then were required to drink a quart of cow's milk before leaving.[116] Their milk was pooled, "just as good dairymen mix the milk of their herds so that a slight deficiency in one donor will be compensated for by the contributions of other donors [allowing the] desired content of fat, protein, carbohydrate and mineral salts" to remain "very even."[117]

The transformation from wet nursing as a service to breast milk as a "unique and valuable market commodity," as an advocate described it in 1929, brought a change in terminology, although not a change in money flows.[118] The former wet nurses were now described as "healthy mothers" engaged in a "profitable business" through the "legitimate trade" in mothers' milk.[119] Parents of babies needing milk still paid, and the lactating women providing milk still received money. As the supplying women were transformed from servants into "healthy mothers" engaged in "business," however, there was a shift in the type of women recruited, as well as in the treatment of human milk. This dual shift can be traced clearly in the history of Talbot's organization.

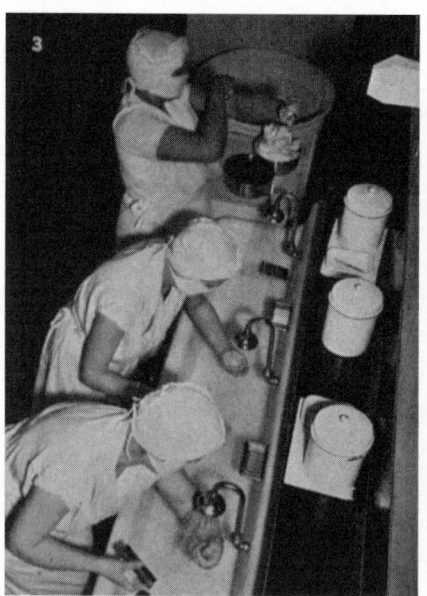 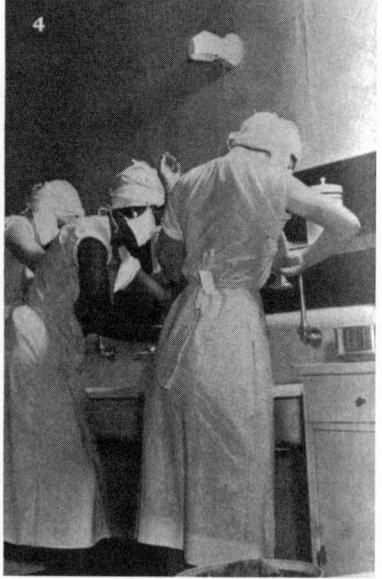

Chicago municipal mothers' milk station—Donor preparation, 1940. *"Saving Lives with Mothers' Milk,"* Hygeia, *May 1940, 426.*

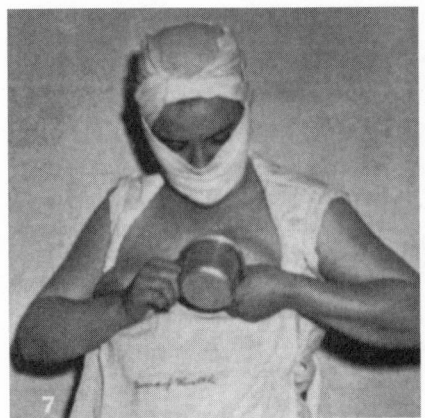

Chicago municipal mothers' milk station—Collecting milk, 1940. *"Saving Lives with Mothers' Milk,"* Hygeia, *May 1940, 427.*

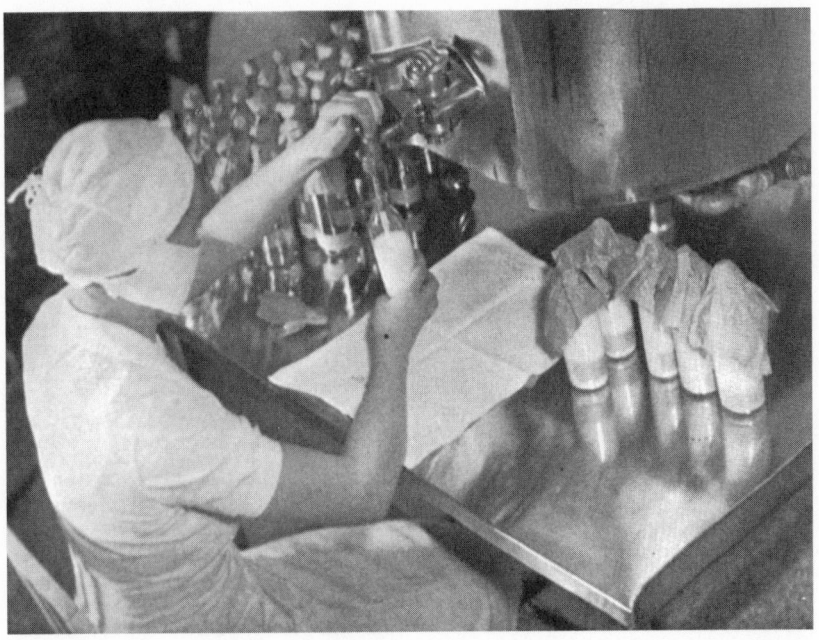

Chicago municipal mothers' milk station—Processing milk, 1940. *"Saving Lives with Mothers' Milk,"* Hygeia, *May 1940, 428.*

Wet nurses were found among the bottom rungs of society—women without husbands to support them or their babies. Part of Talbot's goal in establishing the Directory and its associated home was the uplift of these women. Contrary to traditional practice, Talbot sought to facilitate the ability of his medically managed wet nurses to care for their own babies. The home helped them stay with their babies while waiting for work, and the Directory required hiring parents to allow the nurse to bring her child with her. Talbot told his fellow doctors that he hoped in this way to foster maternal love in "these girls" so that each woman would look after her baby rather than "want[ing] to get rid of the incubus as soon as possible." His project would, he claimed, alleviate the burden on the state, which would otherwise have to provide for these children as abandoned orphans.[120] The Directory employed social workers to advise the women, sought if possible to obtain a financial settlement from the absent fathers, and hoped to launch the women, after their stint of wet nursing, with a nest egg of $50 to $300 saved from their wages. The Directory helped the women find subsequent employment and, if they could no longer keep their own children with them, a place to board their babies.[121]

It was these women, the most desperate, whom the hiring mothers had long feared as possible sources of contamination of their children, bringing disease, disorder, and unfamiliar religious practices and food into their homes. But in switching to bottled milk, the Boston Directory and other milk bureaus also began a switch of suppliers. In her work for Denny and Talbot, Mrs. Henderson had already begun to recruit from a slightly different group of women than the desperate unwed mothers who had become wet nurses. The women she visited week after week to collect bottles of milk were women who had a stable place to live. When the Directory for Mother's Milk closed its home and began to rely completely on women with that minimum level of financial stability, it was switching to a supplier pool drawn from the working poor. Rather than unwed mothers, these women were generally what Talbot described as "healthy married mothers."[122]

When Hoobler began the milk collection effort in New York City that become the Children's Welfare Foundation milk bureaus, he described how the Social Service Department of his hospital recruited and managed "deserving mother[s]," who, while returning to their own homes after their confinement, could in this way earn money rather than needing a charitable handout. He called his milk-selling scheme a "double charity," allowing each milk seller to "support herself and her child," while helping a sick child with the "best food known." He argued that by appearing daily at the hospital to express milk, bringing their own babies to be weighed and examined, these women received more services in the form of advice on nutrition and child care than they otherwise would have gotten, helping them to better rear their own children.[123]

When Hoobler moved to Detroit and worked with the milk bureau there, he encountered women who used the business of milk selling to supplement rather than obtain the basic necessities of life. He described a milk seller in Detroit as enjoying "many comforts previously beyond her reach." One woman reportedly earned "more than $3,500" during a lactation period lasting fourteen months and purchased a house. The Children's Welfare Bureau similarly reported that a mother of three earned "more than $1,700" during her four years of lactation.[124] The "legitimate trade" in human milk was indeed a "profitable business," allowing these married mothers to make significant contributions to their family's welfare at a time when the average annual earnings of all employees (male and female) was $1,420 for nonfarm workers and when men and women in domestic service earned an average of $714 per year for full-time work.[125]

As Talbot had done in the early days of his Directory, supporters of mothers' milk stations reached out to recruit sellers and convince the public to use their product. In a lay magazine published by the American Medical Association, these sums earned by milk sellers were repeated, along with the encouraging words, "It is amazing how much milk can be furnished by one woman, especially if she is taught the proper methods. She may easily increase the supply from 2 or 3 ounces a day to from 15 to 20 ounces or more, in addition to a satisfactory supply for her own baby. The price paid . . . ranges from 15 to 20 cents an ounce."[126] Other mothers would have learned about bottled breast milk as volunteers or through membership in a civic organization. While stations were organized and run by medical professionals, middle- and upper-class women were often involved in supporting the project, such as in Kansas City, where the local Women's City Club sponsored the mothers' milk station, or in Pittsburgh, where the Junior League played that role.[127] In 1934 bottled breast milk achieved international fame when human milk collected in Chicago and Toronto was provided to the Canadian Dionne quintuplets for the first six months of their lives.[128]

This valorization of the supplier as a healthy married mother in business, along with the medicalization of the bottled mothers' milk through pooling and pasteurization and its dispensation by medical personnel, seemed to largely quell the formerly strong anxieties about feeding babies milk from strangers. A troublesome servant had been replaced by a "superior maternal accessory," bottles of standardized, fungible milk with clear market value. Parents seeking this "unique and valuable market commodity" for their own baby could buy it, with a doctor's order, by paying from 14 to 30 cents per ounce, with prices varying by city. Most bureaus also offered milk at reduced prices or free to charity cases.[129] Prices for buying the milk were based on recouping not only the price paid to sellers but other overhead costs. The organizers of the Detroit bureau explained that they were not trying to make the bureau "pay" but kept track of their per unit cost (17 cents), their average selling price (14 cents), and their total budget ($15,000) (1925 figures).[130] The hope was to have enough families paying well over 17 cents an ounce to subsidize those families that paid nothing. Over time, the bureau was able to decrease its per unit cost, and with the help of a hospital that provided space and refrigeration, was "practically self-supporting from its beginning."[131] While wet nursing had been a service provided at market prices, the doctors who sought to create a disembodied human milk supply also sought to control the market for selling and buying milk to achieve their professional ends of treating all needy patients. Just as they allocated their professional services, treating some patients for free while charging others on a sliding scale, they varied the prices for bottled milk. Bottled human milk could have been sold at a profit for whatever price the market would bear, as was true for formulas from commercial milk laboratories and certified milk, but through the medically run milk stations, it was not.[132] As a body product, human milk was a commodity traded within a constrained market designed to promote the ends of the doctors who had succeeded in organizing its supply and controlled its distribution.

Men of Business

As "healthy married mothers" became sought-after participants in the "legitimate trade" in mothers' milk, doctors who were now convinced that blood transfusion was a promising therapy were beginning to focus on their own supply problem. In 1913, as Hoobler was setting up his milk collection program in New York City, one of his first questions for his "experiment in the collection of human milk" was "What price will have to be paid for the milk in order to secure it?"[133] Despite the language of donation used in blood transfusion and the willingness of friends or family members to give blood without any compensation, transfusionists had the same question: How much money was needed to induce people to act as blood "donors"? It seemed self-evident to doctors that money was the appropriate incentive to induce people to become body product suppliers. The transfusionists also needed to decide who should be recruited to become "donors." Without any tradition of blood selling analogous to wet nursing, or physiological limitations to blood selling beyond basic good health, there was no obvious target population of healthy bodies to solicit. As doctors came to think of blood selling as another "legitimate trade" in the 1920s and 1930s, they would come to consider blood sellers as "men of business," making this role almost as strongly gendered as that of the healthy married mothers engaged in the profitable business of milk selling.

Before World War I, when blood transfusion was rare and experimental, most often the procedure was used in urgent, now-or-never situations. Faced with an emergency, doctors used ad hoc techniques to obtain blood, casting about the hospital corridors for a suitable supplier. For his first transfusion, Bernheim recruited an outpatient, offering $100 for his participation.[134] Calling upon the sick to aid the sick was problematic, however. Blood donors were more often recruited from the distraught relatives who had brought the patient to the hospital.[135] Strangers were paid; friends and relatives were expected to supply blood for free, a gift to their loved one.

The $100 Bernheim offered his donor represented the considerable risk and inconvenience to the donor during the period of direct transfusion. Blood transfusion was surgery, performed in an operating theater, where donor and recipient lay close together. The surgeon needed to cut open the healthy body to expose an inch or so of vein or artery, usually working from the wrist, "dissecting out" both donor and recipient under local anesthetic. The procedure left a "considerable wound," which took time to heal, was susceptible to infection, and left a scar. No donor could give again soon from the same place.[136]

Even when citrated blood made indirect transfusion possible and blood transfusion was more common and less hazardous for donors, there were problems finding donors. Frequently a patient arrived without accompanying friends or relatives, or perhaps none of those available was suitable because of age or medical condition. As blood typing became standard practice in the interwar years, the pool of frantic relatives had to be sorted to find those not just willing and anxious to give but those who were biochemically compatible, a process that took time and might result in no match. Doctors began to look beyond their immediate environment and imagine a more organized pool of potential donors, ready to provide blood on demand. Doctors hoped to expand the pool of potential suppliers for any patient by reaching beyond their blood relatives to blood strangers, unknown, unrelated individuals who had compatible blood and were willing to give it up—for a price. The professional blood seller would be a body organized for medical convenience who was in the business of selling blood.

When Bernheim decided to establish a regular supply of paid donors in the era of citrated blood and indirect transfusion, he offered $50. Just as Talbot had looked among the poorest new mothers to find wet nurses, Bernheim targeted poor men living in low- or no-cost men's boardinghouses, whom he characterized as "rovers of the unskilled type."[137] Despite their financial need, these men were unmoved by Bernheim's first solicitation; the role of blood seller was not intuitively appealing. Only after the desk clerk picked out the first group of likely candidates and ordered them to go to the hospital with the "doc," did Bernheim succeed in developing a successful recruitment technique. He came to rely on the clerk to recruit a group each time he called to say that he was preparing to perform a transfusion. Eight to twelve men were needed to ensure finding a match, and it took about three hours for the tests to be done and the donor selected. All men came to the hospital for typing and then waited for the result. The rejected would-be donors were given $1, and the lucky match got $50 when the procedure was finished.[138]

According to Bernheim, "the chief trouble with the system," which he used for several years, was that the donor most often took his money and got "rip-roaring drunk." Like the wet nurses who left the Directory to work in private homes, once away from direct medical supervision, the donors were troublesome. Heavy drinking was not medically advised after bleeding, and Bernheim worried both about his donors injuring themselves and about the negative publicity when a few of the men made the newspapers in stories that linked their sudden wealth through blood selling to drunken brawls. The solution was for Bernheim to personally conduct each donor home, even though Bernheim himself was "usually pretty much of a wreck when the thing was over," and pay the donor only once he was back at his rooming house, where he would be encouraged to stay by the desk clerk.[139]

As transfusions became more frequent, another problem emerged. The time needed to determine blood types was irksome, and after an initial period of blithely ignoring the possibility of transmitting syphilis from supplier to recipient, doctors felt that a negative Wassermann test proving absence of disease was also needed, requiring additional time. While the boardinghouses could offer a reliable supply of willing bodies, the "rovers" came and went, meaning that each call produced first-time sellers who needed to be typed and tested. The solution was a list, like Talbot's Directory for Wet Nurses, of medically processed willing donors, whose blood type had been determined and recorded and who had a recent negative Wassermann test. The paid blood donor was changing from an adventurous bystander, recruited on the spur of the moment, into a medically managed body, selected and prepared for this new role. The money Bernheim was offering to donors attracted another, more appealing population: medical and nursing students. These men and women became even more amenable to blood selling when the practice of "cutting down" on the vein of the donor for direct transfusion began to be replaced with the syringe method, which was less invasive of the supplier's body, did not leave a scar, and reduced the risk of infection.[140] In Baltimore, at least, "students, nurses, and younger doctors had a monopoly of the business" through the 1930s, some becoming "near-professional" donors in the frequency of their donations.[141]

In describing the changes over time in his sources of blood, Bernheim distinguished between the paid "donor" and "so-called professional donors."[142] Though his early donors were often paid, he considered only the repeat blood sellers to be "professional donors." The professional donors were more convenient to doctors, forming "an ever-ready nucleus from which to draw," as well as a more efficient source, typed and screened in advance.[143] As Bernheim and his medical colleagues came to appreciate and cultivate the professional donor, the blood seller acquired a specific set of characteristics: available by phone or otherwise on short notice, free from syphilis, of known blood type, needful of extra income, reliable and compliant—and, usually, male. There was no physiological reason for preferring men as blood donors. Crile had declared in 1909 that "both men and women are suitable," and women had been used as donors since the earliest days of transfusion in the United States.[144] Bernheim admitted women had advantages, being in his opinion less likely to experience a drop in blood pressure and faint. He used female friends and family as unpaid donors, as well as female nursing students as paid donors, but he found women's veins more difficult to work with and "preferred" men.[145] His boardinghouse recruitment system had excluded women, and as the professional blood donor became a more familiar creature nationwide, he was usually male.

What Bernheim described as the practice in Baltimore was followed in other major cities. Doctors drew their blood supply from a mix of the economically marginal and convenient young medical professionals, usually paid, with friends and relatives of patients, usually unpaid. The paid donors were often formalized into a registry maintained by a hospital. The ubiquity of reliance on paid donors led the U.S. House of Representatives to pass a bill in 1926 authorizing the payment of blood suppliers by government hospitals. In suggesting that federal funds be used to reimburse sellers up to $50 per donation, Congress was acting to make sure that veterans and others within the federal hospital system had access to the same care as that provided in other hospitals.[146] Without payments to blood sellers, blood transfusion was not available.

With the medical profession convinced of the need for blood sellers, it supported a national effort during the 1920s and 1930s to establish the status of the professional donor as a heroic and respectable figure. Like the news stories about the new "superior maternal accessory" and the sums earned by milk sellers, this narrative both made the status attractive to those who might consider joining a registry and eased public worries about the qualities that might be transmitted with bought body products. The very term *professional donor* elevated the supplying body's labor, neatly mixing financial reimbursement with an implication of service, matching the ethos of other professionals who worked to serve rather than engaging in a straight exchange of product or time for cash.

Through blood selling, even an uneducated laborer could earn good money while serving others. In 1924 an Ohio newspaper devoted a half-page of its feature "New and Interesting Facts on Science and Life" to an illustrated article, "Earning a Living by Letting Blood." The article lauded men such as John Broady, a "plucky Kansan," earning his way through college by selling his blood.[147] Frank Welch, a factory worker, was acclaimed in

1929 for selling twenty-three and a half gallons of blood over five years for a total of $5,000.[148] Thomas Kane, who had a steady job in addition to his blood work, told the press that his success in selling blood without ill effect was due to the large number of raw onions he consumed.[149] These "professionals" were not "down-and-outers" or "rovers" but strong, healthy working-class men or college boys who sold their blood to supplement their income or to earn tuition in order to advance themselves.[150] The descriptions of these men, which included details such as Broady's stature—he was described as six feet tall and weighing 180 pounds—provided two reassuring lessons to the American public.[151] First, professional donors were admirable physical specimens, whose ability to sell blood affirmed their robust masculinity. Second, any American would want blood from such men, who were bursting with health, vitality, and personal initiative.

Like Talbot describing his "healthy married mothers" who sold their milk, the medical profession aided this positive image of the professional donor, publishing articles for the public about "this business of selling blood," a "new calling" for "healthy, full-blooded young men and women."[152] These sellers "graciously pour[ed] out their blood in the interests of science" as a "unique way of providing bread and butter for the family table."[153] While "full-blooded" women were medically able to sell blood, the author who described this "new calling" noted that only European hospitals bought female blood.[154] The American blood seller was a husband-provider who was "so successful in the business" that he could earn a "fairly steady income" in the big cities, without "the need to engage in any other wage-earning activity." His business was the "manufacturing and selling of blood." To engage in this business, the professional donor could not "lead a life of ease and luxury," however. "He must go through life with a sore arm and must submit to considerable discomfort." And to make his body into an appropriate production mechanism, he must be careful about what he ate and subsist on a "scientific diet of blood-producing foods," with an emphasis on eggs and fresh milk.[155] So fortified, he might give as often as forty times a year. Readers were warned that an amateur, without the benefit of the scientific diet, should give only three to four times a year.[156]

The professional donor was also distinguished from the amateur by his motivation. Before the emergence of the professional donors, news stories and Hollywood films had often lauded blood donors as exceptional heroes.[157] These articles, however, downplayed any idea of "romance" that an uninformed amateur might expect from participating in a transfusion, claiming that "nine times out of ten," blood transfusion was not a life-saving event, and thus suggesting that feelings of heroism were misplaced. In contrast to the "satisfaction" that an amateur might feel, believing that the patient was "beholden to him" for having "helped a brother on the road to health," the professional seller was appropriately motivated primarily by money, treating donation as "a mere matter of business."[158] Doctors wanted business-like, compliant donors, not starry-eyed romantics or unreliable rovers.

The professional donor was lauded as a businessman at a time when many Americans were seeking employment. Although the articles did not put it in these terms, the blood line might be better than the bread line. "Salesmen of blood" continued to be hailed through the 1930s as the solution to the blood supply problem.[159] While doctors did not call payments to professional blood donors a "double charity," like the money earned by married women who sold their milk to augment household incomes during the lean years of the Great Depression, husbands could help provide for their families as "professionals," demonstrating their robust health, business savvy, and masculinity.

Maintaining a registry of professional donors, however, was "cumbersome and elaborate" and "necessitated constant work, supervision and revision."[160] The Mayo Clinic in Minnesota had one thousand donors on its roster in 1923. Donors were categorized by blood type. Further, each registrant received a general physical examination, urinalysis, and a syphilis test every six months. The would-be donors were also queried about their "social habits and social status." About two hundred out of the one thousand processed potential donors were in the "active pool," available on short notice. These active donors gave as frequently as every three weeks. They ranged from nineteen to sixty-two years old and included both men and women, although men age thirty to forty were the most common.[161] In addition to a preference for men, the Minnesota doctors worried about using "boys" who might be too apt "to spend, in exploits, money too easily obtained."[162] As a man of business, the professional donor should have settled habits.

Not all hospitals had the resources to maintain such a screened list. These hospitals relied on commercial agencies that supplied professional donors for a fee, outsourcing the work of creating and maintaining a registry.[163] While doctors certainly agreed that donor recruitment was an inefficient use of their expertise, just as pediatricians had objected to time-consuming searches for wet nurses, they were wary of commercial agencies, some of which were believed to engage in "ruthless exploitation" and "improper technical treatment" of suppliers.[164] A magazine article published in 1939 characterized such bureaus as including "small fly-by-night agencies" conducting a "limited but profitable racket," which involved holding blood suppliers in a state of "quasi-serfdom," "installed in shabby rooming houses, overcharged for meals and sleeping quarters, restricted in their activities and personal freedom, chiseled in their fees and all too frequently bled white by transfusions."[165]

It was in New York City that a medically controlled alternative to both commercial agencies and the hospital registry developed, akin to the existing mothers' milk stations, as a freestanding, medically run institution to recruit and organize supplying bodies. Copying an idea implemented by the British Red Cross in London, Dr. Arthur Coca organized the nonprofit Cooperative Blood Donor Agency out of New York Hospital in 1928 as a "high grade scientific intermediary" between donor and hospital, which would keep the donors "always . . . under proper control."[166] This agency was transformed into a citywide organization, the Blood Transfusion Betterment Association (BTBA), through the efforts of the New York Academy of Medicine and a starting grant from John D. Rockefeller Jr. The BTBA promoted blood transfusion research and operated its own registry, the Blood Donors Bureau, to supply professional donors to multiple city hospitals.[167] One of the Bureau's founders described the advantages over a single hospital service as twofold: it was easier to maintain a supply of donors with more rare blood types and "to regularize the employment of donors."[168] Like nursing mothers who needed financial support to enable them to keep breastfeeding while waiting for employment, to be professional blood donors, the typed, processed recruits, representing an investment of medical time and resources, needed a sufficiently frequent ability to sell their blood to stay with this line of work.

The BTBA opened two offices for the screening and monthly reexamination of donors. Initially each donor was compensated at a rate of $10 per 100 cc, but in no event less than $25 per transfusion. Even if a transfusion was not made, the donor was paid $2.50 as compensation for traveling to the requesting hospital. By the late 1930s compensation had dropped to $7 per 100 cc, with a minimum payment of $14.[169] The professional donor in

New York City, like the professional donor in Baltimore, was male. They were accepted "primarily on the basis of their physical health and the condition of their veins at the elbow, but also on the basis of their appearance, character, accessibility by telephone day and night, and ability to respond to a call whenever made."[170] Similar to their pediatric colleagues seeking breast milk, in creating the professional blood donor, doctors sought to upgrade their suppliers from the most desperate. The BTBA founders worried that "the unsupervised and uncontrolled donors . . . supplied by commercial agencies" were too often "recruited from the less responsible elements of the community."[171] The Blood Donors Bureau tried to do better. About one-quarter of applicants for the job of blood seller were rejected, often on the basis of "unprepossessing habits" or "unpleasant personal appearance."[172] Donors tended to be "students, professional men and workers of all kinds."[173] They were required to provide notice if they left their telephones while on call, and were subject to a three months' suspension for tardiness.[174] To the extent possible, the Bureau sought to standardize and control donor bodies, striving to make a safe and reliable blood supply available to its member medical institutions. Other doctors followed its example, and by 1937 eight other cities had nonprofit donor agencies run by either the local board of health or the county medical society to provide screened professional donors to local hospitals.[175]

The BTBA founders also worked with the city board of health to amplify their efforts to provide standardized donors in New York City. The Blood Donors Bureau could not meet all the need for blood sellers, and commercial registries persisted. At the urging of the doctors, New York became the only government to pass regulations requiring licensing of blood donor registries. In this way, doctors created minimum standards for all professional donors, even those who were not employed by a nonprofit agency supervised by organized medicine. By municipal regulation, the new creature, the professional blood donor, was defined at law as "a blood donor who offers or gives his blood for transfusion purposes for a fee."[176] Each donor was required by law to register with the city and to carry a booklet containing his physical description, blood type, photograph, and signature. The donor had to produce the booklet at each donation, and an entry was then made of the date and the volume of blood drawn. In theory, by means of this book, the frequency of donations could be tracked to protect the donor from selling blood too often for his own health, and dates of physical examinations could be noted to protect the recipient.[177] In 1930 there were over 1,500 registered donors.[178]

This control was not welcomed by all professional donors, at least some of whom preferred the free and easy practices before city regulation. There is anecdotal evidence that donor booklets were shared, sold, and forged to bypass health problems and frequency restrictions. When these not-quite-regulated salesmen of blood appeared at hospitals to provide blood for patients, they did not succeed in convincing everyone that they were professional men of business. By 1938 the public could choose between two possible images of the blood seller. The professional donor, described in such glowing terms to the public at the beginning of the 1930s, was the subject of another laudatory article, "Blood from a Stranger," in the *Saturday Evening Post*. While admitting that professional donors "weren't all angels," the author described how the BTBA and regulations had cleaned up the worst of commercial agency problems. He reassured readers that the dregs of society could not be professional donors; only those with other, regular income were able to eat well enough to meet the health requirements.[179] That same year, however, another popular magazine, the *American Mercury,* offered an alternative vision of down-and-out blood sellers working through seedy commercial agencies. The article, "I Sell Blood," was purportedly written by a newly unemployed man who entered the world of blood selling to save himself from destitution. He described the culture of the "old-timers" who resented the Blood Donors Bureau and deliberately evaded its regulations. He and his fellow blood sellers lived in a squalid boardinghouse, waiting for the next call to bleed. The men he described were not eager young students or budding salesmen but broken failures.[180]

By the time the BTBA began operation, the volumes of blood flowing from suppliers to recipients in New York City were reaching significant levels. It was estimated that 11,000 transfusions were performed in New York City in 1929, averaging a pint each.[181] In 1937 the BTBA alone supplied donors for 9,280 transfusions, and the total number of transfusions in New York may have reached 30,000, a threefold increase in less than ten years.[182] Ottenberg, the "laboratory man" whose early offers to perform blood typing had been ignored, described transfusion in the late 1930s as "so safe and so easy to do that it is seldom omitted in any case in which it may be of benefit." Now that blood transfusion was common, the chief difficulty from Ottenberg's perspective was finding "the large sums of money" needed to pay professional donors.[183] Doctors sought to pass the full price of buying blood to patients, but many patients could not afford this aspect of their care. In a nationwide survey made in 1937, only slightly more than half of hospitals reported that they were willing to bear the cost of transfusions for indigent patients, with one hospital reporting annual expenditures of $25,000 to $30,000 for this purpose.[184] If there were no hospital funds available, the patient could not receive a transfusion. While pediatricians managed mothers' milk stations so that free milk was available for charity cases and could also turn to an array of artificial infant foods if bottled breast milk were not available, doctors in Tennessee reported that charity patients died for want of funds to buy blood.[185] At a cost of $25 to $50 per 500 cc, blood was "economically prohibitive."[186] The professional donor had become the solution to the supply problem for both milk and blood, but for many patients needing an emergency blood transfusion, he was now creating a new problem. For one Chicago doctor, the solution was found in banking.

2

Banks That Take Donations

Now, thanks to the blood bank, no one needs to die at Cook
County Hospital for lack of blood for transfusion.

—Dr. Bernard Fantus, 1938

In 1933 Dr. Bernard Fantus accepted a new job as director of therapeutics
at Cook County Hospital in Chicago. He was an expert in pharmacology
who, in his new position, found himself in charge of blood, a type of therapeutic that had not been in use when he worked as an intern at Cook
County in 1900.[1] The situation at the Cook County Hospital with respect
to blood transfusions was grim. Cook County was a public hospital, treating charity patients. Both its patients and the hospital itself were experiencing unrelenting financial pressures during the Great Depression. The hospital lacked sufficient funds even for sutures with which to sew up patients
after surgery, so surgeons fashioned makeshift substitutes out of cotton
thread.[2] Without funds for professional blood donors, the only option was
friends and family donors. Even when a patient had volunteers to provide
blood, however, a donor might not be found. One patient chart from these
years reportedly recorded, "We have typed 29 people; none of them match.

The family is exhausted and so is the intern."[3] Fantus knew that patients were dying while such futile searches were under way, while at hospitals serving private patients, one phone call would result in the prompt appearance of a typed, screened professional donor. Further, when Cook County doctors did succeed in finding a donor, about one-third of their patients suffered reactions to the transfusions they received.[4] Safe transfusions required not only willing suppliers but also expertise in blood type determination, as well as the careful preparation of sterile equipment and of the sodium citrate solution used in blood withdrawal and infusion.

Fantus was familiar with the constraints on Cook County staff and patients not only from his previous affiliation with the institution but from his own humble past. A native of Budapest who immigrated to Chicago as a young man with his parents, he first worked in a drug store and was able to attend medical school only when his father, a printer, succeeded in trading printing services for his son's tuition. Fantus, like doctors around the country, was disturbed that patients were dying because of their inability to access a quick, safe blood transfusion due to lack of funds for a professional donor.[5] The professional donor was a great boon to doctors, but the person-to-person transaction involved in each blood sale meant that there was no room for the creative billing practices that mothers' milk stations used, allowing medical directors to allocate the bottled milk based on a combination of medical need and ability to pay. Unlike pooled milk, the blood remained the property of the donor as long as it was in his veins, and possession would be transferred to the recipient at the time of transfusion only upon payment of the going rate.

One way to avoid the need for patients to pay professional donors would be to make the blood supply more like the milk supply—and like the supply of other therapeutics that the hospital stockpiled for distribution, such as aspirin and bandages. If the hospital bought the blood itself at market rates, then it could charge patients on a sliding scale, using the wealthier patients to subsidize the poorer. Such an approach, while used successfully in the freestanding milk stations, which served the wealthy and the poor alike, was not an option at Cook County. There simply were no wealthier patients. Those who could afford to pay for medical care went elsewhere. Confronted with what he found to be an intolerable situation, Fantus spent nearly four years developing a different approach, devising a system of blood management designed to eliminate the paid donor altogether. In 1937

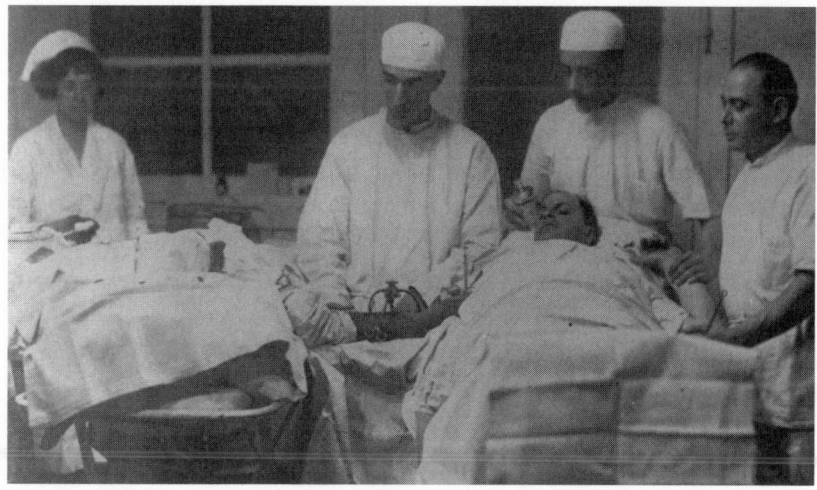

Body-to-body direct blood transfusion, 1929 (donor on right, facing camera). *Herbert G. Harlan, "This Business of Selling Blood,"* Hygeia, *May 1929, 471.*

he explained his system to the medical profession as a "bank." It combined a stockpile of blood controlled by the hospital with a new category of blood donor, motivated neither by love nor by money, but by indebtedness. Cook County patients, unable to pay in cash for blood, would exchange blood for blood.

Storing Blood in War and Peace

"Banking" blood implied deposits and withdrawals from an institutional supply. Such a stockpile was possible only if blood could exist outside the body for hours or days, rather than just minutes. During the 1930s pediatricians and transfusionists alike sought new ways to make the sun stand still and increase the value of body products as therapeutics by making them more shelf-stable. If body products could be stored between collection and use, doctors would be less dependent on undependable bodies. Mothers' milk stations used pasteurization to increase the safety of storing milk on ice, and as refrigeration technologies improved, mothers' milk stations began to preserve milk by freezing.[6] Blood, however, proved much more difficult to preserve, with its tendency to clot and its mixture of delicate cells. When he took charge of therapeutics at Cook County in 1933, Fantus started his effort to solve the blood-cash problem by concentrating on a practical method of maintaining an inventory of stored blood. What became the Cook County "blood bank" began as the Blood Preservation Laboratory.

Fantus's efforts, which ended up taking several years of experimentation and consultation with Chicago-area colleagues, were primarily directed toward convincing himself and his Cook County colleagues that "preserved blood" was safe and effective.[7] As soon as the collection of blood into citrate solution came into use in the mid-1910s, situations had arisen in which a planned transfusion was delayed, or even canceled, leaving the collected blood unused. Doctors, loath to waste this resource, wondered whether it could be stored and used later. In an emergency they could and did perform a transfusion by grabbing a bottle of previously collected citrated blood rather than by contacting a registry and beginning with a warm body.[8] The Baltimore pioneer transfusionist Bertram Bernheim described carrying citrated blood around with him for "several days" at room temperature, so that he always had a pint available.[9] His practice did not come into widespread use, however, as most doctors, already suspicious of citrated blood, looked askance at "stored" or "preserved blood"—blood that not only was chemically modified but had been sitting outside the body for days.

It was intriguing, however, to imagine that blood could be collected days ahead of its use, meaning that it would be immediately available when an accident victim arrived at the hospital or a woman started to hemorrhage during childbirth, without the need to call a professional donor or to start typing friends and family. Laboratory researchers at the Rockefeller Institute in New York City worked on the problem of blood storage throughout the 1910s, experimenting with techniques to keep red blood cells intact and functioning outside the body.[10] Their work found application at the front lines of World War I, where doctors were anxious to save lives by any means possible. Even before the United States entered the war in 1917, "preserved blood" was being tried on the European front. Dr. Oswald Robertson, an English-born American physician who had been working at the Rockefeller Institute, was so enthusiastic about using preserved blood for battlefront transfusions that when his ideas fell on deaf ears in the U.S. Army, he arranged to serve on loan with the British Expeditionary Force.[11] While preservation could not increase the overall quantity of blood available, it could allow stockpiling. Robertson collected blood from lightly wounded patients and stored it in sodium citrate and dextrose on ice for up to twenty-six days before use, in this way managing to have blood on hand for the rush of casualties arriving after a battle.[12]

When the United States joined the war, Bernheim and George Crile, the Ohio surgeon who had published his success with direct transfusion by vascular anastomosis in 1907, were among the American doctors who sailed to France, taking the current practices of blood transfusion with them.[13] The U.S. military designated three-person transfusion teams to transfuse the wounded in preparation for surgery or transport.[14] Blood transfusion was used to treat "shock," itself a newly identified and evolving medical condition arising out of observations of peacetime surgery and the wounds of modern warfare. Distinct from "shell shock," a psychological condition also identified during World War I, shock was a loosely defined condition, marked by pallor, low blood pressure, and the gradual shutting down of body systems, which, if not reversed, could lead to death. Medical professionals believed that it was caused by fluid loss that led to reduced blood flow.[15]

As transfusing patients in "shock wards" achieved success in reducing mortality, the difficulty became finding donors. Both British and American doctors relied mostly on fresh blood collected into citrate from lightly wounded men in the same hospital, from passing troops, or, less optimally, from hospital staff, who were then lost from duty as they recovered.[16] But, like bottled mothers' milk at Boston's Floating Hospital, there was never enough. Bernheim, working as a surgeon for two years with the American Expeditionary Force in France, described in glowing terms the "gallant" life-saving work of the "Shock Teams" but noted too the "need for blood and more blood during and after operation, . . . blood that simply was not to be had."[17] By the end of the war in 1918, the blood supply had become a military problem. Henceforth the U.S. government would consider blood crucial war matériel.[18]

Returning to their civilian practices, American surgeons who had served in World War I sought to apply the lessons of the shock teams stateside, increasingly seeking to use blood as part of general surgical practice. They had seen ample evidence that transfusion aided wounded soldiers, and over time, the soldier, as a victim of sudden blood loss, became the prototype of the patient most likely to benefit from transfusion. Rather than using blood to treat the wide range of patients given blood in the first flush of

transfusion enthusiasm, doctors gradually focused their use of blood transfusion on those who had lost blood through surgery, accident, or hemorrhage.[19] But without the exigencies of battle, during most of the interwar
period civilian doctors did not copy the military use of preserved blood,
relying instead on registries and agencies to coordinate blood donors who
supplied fresh blood. Even military doctors remained suspicious of citrated
blood, let alone of preserved blood, that is, citrated blood that had been
stored on ice.[20] As long as the professional donor system was working reasonably well, stored blood remained a last resort. At the Mayo Clinic in
Rochester, Minnesota, where there was an extensive donor registry, by 1935
doctors "frequently" kept citrated blood in the "ice box" for up to fourteen
days in order to provide a series of small doses to one patient from a single
donor bleeding or to use for an emergency transfusion, but did not rely on
their stored blood for routine transfusions.[21] As late as 1938 a journalist reflected medical attitudes when he asked how "blood which has been standing around in a refrigerator . . . [could] do a patient as much good as the
fresh, warm, live article."[22]

The medical distaste for stored blood was based not only on intuition
that fresh was better than stale and worries about citrate interfering with
natural clotting processes but on the documented increased incidence of
chills and fever in the recipients of preserved blood. It was not until the
1930s that this problem was traced to inadequate attention to sterilization
and cleaning of the materials used to store and transfuse blood rather than
to some property of the preservative itself. In an era before disposable plas-
tic storage bags and tubing, pyrogens—the catchall term for fever-causing
contaminants—could accumulate in reused glass apparatuses and rubber
tubing.[23] With better sterilization and cleansing techniques, medical personnel were able to eliminate this problem.[24] Yet without the urgent demands of war, it took the financial pressures of the Great Depression to
motivate doctors like Fantus to implement the use of stored blood on a wide
scale.

To address the problem of pyrogens, already rampant at Cook County
when using fresh blood, Fantus created the Sterile Supplies Department,
which systemically applied rigorous techniques of sterilization and chemical cleaning of the apparatus used to draw, store, and transfuse blood,
greatly reducing transfusion reactions.[25] These techniques would support
the safer use of stored blood as well as of freshly drawn citrated blood. Just

as stored blood had allowed military surgeons to quickly provide blood to battlefield victims, Fantus thought that stored blood would improve the lengthy and chaotic process of obtaining blood from the uncompensated friend or family donor. He described the process with the same distaste for time-wasting exhibited by the young pediatrician Fritz Talbot in 1908 as he rode street cars around Boston, searching for a wet nurse:

> Donors had to be called for. The response sometimes would be a horde of excited, noisy, gesticulating foreigners. A little blood had to be drawn from half a dozen or even more of these "volunteers" to find one of the blood type to match that of the patient. Should this blood unfortunately give a positive Wassermann reaction [indicating syphilis], which occurred in about 10 per cent of cases, then the whole process had to be repeated. The patient not infrequently expired before blood suitable for transfusion was obtainable.[26]

Fantus was familiar with Robertson's wartime work and also with experiments in Russia using cadavers as a source of stored blood for transfusions.[27] Fantus was intrigued by the prospect of replacing "noisy, gesticulating" volunteers with quiet corpses but quickly decided that American sensibilities would not accept blood from the dead and that corpses were insufficiently abundant.[28] Instead Fantus raised funds to establish the Blood Preservation Laboratory and hired a full-time director, Dr. Elizabeth Schirmer, to assist him in creating systems for storing blood sourced from live bodies so that each patient could have blood when needed. By 1937 Schirmer and Fantus were convinced they could reliably and safely store blood for up to ten days, if it was correctly drawn, quickly cooled in a refrigerator, and maintained at 4°C.[29] In March 1937, using $1,000 from the Cook County commissioners to purchase a refrigerator, the Blood Preservation Laboratory launched a stored blood service.[30]

Supplies of chilled, citrated blood were not new in the 1930s. Since Robertson's wartime work, other American hospitals, like the Mayo Clinic, had adopted stored blood as a backup or supplement to fresh blood.[31] As war returned to Europe with the Spanish Civil War, doctors there again organized supplies of stored blood to aid the treatment of casualties.[32] Although Fantus published his protocols for blood collection and storage, developed during the years of working to prove stored blood safe, it was his way of managing his inventory that was his true innovation.[33] Already by May

1937 Fantus was receiving "inquiries . . . from various parts of the country," as the many Chicago-area doctors knowledgeable about the new service evidently spread the word that Cook County was successfully organizing an unpaid blood supply. As he explained in a bulletin to all Cook County Hospital medical staff, it was the "simple rules" for blood management that were making the new Blood Preservation Laboratory successful. These rules, he explained to his colleagues in May, and to the rest of the medical community in July, made the new stock of preserved blood into a "blood bank."[34]

Learning to Bank Blood

Schirmer, the laboratory director, later recalled that it was when explaining the Blood Preservation Laboratory to an intern that Fantus came up with the term *bank*. The young doctor, when requesting blood for his patients, should approach the laboratory as if it were a financial institution in which he had an account.[35] In the Notice to Medical Staff formalizing the instructions for using the laboratory, Fantus stated, "It is obvious that one cannot obtain blood unless one has deposited blood."[36] Rather than asking patients for money to pay professional donors, Cook County doctors were expected to ask patients for blood—from themselves after recovery or from friends and family. The time of donation need not be tied to the time of transfusion, and the type of the blood deposited in the bank need not match the type of the blood withdrawn. What mattered was keeping the books balanced by matching each debit with a credit.

Fantus introduced his concept for avoiding professional donors and the term *blood bank* to the national medical community in an article published in the prominent *Journal of the American Medical Association*.[37] He explained how blood banking could benefit all patients, wealthy and poor, by switching from reliance on warm bodies to previously collected preserved blood: blood was rapidly available when needed, and blood transfusion became a simpler process. These had been the goals of transfusionists since they began to experience the "resurrection" of their patients after administration of this new body product. There was no question that having bottled, typed blood on hand when a transfusion was needed greatly reduced the time from decision to transfuse to transfusion. The Cook County blood bank could have blood ready for transfusion within thirty minutes of receiving a tube of the recipient's blood for cross-matching.[38]

This increase in efficiency could be accomplished with any stored blood system, including one that relied on blood from professional donors to stock the shelves. To make this efficiency available to all patients, Fantus suggested that in large cities, hospitals too small to support their own laboratory could access preserved blood through the establishment of a central blood preservation laboratory, where professional donors could be bled at "convenient times" to create a common inventory.[39] Fantus's bank, however, was also designed to reduce the *cost* of blood transfusions at his cash-strapped public hospital by requiring in-kind payment of blood debts. Through the elimination of the paid donor, this miraculous therapeutic became available to all patients. "Now, thanks to the blood bank, no one needs to die at Cook County Hospital for lack of blood for transfusion," Fantus announced.[40] This result was due to the power of the bank. Fantus told his medical colleagues that "the term 'blood bank' is not a mere metaphor": "Just as one cannot draw money from a bank unless one has deposited some, so the blood preservation department cannot supply blood unless as much comes in as goes out."[41] By managing blood as if it were money, Fantus replaced the dominant cash-for-blood model with a blood-for-blood model. His innovation was fundamentally a new means of keeping accounts.

At Cook County each department within the hospital (for example, obstetrics or surgery) opened an account with the blood bank. Like any bank account, a new account required a deposit. Staff physicians prepared a deposit by obtaining blood from a donor, who was bled into a flask containing sodium citrate solution. Two small tubes of blood were also collected, one for typing and one for the Wassermann test for syphilis. In the laboratory the blood was typed and tested for sterility and the absence of syphilis. If accepted, the blood remained in the new refrigerator and created a credit in the department's bank account. Any doctor in the department could then draw upon that credit by ordering a unit of blood for any patient. Blood of the correct type would be delivered from the refrigerator.[42] Each department had to maintain an in-flow of deposits equal to its withdrawals, like a bank customer avoiding an overdraft. Through this accounting system, Fantus broke the last direct link between donor and recipient. No longer was a donor, whether the patient's relative or friend or a stranger, paid or unpaid, donating blood for a particular patient. The donor was contributing blood to a bank as a fungible unit, creating a credit. That particular blood

		BLOOD BANK ACCOUNT				
Ward:	Service:		Senior Interne:			
			Junior Interne:			
Debit			Credit		Balance	
Date	Name	Amt.	Name	Amt.	Dr.	Cr.
7-14	H. S.	500			500	
7-14			a. a.	500		
7-15	N. S.	500			500	
7-15			J. S.	500		
7-15			J. R.	500		500
7-15			C. J.	500		1000
7-16	C. J. (False positive)	500				500

Cook County Hospital Blood Bank Account Book, 1938. *Bernard Fantus, "Cook County's Blood Bank," Modern Hospital 50 (Jan. 1938): 58.*

could be withdrawn to be administered to a patient in the future, and in the meantime the patient of concern to the donor would have another unit of stored blood available to him or her.

This system made unpaid suppliers easier to find. For any patient, the treating doctor could bleed the easiest available body.[43] There was no need to search through the "horde" for a match. Fantus explained that patients anticipating a need for blood, such as pregnant women or patients planning elective surgery, could even deposit blood in advance, just as "we deposit in a bank money we do not at the moment need, to be able to draw on it when we do need it."[44] If they needed it themselves, they could receive their own blood; otherwise it would become part of the general stock. Fantus found that by maintaining a few dozen bottles of blood in the refrigerator, his inventory of blood types adequately matched the blood types requested by the transfusing doctors. While the accounts were kept at the department level, patients had responsibility for the blood they received. Any patient who had received blood had been "lent" the blood by the bank and "owed" a return deposit to aid another patient. Particularly patients who had recovered from an infectious disease whose blood might benefit another in the throes of such an illness should accept this "plain duty."[45]

Staff physicians who wanted to use blood needed to convince patients and their families to understand their "plain duty" in order to keep their department's account balanced. Fantus had a Blood Bank Account Book developed, with columns for "debits," "credits," and a running "balance."[46] Through the bank, blood became both like and unlike other therapeutics. Like other medicines received while in the hospital, blood became something the patient got from the hospital itself rather than purchased in a private transaction. Yet unlike other medicines, blood was paid for in kind rather than in the cash charges made by the hospital for other medicines and supplies received by its patients. Even charity patients who were excused from out-of-pocket expenses associated with their care were asked to pay this debt.

The bank was considered an immediate success within Cook County Hospital, where the number of blood transfusions doubled in the year after the bank opened and transfusion reactions continued to drop, having already decreased with the introduction of the Sterile Supplies Department.[47] The hospital could now afford to provide transfusions in accordance with medical recommendations instead of reserving the treatment solely for patients who could provide compatible blood. Within ten years hospital physicians were administering the same number of transfusions per month, approximately 1,200, as they had given in the entire first year the bank was in operation.[48] Admittedly the system was not a cure-all to Cook County's cash flow problems. Banked blood was still not free; in the early 1940s the hospital estimated that each transfusion cost 89 cents, factoring in the cost of salaries and equipment in the blood bank.[49] Still, 89 cents was considerably less than $50. Fantus and those who continued to operate the Cook County bank after his early death in 1940 also struggled with the problem faced by the military shock teams and all subsequent blood bankers: keeping up supplies. In order to meet demand, Cook County Hospital, like many other hospitals, was forced to buy some blood, offering just $10 per 500 cc, which was enough to entice the most financially desperate to sell.[50]

Fantus and his colleagues recognized that a body bank was a radical departure both as a way of talking about the human body and as a way of managing a nonprofit public hospital devoted to providing health care to all. Schirmer remembered that after the *Journal of the American Medical Association* article introduced the term, Fantus was "severely criticized" by some "for using such a commercial term in describing a scientific organization."[51]

Yet on the whole, the response to Fantus's accounting methods was highly favorable. His Cook County colleagues helped to spread the word of his innovation. Several gave a talk on the blood bank service in October 1938 to the American College of Surgeons, and Dr. Schirmer published an article designed to explain the system to the nursing profession in 1939.[52] With hospitals across the country struggling with the expense of professional donors, as well as the need to perform more transfusions more rapidly, the idea of the bank spread like a prairie wildfire.

As two Boston doctors observed in 1939, "For the past two years the medical profession has been extremely interested in blood banks."[53] The appeal of balancing blood bank books rather than paying professional donors was powerful, particularly when combined with Fantus's reported low reaction rates. The public hospitals were among the earliest adopters. A personal conversation with Fantus stimulated the formation of a blood bank in 1937 in Detroit's Receiving Hospital.[54] Los Angeles County General Hospital, another public hospital that was eager to save "thousands" of dollars spent on professional donors, had organized a bank by January 1938, while a public hospital in Washington, D.C., Gallinger Municipal Hospital, had its blood bank operational by 1939.[55] Dr. Alexander Wiener, an expert on transfusion, estimated that by 1939 there had been fourteen thousand transfusions of stored blood withdrawn from banks in operation in cities across the United States.[56]

Hospitals were not only eager to open banks but sought to share their experiences with the new system, as each institution found ways to bring banking into body product management. This exchange was also part of Fantus's vision. In his earliest bulletin to Cook County staff, he had called for the "promptest and most generous exchange of experience," and in his first publication to the medical profession, he urged "extensive cooperative investigation" "to develop this method as rapidly as seems mandatory to save lives now unnecessarily lost."[57] Doctors at the John Gaston Hospital in Memphis published an account of the "problems in blood banking" they had encountered, along with their solutions. In their bank, the technician in charge maintained books that had balance sheets both for individual interns and for patients. The doctors not only received credits and incurred debits but also could loan each other blood, creating an internal trading economy. Each patient was allowed to withdraw blood as needed (that is, to receive a transfusion as ordered by a doctor who had blood credits) but was expected to make up his or her withdrawals by later deposits from friends and relatives.[58] The idea was for both doctors and patients to keep their accounts of red fluid "in the black." This required not only two sets of balance sheets but a bit of fancy bookkeeping; the John Gaston Hospital estimated that it needed to collect about two pints for every one pint transfused, due to wastage, a problem that rapidly became endemic in banking such a perishable fluid. When it all worked as planned (the John Gaston Hospital was plagued by a series of refrigerator breakdowns during the start-up period of its blood bank, and some interns had trouble finding enough donors), blood itself flowed like a new form of cash so that no cash had to change hands.[59] The purpose of all this accounting and the treatment of blood as "capital" in Memphis was the same as in Chicago: to make "the most expensive and the most valuable of all therapeutic agents" "conveniently accessible to the indigent sick without imposing a burden on the tax-payer or on the hospital budget."[60] Like Fantus, the organizing doctors in Tennessee were motivated by the knowledge that lack of funds was resulting in patients dying for want of blood.[61]

As Fantus had recognized, the blood bank required doctors to embrace stored blood. The doctors in Memphis took a pragmatic approach. While acknowledging that stored blood might not be as good as fresh blood, the needs of their charity patients facing acute hemorrhage were so dire that "the question is not one concerning the relative effectiveness of fresh and preserved blood, but of preserved blood and no blood or blood after it is too late."[62] The medical preference for fresh blood, however, threatened to destroy the newly created blood bank at the Johns Hopkins Hospital in Baltimore.[63] Doctors were reluctant to use stored blood if fresh blood was available. The hospital found that its first protocol of typing donor blood before depositing led doctors to use the freshly donated blood if it matched their patient's blood type, sending it to the bank only if it did not match. This practice resulted in fewer transfusions using stored blood, causing the blood that did enter the bank to age on the refrigerator shelf, further compounding the prejudice against it. To make the bank more functional, the blood bank organizers began to require doctors to send freshly collected blood to the bank immediately, before typing, and to withdraw previously typed banked blood for transfusions. This rule applied only to charity patients, however. Private patients who could afford to pay a professional donor could continue to receive fresh blood.[64] Still, as the Depression lingered, other hospital administrators, like Fantus, were successful in enforcing "simple rules" to get doctors to use stored blood.

The rapid and wholesale adoption of the bank model to facilitate access to a blood supply was reflected in medical treatises as early as 1939, when transfusion expert Wiener published a new edition of his earlier treatise on blood groups and blood transfusion. Adding a new section on the blood bank, Wiener endorsed the plan of storing citrated blood of all blood types, as introduced in Chicago, and withdrawing blood from the bank as needed.[65] Most large urban hospitals needed little urging. By 1941, when Dr. Charles Drew, a young doctor who had become perhaps the foremost U.S. expert on blood banking, conducted a survey of facilities, he found multiple banks in the twelve cities he examined.[66] Drew, an African American physician, gained his expertise while pursuing a doctorate in medical science at Columbia Presbyterian Hospital in New York City and had filed his dissertation on banked blood in 1938.[67] The survey updated his thesis and was in its turn rapidly outdated as more banks opened during the early 1940s. In 1942 alone, the *Journal of the American Medical Association* noted new banks opening in Illinois, Oregon, and West Virginia.[68] By that year, to talk about blood transfusion was to talk about blood bank management, and two medical experts on transfusion called their new treatise *The Blood Bank.* The authors repeated Fantus's admonition that "the term 'blood bank' is not merely a metaphor" and detailed the crucial feature of balancing deposits and withdrawals.[69]

The popular press also picked up the phrase. The same article in the *Saturday Evening Post* that described the professional donor in a positive light in 1938 introduced the blood bank as "the latest transfusion development," allowing "blood from any type of donor any old time." In the bank, readers were told, blood was stored much like "raw milk," until needed.[70] By 1939 this latest development was becoming a commonplace concept, explained to the public as functioning similarly to "the common variety of financial bank."[71]

The public needed to understand the blood bank because any member of the public might be called upon to make a deposit. Donors, like doctors, needed to be disciplined in the service of the blood bank. Hospitals sought to regularize the "hordes" of friends and family donors into orderly streams of bank depositors, who, like customers of a financial bank, adjusted themselves to the schedule of the bank. At Philadelphia's General Hospital, for example, would-be donors making deposits for a patient were asked to present themselves at one of three weekly times, increasing the convenience for the blood bank staff. Instead of ad hoc collection at the time of treatment, blood flowed in at these regular collection clinics and flowed out as needed in the form of chilled bottles, neatly labeled.[72] As a depositor, the donor was shifted from the center to the periphery of hospital transfusion practices.

Just as the professional blood donor was becoming a man of business, uninterested in heroics or romance as he carried out his job, the "amateur" friends and family donor also became a much more prosaic figure as he was remade into a bank depositor. A donation to repay a loan was a transaction, conducted during business hours with banking staff. Neither professional nor hero, the unpaid bank donor was simply a source of product, equal to any other producing entity. The bank assumed that the most significant characteristic of a blood donation was its volume, establishing a one-unit credit. Doctors were advised to tell their patients "that, just as when one withdraws money from a bank he does not receive the identical bills he deposited, so their blood [of the patient's friends and relatives], if not suitable for the patient in question, can be replaced by suitable blood from the bank, theirs taking its place [in the bank]."[73]

This explanation glossed over the determination of "suitable" blood. Who decided which blood was "suitable," and on what grounds? On the one hand, the transformation of blood from person-to-person sale or gift to an abstract credit in a bank, in which one pint was equivalent to another, seemed to transform blood into a fungible commodity, like a sack of wheat, that through standardization had value regardless of its origin.[74] The blood bank had an equalizing and universalizing effect on blood flows that two contemporary journalists saw as "a lesson in applied democracy." Not only did blood banks help those without friends, family, or funds access this therapeutic, but the reporters thought that the new indebted donor, giving to the bank rather than to a patient, reinforced "the notion that we are all brothers-in-blood." While such donors still might ask themselves, "Who will get the blood? White man, black or yellow? Christian or Jew?," according to these authors, donors gave without needing to know the answer.[75]

On the other hand, blood banks tracked particularized information about donors with each bottle of stored blood. There was no pooling of product from different suppliers, as was done in the mothers' milk stations, or in a grain elevator as each farmer's wheat harvest was combined before resale.[76] Along with his account book, Fantus published copies of the "donor tags" attached to each unit of blood drawn.[77] In order for blood to retain value in the blood bank, the date of collection, blood type, results of the physical examination, and medical history of the donor needed to travel with the blood. This information indicated that the blood was safe to use. The Chicago bank also recorded the name and address of each donor, a way of tracking the source should a problem arise.

Suitability could also be determined based on other criteria. Without giving any medical rationale, Fantus recorded the sex and race of all donors as a matter of course.[78] It was a constant assumption of medical professionals, reiterated in the medical literature, repeated in the popular press, and used to justify racial segregation of blood products that "laymen have great difficulty believing" that "sex and race make no difference."[79] Maybe donors were unconcerned about recipients, but each recipient, doctors believed, cared about the donor. While there were some anecdotes about recipients caring about the sex of the donor, there is no indication that any blood bank ever separated blood by sex.[80] But based on the belief that "white" patients wished to avoid receiving "black" blood, many banks segregated blood by race.

New York's Columbia Presbyterian Hospital, the institution where the African American Drew studied blood banking, carefully recorded the race of each donor and recipient patient.[81] In Memphis the doctors bemoaned the wastage that occurred because "traditional prejudices" of their patients required maintaining a larger supply of blood than could be used. They claimed that "better cooperation is obtained from both groups [black and white] by requiring each to provide blood for their own patients." Acknowledging that there was no medical reason to segregate blood by race, the Memphis doctors declared that in emergencies "the color line does not hold," for "any available compatible blood" was used.[82] In Baltimore the assumption of the medical staff that what they called "colored" blood could never be used for "white" patients led to similar difficulties at the Johns Hopkins Hospital, due to the significant percentage of African American patients. The hospital created what it called "two entirely separate small banks," one for each race and housed on separate shelves of the blood refrigerator. The hospital departments had separate accounts with each bank, and the hospital tried to maintain the optimal proportion of each blood type on each shelf, without regard to what might be available on the adjoining shelf. The segregation of blood as hospital policy was blandly announced as a matter of avoiding controversy rather than as a means of encouraging debt repayment: "Although there is, of course, no valid objection on biologic or physiologic grounds to the transfusion of patients of one race with blood from donors of another, it has been deemed best to avoid the issue."[83]

Banks in other parts of the country, such as the Irwin Memorial Blood Bank in San Francisco, founded in 1941, did not separate blood by race.[84] Suitability varied by location. The idea of racial segregation of banked blood was sufficiently dominant, however, that the collection of racial data from donors was included as part of the procedures described in the first blood bank manual. *The Blood Bank* treatise set forth as part of the requirements for establishing a blood bank the "essential" need that every flask of collected blood contain a "legible and permanently attached" label with the donor's information, including race.[85] The "lesson in applied democracy" taught in the blood bank included the lesson that a repressive power hierarchy based on popular conceptions of race existed in the United States, in which "colored" blood posed a threat to "white" recipients, although transfusion in the opposite direction was no cause for concern.

From its inception, the banking metaphor sparked these disagreements about blood as a market commodity, as bankers treated bottles of red fluid as abstract, fungible units. In Baltimore "colored" blood and white blood were so distinct as to need separate banks, whereas in San Francisco blood and blood credits could cross racial divides. In Memphis the significance of the race indicated on a blood label varied with circumstance. The blood bank did not create this malleable quality of blood as a body product. Long before the bank was applied to body products, doctors and parents had expressed similar fears and "traditional prejudices" about feeding infants milk from a woman of a different race or ethnicity. Most of the time, parents hiring a wet nurse overcame these fears based on pragmatic considerations; however, in the 1920s the Detroit mothers' milk bureau stopped purchasing milk from African American women, citing the reluctance of white parents to buy milk from black mothers.[86] Mothers' milk stations in other cities found no need to make a similar exclusion, pooling and pasteurizing milk from all women into a fungible commodity that parents accepted as an improvement over the troublesome wet nurse.[87] The significance of race in body product exchange varied by location, even without the use of account books to manage bank deposits.

The blood *bank*, however, caused such fears to surface in new ways. Just as parents had been able to know the source of milk when they hired a wet nurse, patients relying on friends and family as blood donors had always known the source of their blood. Patients who received blood from a professional donor in the days when recipient and donor were in the same operating room also would have met their donor, who might have been from another race.[88] The blood bank, like the mothers' milk station, made unwitting cross-racial body product exchange possible by separating donor and recipient. As the bank transformed blood transfusion from a person-to-person exchange into the receipt of a fungible commodity, it required doctors and patients to decide in a new context how much of the individual characteristics of the supplier traveled with each bottle of blood. This decision was both social and medical, mingling the lay understanding of blood sharing as a marker of kinship with the medical need for sufficient information to determine whether the bottle provided by the hospital blood bank was suitable for a patient.

The differing practices of the first blood banks reflected the ambivalence many doctors and their patients felt about the fundamental assumption of the blood bank that all blood was equal. A blood supply managed without regard to sex or race of donor or recipient was the most efficient, allowing the greatest number of pints to be used by patients who needed them, fulfilling Fantus's original goals. As both Drew and the doctors who ran Johns Hopkins Hospital as a racially segregated facility knew, there was no "biologic" reason to track the race of donors and use that information to decide the allocation of blood. The public good of making banked blood accessible was not served by labeling or segregating blood by race. The Johns Hopkins doctors, however, believed that if patients were able to express their individual preferences in a free market, white patients would prefer to know the race of the blood supplier and to receive blood only from white donors. Fantus's metaphor of the bank, which seemed so simple and useful, was already becoming complicated by the tensions between blood as civic property, with each unit treated as equal in value and allocated by need, and blood as a market commodity, allocated to satisfy individual preferences of patients. These tensions would emerge in new ways as the World War II national blood program emphasized another variation on the blood donor, as one who gave neither for love of a patient nor for money nor to repay a debt, but rather for love of country.

The Nation as a Giant Blood Bank

Even as blood banks in large urban hospitals looked to stock their shelves from indebted donors in the 1930s, what one writer called the "chill impersonality of the blood bank" could not diminish the "fascination of giving blood for somebody else," creating twin links of "gratitude and generosity" between donor and recipient.[89] Just as the amateur donor, selling the occasional pint, expected gratitude and felt a bit heroic, the assumed loving-kindness of a friends and family donor made donations given to pay off a blood debt acts of generosity for which the recipient was, or should be, grateful. Despite the emphasis on the business of blood, the altruistic qualities of the donor remained present in the terminology of professional donors and bank deposits. It was these qualities that hospitals too small to maintain a stored blood supply emphasized, even as they took to calling their lists of as-needed donors "walking blood banks."[90] They were faced with the same conundrum that had motivated Fantus: How could the indigent access blood for transfusion, when the only source of blood was the professional donor or the unreliable friends and family donor? The answer in some of these communities was a new version of the amateur donor, no longer an occasional seller but an unpaid organized donor, motivated by civic-minded generosity to give for a stranger. While in a large city an indigent patient needing a blood transfusion would be expected to supply a donor to repay his or her blood debt, in a smaller town, without a blood bank, if a patient was without a suitable donor among friends and family, he or she might be handed a list and told to find a matched unpaid donor from the registry.[91]

While hospitals and for-profit agencies maintained registries of professional donors, these registries, with their emphasis on altruism, were often organized by civic groups. These charitable "walking banks" or blood donors' leagues, existing alongside professional donor registries, involved donors more interested in social than financial capital. In the pioneering program in Augusta, Georgia, begun in 1937, the donor registry was reportedly crammed with the names of the town's most socially prominent citizens, who all sought a chance to give without payment for indigent patients. This registry, organized by the local American National Red Cross chapter, not only drew from a different socioeconomic stratum than professional donor agencies but also enrolled a significant number of women. One woman, whose veins were found to be suboptimal for donation, reportedly begged a

doctor not to strike her from the list. She wanted to be on record as participating in this new type of philanthropy, no longer limited to "men of business" but a demonstration of beneficence by those who did not need to
work for wages. After 1938 the national Red Cross actively encouraged
other chapters to found such programs.[92]

In Rochester, New York, local media outlets organized a blood donors'
league in reaction to periodic requests they had received to advertise for
unpaid donors. Like Fantus's blood bank, the league was designed to provide blood for those unable to afford a professional donor and without
available friends or family. League members volunteered to be typed and to
give without pay when asked. Radio stations and newspapers in other cities
followed suit, and in small towns male fraternal organizations, including
the Veterans of Foreign Wars and the Knights of Columbus, organized
such leagues, working with a local hospital, which usually did the typing
and maintained one set of the donor records. After reports of the Rochester
effort circulated nationally, similar blood donor leagues were established in
fifty-six communities by 1940.[93]

These experiences laid the groundwork for turning the entire nation into
a "giant blood bank" of civic-minded unpaid donors as the United States
prepared to enter World War II.[94] During the war the domestic collection
of blood for the American armed forces was, at the time, the largest organized medical effort ever undertaken in the United States, with perhaps the
exception of mass vaccination programs.[95] By V-J Day over 13 million pints
of blood had been collected from about 19 million donor visits. During
the war about 60 percent of Americans lived within donating distance of
one of the thirty-five donation centers and their sixty-three mobile units.
About 100,000 volunteers participated in the operation of the centers. For
the duration of the war, Americans were deluged with information about
the blood program, through visual propaganda such as movie trailers and
posters and by direct solicitation at work, at church, and in their homes
by their own children.[96] When the war ended, Americans of all walks of
life had received a "lesson in applied democracy" through unpaid blood
donation.

The giant blood bank began as a limited project, Blood for Britain, in the
months before the United States entered the war. Blood for Britain tested
the limits of American generosity by seeking unpaid blood donors not for
local poor, or even for American fighting men, but for the British. Blood for

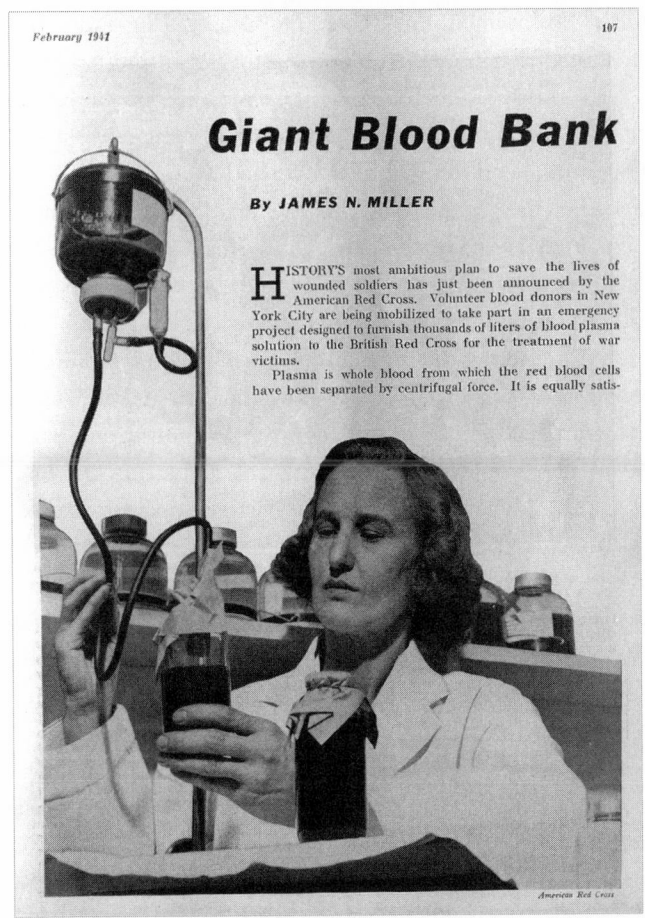

February 1941   107

Giant Blood Bank

By JAMES N. MILLER

HISTORY'S most ambitious plan to save the lives of wounded soldiers has just been announced by the American Red Cross. Volunteer blood donors in New York City are being mobilized to take part in an emergency project designed to furnish thousands of liters of blood plasma solution to the British Red Cross for the treatment of war victims.

Plasma is whole blood from which the red blood cells have been separated by centrifugal force. It is equally satis-

American Red Cross

"Giant Blood Bank." *James N. Miller, "Giant Blood Bank,"* Hygeia, *Feb. 1941, 107.*

Britain was the brainchild of Dr. John Scudder, a physician-scientist involved in blood transfusion research at Columbia Presbyterian Hospital in New York City who collaborated with Drew in blood preservation research. In the spring of 1940, stimulated by reports from the famed researcher Alexis Carrel, now a Nobel laureate, who had recently visited his native France as it prepared for war, Scudder suggested aiding the anti-German cause by shipping blood to Britain and France, working through the existing citywide organizational structure of the Blood Transfusion Betterment Association (soon to be renamed the Blood Transfusion Association).[97]

Scudder's idea seemed outrageous. No one, in England or the United States, imagined that preserved blood as stocked in the new blood banks could survive transport to England. It seemed impossible to supply one continent with blood from another continent. No one understood this better than Scudder. Working with Drew, he had been involved in research to understand the changes that occurred in stored blood over time, and both men were acutely aware of the particularly limited life span of red blood cells.[98] Scudder also knew of the many decades of attempts to find substances other than human blood that would prove equally beneficial to patients, while eliminating the problems of clotting, compatibility, and donor management once and for all. For a brief moment in the late nineteenth century, doctors had turned to milk as a possible substitute, attempting to use the two life-giving fluids interchangeably.[99] During the interwar period, just as the pediatric profession split between doctors focused on optimizing artificial feeding options and doctors advocating breast milk, the blood transfusion field was split into doctors seeking nonhuman blood substitutes and doctors working to optimize the human blood supply. By World War I many doctors, particularly in Britain, preferred saline to human blood as more readily obtainable and less problematic.[100] Building on World War I–era research into blood substitutes and the contemporary understanding of shock as the result of fluid loss, Scudder had been experimenting with blood plasma, a new blood product. His proposal was to ship plasma to Europe as treatment for battlefield casualties.

Plasma is the fluid component of blood. When an anticoagulant, such as citrate, is added to whole blood, and the blood is stored, the red and white blood cells settle to the bottom, and the plasma can be poured off, or a centrifuge can be used to speed the process of separation.[101] Research into blood substitutes in the interwar period had revealed that both plasma and naturally occurring serum (the fluid that separates from the blood cells in the clotting reaction when no anticoagulant is used) shared several advantages over whole blood: they were universally compatible and could be used by any recipient without reaction regardless of blood type, and they could be easily and perhaps indefinitely stored in a refrigerator. While there was disagreement about whether stored blood was best used within one, five, ten, or thirty days, experts readily agreed that plasma was good for one year after preparation.[102] Further, without the need to keep plasma separated by blood type, collected plasma could be pooled. Blood from multiple donors could be combined and processed into this new blood product in batches, facilitating the preparation of large volumes, and then packaged into transfusion-size units, ready for individual use. The ability to pool plasma was ideal for mass production and also further separated this blood product from the origins of blood transfusion. The bank had made donations impersonal, but each unit was still tracked as the product of a particular donor of known characteristics. The use of plasma made each transfusion the receipt of a standardized unit created from raw material provided by many suppliers.

As the Battle of France raged in the spring of 1940, Scudder traveled to Washington along with representatives of the Blood Transfusion Association and the Rockefeller Institute to propose his idea to what would become the key players in the national blood program: the U.S. Army, the U.S. Navy, the National Research Council, and large pharmaceutical and biological firms.[103] Carrel also lent his prestige to the project in its initial stages, participating in the planning as both a French national and a prominent medical researcher.[104] While the federal government was very interested in a project that would test Scudder's theory that plasma would be an effective whole blood substitute, with obvious application to anticipated U.S. military involvement in Europe, the program was started with private monies. The Blood Transfusion Association committed $15,000, and the American National Red Cross, with its mission of aiding victims of war and its growing experience organizing blood donors, contributed $25,000.[105]

By the time the program launched in August 1940, France had fallen to the Germans, and the project became Blood for Britain. For five months, from August 1940 to January 1941, the American Red Cross in New York City advertised for volunteer donors to give a pint of blood for the British. Donors were urged to call a central office, and receptionists scheduled donors for appointments at participating hospitals. Volunteer medical personnel staffed the collection hours, processing over seventeen thousand donations from philanthropic New Yorkers.[106] The program managers then had to separate the plasma from the blood cells and get it safely overseas.

Despite plasma's advantages over whole blood, its collection and transport across the Atlantic Ocean was still a challenge. Drew, who was recruited as the full-time medical director of Blood for Britain, worked quickly to find ways to manufacture plasma from whole blood in bulk, and then to package it, all the while preserving its sterility.[107] Another organizer for the project explained that at the outset the doctors had "received the impression that preparing plasma would not be much more difficult than mixing a cocktail, but we soon learned, much to our distress, that such was not the case." The "mass production of plasma for shipment abroad, to be used after a relatively long period had elapsed . . . was a vastly different proposition than the production of small quantities of plasma in a hospital for prompt use on the premises."[108] The administrators wrestled with scaling up plasma production, with the choice of materials for bottles, labels, and cartons, and with the requirements for donors. One open question remained whether Blood for Britain would accept blood from African Americans. Eventually it was decided that if African Americans presented themselves as donors, their blood would be taken but would be labeled as "Negro blood." In practice "Negro blood" was not included in the pools used to make plasma, presumably to protect the sensibilities of British casualties, but with scant regard for Drew's feelings. Drew later spoke out against the racial segregation of blood supplies in the national blood program.[109]

Once manufactured and packaged, the liquid plasma needed to be kept cool while transported by boat and the glass bottles protected from breakage. It is unclear how much plasma reached England in usable form, although it was later estimated that less than 10 percent arrived contaminated.[110] The British medical officers were much too busy treating the wounded to collect systematic data on their use of the American plasma—a form of aid that they had not requested—but the limited information received back in the States indicated that some plasma had arrived safely and been used successfully, although the project may have been of only minimal help to the British.[111] Any information about the potential usefulness of a blood product that could substitute for more fragile whole blood was valuable.

Even before Blood for Britain began, in March 1940 the U.S. Army and U.S. Navy had begun planning for the use of blood should the United States enter the war. Each appointed a medical officer to be in charge of blood and the new medical category, "blood products," and the surgeons general asked the National Research Council to advise them about blood transfusions. In response, the Council first established the Committee on Shock, indicating its understanding of why the army and navy were concerned with the issue. Then the medical researchers on that committee immediately created the Subcommittee on Blood Substitutes, signaling the

anticipated importance of blood substitutes in global warfare.[112] This subcommittee ended up supervising the entire U.S. military wartime blood
program, but as one of the participants described it later, when the subcommittee was established, the very idea of blood substitutes was "little more
than wishful thinking."[113] No one was producing or using blood plasma or
serum outside of small research projects, that is, no one but the civilian
Blood for Britain project. Due to both pessimism about the use of whole
blood at the front and optimism about the promise of blood substitutes,
U.S. military doctors threw themselves into a blood plasma program as the
dominant portion of the World War II blood program. Of the 13 million
pints of blood collected during the wartime blood program, about 75 percent was turned into plasma and used by the army in the first widespread
reliance on plasma for treatment of shock and hemorrhage.[114] A further 17
percent were processed into serum, the focus of the much smaller navy
blood program.[115] Only near the end of the war, as doctors realized that
neither plasma nor serum was as effective as whole blood in saving lives, did
the military work to develop blood banks abroad and to ship whole blood
collected in the United States to the troops overseas.[116]

While liquid plasma was difficult to ship, researchers in the 1930s had
already begun working on a way to dry plasma for later use in a reconstituted
form, a technique that would greatly ease storage and transport issues.[117] A
powdered blood product, like powdered milk, would be lighter, less fragile,
and shelf-stable without refrigeration, key advantages for both transport to
and use at the battle front. Once Blood for Britain convinced the military
that plasma was an effective blood product, the wartime effort focused on
processing blood into dried plasma.

The brief Blood for Britain project became the template for the national
blood program. In early 1941, when Britain notified the organizers that it
would be able to meet its own blood needs, without pause Blood for Britain
officially became a national program to research the collection, storage, and
use of plasma.[118] It was too valuable to those who were planning for U.S.
military involvement in the war to let lapse. Even before the United States
entered the war, blood centers were established in Bryn Mawr, Pennsylvania, Ann Arbor, Michigan, Nashville, Tennessee, and Iowa City, Iowa, at
hospitals where prominent blood researchers worked, to further prepare for
a national program.[119] The order went out in 1941 to determine the blood
type of all recruits and to inscribe that information on their identification

tags, preparing each body to be either a donor or a recipient.[120] Drew, the
Blood for Britain director, was asked to stay on and write up a detailed report for the benefit of future organizers.[121] After the bombing of Pearl Harbor in December 1941, the project quickly became the program that the
planners had been anticipating since 1940, expanding into a national network of collection centers and processing plants. This program could rely
on Drew's work on the manufacture, processing, and shipment of plasma
and on a newly formed coalition among the Red Cross, the medical profession, the armed forces, biomedical research laboratories, and private enterprise. It could also rely on the new form of amateur donor, the unpaid
blood bank donor, motivated by patriotism.

As the national blood program replaced Blood for Britain, extending
collection efforts from New York City to most of the country, the blood
collection goals became staggering. At the peak of the program, the Red
Cross centers were bleeding 100,000 donors per week, collecting a pint of
blood every two seconds somewhere in America.[122] For Americans who
were being advised to buy war bonds, plant victory gardens, and submit to
rationing programs, blood donation was another wartime obligation. But
blood donation was portrayed as unique in its highly personal nature. Even
as the blood bank and the pooling of collected plasma severed the personal
link between donor and recipient and even the one-to-one relationship between a pint given and a pint received, the national blood program sought
to avoid the "chill impersonality" of the blood bank with its balanced account books. Instead, beginning with Blood for Britain, as the Red Cross
strove to attract these new unpaid donors, it told them that their blood was
not just like cash or another market commodity but rather "a gift which
was literally part of each donor . . . of a more personal nature than any
contribution of money or articles could be."[123]

Despite this emotional appeal, "from the beginning to the end of the program, the major problem was to obtain an adequate number of donors. . . .
Only unceasing efforts enabled the [blood donation] centers to meet their
quotas."[124] These efforts included explaining to the public their new role as
potential donors. For example, a radio interview given by a Red Cross official and reprinted in a popular journal in 1943 began by describing the fate
of the collected blood. The official explained the process of plasma preparation "in a centrifuge—an instrument somewhat similar to a cream separator
and working along the same general principles." The plasma was then dried

"by a carefully devised process which has been adopted after many trials," using "quite expensive" equipment. The result was a product that "occupies a small amount of space, can be easily preserved, transported, kept sterile and readily prepared for administration, and it is universally adaptable." The interviewee then reassured potential donors that "giving of blood in reasonable quantities by normal persons is not harmful. . . . The idea that there may be some permanent bad effect is simply not true." The benefits, in contrast, were enormous. The blood program was "revolutioniz[ing] the early treatment of battle casualties," reducing "the deaths of American wounded to an almost unbelievably low figure." "People should realize that when they give blood they are actually taking part in establishing this marvelous record" and in fact "are saving lives just as effectively as the doctors at the front!"[125]

The valorization of the professional donor as the uniquely robust man of business was gone, replaced by every man and every woman who could save lives by their personal gifts. An article memorializing the one-year anniversary of the blood donor center in Boston, for example, inventoried a long list of donor types, beginning with the governor and his wife and continuing with "housewives who leave their children with neighbors and spend an hour at the Center; students who come in between classes at nearby colleges and schools; servicemen giving up precious hours of their cherished leave; business men and women coming in during lunch hours and after work; war factory and shipyard workers who arrive directly from their strenuous work on military materiel." Far from emphasizing the unusual physical vigor of donors, the Red Cross also celebrated a donor in a wheelchair.[126] While the professional donor was presumptively male, the wartime program relied on recruiting women to become donors in much greater numbers than in their prewar proportions. Like so many other occupations, the role of blood donor was newly available to women during the war, and women provided about half of the blood collected.[127] In the uncompensated world of gifting blood, they too could now be "champion blood donors," getting their name printed in the newspaper for giving five pints.[128] The women's fashion magazine *Vogue* ran a first-person account of a woman giving blood to the "plasma bank," reacting to the drafting of her husband by doing "the easiest and most needed thing any civilian could do in this whole war." Admitting that she was "plain scared," the narrator described the "especially nice nurse," who took the time to reassure the timid, and her resolve to return to give again and repeat "an absorbing and exciting experience."[129]

The new amateur blood donor who was neither working professional nor anxious friend or family nor blood bank debtor required new recruitment tactics. Even though the goal of the national blood program was shelf-stable dried plasma, the program still required a controlled flow of donors. The problem was no longer the "ageing out" of collected but unused blood on the refrigerator shelf, the worry of blood banks, but the capacity of the plasma-processing facilities. Fresh blood was now a raw material for an industrial process. The Red Cross, as the national coordinator of donors, was charged with providing blood to the manufacturing plants in a predictable stream. Ideally each drawn unit of blood would be shipped to the processing plant, processed into plasma, dried, and packaged without interruption, and for each shipment of plasma leaving the plant, a fresh lot of blood would arrive. The Red Cross directors spoke explicitly of the process as a "mass-production, assembly-line type of project."[130] To achieve the optimum assembly-line production of blood product, the donors had to be similarly optimized and organized into a steady flow, neither too thick nor too thin. Key statistics were the losses at each stage of blood collection: the no-shows, the can't-bleeds, the discards. The Red Cross calculated how many donors had to be recruited each day to yield the number of successfully collected and retained pints to meet the requirements of the processing facilities. Eventually it was determined that 150 donors were needed for each 100 pints of blood.[131]

Each blood collection center had been located because of its proximity to a processing plant, and the output of each center was assigned to one or more specific plants. The collected blood was stored in refrigerators until packed by "trained blood custodians" and sent to the plant on a "prearranged express schedule" along with a daily shipping list in triplicate, containing each donor's name and serial number. Processing would begin the next day.[132] The flow of blood from donor to plant depended not just on volume but on a carefully managed supply chain, in which the collected blood was appropriately handled in shipment by truck or train to the plant, allowed neither to warm up nor to freeze, either of which could destroy the blood. Because of the transportation arrangements, there was little flexibility to send extra blood to an underutilized facility; each center and its plant(s) had to be optimized as an individual unit. The processing facilities were commercial laboratories working under federal contract. By December 1943 a network of nine different companies was engaged in this work, for which the government paid a per unit price.[133]

To serve this industrial enterprise, the Red Cross worked to standardize the processing of each donor. Its goals were to maintain donor safety, encourage donors to return, and harvest sufficient raw material to meet the government quotas of product. The means of standardizing suppliers were developed over time, beginning with the Blood for Britain project. Managing donors was always tricky and required constant compromises. While it was ideal if donors did not eat for four hours before donating, or at least did not eat fatty foods, a fasting requirement quickly proved impractical.[134] Similarly there was concern about the transmission of blood-borne diseases such as malaria and syphilis, which not even the most careful screening, either by questioning or testing, could keep out. A person newly infected with syphilis might have a negative Wassermann test but be contagious. Yet it was rapidly concluded during Blood for Britain that the genital examination that might find such persons—and which was required for professional donors under the New York City sanitary code—was an unacceptable way to treat voluntary donors, when "over 50 per cent of the donors were women, many socially prominent and some unmarried."[135] Donor bodies were unreliable, potentially dangerous, and always prone to resist the discipline of the supply chain.

When Blood for Britain began in New York City in 1940, no one could predict the response to an appeal for unpaid donors. Part of the motivation for the blood donor registries and leagues organized in the late 1930s was dissatisfaction with the results of ad hoc appeals in the media, which could result in either no response or an overresponse. The New York City–area Red Cross chapters had to overcome these problems. They organized publicity by radio, newspapers, and magazines, urging potential donors to call for an appointment. Because blood donation was an unfamiliar experience to most New Yorkers before the war, the staff answering the phones was trained to provide detailed information about the Blood for Britain project and the process of blood donation, encouraging the doubtful and timid to proceed. Too much interest, however, would overtask the capacity of the hospitals to draw blood and discourage potential donors when they were told they could not get an appointment soon. Too few donors discouraged the doctors and nurses who volunteered to work overtime and staff the collection points, leading to diminished capacity as the medical personnel dropped away. There was a constant battle too with "absenteeism," would-be donors who made appointments but failed to appear.[136] During Blood for Britain, the Red Cross learned to estimate the effect of particular forms of publicity on donor interest and to plan publicity to generate 1,200 to 1,300 donors per week.[137] In just this limited experience, the organizers concluded that the donor needed to be coaxed "by intensive and continued newspaper publicity and radio appeals." Simultaneously the organizers believed that when Americans were appropriately coaxed, donor enthusiasm was high, grounded in "a spontaneous expression of deep public sympathy . . . and a keen desire to lend help."[138]

The Blood for Britain project also pioneered several other ways of managing donors that became part of the national standardized process. The Red Cross sent volunteer "Gray Ladies" to the hospitals to act as hostesses for the donors. For many donors, the experience was their first visit to a hospital, as well as their first experience with blood transfusion, and they arrived "with a spirit of determined martyrdom."[139] To better-off Americans, the hospital was often unknown territory, the site of care for the deserving poor rather than the site of delivery of modern medicine it would become in the postwar period. Unless they were delivering a baby or having their adenoids, appendix, or tonsils removed, they never set foot in such places.[140] Even before Blood for Britain, in its walking blood bank projects, the Red Cross had come to realize the need to give donors "every consideration."[141] The Gray Ladies made sure this consideration had a feminine touch. After their hospital donation, Blood for Britain donors were offered some "light refreshment," such as milk, eggnog, or whiskey (the whiskey was dropped from the national blood program).[142] The goal, as described by Drew in his final report, was "to treat each donor as an individual worthy of every consideration, and at the same time introduce methods which resemble in some degree a factory line."[143]

In the expanded national blood program, the Red Cross strove to meet this goal through written rules of "blood procurement" intended to standardize the process across its collection centers, rules that changed as the organization gained more experience.[144] At the outset the national blood program adopted the recommendation made by the Blood Transfusion Association at the conclusion of Blood for Britain to move blood collection out of hospitals into freestanding centers.[145] Since the advent of the surgical method of direct transfusion, blood donation had always occurred near the bedside of the patient in the hospital. With donation now minimally invasive, and the blood bound for a processing plant rather than a local body, there was no reason to make donors come to the hospital, an uncomfortable space for many. The Red Cross rented general-purpose buildings in areas accessible to donors and set up blood centers within those buildings according to standardized criteria for spatial organization to better process donors. The procurement rules also specified the nature of the bodies that could serve as donors. Donors could not have an elevated temperature, high blood pressure, low hemoglobin, or an irregular pulse. They could be of either sex, but they had to be between twenty-one and sixty years of age and demonstrate in a predonation examination that they did not fall outside certain fixed measures of health. These fixed measures changed over time, as the reactions of donors to donation were better understood. For example, a minimum weight of 110 pounds was added to reduce fainting, and as more donors were needed, the age limit was dropped to eighteen with parental permission.[146] Another aspect of the rules that shifted was the acceptability of blood regardless of race and whether blood collected would be labeled by race. Generally, as in Blood for Britain, blood was collected regardless of race, but African American blood was labeled "AA" and segregated in processing and distribution.[147] Collection teams composed of "a physician, four nurses, a secretary, and one or two shipping clerks" managed each collection site, and with each team member having assigned duties, centers could process one hundred donors in four to five hours.[148]

These teams were trained to process donors in an efficient, assembly-line manner that maintained a uniform donor experience across centers. The donor began in a reception area, then passed into a record-keeping room where his or her personal identification was noted and a "standard, serially numbered registration card" was prepared. A physical examination took place in a third room, where the collected health data were noted on the card, and then donors were admitted to a common bleeding room. After bleeding, the donor was requested to rest and recuperate in the canteen, where Gray Ladies or other volunteers served refreshments. Here donors acted as if they were "groups of old friends," evincing high spirits and camaraderie resulting from their charitable act and embodying that "democratic" spirit of the blood bank.[149] Efforts to humanize the experience were successful enough that the author of the *Vogue* article testified, "There was never the slightest feeling of being ground through a mill."[150]

A full-time assistant director of the Red Cross managed donor recruitment on a national level, in charge of producing "posters, leaflets, car cards, pamphlets, motion pictures, photographs, radio transcriptions and announcements, recruiting plans, and publicity kits" for use by all the regional centers.[151] One part of this promotion included a new way of making the "gift of blood" a personal one, restoring some of the intimacy that had been stripped away in the transition to the use of stored blood. Beginning in December 1944, all donors were asked if they would like to inscribe a carton of dried plasma, signing their own name as the gift giver and naming a particular soldier or sailor whom they were honoring or memorializing by their gift. The text read, "The plasma contained in this package was processed from the blood of volunteer donors enrolled by the American Red Cross and symbolizes in part the blood gratefully donated by _____, in honor of _____ of the United States Armed Forces."[152]

While the labeled box probably would not hold any material from the inscribing donor, this option gave the reconstituted body fluid an individual identity and strengthened the link of generosity and gratitude between donor and recipient threatened by the more commercial terms of the banking metaphor. About one-third of donors filled out labels when the option was given to them, seeking to make that personal connection.[153] These donors believed General Jacob Devers, the commander of the U.S. Ground Forces, who told the American public, "When your blood flows into the veins of a wounded soldier, that soldier knows it is more than medicine for his body. It is a part of you that you are giving to help keep him alive. The psychological effect is tremendous."[154]

The recipients also believed General Devers. When, late in the war, the army began collecting whole blood for shipment to the front, it allowed donors to inscribe a tag with their name, which was affixed to the jar containing their blood. These tags became keepsakes of those who received the blood. At a marine field hospital on Iwo Jima, "many of these tags are now in the wallets of wounded marines who swore to hospital attendants that they would some day find and thank their benefactors." One soldier, treated in England with a pint of blood collected from a military wife in Boston, got a chance to shake her hand in thanks in a meeting at the Boston Red Cross center upon his return home, but some of the marines evidently hoped for more. Noting that "most of the donors are girls," the pharmacist's mate in charge of the blood bank for the field hospital predicted that "some romances may develop from this."[155]

World War II National Blood Program plasma dedication program. *American Red Cross donor recruitment pamphlet, as reproduced in Douglas B. Kendrick,* Blood Program in World War II (Supplemented by Experiences in the Korean War) *(Washington, DC: Office of the Surgeon General, Department of the Army, 1989), 123.*

With the intended recipient the wounded military body, the giant blood bank successfully called on notions of patriotism and collective sacrifice to extract blood from thousands of American bodies stateside. Although informally explained as a bank and designed to achieve Fantus's twin goals of safe, efficient dispensation to those who needed it at minimum cost, the national blood program had little connection to institutions of capitalism, at least from the perspective of the donors and recipients. Blood was not being traded for cash, and neither was it being treated as cash; there were no deposits and withdrawals or debts in the flow of blood from home front bodies to distant battlefronts.

There was, however, money being made. For-profit companies were paid a per-unit price for the dried plasma they prepared. In the postwar era, these same companies would remain in the blood product industry, applying wartime research into the fractionation of blood plasma to the manufacture of multiple specialized blood products, including the clotting factors used to treat hemophilia.[156] The unpaid donor of blood to strangers had first been recruited to aid local indigents, and then, through Blood for Britain, had been used to help the hard-pressed British at a time when the United States was refusing to offer direct military assistance in the fight against Germany. The national blood program normalized donating to banks without compensation or expectation of personal benefit, enlisting thousands of Americans in this new role. It also used these highly personal gifts as raw material for for-profit companies. The federal government could have bought the blood it used, just as it bought uniforms, penicillin, and other materials for the armed services, or allowed its plasma suppliers, like other government contractors, to pay for raw materials and factor that cost into the price of the final product. Instead, like the prewar hospital blood banks, the national wartime program kept blood and blood products in a separate category of medical therapeutics. In the civilian world, they were the only therapeutic patients might be required to repay in kind or to supply themselves, from friends and family, or from a donor registry. In the wartime program, they were the only military matériel sourced from unpaid volunteers.

Through the giant blood bank, American blood was treated as a public collective resource, taken without compensation from those who had it and distributed to those who needed it in the service of the goals of the federal government. Boxes of dried plasma were classic market commodities, fungible and capable of being sold—home front hospitals looked enviously on the military stocks of this new product—but their manufacture and distribution was centrally controlled. In the prewar hospital blood banks, it was administrators like Fantus who controlled supplies, using the bank to allocate inventory in ways impossible when transfusion was a person-to-person exchange. During the war government bureaucrats used the ability to amass an inventory of this new body product to own and control this war matériel, greatly improving the ability of military doctors to use blood transfusion to treat casualties. Through the national organization of the Red Cross, the army and navy could mobilize supplies from across the United States and move them to where they were most needed, for example, funneling all blood collected to California in the last months of the war, where it would be shipped to Guam as battles continued in the Pacific theater after Germany's surrender in Europe.[157]

The national blood program borrowed terminology and techniques of blood procurement and preservation from preexisting banks, but the administrators of the giant blood bank ignored Fantus's admonition and treated the bank as a "mere metaphor." Fantus and other administrators who copied his careful method of accounting in civilian hospitals across the United States relied on an understanding of blood as a market commodity, which, like agricultural commodities, had a per unit value to suppliers, recipients, and bankers alike. The blood bank had transformed blood exchange from individual transactions conducted by salesmen of blood into organized banking businesses, in which donors and recipients alike were guided by the model of the financial bank to interact in business-like ways. The blood bank relied on liberal economic theory, harnessing individual preferences to avoid donor fees in order to obtain and allocate a blood supply. In the giant blood bank, however, there were no individual accounts that had to be balanced or debts to be paid. Rather than managing a market, the U.S. military used central planning to extract a blood supply from the population for use as a public resource, which it then allocated in the service of national ends, shipping plasma and blood to the front lines and to military hospitals. In the postwar world the question of the preferred mode of allocating blood resources—central planning or market forces—erupted into controversy.

3

Blood Battles in the Cold War

Any provision of free medical service or supply to everyone without regard to ability to pay is in opposition to the principle that it is the responsibility of an individual to assume the obligations of medical expense just as he does for other living expense. We deplore the use of the term "free blood."

—American Medical Association House of Delegates, 1948

On December 7, 1941, Mrs. Bernice Hemphill found herself standing in a long line outside the Queen's Hospital. Like hundreds of other residents of Honolulu, the young navy wife had headed straight to the hospital when she realized that the island was under enemy attack, seeking to give her blood as a way to be of immediate service to the many wounded in the early morning bombing raid on Pearl Harbor. Unlike the others in line, Hemphill was certified by the State of California as a laboratory bioanalyst, trained to run a clinical laboratory. After about an hour of standing in the unmoving line, she decided to go into the hospital and find the blood-processing laboratory. She found a hospital experienced only with a low volume of person-to-person blood transfusions, without any blood bank or plan to create one. As she described that day decades later, she went straight to work processing the donations, typing blood, making blood storage solution, and collecting and sterilizing makeshift containers for blood. She did not return to her home for six days, working long hours and sleeping at the hospital as a blackout and curfew made travel difficult. By January she was on the payroll, running the laboratory and creating a blood bank that became the "hub" for blood supplies in Honolulu. Hemphill's career in blood banking would continue for the next forty years, earning her the title "the mother of blood banking," or sometimes simply "Mrs. Blood."[1]

From the beginning of her career to its end, Hemphill thought of the blood supply in terms of banking. Her wartime experiences left her with a lifelong antipathy toward the American National Red Cross and its blood collection efforts. While she later claimed that she disliked the Red Cross because it was too bossy in managing its volunteers, her fundamental, if unrecorded, objection may have been that in the standardized staffing of the wartime Red Cross blood collection centers, there was no obvious role for a trained laboratory bioanalyst.[2] In the world of blood banking, she found it easy to put her training and intelligence to work and to gain a paid position of importance. When she returned to her native San Francisco with her husband in 1943, she declined to work for the national blood program and instead began volunteering at Irwin Memorial Blood Bank, one of the early banks that Blood for Britain director Dr. Charles Drew had included in his survey of blood banking in 1941. By 1944 she was on Irwin's staff and eventually became its executive director, serving until 1982, always, according to one of the doctors affiliated with the bank, "beautifully dressed in the latest style" with "never . . . a hair out of place."[3]

Hemphill earned her "mother of blood banking" title by becoming one of the leaders of the Cold War movement to take the banking metaphor seriously, emphasizing the free market as a superior way to manage the blood supply. As the only permanent officer of the American Association of Blood Banks for over two decades, Hemphill led blood banks in their fight against the Red Cross and its scheme to develop the wartime "giant blood bank" into a peacetime blood supply based on the unpaid civic-minded donor.[4] Organized medicine, represented by the American Medical Association (AMA) and state and county medical associations, entered the fray alongside the blood banks, as part of its dogged resistance to what the AMA called "socialized medicine."[5] In the Red Cross plan of collecting blood from all willing to give for the benefit of all those in need, the AMA and the blood bankers saw a fatal severing of the relationship between body products and markets that suggested a single-payer model of delivering health care and undermined the obligation of patients to pay for all medical treatment. The federal government, on the other hand, supported the Red Cross plan to organize the blood supply nationally, because the U.S. military was eager to have access to blood when the anticipated next war began.

World War II had cemented the importance of blood as critical war matériel, first suggested by its use during World War I. The importance of blood supplies was so central that when the United States was preparing for the invasion of Europe in 1944, the crucial advance that the Allies hoped would turn the tide against Germany and the Axis Powers, the director of military blood services was one of the few officers entrusted with advance knowledge of the invasion date so that he could begin to stockpile perishable whole blood in England, ready to supply the craft landing on the beaches of Normandy.[6] Although the wartime blood program was dismantled when the war ended, the military remained intensely interested in the giant blood bank "circulating in the veins and arteries of the living American public."[7] As the Cold War quickly became a nuclear showdown between the United States and the Soviet Union, the military began to plan for atomic warfare anywhere in the world. Based on data collected in Japan after the United States exploded atomic bombs over Hiroshima and Nagasaki, the military estimated that one million pints of blood a week, for three weeks, would be necessary in the aftermath of a nuclear attack on the United States. In such an event, a popular science weekly explained in 1948, the giant blood bank was the "only . . . blood bank in the world" that could meet such a need.[8]

At the same time that blood was being integrated into Cold War military planning, the many doctors in the armed services were returning to their civilian practices. Having had ready access to blood and blood products in the military, they found that the difference between practicing with a ready supply of stored blood and practicing without one felt like "the difference between the use of a horse and buggy and the modern automobile."[9] They wanted blood banks in their communities. In the postwar decades banked blood was no longer limited to charity patients forced to rely on stored blood but became a taken-for-granted aspect of treatment for all patients that allowed the procedures that replaced blood transfusion as front-page news: open heart surgery, renal dialysis, and eventually organ transplants. With these new treatments came ever-increasing demands for blood.

In the early Cold War the immediate problem for both civilian doctors and federal planners was establishing a blood supply. Doctors, hospitals, and the government each wanted the power to access and allocate the blood supply for their different purposes. The government saw blood as a public resource, necessary to support national political and military ends, best organized centrally. Organized medicine saw blood as a vital therapeutic, integrated into the private practice of medicine and part of the arsenal of each individual physician, to be allocated as he or she saw fit. These dual visions created tensions in blood banking focused on the relationship between blood and cash, which had been made central in 1937 when Dr. Bernard Fantus at Chicago's Cook County Hospital told his colleagues that they ought to treat blood like money in the bank, accounting for credits and debits. As demand for blood and blood products increased, what had been the quiet coexistence of the Red Cross blood program using patriotic donors and blood banks using a combination of indebted donors and professional donors turned into "the battle of the blood banks."[10]

The most heated issue of the battle was whether a patient who received blood had any obligation to pay for it. The Red Cross advocated for free blood to all who needed it, without obligation, while the medical profession and the blood bankers insisted that blood was a "personal resource" that had to be paid for, just like any other aspect of medical care.[11] Hemphill and her fellow blood bankers preferred payment in replacement pints of blood, but they would also accept cash that they could exchange for blood by paying donors. In the words of one contemporary observer, the "basic problem" was "free or pay."[12] Coexistence seemed impossible because in these heated debates about the blood supply, blood became a proxy for discussions about medical services generally. Was health care a universal right, a public good to be provided to all citizens by the government? Or was it a market commodity, to be sold by providers to those with the ability to pay? Because of the medical profession's commitment to avoid any central planning and government subsidization for medical services, doctors and blood bankers pilloried the Red Cross program as fostering irresponsibility and social decay. They focused instead on making the blood supply system ever more like financial banking. In the process of making sure that the bank was not a "mere metaphor" when applied to blood, organized medicine emphasized the nature of banked blood as market property to such an extent that its advocates lost sight of Fantus's original vision of the blood bank as an institution that facilitated the availability of blood for all who needed it without regard to ability to pay, using markets to promote blood as civic property.[13]

Stocking Hospital Blood Banks

Hospital blood banks were the front lines of the blood battles. As medical care moved from the home to the hospital, even for well-to-do patients, the hospital was the locus of blood transfusions. When fresh blood was used, donors were bled at the hospital, close to where the transfusion would occur. Fantus, as a hospital director of therapeutics, was concerned with managing a blood supply for patients of his employer, Cook County Hospital, and it was largely other hospitals that copied his innovation. Even while the national blood program was pioneering the freestanding blood center to collect blood for processing into plasma, hospitals continued to establish blood banks, eager to provide blood to their civilian patients more efficiently. The number of home front hospitals with a blood bank doubled between 1941 and 1945, to about four hundred. After the war the total rapidly climbed to nearly one thousand by 1956.[14]

Blood bank experts initially recommended that only the largest hospitals, those with more than 350 beds, start blood banks, because otherwise blood usage would be too low to maintain a sufficiently fresh inventory.[15] Because even as late as 1965 only one-fifth of U.S. hospitals had more than two hundred beds, this recommendation would seem to consign most hospitals, and the doctors who practiced at them, to the "horse and buggy" approach of donor registries.[16] In the 1950s, however, as the expectations of both doctors and patients for blood on demand increased, wartime developments in blood preservation also increased the shelf-life of stored blood, reducing the "ageing-out" problem. In this new era medical professionals increasingly believed that "every hospital must maintain its own blood bank or have a constant source of blood supply available," either from a regional blood center or from a nearby hospital.[17] If there was no external source of supply available, even the smallest hospitals developed this hallmark of modern medical care, increasing the number of communities with access to banked blood. In Henderson, Kentucky, the eighty-bed Methodist Hospital set up a bank in 1950. Just like Fantus in 1937, the administrators found that the most expensive start-up cost was the purchase of two refrigerators, one that they filled with blood and kept under lock and key, and the other containing the chilled preservation solutions into which the blood was collected. Using existing staff to collect and manage the blood supply, and a combination of indebted donors and civic-minded unpaid donors, the hospital was able to keep an adequate inventory and proudly deemed their "small hospital blood bank" a success five years later.[18]

Whatever the size of the blood bank, improved access to blood led to increased demand. By 1957 "almost all hospitals transfuse[d] more blood than they collect[ed]," requiring them to look elsewhere in the blood supply system to balance their blood flows.[19] This imbalance in blood flows was supportable because, unlike in 1937, hospital blood banks no longer existed in isolation but operated within a matrix of other blood supply institutions. Hospital blood banks were drawing only an estimated 30 percent of the blood collected annually in the United States, although they were dispensing virtually all of the blood patients received.[20] They were obtaining blood from community banks, which drew almost 25 percent of the blood collected, from Red Cross blood centers, which drew about 50 percent, as well as from commercial banks, that is, for-profit enterprises. The blood battles were waged between the two main external sources of the hospital blood supply: the Red Cross blood centers and community blood banks. They were battling not just to be the major source of supply for hospital blood banks but also to establish their philosophy of blood supply management.

The community blood banks, such as Hemphill's employer, Irwin Memorial Blood Bank, were the successors to the prewar Blood Donors Bureau in New York City organized by the Blood Transfusion Association and the philanthropic blood donor leagues established around the country. These organizations were freestanding nonprofit agencies created to provide medically supervised donors to multiple hospitals, sparing each hospital the need to recruit and type donors. In the new world of banked blood, hospitals found it convenient to outsource collection and processing to community blood banks, just as they had previously outsourced donor recruitment and management to donor bureaus and leagues. Rather than medically supervised donors, the community banks provided bottles of stored blood. By 1940 there were already four community blood banks, and by 1944 the number had climbed to about twenty-five.[21] Doctors often founded these banks, working through their local medical organization. For example, the Inland Empire Blood Bank opened in Spokane, Washington, in 1945 under the auspices of the county medical society and with fundraising help from the local Lions Club.[22] Between 1945 and 1956, when the number of hospital blood banks was skyrocketing, the number of community blood banks tripled.[23]

Not only did the number of such banks increase, but they also processed more blood over time. Irwin Memorial, which also was organized by a county medical society, was collecting blood from about two hundred donors per month when it opened in 1941. By 1950 it was processing three thousand donors per month.[24] The hallmarks of these banks were their local control and their steadfast adherence to Fantus's injunction that the bank was not a mere metaphor. These freestanding nonprofit institutions struggled to keep cash and blood in balance. Like Fantus's original blood bank, the community blood banks relied on the indebted donor to pay back blood loans in kind.

After 1948 the community blood banks had competition from Red Cross blood centers that emerged from the wartime donor centers that collected blood for military use. These institutions were also freestanding, in that they were not part of any hospital, but they were part of the American National Red Cross. During the war, the Red Cross blood collection centers had never formally adopted the bank terminology or its philosophy of accounting, although the press and the public adopted the term *bank* to explain the national blood program's vision of the citizenry as a vast reservoir of blood, ready to be tapped in the service of the national interest.[25] Soon after World War II ended, the Red Cross chose blood procurement as the "core of its peacetime activities," providing an ongoing mission for an organization founded to provide aid to prisoners and civilians during times of war.[26] Its administrators rightly believed that they had accumulated considerable expertise in blood collection, processing, and distribution, and that, as an organization, the Red Cross had the national infrastructure and perspective that could be used to manage what the government liked to call "the national blood supply."[27] The federal government encouraged the peacetime ambitions of the Red Cross because the military was eager to maintain access to the veins of the American public. Although the Subcommittee on Blood Substitutes that had directed the wartime blood collection efforts was disbanded, by 1948 the National Research Council had constituted a new Committee on Blood and Blood Derivatives. The Committee, which included representatives from the army and the navy, recommended to the secretary of defense that the Red Cross resume its official role as blood collection agency for the military.[28]

Even before it received this official invitation, and as the federal government was asking the Red Cross to wind up its wartime program, the Red Cross had been authorizing local chapters to begin civilian blood collection programs. By June 1947 there were sixteen such Red Cross programs, run at a municipal, county, or state level, and plans were under way for twenty-five more.[29] The Red Cross had bigger plans, however, to coordinate the civilian blood supply nationally, as it had coordinated the military blood supply. In 1948 it launched the Red Cross National Blood Program with great fanfare and the blessing of the federal government.[30] The inaugural Red Cross center opened in Rochester, New York. In his dedication address, the president of the American National Red Cross told his audience that the program was designed "to provide blood and blood derivatives, without charge for the products, wherever needed throughout the nation."[31] Through its program, the Red Cross "present[ed] the opportunity to all our citizens to contribute directly to the saving of life and the prevention of suffering—not as an ideal but as a concrete act of generosity."[32] Like the wartime donations for the troops, this generosity was cast by another Red Cross administrator as a civic-minded act, a service "of the people, by the people, and for the people."[33] In direct opposition to the community banks, the hallmarks of the Red Cross were national organization and a commitment to free blood to those who needed it, without obligation to pay in cash or blood.

As the Red Cross worked to market its program to medical and lay audiences, it provided a vision of blood as a unique therapeutic taken from the generous and given to the sick, regardless of financial status. After the Rochester launch, Red Cross officials gave speeches to medical groups, generated pamphlets, and courted press coverage.[34] An educational pamphlet about the Red Cross program, *Blood's Magic for All*, explained that "blood [is], or should be, a pillar of national health." It told all Americans that they had an opportunity to "give the most unselfish gift of your life," a gift that "gives you a personal share in fighting death and disease" and "makes you an active partner in the progress of medicine." Donors were promised, "The person receiving your blood or blood medicine will *not* be charged for it. The only charge will be the fee of the physician or hospital administering the blood or blood product." Participation "admits you to a modern kind of democratic citizenship."[35]

The popular weekly *Science News-Letter* published a glowing three-part series about the Red Cross program in 1948. Its author portrayed its advantages by examples from the first months of operation in Rochester.[36] "Mr. X," a forty-five-year-old hemophiliac from a small upstate town, was slowly dying of blood poisoning and starvation because of badly infected teeth. His doctors and dentist were unwilling to remove his teeth because he had nearly died of blood loss after a previous tooth extraction. But thanks to the Red Cross program, they had access to ample free supplies of antihemophilic globulin and fibrin foam, two of the newest blood products useful to promote clotting. Using these blood products, Mr. X was "saved" from a slow death by successful oral surgery. Once again "up and about," he felt "like a million dollars." His experience was described as "unique" but soon to become common, once the national Red Cross blood program was up and running, bringing the most modern blood products to cities, towns, and farms across the country. The parents of six-year-old Bobby in Elmira, New York, were also described as freed from worry by the new blood center, as their hemophiliac son now had blood available whenever he needed it, also free of charge. Another small-town boy, suffering from kidney disease, needed multiple treatments of serum albumin, another new blood product which was available only from commercial suppliers at $80 per treatment, more than his parents or the local hospital could afford. The Rochester center made the product available to him without charge, transforming an untreated child into a recovering child.[37] In the Red Cross program blood was not itself equated with cash, although the results might be worth "a million dollars." Gifts from donors would allow patients and hospitals to avoid crushing bills for life-saving therapeutics.

Initially, organized medicine accepted this alternative approach to the blood supply problem. The Red Cross obtained approval from the AMA for its program before the Rochester center opened, and the AMA joined the effort to educate the American public.[38] The author of *Blood's Magic for All* published an article in the November 1948 issue of the AMA lay magazine entitled "The Gift of Miracles." Like the pamphlet and the *Science News-Letter* reports, this article explained how, through the gifts of their neighbors, Americans would receive life-giving blood and blood products without paying a penny as part of "a distinctive kind of peacetime battle against death, disease and pain." "In cities, towns and hamlets over the country, the postman, housewife, farmer, banker, preacher and men in prison cells" could give these gifts, allowing the Red Cross "to bring blood and blood products to anyone needing them, anywhere." As during the war, men and women from all walks of life, recruited from the farmhouse and the jailhouse, could participate as donors in a program that expanded the notion of the soldier-recipient to include all patients as casualties in a "peacetime battle" against disease and death.[39]

With medical support, the Red Cross program at first proceeded quickly. In Stockton, California, two doctors "squawked" to their local medical society for a blood bank, when on successive days each had the experience of treating a young woman who died from hemorrhage before they could arrange blood for transfusion.[40] One of these doctors, Dr. Donald Harrington, had been trained in body-to-body transfusions by syringe in his residency, but while serving in the Army Air Corps during World War II had learned to value the speed of using stored blood. The discussions within the medical society to create a community blood bank coincided with the Red Cross announcement of its plans for regional blood centers, and with the help of another local doctor who was chair of the local Red Cross chapter, Stockton became the site of the second Red Cross regional blood center in February 1948.[41] These doctors, eager to have a reliable blood supply, were happy to take Red Cross help, even though the California Medical Association took the position that all blood banks should be run by local medical societies.[42] Eleven more Red Cross centers were collecting blood by October 1948, and the total more than tripled in the next two years, with centers in locations as widespread as Kansas, Georgia, Massachusetts, Washington, D.C., Nebraska, Missouri, and North Carolina, as well as two more in California.[43]

When the Korean War began in 1950, the Red Cross easily redirected its existing blood supply chain to serve military objectives, as the federal government had hoped. Under a formal agreement with the military, the Red Cross resumed large-scale blood drives, collecting whole blood for shipment overseas, a role it would play again during the Vietnam War.[44] Between wars the Red Cross continued its efforts to extend its civilian program nationally. By 1963 about half of the blood collected in the United States was collected by a network of fifty-six regional Red Cross centers.[45] The rate of formation of Red Cross centers dropped off markedly after 1955, however, and many of the Red Cross centers failed to supply all the blood used in their region, instead serving only in a supplementary role for hospitals that also collected their own blood and/or received blood from elsewhere.[46] While the Red Cross thus had more control over the nation's blood supply than any other entity, it failed to achieve its goal of managing the nation's blood supply as a single public resource. Despite its concerted marketing push and its favorable beginning, the Red Cross blood program had been thwarted by determined opposition from community blood banks and organized medicine.

Fighting Communism with the Blood Bank

The phrases *national health* and *free of charge* repeated by the Red Cross during the postwar years quickly cost the organization the initial support it had gained from the medical profession. These were fighting words, associated then (as for decades thereafter) with what the AMA called "socialized medicine." Since the early twentieth century the AMA had fought any government funding of or control over medical services as a threat to professional autonomy, status, and profits.[47] In response to this perceived assault from the Red Cross, organized medicine and the community blood banks fiercely embraced the banking metaphor and its implication of deposit and withdrawal. They emphasized the similarity between blood banks and financial banks to explain their preferred method of blood supply management as part of free market capitalism, in opposition to what they portrayed as the harmful socialist approach of the Red Cross.

The American Association of Blood Banks (AABB), the professional organization that allowed scattered banks to share information and philosophies, led the opposition to the Red Cross plan of a national blood supply. At the founding meeting in 1948, sponsored by the Baylor University Hospital blood bank in Dallas, the dean of Baylor's medical college told the assembled blood bankers that he favored community blood banks over regional centers in peacetime as a way of promoting local self-sufficiency.[48] His audience agreed. Many of the hospital blood bankers present appreciated the assistance of the Red Cross in donor procurement, and the organization passed a carefully worded resolution inviting the Red Cross to join the AABB in recognition of that role. Just as the Red Cross was opening its first peacetime collection centers, however, the AABB issued a statement declaring its strong opposition to blood collection and distribution by the Red Cross: "No service is offered or proposed by the Red Cross that is not, or could not be, done better by independent, non-profit blood banks working in cooperation with one another."[49]

The issue was not just local control but medical control. A blood bank administrator who attended the Dallas meeting and was elected to the executive board of the newly founded organization, Dr. Julius W. Davenport Jr., returned to New Orleans and explained to his medical colleagues that they ought to think about this issue similarly to the doctors belonging to the California Medical Association: "Blood banking is a part of the practice of medicine and as such can best be administered under local control of responsible, independent, nonprofit institutions under the professional supervision of local medical societies." The Red Cross, in his view, was attempting "an invasion of medical practice by a lay organization."[50] The problem was not that the Red Cross failed to employ doctors and other qualified medical personnel to supervise blood collection and management; the Red Cross blood program was under the supervision of a medical advisory committee, and each center had a medical director.[51] The problem was that the American National Red Cross itself was not a medical organization controlled by doctors. This lack of ultimate medical control was an objection that the AMA had raised previously to bolster medical opposition to any form of government-directed health care. According to the AMA, administration of any aspect of medical care by a "lay organization" was a direct attack on the autonomy and prestige of the medical profession. The AABB used the twin pillars of local management and supervision by organized medicine to distinguish both hospital and community blood banks from the Red Cross blood centers.

The AABB membership, however, focused most of its ire on the difference between blood *banks* and blood *centers*. At a time of great tension between the United States and the Soviet Union, the AABB used the bank to link local control and medical supervision to capitalism as a cornerstone of democracy. It cast the blood bank wars as yet another battle in the struggle against communism as both an economic system and an oppressive political system. Though framed in the language of Realpolitik, the blood battles might be better understood as another front in the fight of professional medicine against any form of government-run health care.

Organized medicine's support for government health insurance in the early twentieth century had soured around the time of the U.S. entry into World War I, and the opposition of organized medicine to any and all such plans would continue throughout the twentieth century, helping shape the American medical complex and, within it, what would soon become known as the "blood business."[52] During the first half of the twentieth century, the AMA had melded a weak and diffuse profession into a strong, respected profession with high prestige and high earning potential. Medical profits were steeply increasing after 1945, with the net profit from medical practice quadrupling between 1945 and 1969 and medical incomes rising much faster than the consumer price index.[53] Doctors were in control of the money flow surrounding medical care, setting fees for procedures such as transfusion and participating in the rise of the modern hospital. "Free blood" and nationally coordinated medical care suggested another way that health care dollars could be allocated, a way fewer of those dollars might flow to doctors.

During World War II the AMA had fought an antitrust lawsuit by the federal government, defending its practice of penalizing doctors who participated in insurance plans or who even advocated for government health insurance.[54] After the war the increasing economic pressures on the medical marketplace were driving a renewed national discussion about a government health care system. The rapid rise of blood banks was part of the changing nature of medical care in the United States, part of the transition to modern hospital-based medical care.[55] Partly because of the advances in surgery made possible by blood banking, and partly due to the revolution in drug therapies, medical care expenses had begun their startling rise, which would continue for the remainder of the century.[56] Most Americans lacked health insurance at the end of the war, and even as the percentage with hospitalization insurance increased in the 1950s and 1960s, any hospitalization could easily result in expenses beyond the means of many.[57] The debates over how to pay for modern health care involved the same complex of issues as the battle of the blood banks: who paid, who controlled access, and on what level that control was exercised. The AABB, supported by the local medical societies that sponsored many of its member banks, believed that the patient should pay for blood, the doctors should control access to blood, and the control over the blood supply should be local. The Red Cross advocated that costs be shared by all citizens and that control of the blood supply be held by a private philanthropic organization at the national level.

At the heart of the issue was the relationship between patients who received blood and the blood supply. Representatives of organized medicine categorized the Red Cross approach as "something for nothing," which they contrasted unfavorably to the "pay as you go" ideal of private enterprise used by the banks.[58] Hemphill and her colleagues did not give patients blood; as Hemphill explained, "We loaned it to you."[59] Davenport cried "Bosh!" to the idea of "free blood for charity patients." His bank at Southern Baptist Hospital in New Orleans was willing to waive service charges for indigent patients, but "we cannot perceive how the status of being a charity patient in any way relieves the relatives of such person from the valid obligation of seeing that the loan is repaid."[60] Every recipient was equally obligated to become or find an indebted donor to repay "blood loans" in kind, but if unwilling or unable to do so, was obligated to pay a steep "replacement fee" to satisfy the debt.[61]

With such opposing viewpoints, by 1949 meetings between the Red Cross and the blood banks to discuss the blood supply were less attempts to cooperate than skirmishes in a high-stakes war.[62] As America's wartime allies—most prominently Great Britain—adopted government health plans, organized medicine stepped up its rhetoric, casting the differences between AABB blood banks and Red Cross blood centers not only in terms of the practical question of how to fund blood procurement but as matters of political philosophy and morality. At the time of AABB's founding, Davenport had warned that "American free enterprise" was at risk if the "fundamental responsibility for replacement of blood bank loans" was not assumed by the borrower, a threat parallel to that posed by a borrower from a monetary bank defaulting on a loan. His blood bank was just like "the Republic National [financial bank]—it must receive deposits if it is going to stay in business."[63] "Free blood" was part of the threatened "federalization of medicine." Such federalization not only threatened medical control of health care and physician profits but, according to Davenport, also had profound political implications. It would lead to a "police state" and "ultimately a form of existence by directive," weakening America's moral fiber.[64] In a Cold War world in which these phrases referred both to the dictatorial regimes of the recently defeated enemies, Nazi Germany and fascist Italy, and the central planning of the new archenemy, the Soviet Union, these were strong words indeed. Instead of being courted with the promise of "blood's magic for all," bringing relief to sick children through a "gift of miracles," the public must be "indoctrinated with the idea that blood cannot be replaced by money and must be aware of the moral responsibility of the recipient or his family to see that all loans are repaid to the bank."[65]

During the Cold War the battle of the blood banks thus was cast as part of an ongoing worldwide conflict with the Soviet Union, in which "free blood" and the loss of local, private, and medical control over the blood supply threatened capitalism and thus democracy, corrupting the United States from within. Dr. Lester Unger, who had been involved in blood transfusion medicine in New York City since 1916, thought the replacement fee that Davenport and others levied on debtors as an incentive to repay in kind could be "overdone," causing a "greater burden on a man who wants to pay his bill and cannot get relatives or friends to replace blood" or on hospitals who pay the blood bank bills for indigent patients. At the New York Post-Graduate Medical School and Hospital blood bank, Unger charged only $7.50 as a replacement fee, rather than the $25 other blood banks charged.[66] Despite his sensitivity to those who lacked both cash and blood, Unger joined Davenport at the Dallas meeting in explaining the dangers posed by the Red Cross approach: "Under a plan by which everyone irrespective of his financial status, gets so-called 'free blood' this therapeutic agent is singled out as the only medical gratuity given to self supporting individuals. If that philosophy is correct, then 'free' obstetrics, 'free surgery,' 'free medicine,' for that matter, 'free everything' should be available to all regardless of financial ability."[67] "Free blood" was the start of a slippery slope, at the bottom of which Americans would find themselves sheep-like victims of a police state, initiative and private enterprise destroyed. To the doctors battling any suggestion of socialized medicine, bottled blood should not be a unique item, a special "gift of life," but a therapeutic like any other for which patients paid unless the medical establishment decided they were eligible for charity care.

When the AABB and the AMA argued that the Red Cross national blood program was an un-American rejection of market capitalism, they were making a potent form of criticism in the years when the House Committee on Un-American Activities and Senator Joseph McCarthy were each searching for communist spies in the highest reaches of government as well as in Hollywood.[68] In this framing of a "free blood" system, a gift of, by, and for the people was transformed from an act of democratic citizenship into a handout that threatened American democracy. It was an attack on the capitalist principle that markets, not governments, allocated goods. In this battle the medical profession's initial allegiance to blood banks as institutions that increased access to a needed therapeutic without regard to ability to pay was transformed by market rhetoric. The normative vision of improved access that this new property had been created to serve was replaced with a different vision of each patient taking individual responsibility for his or her medical needs. Blood, in the arguments of the medical profession and the blood banks, was market property, part of a capitalist system in which implementation of liberal economic theory, with its focus on individual actors, was regarded as a patriotic and moral imperative.

By the late 1950s the blood battles had resulted in a patchwork quilt of institutional control over the blood supply. Each region of the country experienced the collection and management of the blood supply differently. The Red Cross was collecting about 70 percent of the blood in New England, while in the Southwest it drew virtually no blood; in that region community blood banks and hospital blood banks were splitting the blood procurement.[69] This geographic separation did not reduce the battles. Because the question of national health care was so important to organized medicine, it refused to relinquish its opposition to the Red Cross. On the other hand, national coordination of the blood supply to render blood flows more efficient was of interest to all doctors and hospitals that wanted blood for their patients, just as national coordination of financial banks aided all banks. This promise of improved efficiency for all hospital blood banks kept the two sides skirmishing, as cooperation held promise as well as threat.

This promise had allowed the Red Cross national blood program to launch with AMA support, so that doctors would be sure to have blood flowing in their communities. Yet soon after the Rochester center opened, "rumblings of discontent" within the AMA led first to a heated debate within the organization about whether to withdraw support altogether, followed by a list of conditions for continued AMA support.[70] These conditions included the requirement of the consent of the local medical society before opening a new Red Cross blood center. Numerous county medical societies rapidly rejected Red Cross proposals to open blood centers in their areas. In California, where the state medical association reiterated its support for locally controlled banks, the Red Cross was welcome to assist in procuring donors only. At the AMA annual meeting in June 1948, one of the "stormiest" sessions focused on the continued AMA support of the Red Cross blood program.[71] Between 1948 and 1955 the AMA House of Delegates passed at least twelve resolutions reiterating its support for control of blood banks by local medical societies and registering its continued opposition to the Red Cross program goals.[72] One such resolution put the AMA on record declaring that any free medical service or supply offered to all without regard to ability to pay violated the principle "that it is the responsibility of an individual to assume the obligations of medical expense just as he does for other living expense."[73]

The clarity of the battle on the national level, though, disguised considerable cooperation locally. Despite the AABB rhetoric emphasizing lay leadership at Red Cross blood centers, many doctors were involved with their local Red Cross, and quite frequently there was overlap in membership between local Red Cross chapters and county medical societies, the type of overlap that had led to the opening of the second Red Cross center in Stockton, California, in response to physician interest.[74] The Red Cross continued its policy of "permissive" local involvement in blood banking, and in 1950 over 150 local Red Cross chapters were involved in blood work outside of the national Red Cross program, mostly conducting donor recruitment for banks.[75] In Detroit even the opening of a Red Cross regional blood center did not end the promiscuous intermingling of a local hospital blood bank and the local Red Cross chapter, which included Red Cross motor corps driving donors from the hospital to the Red Cross center, Red Cross personnel drawing blood at the hospital, and eventually a mixed procurement system at the hospital, with some donor hours staffed by the Red Cross and some by the hospital.[76] While doctors at a philosophical level were committed to private medicine and personal responsibility, in their day-to-day practices many simply wanted blood for their patients by any practical means.

Doctors also saw the virtue of thinking about the blood supply at the national level. In 1949 the standing AMA Committee on Blood Banks made the first of two nationwide surveys of blood banks, with the participation of the Red Cross, the AABB, and associations of hospitals, pathologists, and surgeons.[77] Then, in July 1950, the Medical Policy Committee of the American National Red Cross called a meeting in Boston "to discuss a plan of cooperation among all blood banking personnel and facilities in this country." The meeting was attended by representatives from the AMA, the American Hospital Association, and the AABB and resulted in a signed agreement of cooperation.[78] The so-called Boston Agreement provided both for peacetime cooperation and for wartime planning, setting out the theoretical contours of a system that blood centers and banks would struggle to implement for decades to come: a way to exchange blood between collecting entities. Just as a dollar bill had the same value in any financial bank, units of blood should be exchangeable between banks, with each banked bottle of equal worth no matter which entity collected the blood. If the blood banking system became national, blood could flow from places of high supply and low demand to places of low supply and high demand, smoothing the inevitable problems of maintaining an inventory of a perishable commodity.

Within weeks, however, a follow-up was needed to clarify the Boston Agreement because "a number of misunderstandings [had] arisen at hospital and community levels between members of the American Association of Blood Banks and persons engaged in American Red Cross transfusion activities."[79] Cash flows were getting in the way of blood flows. The Boston Agreement specified that blood shipped from one bank to another as part of an exchange became the property of the receiving bank, "to be used in accordance with its usual policy."[80] The hospital and community banks wanted to charge their usual processing and replacement fees for any pint they dispensed—that is, to require the recipient to pay for the blood, in kind or in cash. The Red Cross wanted its blood to remain free, no matter which entity transfused it. To do otherwise would violate its promise to donors.

There was also concern about the operational standards of other banks. In order for units of blood to be fungible, they must be perceived as equal in safety and reliability, which required receiving banks to trust the laboratory work, handling procedures, and labeling of the sending bank. Both the AABB and the Red Cross hoped that the federal government through the National Institutes of Health would establish national standards for blood products and inspect and certify blood banks.[81] Through such a federal licensing program, banks could rely on blood collected by any participating bank. During the 1950s, however, the federal government did not create such standards, greatly hampering implementation of the national system developed in principle by the Boston Agreement.

Throughout the decade efforts to bring order nationally remained at the level of talk rather than action. The AMA took the lead in forming the Blood Foundation in 1955, bringing together representatives of organized medicine (including the American Hospital Association and the American

Society of Clinical Pathologists), the AABB, and the Red Cross to discuss blood supply issues. The Foundation was transformed into the more formal Joint Blood Council in 1960.[82] As the blood bank battles remained unresolved, preventing any truly national coordination of the blood supply, this organization did not succeed at much beyond making another survey of blood banks in 1957.[83] The survey, published in 1960, revealed that the ongoing battles were resulting in a draw, with the Red Cross stalled at collecting about half of the blood supply.

While the hoped-for federal licensing program for blood collection and storage organizations did not materialize, the federal government did develop a program that regulated disembodied blood and blood products as "biological products" under its federal authority over interstate commerce. These regulations required facilities that shipped blood interstate to obtain federal licenses.[84] All Red Cross blood centers operated under a single federal license. The Joint Blood Council survey in 1957 found that three-quarters of community blood banks had licenses. Hospital blood banks, on the other hand, which obtained blood directly from donors or from the local blood center or community bank, saw no reason to obtain a federal license, and fewer than 10 percent of hospital blood banks were licensed.[85] Blood that was flowing into hospitalized bodies thus might or might not meet federal standards, depending on where it was collected.

In addition to the unsuccessful attempts to organize the blood supply on the national level and the on-the-ground local cooperation of some doctors, hospitals, community blood banks, and Red Cross chapters, some states intervened, seeking to bring some degree of order to the blood supply within their boundaries. During World War II, while the federal government planned blood supplies for the troops, states had included the blood supply in their civil defense planning. In Florida, for example, the state had developed a network of five community blood banks to provide blood and blood products to its residents in the event of enemy attack.[86] With the coming of peace, many state legislatures sought to ensure access to this modern medical technology for their citizens, either by continuing wartime programs, as in Florida, or starting new ones. By 1947 nine states had some form of a statewide blood or plasma program, and another eleven states were considering such a program.[87] The shape of such state plans, however, varied based on local factors, most prominently how the first blood banks in the state had been organized.[88]

North Dakota's state plasma program used a top-down approach to support blood therapy in a largely rural, sparsely populated state with little prior experience with blood banking. During World War II North Dakota residents had not participated in the national blood program; there simply were not enough potential donors to make a blood donor center in the region worthwhile. Yet doctors in the state felt that their patients should have access to stored blood and blood products and that dried plasma was an ideal blood product for storage and shipment in their state, allowing towns too small to support a blood bank to maintain a stock on hand. The doctors turned to the state legislature to fund and manage a blood program, and in 1944 the state health department began a statewide free plasma service. Using state funds for staff and facilities, the program relied on unpaid donors for its supply and provided dried plasma, free of charge, to any state resident who needed it. Here was a free blood product, provided by the government, but rather than opposing it, the state medical society "wholeheartedly and enthusiastically" accepted it.[89] In North Dakota the state was not providing something for nothing that doctors could otherwise provide for a fee; it was providing something that had been unavailable at any cost. By 1950 the North Dakota program was augmented by eight hospital banks in six cities.[90]

In Massachusetts, a geographically small state with one urban center, the early experience had been much different. Boston hospitals had been among the pioneers of blood banking in the 1930s, with the bank at Massachusetts General Hospital the state's largest.[91] During the war the Red Cross operated a blood donor center in Boston, staffed by local volunteers and relying on area residents to meet ever-increasing quotas for donation.[92] After the war doctors working through the Massachusetts Medical Society developed the nation's first statewide whole blood program in 1946, using local Red Cross chapters for donor procurement even before the national Red Cross launched its program. Under the Massachusetts Regional Blood Program, the state licensed all blood banks. The program combined mobile Red Cross collection clinics, the regional Red Cross donor center, and a central state-run laboratory for processing blood with the original hospital banks, which continued to collect, store, and dispense blood. Eventually the Massachusetts blood supply was largely coordinated by the Red Cross regional center as part of the Red Cross national program.[93] The Red Cross center provided much of the blood supply, but the hospitals remained able to call upon their own donors and draw blood themselves as necessary. Through this system doctors retained local control and reduced anxieties about blood shortages. In more rural areas of the state, hospitals often relied upon the Red Cross to provide their entire blood supplies, while the Boston hospitals drew over half of the blood they used, relying on the Red Cross for the remainder.[94]

A Massachusetts physician explaining his state's program to blood banking colleagues at an AMA-sponsored conference described the cooperation between the Massachusetts Medical Society and the Red Cross as "complete."[95] The ability of Boston hospitals to draw and process their own blood became significant as the need for blood stored less than twenty-four hours became acute with the advent of open-heart surgery. With the Boston hospitals performing about twenty such operations per week, each case requiring an average of twenty pints of blood, the hospital blood banks relied upon their own donors or called upon two blood donor registries in Boston, which could supply walk-in donors for a fee.[96] Pointing out that the medical director of the regional program was always appointed by the Massachusetts Medical Society, the Massachusetts doctor tellingly titled his presentation "Medical Sponsorship and Supervision," emphasizing the ways the program met the hallmarks of AABB blood banks. This hybrid program blended the prewar hospital-based system with the convenience of statewide blood procurement using the Red Cross civic-minded donor model and added a state-financed central laboratory to manufacture the new blood products. The doctors were happy to rely on state money to support the blood laboratory and on supplies from donors giving blood "for free" when they felt that control of the blood supply remained both local and medical.

In contrast to Massachusetts, which had no community blood banks, in California community blood banks came to dominate the blood supply, largely through the influence of the mother of blood banking, Bernice Hemphill. The state legislature had surveyed the blood bank situation in 1946 and found that there were twenty-eight blood banks in California. The banks were clustered in and around San Francisco and Los Angeles, and more than half of the hospital beds in the state were unserved by any blood bank. What banks there were also varied in quality, measured by indicators such as routine testing for Rh factor and the ability to monitor the temperature of stored blood. Five of the banks were community blood banks, and four of those were in the Bay Area. These four banks, encouraged by Hemphill, collected about as much blood as the other twenty-four banks combined.[97] The success of these community blood banks led the legislature to recommend a state blood banking system based on community blood banks, under which the state would be divided into fourteen areas with at least one community blood bank in each—a form of centrally planned local control. Reflecting Hemphill's personal philosophy, the guidelines stressed the use of local, nongovernmental funds for start-up, the satisfaction of ongoing budget needs through processing and replacement fees, and local control. The report defined a blood bank as operating on the "essential principle" "that beneficiaries repay loans through a service charge and with a similar amount of blood," endorsing the individual responsibility approach.[98] The role of the California state government was to be limited to consulting, establishing standards, and perhaps providing interest-free loans for start-up funds, while local medical societies provided direction.[99] By 1963 California also licensed blood banks, providing state standardization.[100] In the four years following the state report, the number of nonhospital blood banks in California nearly tripled to fourteen, even as the Red Cross opened three centers in the state.[101]

Perhaps the least successful attempts at state-level coordination of the blood supply were made in New York, where repeated efforts failed to manage the challenge of rationalizing a blood supply in dense metropolitan areas and underserved rural areas. The blood supply in New York City had long been premised on the professional blood donor, organized both by the Blood Transfusion Association donor bureau and numerous for-profit donor agencies. As donor registries were replaced by blood banks, at least one for-profit bank, the successor to New York's professional donor registries, was created, as well as numerous hospital banks, which used professional donors and also encouraged patients to repay their blood "loans" in kind. The heavy recruitment of the New York metropolitan-area population as unpaid donors to the wartime blood program, first through Blood for Britain and then for the U.S. military, served to entrench the professional donor in civilian medicine, as throughout the war domestic blood needs continued to be met by paid donors.

As elsewhere, reliance on the professional donor for blood flows created problems of cash flows. During the war the state medical society had created a special committee on blood transfusion with the goal of making blood available at the lowest possible cost by better coordination of blood collection efforts. After the war this committee's report became the basis for a statewide plan to distribute blood. The state offered technical assistance and limited funding to open banks in underserved areas and urged an "individual responsibility" model, relying on strict adherence to the principle of loan repayment to meet the goal of providing blood to all state residents without reliance on professional donors.[102] Unlike in California, New York encouraged each hospital to have its own blood bank, with a coordinating organization, the Blood and Plasma Exchange, to facilitate sharing of blood among them, particularly within New York City. As this plan was implemented, one urban hospital blood bank, at the New York Post-Graduate Medical School Hospital, became a regional center, supplying over two hundred hospitals with blood that it collected from donors twenty-four hours a day, seven days a week, using a paid staff of fifteen and relying on a fleet of cars to deliver blood across the city.[103] In the rural upstate regions the individual responsibility model did not take hold, despite the plan. Instead the Red Cross was critical in maintaining the blood supply there; its first blood collection center was in Rochester in 1948, soon followed by centers in Buffalo and Syracuse.[104]

A reassessment about ten years later found that, especially within the New York metropolitan area, matters had not improved. In the city over 150 agencies involved in blood collection and transfusion evidenced "mutual disregard, lack of confidence [in each other] and even competition."[105] In 1958 New York City was still relying on paid donors for over 40 percent of its supply, at a time when the rest of the country was estimated to use, on average, only 2 to 14 percent paid blood. Charges for a unit of transfused blood ranged from $14 to $60 among the city hospitals.[106] Despite sixty recommendations for improvement developed by the New York Academy of Medicine, not much changed. In 1964 an administrator at the newly established New York Blood Center, a community blood center charged with developing an "integrated blood program for the metropolitan area of New York," admitted that it was "no secret" that "New York has a chronic and grievous problem with blood."[107]

A decade after the battle of the blood banks had begun, not all areas of the country were experiencing "chronic and grievous" problems, yet most agreed that blood banking was still in "a chaotic period" through the 1950s and into the 1960s.[108] It was apparent to all participants, from the most fervently free market administrators of community blood banks to the Red Cross center directors attempting to manage blood as a public resource and the hospitals and doctors who sought to use banked blood on a daily basis, that regional, if not national, coordination would benefit everyone. Despite the apparent success of the Massachusetts Regional Blood Program, state programs were necessarily limited; the New York metropolitan area, for example, encompassed parts of Connecticut and New Jersey. Blood that crossed state lines could be coordinated and regulated only on the federal level. Federal cooperation necessitated an agreement on the nature of blood. Was it free market property, flowing to those who took responsibility to pay, or civic property, flowing as a communal resource from the civic-minded to those in need? The lack of agreement on this philosophical question kept the situation chaotic. The sticking point remained the focus of the AABB blood banks on what they called the "replacement donor."

The Replacement Donor

The community blood banks took Fantus's admonition that "the term 'blood bank' is not a mere metaphor" very seriously, more seriously than Fantus himself, as they accounted for blood flows and cash flows.[109] As free-standing entities, they were more like financial banks than hospital blood banks. Fantus himself had responsibility for all therapeutics within Cook County Hospital, working within an institution that had multiple sources of income. A community blood bank director, however, like Hemphill, managed an entity for which all expenditures and incomes were directly attributable to the collection, storage, and dispersal of blood. Like Fantus, community blood bank administrators believed that no one should be allowed to withdraw from a bank unless he or she made a deposit, and unlike Fantus, who set up accounts for each department in his hospital, the freestanding blood banks considered each patient to be an account holder, obligated to stay out of the red by paying back his or her loan. The Red Cross, however, did not use the term *bank*, even metaphorically. It promised that any patient who received blood drawn at a Red Cross center would not be charged for the blood itself. Patients were not bank customers or debtors but recipients of "gifts of life." This philosophical difference meant that Red Cross blood and blood from AABB member banks might be fungible therapeutically, as a body product, but was not fungible from an accounting point of view. If an AABB member bank accepted a pint of Red Cross blood to meet a supply deficit, promising to replace it at a later time, it wanted to treat that pint like any other pint it dispensed and require repayment. Otherwise, according to its business model, the bank would run dry. Each recipient needed to be what banks came to call a "replacement donor," paying back a debt or earning credit in anticipation of a future debt. This approach was the essence of the "pay-as-you-go model" that the AABB and AMA preferred over the "something for nothing" approach of free blood that they considered socialized medicine.

In the postwar years, as blood banks tried to keep blood and cash flows balanced patient by patient, they developed the "replacement fee" as their preferred means to ensure that patients met their individual responsibility. Fantus had warned the doctors at Cook County Hospital in 1937 that without deposits, they would lose withdrawal privileges. Most patients were not often repeat customers at the blood bank and thus needed a different form of incentive. The replacement fee was part of a two-tiered charge for blood. Even the Red Cross acknowledged that blood from its centers might come with a fee from the hospital or doctor who administered the transfusion. The blood banks kept that service or processing fee separate from the replacement fee. The service fee was to cover overhead costs; what Fantus had estimated as 89 cents in his hospital blood bank in the 1930s became $10 to $15 in many postwar banks.[110] The replacement fee was different; it was the dollar value placed on the blood withdrawn, which could be paid in cash or in kind. The goal of the blood bankers was to keep the replacement fee high enough that patients chose to become indebted donors. Motivated to avoid the fee, they would either give blood themselves after recovery or recruit friends and family members to donate and pay off their debt as a way of diminishing an already hefty hospital bill. For the few patients who were repeat customers, particularly hemophiliacs, the replacement fee caused a serious financial burden as they exhausted the ability of friends and family to make in-kind repayment, but for other patients, it provided an incentive to supply blood.[111]

When the Inland Empire Blood Bank opened in Spokane in 1946, it charged $12.50 per unit, plus a refundable "replacement charge" of $25 per unit. About three-quarters of blood debtors provided blood in order to obtain a refund, and the director used the cash collected from replacement charges paid by the remainder to buy blood from professional donors, keeping the blood books balanced.[112] When it proved difficult to operate the bank and maintain blood supplies using only the $12.50 processing fees and the limited replacement fees collected, the administrators, like Fantus, created novel accounting solutions to increase inventory levels without spending money on professional donors. Their solution was to supplement their program of bank "loans" with another idea borrowed from modern capitalism: insurance. Anyone who had not yet accumulated a blood debt could donate a pint and thereby earn a credit of one unit of blood. For one year the donor or anyone in his or her immediate family could receive a pint of blood without any replacement charge, a form of in-kind medical insurance.[113] What became known as the "replacement donor" donated blood in order to repay either a present or a future debt. Through this broadened category of the indebted donor, Fantus's concept of creating a communal inventory from patients and their friends and family was expanded from current patients to include those who feared being patients in the future and the indebtedness they would then face. Healthy individuals could not only help their ailing friends and relations pay off debts already incurred; through the credit system, they could also help themselves by creating a deposit account.

The Inland Empire's donor credit program, begun in 1947, expanded in 1948 to a group credit plan. In such plans donors gave blood as members of an affiliated group such as the Lions Club, a church, or employees of a corporation, adding to an account in the name of their group that could then be drawn upon by any member of the group and his or her family members. Inland Empire preferred such group plans because it could then schedule a mobile unit visit to one location where donors recruited from the group would fill the beds in a targeted blood drive. By periodically scheduling such visits to groups of known size, Inland Empire could maintain a constant and predictable blood supply. These strategies were so successful that the bank was able to reduce its nonrefundable processing fee to $10 per unit in late 1949.[114]

These two strategies of the refundable replacement fee and blood credit plans (usually called "blood assurance plans" or "blood service plans") came to be widely used by community blood banks, crystallizing the accounting differences between these banks and Red Cross blood centers.[115] Donor credit plans could become quite elaborate. The entrepreneurial administrator of the Salt River Blood Bank in Phoenix developed such formalized

Bank your Blood as you would your money!

Start Your
Blood Reserve Fund Today!

JACKSONVILLE BLOOD BANK, INC.
536 WEST 10TH STREET
JACKSONVILLE, FLORIDA
Phone EL 3-8263

"Bank Your Blood," undated donor recruitment material from Jacksonville Blood Bank, Jacksonville, Florida. *As reproduced in Richard A. Martin,* Jacksonville's Silent Service: A History of the Jacksonville Blood Bank and Florida-Georgia Blood Alliance, 1942–1992 *(Jacksonville, FL: Centurion Press, 1992).*

blood assurance plans to manage his cash and blood flows that the bank established a separate business entity to manage its plans, and the state of Arizona claimed jurisdiction to regulate the plans as a form of insurance.[116] The community blood bank in Stockton, which found using professional donors even more efficient than targeted blood drives, gave local residents a choice: they could buy into its blood assurance plan with blood or money. In 1957 the bank collected $1 per person or $4 per family for an annual membership and used the money to buy blood as needed.[117]

In establishing credit plans, using paid donors, and setting fees, the administrators of each blood bank responded to local conditions of supply and demand to keep the blood available that local hospitals needed. This type of local control was a hallmark of how organized medicine and the blood bankers thought that body products, like other aspects of medical care, should be managed. Each city and region had unique needs for blood, which fluctuated over time. While the commitment of these banks to the replacement donor made any coordination with the Red Cross difficult, they hoped it would be possible to assist each other in their constant search for replacement donors, by allowing friends and family anywhere in the country to pay back a blood loan, earning credit at the dispensing bank. Hemphill, one of the most insistent advocates of the bank as no mere metaphor, thought that AABB members, by acting even more like financial banks, could more efficiently manage their perishable inventory, enhancing blood flows for all banks.

Hemphill envisioned a patient in San Francisco recruiting blood donations from family or friends in Florida and Illinois, resulting in credits transferred to Irwin Memorial as the supplying bank, even if no actual blood crossed state lines. On a monthly basis the credits and debits exchanged between banks would be reconciled, and actual cash or blood would flow between banks to balance the books.[118] Taking her role as banker literally, Hemphill asked her personal banker how banks transferred monetary credits represented by checks. Once she learned about the national banking clearinghouse system, she called the Federal Reserve Bank to get a further explanation and got sample forms that she adapted for her blood clearinghouse.[119]

Like the first blood banks, the blood clearinghouse was essentially a method of accounting. As Hemphill explained it, "The district clearinghouse is primarily a bookkeeping agency, responsible for keeping a daily debit and credit record of all reciprocal transactions handled for each of its participating blood banks and for arranging monthly settlement on all inter-bank exchanges."[120] It was a way of tracking credits and debits on a bank-by-bank basis. Just as the banking metaphor assumed that all blood was fungible, the clearinghouse relied on the complete fungibility of collected blood, regardless of its institutional source. To bolster the ability of banks to treat other banks' blood as equivalent to their own, Hemphill created standards for blood collection and preservation for clearinghouse members. She arranged shipping mechanisms and established transaction fees. The clearinghouse, like a financial clearinghouse, followed a pay-as-you-go model. Sending and receiving blood through the clearinghouse required payment of a fee. The transaction fees initially paid the salary of one full-time employee to keep the books. The clearinghouse began among California banks, and then, through the AABB, Hemphill's organization was expanded nationally in the 1950s, using regional offices to coordinate blood supplies by district.[121] The ability to transfer blood among banks nationally made the need for national standards pressing. In the absence of federal regulation, the AABB drafted its own standards beginning in 1955 and established a voluntary accreditation program for its members.[122] Accreditation qualified them to participate in the clearinghouse.

As Hemphill recalled later, the accreditation standards specified the minimum requirements for blood collection and processing, as well as important details such as "the shipping containers, the preservatives, [and] who would pay the cost, the shipper or the receiver." Yet the standards did not address the issue of whether collected blood came from replacement donors, paid donors, or civic-minded donors.[123] Like doctors in the era before the blood bank, the postwar blood bankers did not attach any stigma to exchanging cash for blood. Blood could be fungible whether it came from paid professional donors or unpaid replacement donors, and the ratio between these two possible sources was driven by the bottom line in an atmosphere where the equation of cash and blood was celebrated as the key superiority over Red Cross blood centers. Thus the Inland Empire Blood Bank in Spokane attempted to limit reliance on professional donors because the bank was short of money; new incentives were created for unpaid donors in order to increase blood flow into the bank with less cash outflow. In Stockton, where the Red Cross had ceased to operate the blood center after the Korean War ended, the community blood bank that was formed to take over its role, the Delta Blood Bank, found it impossible to recruit sufficient unpaid donors in the absence of the patriotic appeals of wartime, leading it to rely heavily on professional donors, even as it continued to encourage replacement donors.[124] In Phoenix the same adminis-trator who created the largest blood assurance corporation believed he could procure, process, and distribute blood at the lowest cost per pint using paid donors, who would show up to be bled at the times requested by the bank, rather than spending money on blood drives and donor recruitment. His Salt River Blood Bank thus switched from a mostly unpaid donor pool in the 1940s to professional donors.[125]

In the broadening of blood bank depositors beyond friends and family of individual patients who had received blood, the postwar banks were coming closer to the Red Cross centers in considering the entire "living American public" as potential donors, but their characterization of and explanation for blood donation was very different. Rather than stressing the "opportunity" of everyone to participate in a community-building exer-cise to create a shared resource, the community banks focused on the *use* of blood by casting all donors as either current or future blood debtors—all giving was related to receiving. Rather than appeal to generosity, the banks appealed to self-interest, using market-based solutions to manage this form of market property and believing that the invisible hand of the market would create the most efficient blood supply. It was the fear of overwhelm-ing medical bills—or their actuality—that would bring donors into credit plans or lead them to repay their "loans." The personal responsibility to pay for blood was just the same as if the banks "were selling silver teaspoons or carrots," explained the administrator of the Blood Bank of Hawaii.[126] The relationship between donor and recipient was not characterized by grati-tude and generosity. Instead each was involved in a commercial transaction for a body product with the bank, which owned and controlled the inven-tory of disembodied blood.

Although no cash was given to the replacement donor, he was essentially an extension of the professional donor, giving for personal benefit rather than for the public good. And like the professional blood donor, the re-placement donor was presumptively male. The blood banks looked to the male portion of the "living American public" for their replacement donors. Though women were not excluded from donating, the blood credit plans, targeting fraternal organizations and places of employment, were focused on enrolling men. The masculinity of the role was evident in the change in the donor population at the community blood bank in Denver, as the bank changed its donor recruitment approach. When the Belle Bonfils Blood Bank was founded in 1943, the bank followed the Red Cross model, collecting blood from civic-minded volunteers and providing it to those who needed it without charge. Like the wartime Red Cross program, the bank had nearly as many women donors as men. But by 1947, after the bank had set up a fee structure for patients based on repayment of blood debts, fewer than 25 percent of its donors were female.[127] After the war ended even the Red Cross blood program found that women constituted only 25 percent of its donors; in 1957 less than 20 percent of the nation's banked blood came from women.[128] Just as the professional donor of the Depression years could provide for his family by selling blood, the working husband and father during the Cold War could provide for his family by purchasing blood credits with his donation.

Women's role in the blood supply was in the blood bank itself. No longer the province of laboratory scientists using rare and tricky sera, blood testing and matching became routine work performed by less-educated workers, eventually to be gathered into the occupation of "medical technologist," a job category, like nursing, much more accessible to women than that of physician.[129] Hemphill's training as a laboratory bioanalyst in the early 1940s heralded this change. The wartime blood program had also developed the gendered role of blood bank hostess, as the assembly-line management of donors at blood collection centers was softened by the solicitude of the volunteer Gray Ladies. In the postwar decades women filled almost all of the paid and unpaid roles in blood banking except that of medical director, a position reserved for those with medical degrees, a largely male population.

Hemphill remembered Irwin Memorial as "a female dominated organization." As executive director, she ran the day-to-day organization with the aid of a handful of female support staff to manage the office, the accounts, and the volunteers.[130] There was a male medical director and "male employees—physicians, technologists, the custodial group—but it still was a very dominant women's organization in the management and in the leadership."[131] The nurses who drew the blood were women, as were the majority of the technicians trained to do the associated laboratory work. The volunteer labor on which Irwin Memorial crucially relied—those who transported blood and donors, staffed the canteen where donors recuperated, and aided the nurses—was entirely female.[132] In 1948 Hemphill relied on twenty-five paid employees and sixty-five volunteers. By 1950 there were seventy-five such volunteers, mostly physician's wives, under the direction of Mrs. Curtis Smith, herself an unpaid volunteer and wife of one of the doctors at the bank.[133] At the Mayo Clinic in Rochester in the 1960s the Blood Bank Society, the fifty-member organization of Mayo blood bank "technicians, nurses and secretaries" and other "interested persons," was so predominantly female that it held its monthly meetings in the Women's Club and had women filling all the officer positions.[134] The same feminization of blood banking occurred in Jacksonville, Florida, where the all-women civic organization, the Junior League, provided volunteers.[135]

This gendering of donors as male and those who recruited, bled, and cared for them as female pervaded the postwar blood procurement system in the United States. The dominance of women in the nursing and volunteer staff led to a newspaper article about the Jacksonville bank headlined "They Call Themselves Lady Draculas."[136] In 1965 the Association of American Blood Banks publicized the fact that five out of six blood bankers were women, "thousands of women out for your blood."[137] This gender difference was used to provide a little sexual spice as part of the blood donation experience, as suggested by the "Lady Dracula" nickname. The "pretty nurses" at a Chicago bank were mentioned in a news story describing blood donation as a positive experience, the pulchritude of the help another draw alongside a "pleasantly decorated lounge." The author felt that being interviewed by a "pretty nurse" eliminated the apprehension of most male donors, who could relieve any residual anxiety by staring at a mural of a "bathing beauty" on the ceiling while their blood was being drawn.[138]

The gendering of the postwar blood donor as masculine continued the prewar gendering of the professional blood donor as a "man of business." In these decades before the gift/commodity dichotomy became dominant, the unpaid replacement donor was not considered the opposite of the professional donor, someone gifting rather than selling his body product. To the contrary, even though he was not receiving cash, because of the emphasis on the blood bank as a capitalist institution, the replacement donor was treated as someone transferring ownership of his private property for a personal benefit, taking individual responsibility for his debt. The market

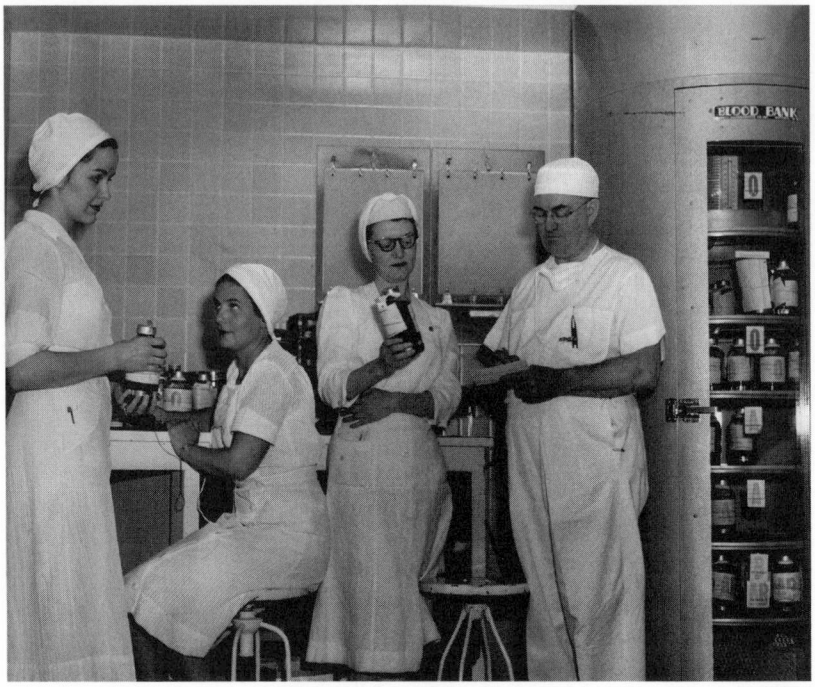

Female blood bank employees with male colleague, Mayo Clinic, Rochester, Minnesota, undated photo. *Used with permission of Mayo Foundation for Medical Education and Research, Rochester, MN.*

property understanding of blood perpetuated the gendering of the blood donor as masculine. Like the professional donor, the replacement donor was motivated by practical business sense rather than generosity and could receive gratifying reinforcement of his masculinity by assuming this provider role. The chief distinction was that the replacement donor role was much more accessible. Before the wartime increase in demand for banked blood, professional blood donors had been described as extraordinary men, able to accomplish feats of physical vigor unmatched by the occasional blood seller. After the war, with blood banks in every town, just like financial banks, almost any man could make a deposit in the blood bank as he would in a financial bank. By acting as a replacement donor, he was showing the same fiscal responsibility and ability to care for his family as he showed by maintaining a savings account. The banking metaphor helped maintain the blood donor as a *man* of business.

Blood Business

The man of business was supplying blood to bankers who took their business seriously. And businesses traded with those who had something to exchange; they did not give out something for nothing. By rejecting the Red Cross's vision of blood as a public resource, organized medicine and the AABB also rejected Fantus's original vision of the bank as a means of increasing access to medical care. At the AMA-sponsored Conference on Blood and Blood Banking in 1964 the participants reiterated the same points made in Dallas almost two decades previously about the need to treat blood as market property in support of personal responsibility and the fabric of American life.[139]

According to one community blood bank administrator, the relationship of donor, recipient, and bank was appropriately one of commerce:

> The legal tender in blood banking is blood and not money. Actually then, a donor does not *give* his blood to the blood bank; he is a depositor who receives a legal credit in terms of blood. Conversely, when blood is issued to a patient he contracts a debt repayable at the blood bank where the legal tender is blood. If he has a deposit of blood in the bank, or if some other depositor transfers his credit to repay that loan, the transaction is finished.[140]

A blood bank colleague agreed and made the case again for individual responsibility:

> We believe the individual should meet his own obligations to replace blood for his friends and family. We further believe the misguided trend of making the community responsible for blood replacement of the individual that is not only an unpalatable, socialistic approach which encourages the shiftless minority to shirk their responsibility, but this approach could ultimately destroy hospital blood banking and the replacement donor system. Therefore, we believe the individual must be encouraged to shoulder his blood replacement obligations, and it should in no way be left up to the community to help him with his rightful responsibility.[141]

Those who needed blood but lacked the resources to pay for it in blood or in kind were the "shiftless minority" rather than the desperately ill. Within the reality of day-to-day medical care, this rhetoric could ring painfully false. Hemophiliacs like "Mr. X" and little Bobby needed blood often, withdrawing many more pints of blood than the patient's family could repay.[142] A single accident or operation could result in a patient's receiving twenty to one hundred pints of banked blood, creating an overwhelming blood debt.[143] The Inland Empire Blood Bank assisted a patient needing nine transfusions a month by waiving the service charge, though not the replacement fee.[144] Irwin Memorial Blood Bank did not waive its repayment demands for hemophiliacs but tried to work with the local hemophiliac community to help them meet their heavy blood debts.[145]

Just as the attempt of blood bankers to maintain their banks as more than a mere metaphor was challenged by these medical realities within the patient population, their attempt to create a national blood banking system just like the financial banking system was hindered by the failure of the AABB to convert all hospitals and doctors to its position. The AABB fought the Red Cross to a draw but could not defeat it. The many hospital blood banks that relied on Red Cross blood for some or all of their inventory, and the doctors who experienced the benefits of local cooperation with the Red Cross, kept the vision of blood as "silver teaspoons" and the replacement donor as a man of business from becoming universal. The philosophical clash between blood as private market property and blood as a public resource that could be managed as a form of civic property continued, fought not only between the AABB and the Red Cross on an institutional level but within the hearts and minds of doctors themselves, who might wholeheartedly endorse individual responsibility and pay-as-you-go medicine but also worried that the replacement fee might be "overdone" when it disproportionately burdened the medically neediest.

With this continuing battle over blood, the national blood landscape remained chaotic. Despite Hemphill's efforts to establish a national clearinghouse, in 1960 less than 5 percent of the nation's blood supply was subject to reciprocity.[146] In yet another skirmish in the blood battles, the Red Cross joined the clearinghouse but insisted that it would forward only one unit of blood to replace each unit received by a patient, no matter how many units were donated on that patient's behalf. As many blood banks required more than one-for-one replacement to clear a patient's account (a way of maintaining inventory when some blood inevitably aged out or was otherwise unusable), this policy caused constant problems as patients attempted to clear blood debts by donations to Red Cross centers. Eventually, after much discussion, the Red Cross allowed the replacement of 1.5 units for each unit drawn, still far less than the three- or four-to-one ratios required by banks struggling to balance blood flows.[147] With disagreement about the obligation of a recipient to replace or pay for blood continuing to fester, in 1976 the Red Cross withdrew from the clearinghouse.[148]

In response the AABB published a position paper reiterating that blood must be considered a "personal resource," just as money was a "personal resource."[149] The blood bankers had elevated Fantus's statement that the bank was no "mere metaphor" to gospel truth. Yet their glorification of market-based conceptions of blood as a body product had not created an efficient market in which the invisible hand allocated blood where it was most needed. Reflecting the general disorder in the medical marketplace in the United States, the blood supply system was described in a federal report in 1972 as "a vast complex of organizations collecting, processing, and distributing blood products," functioning in "unsystematic and unregulated" fashion, "often resulting in an uneven distribution of the blood supply."[150]

As more Americans began to take a critical view of their blood supply, the debate shifted from the perennially irresolvable discussion about whether blood, like health care generally, should be a public resource or a private responsibility, to a more focused and seemingly more easily answered question: If prudent and responsible Americans were replacement donors, was the professional donor, motivated by quick cash, the true source of disorder within the blood system?

4

Market Backlash

What are the consequences, national and international, of treating human blood as a commercial commodity? . . . Should men be free to sell their blood?

—Richard M. Titmuss, *The Gift Relationship: From Human Blood to Social Policy,* 1971

"Should men be free to sell their blood?"[1] When Dr. Bernard Fantus conceived of the blood bank at Cook County Hospital in 1937, he did not concern himself with this question. Neither did the physicians who had been attempting to use blood transfusion to treat their patients in the decades before Fantus's innovation. Fantus's problem was not with blood selling but rather with blood buying, that is, how to provide blood for patients who could not afford the market prices for blood. The blood battles of the 1950s and 1960s did not turn on this question either. When a Massachusetts pathologist summed up the "basic problem in blood banks" in 1955 as "free or pay," he was not talking about blood donors.[2] Bernice Hemphill, the mother of blood banking, and her banker colleagues who deplored free blood were, like Fantus, focused on the distribution of blood: whether the *recipient* should pay for blood once it had been turned into a body product through the blood bank. When British sociologist Richard Titmuss asked this question in 1971, however, it was becoming the dominant question in blood banking.

The transition from relentless focus on user payment for banked blood to deep concern with payments to donors for embodied blood emerged out of a backlash against the medical enthusiasm for banked blood as a market commodity. The greatest about-face occurred among the population most committed to treating the blood bank as no "mere metaphor": the medical profession.[3] Doctors and blood bankers considered themselves professionals who were paid for their expert services in providing and using banked blood, just as in other aspects of providing medical care in a hospital setting. Their commitment to medical expertise in blood banking had contributed to their opposition to Red Cross "free blood" as not sufficiently medically controlled. This assumption of blood as part of medical services collided with their advocacy of "paid blood" as a market commodity when they found themselves regarded by the law as manufacturers of that useful therapeutic, banked blood. In the courtroom patients seeking compensation for blood transfusions gone wrong argued that they had purchased a defective product. To their consternation, doctors and blood bankers found their actions judged under product liability law, food and drug law, and unfair competition law, that is, laws that regulated businesses, consumers, and commerce. Just as the blood bank made the *bank* the dominant way of understanding body products in medicine, so banked blood became the model for understanding body products in law. In order to avoid the unanticipated legal consequences of "paid blood," medical professionals and blood bankers rethought their rhetoric and their practices, seeking to break the connections between money and blood among supplier, bank, and recipient that lent support to such lawsuits.

The medical profession successfully sought passage of state laws defining banked blood as part of the "service" of providing medical care rather than a possibly "unreasonably dangerous" "product."[4] These so-called blood shield laws have shaped body product exchange in the United States ever since by making the terms of the transaction between patient and body bank legally irrelevant. Blood bankers and hospitals also changed their practices, seeking to lessen any implication that they bought and sold blood. In addition to changing the wording of bills received by patients, blood banks decided voluntarily to eliminate the professional donor. These shifts in law and medicine made the question of blood sales by donors newly important.

The medical profession was not alone in its developing concern with blood selling. As the chaotic state of the American blood supply brought increasing public criticism, and the realization that hepatitis was a serious disease transmissible by transfusion increased worries about blood suppliers, Americans began to wonder if treating blood as a market commodity was advisable. In 1971 Titmuss's critical comparison of the blood supply system in the United States with that of Great Britain, *The Gift Relationship: From Human Blood to Social Policy,* was published in the United States. The British sociologist argued that allowing blood sales promoted egoism over altruism, corrupting society.[5] His book immediately became influential because it crystallized existing American concerns, and in so doing signaled a refocusing of the relationship between body products and cash. The national conversation about banked blood in medicine, in policy circles, and in the popular press shifted to whether blood should be given or sold to the bank, that is, as Titmuss helped frame the debate, whether blood should be a gift or a commodity. The gift/commodity dichotomy challenged the basic rationale of the body bank, manifested in its ledgers recording deposits and withdrawals, that a body product from a stranger would have equivalent therapeutic value to the receiving body, regardless of its source. Aided by the medical profession, by Titmuss's critique, and the resurfacing of racial fears, Americans began to divide body products into two unequal categories, equating purchased body products with contamination and disease, and gifted body products with purity. Like the blood shield laws, fear of the professional donor had repercussions in law and society that reached beyond blood and have continued to the present.

Good or Service?

As the body was becoming bankable in the first decades of the twentieth century, medical professionals were well aware of possible legal liability to their patients if something went wrong. Under medical malpractice doctrines, when any medical treatment caused harm, doctors could be required to pay compensation if their patients could prove that the care they received failed to meet the standard of care in their local community. If a patient was injured while in a hospital, however, the institution usually escaped any liability. Many states applied what was known as the charitable immunity doctrine: hospitals, as charitable organizations, were generally not held responsible for any errors of their employees, unless it could be proven that they had been negligent in hiring those employees.[6] While the body product donor was a new addition to the traditional doctor-patient dyad, courts had no difficulty extending traditional legal principles to decide that when a donor suffered harm, the doctor who harvested the body product might be liable.

In the early years of blood transfusion, when the invasive method of direct transfusion was used, these liabilities could be sizable. In 1922 a young California woman who had given blood to her dying neighbor recovered $1,500 ($20,000 in today's dollars) from the neighbor's estate after the wound in her arm failed to heal for months, causing her to give up her job in a telegraph office and remain out of work for over a year. While the donor looked to the estate of the blood recipient rather than to the doctor for compensation, the amount of her reward indicated the scale of damages possible.[7] Another donor from Georgia sought $30,000 ($400,000 in today's dollars) in compensation from the treating doctor in 1925 when her wound did not heal well. She claimed that while she had willingly consented to give blood to treat her husband, she had consented only to donate blood by the indirect method and that the doctor had cut her arm to expose a vein without her consent.[8] When a former University of California crew team member, who had been a professional blood donor since his college years, died of septicemia after selling his blood for a transfusion in 1933, the jury awarded damages of $58,000 (over $1 million in today's dollars) to his widow and mother in a lawsuit against the doctors who performed the transfusion and the hospital where it occurred.[9]

The scattered published legal opinions about such disputes reflect only those instances in which a harmed donor brought suit, there was a trial, and one party chose to appeal the verdict. Other instances must have resulted in out-of-court settlements or in jury verdicts without a published appellate opinion.[10] A survey of hospitals in 1937 found that out of 350 hospitals, forty reported transfusion "accidents," with a total of sixty such incidents, including sixteen patient deaths and one donor death.[11] During these decades, however, the medical profession considered the threat of malpractice litigation an "annoyance" rather than a serious problem, even though there was a "slow, but steady rise" in the number of medical malpractice lawsuits.[12] The new use of body products for treatment, and even the advent of the body bank in the late 1930s, did not create any new legal wrinkles or, for the most part, heightened medical attention to legal matters. Even in New York City, with its municipal regulation of the professional blood donor, the doctors who had sought such regulations focused on improving the control of donors who practiced their profession outside of the medically run Blood Transfusion Association's Blood Donors Bureau, not on limiting the legal liability of doctors and hospitals.[13]

The legal landscape shifted considerably in the postwar years, however. In the explosion of blood banking after World War II, doctors at first almost completely ignored legal issues as they discussed how best to establish and run blood banks. When the American Medical Association (AMA) published a guide to starting a blood bank in 1951, the only mention of law was a reminder that if a bank intended to ship blood to another state, the federal regulations on interstate commerce in biologics needed to be followed.[14] This state of affairs did not last long. More blood banks meant more transfusions and more lawsuits.

In 1953 the AMA estimated that 3.5 million blood transfusions were given annually in the United States. Most of these proceeded without mishap. Transfusion was much more routine than it had been in the days of donor registries, and with direct transfusion no longer used, harm to the donor had become quite rare. The procedure was still risky to the recipient, however, with a rate of death of about 1 in every 1,000 to 3,000 transfusions, a similar risk to dying from appendicitis or from the effects of anesthesia. Death could result from using the wrong type of blood or from the transmission of a blood-borne disease. Even if a blood-borne disease did not prove fatal, the recipient might still turn to the law for compensation. While doctors had long worried about transmitting syphilis and malaria by transfusion, by the 1950s it was hepatitis that was the biggest concern, with doctors estimating that as many as 1 in 200 transfusions would transmit hepatitis to the recipient, and that 1 in 6,000 recipients would die from hepatitis.[15] When providing advice to other blood bank administrators in 1951, the administrator of the Henry Ford Hospital Blood Bank in Detroit listed hepatitis as the most common reason to reject a donor.[16] A lawyer, surveying all reported cases involving transfusion-related injuries in 1961, found only one lawsuit alleging transmission of syphilis and none alleging transmission of malaria.[17] It was hepatitis that was the major source of concern for the medical profession and for lawyers who defended doctors and hospitals.

The medical profession became focused on possible legal liability arising out of blood transfusions not just because of the increasing number of transfusions. The law was also changing. The charitable immunity doctrine, which had largely shielded hospitals from claims by patients, was crumbling. Courts were more willing to find hospitals liable for the negligence of their employees. In 1946 an appellate court in New York upheld a jury award of $6,500 against Genesee Hospital. The plaintiff, Mrs. Necolayff, age forty-two, was nearly recovered from a successful kidney operation at the hospital when a student intern and a nurse entered her room and announced that she was going to receive a blood transfusion from her daughter, Lillian. When she protested, accurately, that she did not have a daughter, they proceeded with the transfusion regardless, giving Mrs. Necolayff blood intended for a woman down the hall, which was incompatible with Mrs. Necolayff's blood type. Mrs. Necolayff suffered a transfusion reaction, which she claimed resulted in her admission to a mental asylum. The hospital, the court ruled, could be liable for such a mistake.[18] Courts in the District of Columbia and Mississippi agreed, finding hospitals liable when their blood bank technicians made errors resulting in the transfusion of incompatible blood and patient deaths. The family of Mrs. George Holmes, a thirty-five-year-old housewife and mother, was awarded $25,000 in compensation for her death in a transfusion accident.[19] The *Necolayff* and *Holmes* cases, among others, were discussed in the pages of the *Journal of the American Medical Association*. Although not all patients were successful in recovering for injuries they received from blood transfusions, the *Journal* reported to its members in 1957 that only about half the states continued to recognize the charitable immunity doctrine.[20]

Injured blood recipients, as potential plaintiffs, had a significant new legal weapon in the post–World War II era: product liability law. This new doctrine, developed by courts at midcentury, emerged out of cases in which consumers were injured while using an unsafe product but could not prove any negligence in the manufacture of the product. Faced with a choice between innocent individuals bearing the costs of their injuries or imposing the obligation of compensation on manufacturers, courts developed a theory that all products came with an implied warranty of fitness for their intended purpose, which, if breached, entitled the injured consumer to compensation from the seller without any need to show negligence.[21] Suddenly it was significant that body banks created body *products.*

Product liability law provided a way for patients injured by blood transfusions to sidestep the traditional rules of medical malpractice regarding standard of care, the need to show negligence, and, in states where it was still in force, the doctrine of charitable immunity that protected hospitals. Banked blood, plaintiffs' attorneys argued, was a product, and if it contained hepatitis or was the wrong type, it was not fit for its intended purpose and was "unreasonably dangerous."[22] Under product liability law, the hospital that sold the blood to the patient and the doctor who supplied this unsafe product were liable, even if all possible care was taken in screening the donor and processing the blood. The same medical arguments made in opposition to "free blood"—that blood had to be bought and paid for just like silver teaspoons—could be turned against doctors and hospitals. If blood was sold to a recipient who had a personal responsibility to pay for it, then the recipient had legally protected expectations that the blood was safe.

One of the first cases to apply the product liability doctrine to banked blood involved the blood supply in New York City. Mrs. Perlmutter sued Beth David Hospital, claiming that a pint of blood she had received in a transfusion while a patient had given her hepatitis. She had been charged $60 for the blood, and she claimed that, having sold her a defective product, the hospital was liable for all her resulting harm, estimated at $50,000.[23] The hospital asked the trial court to dismiss her lawsuit for failure to state a legally cognizable claim for relief, no matter what facts Perlmutter was able to prove at trial. The opinions in the case therefore assumed that everything Perlmutter alleged was true and addressed the legal question whether such a scenario could ever be a breach of implied warranty. Both sides agreed that under state law, there was an implied warranty that "goods sold are reasonably fit for the purpose for which the buyer requires them," as long as the buyer lets the seller know her purpose and "relies on the seller's skill or judgment." In 1953 the trial judge ruled that Mrs. Perlmutter's claim fit within this established law of sales in New York. Buying blood from a hospital blood bank for the purposes of transfusion, the judge reasoned, was exactly this sort of transaction. The hospital-seller understood the purpose for which the blood was purchased, and the patient-buyer relied on the skill and judgment of the seller in providing safe, matched blood. Mrs. Perlmutter was therefore entitled to a trial at which she could prove that she had purchased the blood and that the implied warranty had been breached. The appellate court affirmed.[24]

The state's highest court disagreed, accepting the argument of the hospital that the relationship between patient and hospital was one of recipient and provider of *services,* not of goods. The majority explained, "Concepts of purchase and sale cannot separately be attached to the healing materials such as medicines, drugs or, indeed, blood supplied by the hospital for a price as part of the medical services it offers. That the property or title to certain items of medical material may be transferred, so to speak, from the hospital to the patient during the course of medical treatment does not serve to make each such transaction a sale."[25] Blood was property, and ownership of that property may have changed from the hospital to Mrs. Perlmutter in return for cash payment, but there was no sale of a good. "Not every transfer of personal property constitutes a sale." In this case "the essence of the contractual relationship" was that "the patient bargains for, and the hospital agrees to make available, the human skill and physical materiel of medical science to the end that the patient's health be restored."[26] "It was not . . . blood . . . for which [Mrs. Perlmutter] bargained," argued the majority, "but the wherewithal of the hospital staff and the availability of hospital facilities."[27] Even if Mrs. Perlmutter could prove that she had contracted hepatitis from the blood provided by the Beth David Hospital blood bank and had suffered $50,000 in damages, she was not entitled to collect any damages from the hospital. The judges in the majority were not worried about treating blood as property, but they accepted the argument of the defendants that imposing liability on the hospital "would mean that the hospital, no matter how careful, no matter that the disease-producing potential in the blood could not possibly be discovered, would be held responsible, virtually as an insurer, if anything were to happen to the patient as result of 'bad' blood."[28] Holding the supplier of a dangerous product liable for individual harms that might result regardless of the care taken was the essence of the developing new law of product liability. With respect to other products, courts during these decades reasoned that the manufacturer was better able to bear this risk and to take steps to minimize it than consumers, who also had no way of discovering that the blood they were receiving was "bad." By a slim majority, the New York high court distinguished hospitals from restaurants, which, the dissenting judges pointed out, were liable for "bad" food sold to patrons, even if they were selling the service of dining rather than individual food items, and even if they took all possible care.[29] Although the charitable immunity doctrine no longer acted as a complete shield to hospital liability, the majority of the New York court still considered hospitals to be legally different from restaurants.

Fantus would have agreed with the majority's reasoning. At Cook County Hospital in the 1930s, where the blood bank maintained accounts with doctors, not patients, the end that he shared with his medical colleagues was restoring health. The ready provision of high-quality stored blood was a means to that goal. The Red Cross blood program directors also would have agreed, particularly that the receipt of the blood it collected from uncompensated volunteers was not a sale to the patient, but a gift. In this case, despite the hospital charge of $60 for the pint of blood—a sum probably chosen to encourage Mrs. Perlmutter or her friends and family to become replacement donors and thus clear the debt—the hospital, and the Blood Transfusion Association, which had become a party in the case, also agreed that there had been no sale of a product to Mrs. Perlmutter. Despite the desire of blood bankers to charge for blood just like silver teaspoons, they agreed with the majority of the highest court in New York state that the trial judge had gotten it wrong. Paying $60 for a pint of blood was not a sale of property like any other, but part of the provision of services by trained professionals.

Organized medicine, hospitals, and blood bankers wanted to have it both ways: they wanted blood to be treated as a market commodity by patients but as a special sort of "therapeutic merchandise" by the courts.[30] Medical professionals recognized that body products were unique in an important way: they were sourced from human bodies. It was this unique quality, and the perceived difficulty of managing a supply dependent on troublesome and independent-minded individuals, that had led blood bankers to stress the market nature of body products so heavily. They were convinced that the invisible hand of the market was the best motivation to keep Americans participating in the supply chain at the levels necessary to have adequate amounts of this therapeutic. On the other hand, medical professionals wanted to be able to treat such products as *non*-unique. There was to be no "free blood" because there was not, and should never be, "free surgery" or "free medicine."[31] Blood was a medical therapeutic like any other, to be paid for like any other, despite its source. Further, doctors agreed with the court that any therapeutic that was made or processed in the hospital, such as banked blood or other intravenous solutions, was only incidental to the expert provision of medical services and did not make the hospital into a manufacturer in the same category as Bayer Corporation, a manufacturer of aspirin.[32] The category these doctors and hospitals wanted shielded from commercial law was medical therapeutics supplied by hospitals and medically controlled organizations, like community blood banks. They wanted to be free to sell or give away such therapeutics in their professional discretion, without implicating the law of property and sales.

In the *Perlmutter* case the highest court in New York agreed with this reasoning: the hospital could sell a pint of blood for $60 without accepting the same obligations as other product manufacturers to make customers whole in the event that the blood was, as Perlmutter claimed, "injurious" rather than healing. While the final outcome in *Perlmutter* was reassuring to all the blood banks and hospitals in New York, it was also worrisome because the hospital prevailed only after two contrary rulings, and by only one vote. Even before the trial court decision in the *Perlmutter* case, the AMA Committee on Medicolegal Problems had prepared a report that was published in the *Journal of the American Medical Association,* summarizing recent lawsuits involving banked blood and reviewing all the harms that could be suffered by donor and recipient.[33] In the wake of the *Perlmutter* decision, blood banks, hospitals, and their supporters moved quickly to limit potential product liability as much as possible. California was the first state to pass a responsive law, declaring in 1955 that the provision of banked blood for transfusion was a service and not a sale.[34] For those involved with banked blood in other states, the AMA advised changing billing practices: "Instead of making a charge for blood, the hospital should make an equivalent and specific charge for the use of its facilities and services of its technician." Hospitals should still collect the money, but call it something else. Further, the AMA recommended getting signed consent forms from patients that the blood supplied for transfusions was "incidental to the provision of services" and no "warranty of fitness or quality" applied."[35]

The medical profession was appropriately worried. Its victory in *Perlmutter* was repeated in other states, where courts refused to find the purchase of blood by a patient to be a "sale of a good" subject to the usual warranties, accepting the arguments of hospitals that they should not be subject to the risk-shifting purposes of product liability law.[36] But as product liability doctrine became better established in American law, legal commentators disagreed with the refusal of courts to include banked blood within its contours. While one early legal commentator, summarizing the *Perlmutter* case for New York lawyers as the appeal in the high court was pending, found it "clear" that the provision of blood by Beth David Hospital was not a "sale," the decision was widely criticized by other legal scholars who argued that the trial court judge had been correct, and that Mrs. Perlmutter should have been able to argue her claim to a jury.[37] The legal experts of the AMA found articles published in the *Harvard Law Review* and elsewhere during the 1950s that considered "bad" blood a risk appropriately imposed on hospitals and blood banks rather than on patients who happened to receive the one disease-ridden bottle lurking within every two hundred stored bottles of blood.[38] Over time other courts agreed, finding the argument that blood was part of a "service" and thus not a "good" an unconvincing attempt to avoid the plain law of sales.[39] A Florida court found that while the distinction might apply to a hospital like Beth David, it should not be extended to a community blood bank.[40] An appellate court in the state of Washington scoffed at the *Perlmutter* reasoning, stating in a case against a community blood bank, "If the operation of respondent in extracting, typing, bottling, storing, matching, delivering, and charging money for blood is characterized as a service, it is only for the purpose of avoiding the strict liability rule."[41]

It would be a decade before any other state followed California's lead in enacting a law to shield suppliers of banked blood from the product liability doctrine. Sensing a possible means of recovery, lawyers for injured patients continued to press such claims. The insurance defense attorney Sidney Zipser, who had represented Beth David Hospital in its ultimately successful appeal to the New York high court, felt that during the 1960s litigation involving blood transfusions was increasing with "geometrical progression."[42]

The Blood Trade

If banked blood was a good being bought and sold, the legal ramifications reached beyond patients making breach of warranty claims against doctors and hospitals. To the widespread consternation of organized medicine and blood banks, in the 1960s the Federal Trade Commission (FTC) began to consider the "blood business" a type of commerce.[43] Again it was the market-based approach of the American Association of Blood Banks (AABB) and its allies that made this legal intervention possible. Despite the ongoing difficulties with the national blood clearinghouse Bernice Hemphill had established, the clearinghouse did promote interstate shipment of blood, as participating banks sometimes shipped blood to other banks to clear their accounts. All such shipments were done under licenses from the federal government granted to Red Cross and community blood banks as participants in interstate commerce in biological products. Hemphill estimated in 1964 that 500,000 pints of blood had been donated at one facility as replacement pints for a blood loan elsewhere. While many of these were traded as credits, some fraction had been shipped between banks. Any participating bank could borrow and loan blood across state lines when it experienced an imbalance in supply and demand.[44] Given this reality, the FTC concluded that "the clearinghouse program of AABB facilitates the movement of blood from one bank to another in *commerce*" and therefore that it had jurisdiction over a local dispute in Kansas City, Missouri, involving clearinghouse participants.[45]

The dispute involved a boycott of two for-profit blood banks by local hospitals, doctors, and a newly formed nonprofit community blood bank. Commercial, for-profit blood banks were the successors to the for-profit blood donor agencies, which had been part of the blood supply system since the 1920s. In New York City doctors had used municipal regulations to exert control over such agencies, creating minimum standards for the agencies and their donors that mimicked the procedures used at the nonprofit, medically founded, and medically controlled Blood Donors Bureau. Decades later doctors still worried about blood sourced from blood banks not under control of medically run institutions. Since its founding, the AABB had promoted "independent, non-profit blood banks" "under the professional supervision of local medical societies."[46] While in 1947, when the AABB was founded, the primary problem had been perceived as the lay-run Red Cross centers, which, while nonprofit, were under the ultimate control of a nonmedical organization, after 1950, as the number of commercial banks increased, that early commitment to nonprofit banks increased in significance.[47]

In Kansas City the commercial banks had opened to fill a local need. As the demand for blood grew during the postwar decades, there was no "independent, non-profit blood bank" "under the professional supervision" of the local medical society. Due to disagreements among the county medical society and the local hospitals, a nonprofit community blood bank, though formally organized in 1953, did not open until 1958.[48] In its absence, two for-profit blood banks opened, seeking gain while helping to keep the local hospital blood banks stocked. Each obtained a federal license to ship blood in interstate commerce, as did the community bank when it opened.[49] Once there was the option of using blood from the community blood bank, however, the doctors, the hospitals, and the nonprofit bank attempted to prohibit all participation of the for-profit banks in local blood flows. Rather than seeking regulation, as doctors had done in New York City, the doctors in Kansas City simply agreed that they would no longer use any blood from the for-profit blood banks. Not only did doctors refuse to transfuse blood drawn at those banks, but the hospitals told patients who received blood that they could not repay blood debts by making donations at the commercial banks, and the community bank told the AABB clearinghouse that it would not accept pints collected by those banks.[50]

The for-profit banks complained first to the Better Business Bureau and then to the FTC that these actions were unfair competition in restraint of trade and a violation of federal antitrust law. The banks argued that the actions of the doctors and hospitals constituted a conspiracy to boycott their businesses, a type of concerted refusal to deal that courts had long considered a per se violation of the antitrust laws, even when the alleged conspirators claimed lofty, or at least noncommercial, motives.[51] In 1962 the FTC agreed and issued a detailed complaint against the city's nonprofit blood banks (the community bank and the hospital banks), charging them with unfair trade. The complaint was followed by a cease-and-desist order by the full commission in 1966.[52] The FTC reviewed the contracts between the nonprofit blood bank and hospitals and found that they described "commercial transaction[s]."[53] Although the doctors opposed to the commercial banks protested that they had a moral objection to a trade in blood as "not consistent with the dignity of the human being," the evidence showed that the nonprofit community bank traded in blood just as much as the commercial banks.[54]

To explain its conclusion that the hospitals and the community blood bank were engaged in the blood trade, the FTC detailed the ways cash and blood flowed among the hospital banks and their nonprofit supplier. During the period in question, the community blood bank paid 17 to 40 percent of its donors and also maintained a "donors club" at Leavenworth Prison in neighboring Kansas, buying blood from inmates.[55] It charged hospitals more per pint than it paid donors. Each patient who got blood from the nonprofit bank (via a hospital blood bank) was charged $25 per pint, plus a $9 processing fee, both of which could be paid in kind through blood donations at the community bank or through any clearinghouse bank in the country, including Red Cross centers. According to the FTC, the nonprofit blood bank made a net profit of $3 per pint on blood it received from the Red Cross and either $6 or $16 per pint on all replacement pints.[56] The FTC concluded that both the for-profit banks and the nonprofit banks, when "acquiring, processing, and supplying whole blood (human) to hospitals," were "parts of a 'business' rather than parts of the practice of medicine."[57] This view was echoed in the popular press, which during this period referred to the "blood business" and "blood traffic" to describe blood banking generally.[58] The legal literature too agreed that the FTC was appropriately concerned with nonprofit corporations that competed with for-profit corporations: the motivations and ultimate nonprofit status of organizations should not permit such entities to enter markets and engage in behavior not permitted by for-profit participants.[59]

Despite the apparent legal weakness of their case, and supported by hospitals and blood banks around the country, the Kansas City nonprofit banks appealed the Commission decision to the courts. In 1969 the Kansas City nonprofit banks finally persuaded a federal appellate court to overturn the FTC finding, on the grounds that the hospitals and the community blood bank, as nonprofit institutions, were not subject to the jurisdiction of the Federal Trade Commission. In a ruling that turned on detailed legal analysis of statutory language, the court found *not* that the FTC had gotten the facts wrong about the "blood trade" but that there was a federal statute prohibiting the Commission from regulating nonprofit corporations, even if those corporations were engaged in "business."[60]

During the years that the case was pending, this federal action prompted much outcry within blood banking over the idea that blood banking was "commerce" and that hospitals might be forced to take "bought blood."[61] From two thousand miles away, the nonprofit community blood bank in Spokane had contributed to the defense fund, and the AABB filed a brief before the federal court in support of the Kansas City community blood bank and hospitals.[62] Using the same argument they had made against claims by injured patients, blood bankers insisted that their organizations provided a *service* rather than a *product* and therefore that there was no trade in blood that was being illegally restrained. Because the FTC had examined the flows of money between donors and banks, as well as between banks and patients, however, the case helped shift medical attention from the earlier insistence on "paid blood" to a new concern about "bought blood." Ignoring the fact that the Kansas City community blood bank, like almost all other nonprofit banks around the country, bought some of its blood, and that the for-profit banks were willing to accept blood from unpaid replacement donors, the medical profession distinguished its preferred nonprofit banks from the for-profit banks on the relationship between donor and bank. Most community blood banks relied primarily on the replacement donor, while the for-profit banks sought the professional donor. In the Kansas City case the defendants had brought evidence that the for-profit blood banks had advertised for paid donors in the *Kansas City Star,* which the local doctors found offensive.[63] No one seemed to remember that reputable medically run organizations, such as the Mayo Clinic in Rochester, Minnesota, had in the past used newspaper advertisements to recruit paid donors for nonprofit blood banks.[64] In emphasizing this difference between for-profit and nonprofit banks based on "bought blood," the blood bank community began to cast the professional donor, that "man of business," in a negative light.

The basic problem was that these legal challenges threatened to upend the ways that AABB blood banks ran their banking businesses and the philosophy they had developed to justify their approach. In response, the medical profession found itself engaged in disordered backpedaling throughout the 1960s. The market rhetoric that had served its professional ends in opposing government-sponsored medical care was creating legal problems. In 1955 the party line of opposition to the Red Cross and "free blood" was that "the hospital or community blood bank is based on the philosophy that blood is a biological *product,* like penicillin or any other commodity, and as such should be handled on economic principles."[65] Blood was a product that must be bought and paid for, just like all other therapeutics. By the 1960s the doctors involved in organizing the community blood bank in Kansas City were arguing that not only was banked blood a service, not a product, but that "paying for blood was morally wrong."[66] At its annual meeting in 1962 the AABB adopted a Statement of Principles of Blood Procurement, which, while affirming the reliance on "voluntary donor replacement" and blood insurance programs, those market-based incentives used to maintain blood supplies, began by disavowing the commodity nature of blood: "Blood for transfusion is a human living tissue and is not a commodity. Blood does not carry an expressed or implied warranty. Blood used for transfusion is a service. Blood is an integral part of the rendition of medical services to the individual."[67]

Even Hemphill, that AABB stalwart who never wavered in her opposition to the Red Cross and her emphasis on the replacement donor, lent her name to a lengthy position paper sent to the California state legislature in 1963, explaining that for-profit banks introduced "commercialism" into blood banking and caused "socio-economic problems" in advertising for paid donors who might not be physically fit to give. The position paper was described to the legislature as a statement by "the five oldest, nonprofit, medically sponsored, community blood banks in California," emphasizing the nonprofit bona fides of its authors.[68] Further, Hemphill testified before the U.S. Congress that the "laws *and terms* of the marketplace" should not apply to blood banking.[69]

For Hemphill to accuse the for-profit banks of introducing "commercialism" into the blood system after she had deliberately crafted a clearing-house based on commercial banking, and for Kansas City doctors to raise moral objections to paying for blood while both requiring their patients to pay for blood and sponsoring a bank that bought blood appears hypocritical in retrospect. In the early 1960s, however, no one raised that accusation. The positions of blood bank administrators and doctors were awkward and apparently self-contradictory because the terms of the developing debate—good or service, free or paid—did not adequately capture the medical position they espoused. Despite the testimony of one Kansas City doctor that he had opposed paid blood since his physician father had forced him to return the money he had received for selling his blood as a student, the shared objection of the hospitals, doctors, and county medical society was not simply to the buying and selling of blood.[70] They knew that the local hospitals had long paid for blood when there were no freestanding blood banks and that the nonprofit community bank that they had helped to establish and were happy to rely upon to stock hospital blood banks also bought and sold blood. The president of the AABB who came before Congress to testify that blood was not a commodity in 1964 was also president of the Detroit Blood

Service, a nonprofit blood bank in Detroit that, like the for-profit banks in
Kansas City, depended on paid donors for its inventory. He testified that he
"was not happy about" using bought blood but that it was necessary because the Red Cross could not meet all needs in the city.[71]

The objection of the Kansas City doctors was to the idea of *profit* from
the buying and selling of blood, that each of the for-profit banks was "en-
riching its owners" through its sales.[72] Both the hospitals and the community blood bank were nonprofit institutions, even though they bought and
sold banked blood. When the doctors complained that the proprietors of
the for-profit banks were inexperienced in blood banking, the real problem
was that they were insufficiently compliant with the norms of the medical
profession with respect to blood. It was clear that in the absence of a community blood bank in Kansas City, there had been money to be made in
collecting blood and having it ready for use by local hospitals, and in classic
free market fashion, these proprietors had stepped in to meet market demand and, thereby, to make a profit. This approach was the same as that
taken by commercial donor agencies of the 1930s and 1940s. Despite the
passionate free market rhetoric of organized medicine during the 1950s, the
Kansas City doctors were disturbed by the undiluted management of blood
as property that brought income to those who provided banked blood
for hospital use. While they, like New York City doctors earlier, might be
forced to use blood collected by such profit-seeking businessmen when no
other blood was available, they viewed banked blood as appropriately civic
property, to be managed for the common good as defined by the medical
profession, even if it was bought and sold as a personal resource. The problem was not commerce or markets but the end result of market exchanges.
Blood flows should be managed by the market, but a market controlled by
medicine in the service of its professional ends, not as part of unrestrained
private enterprise. In New York City the medical community had been able
to use regulation to constrain for-profit donor agencies. In Kansas City,
once the medical society had been able to launch a nonprofit community
blood bank and there was an alternative to the unregulated for-profit banks,
doctors preferred to use the blood bought and sold by the nonprofit bank,
seeing its administrators as participating in a medically controlled market
and sharing the goals of the doctors and hospitals.

This distinction between blood as market property and as civic property
was deeply rooted in medical professional ethics. During the blood bank

battles, when the enemy was "socialized medicine," the medical profession had elided the distinction, focusing on the market nature of body products in order to serve the goal of maintaining local medical control of medical practice and medical funding. As commercial blood banks, the courts, and the Federal Trade Commission took the banking metaphor at face value, however, the distinction reemerged as doctors and blood bankers tried to articulate why banked blood, though market property in that it could be bought and sold, was *not* just like silver teaspoons. The ramifications of "paid blood" at law revealed the limitations of the medical embrace of free market ideology as a means of allocating medical care. While doctors opposed "free blood," they also were uncomfortable with the free hand of the market, without medical control. In response to these legal challenges, the medical profession reinterpreted its adoption of the banking metaphor, incorporating the new distinction between goods and services while downplaying the language of personal property and products.

Adopting the language of service rather than of goods and products, while an abrupt change, still fit the banking metaphor. Financial banks are part of the financial *services* industry, and community and hospital blood banks had always thought of their role as providing services to the medical profession. The medical profession and blood bankers began to discuss the *services* they provided and to charge "service fees" for the processing of blood, while at the same time continuing to treat banked blood as a fungible product that could be traded through the clearinghouse and as property for which patients needed to pay, in cash or in kind. The key was to reemphasize that banked blood was a means to an end, not an end in itself. The AMA explained the revised philosophy in congressional testimony at a hearing on a bill proposed by Senator Edward V. Long of Missouri in response to the Kansas City case. Before the federal court issued its decision, Senator Long proposed to amend the law to exempt nonprofit blood banks from FTC jurisdiction and held extensive hearings on the bill. The AMA representative testified, "In the interests of the public welfare, and as a matter of public policy, the transfusion of life-saving human tissue should not be regarded as the transfer of a commodity passing in the channels of commerce. . . . Blood, of itself, is an integral part of that medical service and should not be the subject of barter or sale."[73]

The medical profession found some support from another federal agency, the Internal Revenue Service (IRS). As early as 1942 the IRS had determined

that the donation of blood was a "personal service" rather than the donation of "property" and had steadfastly refused to allow blood donors to
nonprofit banks to deduct the value of their blood as a charitable contribution, even as the Red Cross had lobbied for the recognition of such a tax
deduction, believing that it would increase donations.[74] While Senator
Long's proposed bill did not pass in 1964, the federal decision overturning
the Kansas City order in 1969 on the grounds of lack of agency jurisdiction
over nonprofit corporations called a halt to further Federal Trade Commission regulation of nonprofit hospitals and community blood banks.

The bigger problem was the laws and courts of the fifty states. It was too
easy for state courts, like the dissenting judges in *Perlmutter,* to find banked
blood subject to product liability law. The Pennsylvania Supreme Court did
so in 1970, finding that the estate of a patient who died from hepatitis after
receiving a transfusion could sue the treating hospital for selling a dangerous product. While the trial court rejected the claim as "the application of
legal principles to what is so basically a purely nonlegal exchange of an item
of human inventory that it defies classification in commercial terms," the
higher court disagreed, finding it "a distortion to take what is, at least arguably, a sale, [and] twist it into the shape of a service."[75] A statutory amendment to the commercial code of each state could solve the problem. Following California, and as part of a concerted push by state medical societies in
the 1960s and early 1970s, supported by the AABB and the AMA, many
states enacted blood shield laws, designed to remove banked blood from the
laws regulating sales of goods.[76] These laws generally adopted the medical
argument that banked blood was part of a service and not a good, even if
it was sold. With a bill sponsored by the California Medical Association,
California led the way by amending its earlier law in 1963 to specifically
state that any "distribution" of blood, including any "sale or exchange," "is
declared to be, for all purposes whatsoever, the rendition of a service by any
person participating therein" and "is declared not to be a sale."[77] After lobbying by the Illinois State Medical Society, the Illinois legislature over-
turned a previous state supreme court decision by passing a blood shield law
in 1971, and Pennsylvania overruled its supreme court in 1972.[78] By 1973 all
but six states had passed similar legislation.[79] Blood remained a body product legally bought, sold, and traded by banks, but under federal and state
law, and thanks to medical efforts, it was no longer legally a commodity.

As the medical profession reacted to the threat of legal liability that its insistence on "paid blood" had helped to create, it did not limit itself to fights in courtrooms and in state legislatures. The new focus on cash for blood exchanges brought renewed medical attention to that stalwart of the blood supply, the professional donor. From the supplier perspective, the question was not good or service. Able-bodied donors were clearly not receiving medical services when they submitted to bleeding. The question was rather gift or sale. When Richard Titmuss's book comparing the British and American blood supply systems became popular in 1971, the terms he used, *gift* and *commodity*, were widely adopted to explain the tension surrounding the donor. Both terms in the gift/commodity dichotomy, however, were misleading in the way that they came to be used in American policy discussions.

Titmuss himself was aware that although he described the gift as an expression of altruism without any expectation of reward, anthropological research had already complicated this simplistic view by analyzing the social function of gifting.[80] Gifts are often given with the expectation of future reward or in recognition of past benefits. To pretend that an unpaid donor had no motivation other than altruism was to make an unrealistic assumption. Titmuss created a typology of donors, from the "paid donor," receiving cash, to the "voluntary community donor," motivated by the desire to contribute to his or her community. He included only blood from the voluntary community donor in the category of gift, excluding not only "bought blood" but also blood from the replacement donor and the "family credit" donor as other forms of compensated donation.[81] No American blood collection organization, even the Red Cross blood centers, was completely supplied by voluntary community donors.[82] Further, any banked blood, even if provided as a gift by a voluntary community donor, became a commodity in all respects except legally in that it was processed into a fungible body product, which could be billed out to patients, traded between banks, or even sold to for-profit companies that used whole blood to make other blood products.[83] Its origins in an unpaid donation did not keep blood from being treated as a commodity; blood sourced from voluntary donors as well as from replacement donors and paid donors became a commodity. The difference was only in the transaction between supplier and bank, not in the ultimate treatment of the blood.

Ignoring this variety in the ways donors were compensated and the fate of all banked blood, the question became whether the blood was from a professional donor, paid per pint, and called a "commodity," or whether the blood was given without compensation and called a "gift." In these discussions the key feature was cash. Ignoring Titmuss's acknowledgment that many donors who did not receive money were still receiving a quantifiable benefit in return for their blood, in the debates that emerged in the 1960s and have persisted ever since in discussions about body product management, Americans have uncritically lumped together in the category of the gift unpaid directed donations by friends and family for a patient, uncompensated donations by a citizen for use by anyone in need, as well as donations by replacement donors, blood assurance program members, and others who receive credits for their donation. As long as there was not cash provided to the supplier, the blood was a gift, separable from the commodity provided by donors who received money.

Although litigation-shy doctors began to focus on the cash received by donors in the 1960s and 1970s, they did not originate the critical perspective on blood sales. In many ways, the gift/commodity debates were simply a reformulation of long-existing sociocultural anxieties about body product exchange that the body bank had sought to dispel but had never completely eliminated. The adoption of the banking metaphor, with its assumption that all blood was equivalent, had never been strong enough to resolve the deep-rooted cultural anxieties that all blood was *not* the same, that the transfer of blood would also transfer qualities from perceived inferiors into a vulnerable patient. The incorporation of racial segregation of blood into the earliest blood banks by Fantus and others was based on powerful and persistent conceptions of blood as constitutive of human identity and, in American law and culture, of race.[84] Even the routine nature of blood transfusion in the postwar era could not dispel the notion that aspects of the supplying body lingered in the disembodied fluid. During this period, continuing suspicions of blood from the "other" were reformulated into fear of "bad blood" from those who sold it rather than those who gave it. The "other," as Hemphill and her nonprofit blood banking colleagues euphemistically explained it to the California state legislature, could be anyone with a "socio-economic problem," inferior because of poverty and lack of education. In the United States, with its history of racism, however, the "other" most feared by the European American majority was the African American blood donor.

The World War II blood program had bolstered this anxiety. Its continuing rhetoric of blood as a personal gift, reinforced by the ability to personalize the gift with a dedication, emphasized that the individual donor mattered. The wartime program also nationalized previously regional Jim Crow practices with respect to blood and reinforced racial prejudices by first refusing to accept African American blood, and then by keeping Red Cross supplies racially segregated, with African American blood labeled "AA."[85] Race and the blood supply had been a festering issue in the wartime blood program and did not disappear when President Harry Truman desegregated the armed forces in 1948, nor as blood banks became an omnipresent feature of civilian medicine.

Rather, when the Red Cross began its peacetime blood program in 1948, it announced its official policy as follows:

> Inasmuch as, on the basis of recorded scientific and medical opinion, there is no difference in the blood of humans based on race or color, the plan does not require the segregation of blood; however, whenever necessary to insure the success of the plan, which is to make available blood and blood derivatives to all the people of the United States regardless of race or color, chapters will collect and hold blood in such a manner as to give the physician and the patient the right of selection at the time of administration.[86]

In other words, racial labeling and segregation would continue in those areas of the country where it was already practiced and as part of the national blood program. The touted collection of gifts "of the people, by the people, and for the people" would include bags of blood labeled "white" and "colored."[87] According to the Red Cross, the knowledge that blood carried race was folk knowledge, unscientific and nonmedical, but still worthy of respect. This policy formally changed in 1950, when the Red Cross dropped its record keeping of donors by race.[88] With the Korean War increasing the need for blood, and with the armed forces now integrated, the federal Office of Defense Mobilization told potential donors in a publicity manual that as long as blood types match, "it doesn't matter whether the blood [for transfusion] comes from a Japanese, a Scotsman, a Negro, or an East Indian."[89] In the northern states the American medical establishment and mainstream white newspapers denounced any discussion of racial or ethnic differences in blood.[90]

On the local level, however, blood segregation continued into the 1960s. The AABB, dominated by community blood banks in the West and Southwest, did not recommend that information on a donor's race be collected in donor histories or included on blood labels as it developed blood bank certification standards.[91] But in other parts of the country, blood for civilian use had been routinely racially labeled and segregated. AABB founder Dr. Julian Davenport, who practiced at the Southern Baptist Hospital in New Orleans, called it "ridiculous" from a scientific perspective to segregate blood, but in 1949 he wrote that "those of us who live in the South" must bow to "long standing social attitudes" and segregate banked blood, even though he recognized that many southern hospitals sometimes transfused blood purchased from northern banks that did not racially label or segregate blood.[92] Along with maintaining separate waiting rooms for "colored" and "white" patients, the public Charity Hospital in New Orleans had a policy of never giving cross-racial transfusions, even with patient permission.[93] In the 1950s and 1960s the power of blood as a marker of heredity and race became increasingly emphasized in the segregated American South. Rather than a medically tolerated practice by doctors seeking to avoid controversy, blood segregation became a political statement. As the civil rights movement gained momentum, segregationists saw racial segregation of blood as a positive step that could be taken to shore up white supremacy. For the first time states passed laws *requiring* the racial segregation of blood into "white" and "Negro."[94] In Louisiana, as part of a cluster of new segregation laws intended to signal state opposition to the national push for racial integration, the legislature passed a law requiring all blood to be racially labeled and, under threat of fine or imprisonment, requiring the transfusing doctor to inform the patient of the race of the donor before transfusing blood.[95] At Charity Hospital this new law only bolstered existing practices.[96] The Civil Rights Act of 1964, one of the primary legislative results of the civil rights movement, became a weapon to stamp out Jim Crow in blood supplies. The federal government quietly let southern hospitals know that their receipt of federal funds under Medicaid and Medicare obligated them to cease the segregation of blood, but as late as 1969 Louisiana hospitals continued the practice.[97]

It was just as formal racial segregation of blood was ending that the professional donor was coming under increasing scrutiny in medicine and among the lay public. Cash became a proxy for contamination. While fear of racial contamination was grounded in unscientific folk knowledge and politically unpalatable segregationism, fearing blood from those desperate enough to sell blood was rational because of the danger of blood-borne disease. Especially given the links long assumed between "Negro blood" and disease in American medicine and society, opposition to the professional donor was an example of what has been called the "'new,' subtler forms of racism" that emerged in many areas of American life in the 1960s.[98]

Paid Donor and Disease

Despite Fantus's original goal of using the blood bank to reduce the need for professional blood donors, the paid supplier, present at the earliest beginnings of modern transfusion therapy, had persisted. By the 1960s the situation nationwide echoed that in Kansas City: there were some for-profit blood banks that unabashedly paid almost all suppliers, and almost all non-profit banks also paid suppliers some of the time—with the exception of the Red Cross centers. In 1964 Hemphill testified before Congress that Irwin Memorial, the first community blood bank, paid donors for about 7 percent of the blood it collected and that 15 percent of the fresh blood it collected for use in open-heart surgery came from paid donors.[99] Paid donors not only were used to deal with temporary dips in inventory but could be counted on to show up when requested, a necessary feature when the bank needed to supply freshly collected blood to a hospital performing open-heart surgery. Just as payment for breast milk bought doctors the ability to supervise milk sellers, making sure they were sufficiently sanitary, it bought blood bankers the ability to control donors by making donation a job that needed to be performed at a particular time. Irwin Memorial was not alone in its modest reliance on paid donors. The Henry Ford Blood Bank in Detroit, one of the first blood banks, had initially paid donors and later bought blood from a for-profit blood bank when necessary.[100] The University of Pennsylvania blood bank paid donors.[101] The Junior League Bank in Milwaukee, founded with philanthropic dollars and staffed by volunteers, paid donors.[102] Hundreds of hospital blood banks paid donors.[103]

The Joint Blood Council survey in 1957 had found that about one-sixth of blood suppliers were paid nationwide.[104] This action had always been as morally neutral as paying interest on bank deposits. Banks did what they needed to do to maintain supplies, including paying donors when necessary.

The widely respected Mayo Clinic paid blood donors as part of its ongoing effort to maintain a blood supply in a sparsely populated rural area, advertising this means of earning money in the newspapers when necessary. In 1971 the Clinic offered $25 per donation, and donors in its pool usually gave two to four times per year.[105] This policy attracted the financially needy, who were not necessarily those who might be considered a "socio-economic problem." For example, the congregation of the Greenleafton Reformed Church in rural Preston, Minnesota, sold its blood to the Clinic as a fundraising endeavor, organizing periodic caravans of members to Rochester and, according to a local newspaper report, raising $27,000 over eight years to help pay for a new church building after a fire.[106] In the 1950s the blood bank divided its donors into three classes—professional, replacement, and church—with church donors receiving cash payments that were intended for a community project. In 1951 the bank reported a waiting list of groups hoping to join the ranks of church donors and send members to sell their blood at scheduled intervals four times a year.[107]

During the 1960s buying blood became more suspect, as "bought blood" became synonymous with what was called "bad blood," that is, diseased blood.[108] In part the criticism against bought blood was an attack on commercial blood banks as improperly motivated by pursuit of the all-mighty dollar rather than by providing medical treatment to those who needed it. In addition to the fight in Kansas City against the commercial blood banks, waged in part on the objection to their recruitment of paid donors, in 1970 the nonprofit community blood bank in King County, Washington, unsuccessfully sued a local for-profit blood bank using the novel legal theory that its purchase of blood from donors for $5 per pint was depleting a public resource, analogous to taking water from a river to the detriment of downstream users.[109]

But the criticism against paid donors was not limited to medical opposition to for-profit banks, nor was it based solely on racially motivated fearmongering. The popular press reported disturbing information about the donor and blood management practices of commercial banks, who were a significant source of bought blood in the American blood system. In 1961 the National Institutes of Health, the Public Health Service, and the Department of Justice investigated four commercial banks for supplying expired blood to hospitals, using falsified collection dates.[110] In another blood scam a few years later, a New Jersey commercial bank was found to have been supplying blood falsely labeled "negative for syphilis."[111] In New York City the transmission of malaria to a heart patient via blood from a professional donor occasioned a citywide search for the donor in 1963. Located in a homeless shelter, the named donor was found not to have malaria and admitted to loaning his donor card to one or more acquaintances to allow them to sell their blood under the New York City regulations, providing ample opportunity for the press to explore the seedy side of blood sales.[112] When there was money to be made, public health was unquestionably sometimes compromised in the rush to maximize individual profits.

Just as the paid blood supplier was not new during the 1960s, concern about disease transmission by blood transfusion was not new. The case of malaria in New York City only reaffirmed the medical concern with avoiding transmission of both malaria and syphilis that had existed since the first years of the twentieth century. Doctors and blood banks attempted to screen for the former through medical histories and the latter by the use of the inexact Wassermann test. The authors of the first blood bank manual, published in 1942, had discussed these dangers.[113] But the experiences of the wartime blood program had revealed a new danger: hepatitis. Because plasma was prepared by pooling blood from many donors, the risk of hepatitis infection was much greater from plasma than from whole blood, as a single infected donor could contaminate an entire batch of plasma. The large-scale production and use of plasma during World War II caused the incidence of hepatitis in transfusion recipients to jump.[114] After the war hepatitis became the primary medical concern about the blood supply, leading to lawsuits such as the one filed by Mrs. Perlmutter, as patients found themselves facing a new health threat as a result of their treatment.

At first the threat seemed minimal. In the 1956 edition of its technical manual, the AABB warned its members that both hepatitis A and B could be transmitted by blood transfusion either from blood itself or from incompletely sterilized equipment. But the AABB estimated that fewer than 1 percent of donors carried the disease, minimizing its risk to recipients of whole blood.[115] Over time, however, doctors began to realize that hepatitis was a more dangerous disease than they had first believed, causing not just an initial flu-like attack but the possibility of long-term liver damage as the virus lingered, leading to death in about 10 percent of cases. Further, they realized that the lingering virus could infect others via blood donation well beyond the initial onset of symptoms, greatly broadening the population of seemingly healthy donors whose blood might transmit this disease. The fear of potentially fatal disease from "bad blood" grew during the 1960s because the knowledge of the threat outpaced knowledge of ways to eliminate it. Virtually the only screen was the donor's ability to confirm or deny a past case of hepatitis, what one doctor called "the hurried testament of the donor," unless the donor was actively experiencing symptoms at the time of donation.[116] Because the symptoms were so mild in many people, many "innocent carriers" were unaware that they had contracted the disease.[117] Only in 1971 did it become possible for blood banks to screen blood for the presence of hepatitis, and even then the screen caught only about 60 percent of infected blood, reducing, but not eliminating, the risk of hepatitis in the blood supply.[118]

Therefore, during the 1950s and 1960s and into the 1970s Americans were forced to rely upon stereotypes and assumptions rather than science or medicine to avoid this invisible killer. The association of disease with filth, squalor, and poverty had been reinforced again and again in American history.[119] It seemed only logical that paid blood suppliers from the wrong side of the tracks were the problem. Hepatitis could spread through contaminated needles, and thus intravenous drug users were a high-risk population, and perhaps overrepresented among those seeking a quick means of earning cash through blood sales. Soon doctors were looking hard at the professional blood donor as a source of disease. A Boston study, published in 1959 and looking retrospectively at hepatitis cases in veterans hospitals between 1953 and 1957, showed a link between one for-profit blood bank and an increased incidence of transfusion-associated hepatitis in patients.[120] But even as some correlation was shown, not all the evidence agreed. The same Boston study showed no correlation between blood obtained from two other for-profit sources and hepatitis.[121] The best way to know if an asymptomatic supplier would transmit hepatitis was whether his or her blood had transmitted it before. Professional donors, as repeat suppliers, could therefore be considered "clean" donors, tested in the most reliable way possible—after their first donation, that is. In 1964 an administrator of a chain of for-profit blood banks presented data to his blood banking peers that at his banks, about two-thirds of the donors were repeat donors, thus rendering them, he argued, "good, safe, low-risk" donors.[122] An administrator of a nonprofit blood bank who used significant numbers of paid donors also argued that the riskiest donors were those who had not donated before, whether paid or unpaid, and pointed out that it was much easier to turn away a potential donor seeking $5 than a well-meaning family member seeking to repay a blood debt for a loved one.[123]

As the argument about the safety of paid donors percolated through the medical literature and through the blood banking world, it also surfaced in the popular press. Newspaper headlines informed the public both that "Hepatitis Is Traced to a Professional Donor" and that the "Best Blood Is Given by Pros."[124] In Illinois the multiple for-profit banks in Chicago were the subjects of several exposés in the *Chicago Tribune* during the 1960s.[125] One article, illustrated by a photograph of disreputable-looking men waiting outside a blood center in a poor neighborhood, was a first-person account of being an alcoholic in Chicago, which included a description of how the narrator, incarcerated for public drunkenness in the county jail, was helped by jail administrators to make an appointment to sell blood upon his release.[126] These stories of down-and-outers were in sharp contrast to the images provided in stories about a suburban Chicago blood "co-op," where white matrons and businessmen could give blood in exchange for free blood if needed—a circulation of blood flows that appeared to eliminate those of darker skin and less comfortable incomes and provided members with what the newspaper called a "premium vintage," allowing them to avoid the potentially contaminated blood from the inner city.[127] This distinction between bought blood and given blood was not just a matter of cash and disease but of race and class.

An article about blood sales in Chicago's African American paper, the *Chicago Defender,* was more sympathetic to the professional donor, distinguishing the "winos" from the temporarily unemployed selling blood for food and rent money. Those "down on their luck" were a necessary part of a "life-saving process," benefiting others much more than the $5 they earned helped themselves. The *Defender* was willing to state what was usually left unstated in the discussion of paid donors: that if direct body-to-body transfusion were still in use, "many a patient might refuse blood from donors such as are seen at blood banks." Their skin color and shabbiness created fear, but the reporter argued that "once tested and found safe," their blood was as good as that from the most "immaculate donor" and bore no evidence of the race of the donor.[128] The Delta Blood Bank in Stockton was so sensitive to the public fear created by the appearance of its paid donors that it managed its schedule so that replacement donors would not be donating at the same times as professional donors, and its staff drove paid donors to the clinic to avoid disturbing the clinic's neighbors with the sight of down-and-outers congregating outside in anticipation of bleeding hours.[129]

Like the Progressive-era mothers' milk station administrators who saw milk selling as a way to keep women and their infants off the public charge, the *Defender* article pointed out the positive role that selling blood played in the lives of those on the margins, helping them remain self-supporting. Even the *Cedar Rapids Gazette* in 1953 provided its Iowa readers with the tip that selling blood might be a good option if one ever found oneself "stone broke" in a strange community.[130] In much of the popular press, however, professional donors were no longer the Depression-era enterprising "men of business" choosing an unusual way to put food on the table; in the prosperous postwar decades, they had become feared and pathetic figures.

This growing lay and medical distaste for bought blood initially brought more hand-wringing than action. Doctors could not imagine the blood supply without the paid donor. In New York City by the late 1960s hospitals relied on paid donors for about 50 percent of all blood collected.[131] Even as a medical researcher in Los Angeles published his results that any patient receiving a transfusion at his hospital had an approximately 20 percent risk of contracting hepatitis and linked that probability to reliance on for-profit blood banks, he admitted that "commercial banks provide a valuable service because voluntary agencies are not able to keep up with the demand."[132] Blood bankers and the doctors whom they supplied believed that only cash for blood could produce enough willing blood suppliers. The Kansas City doctors who chose to boycott the for-profit banks in their city had a luxury of choice not available to doctors in larger urban areas with greater demands for blood.

The worry about the paid donor, originating among doctors, was also transmitted to the American public, who were told that their blood supply was not only potentially dangerous but also perhaps insufficient and misallocated. In an article entitled "6,000,000 Pints Is Not Enough," the *New York Times* reported in 1964 that even vital operations were being postponed due to lack of blood and that sometimes doctors took risks, using unmatched blood because nothing better was available.[133] In 1965 the AMA made another of its periodic surveys of blood banks and attempted to account for all blood drawn. The researchers estimated that almost one-third of collected blood was discarded unused, a figure that was reported to the public as "wastage."[134]

These newspaper stories amplified the negative public perception of paid blood donors and reinvigorated the sense of individuality in the act of blood transfusion. Blood was not fungible but divisible into "bad" and "good" categories that mapped onto "commodity" and "gift." "Bad" bought blood came from bodies that were urban, poor, and possibly dark-skinned. The "blood business" became a derogatory term, describing a "bloody mess."[135] It was a mess because it was disorganized and because "down-and-outers" and "Bowery bums" were relied upon for paid donations.[136] "Whose Blood Was That?," a "shocking account of the scandalous conditions" surrounding blood collection, reminded Americans that they had no idea where the blood they received originated.[137] A New Jersey patient who contracted hepatitis after five transfusions associated with major surgery found that she had received blood supplied to the hospital from two different blood banks. Only one pint had been drawn by the local nonprofit community blood bank. Of the other four units, supplied by a for-profit bank, two units had been purchased directly from donors in New Jersey at $8 a pint, and two units had been shipped from the Interstate Blood Bank of Memphis. The for-profit bank sold all four pints to the hospital for $18 a pint, which in turn sold the blood to the patient for a $25 replacement cost and a $20 service fee, only the former of which was payable in kind.[138] A bloody mess indeed, in which everyone but the patient seemed to be making money in the blood trade and in which the patient was left without legal remedy in many states (although not New Jersey) because of the blood shield laws.[139]

It was the most overtly commercial part of the blood system, the for-profit banks, that was the first target of political action. Two New York legislators proposed state and federal legislation to eliminate commercial blood banks in 1967, a proposal that was resisted by the New York blood bank community.[140] In Illinois the state legislature commissioned a report on the feasibility of regulating the blood supply in 1965, and the commission proposed a licensing system for blood banks that would have forbidden all advertisement for blood donors, except for preapproved "brief factual announcements that donations of blood are being accepted," a provision aimed at the business model of for-profit banks.[141] California proposed a state blood bank licensing system in 1963, which was supported by the nonprofit community blood banks but opposed by commercial banks on the grounds that they were already licensed federally because they, like the Interstate Blood Bank of Memphis, shipped blood across state borders. They resisted the requirement to conform to two separate licensing schemes, arguing that if a state-by-state licensing system were created, the blood system would be even more chaotic.[142]

Without waiting for legislative action, Americans took matters into their own hands, opting out of the general blood supply by joining co-ops, like the one in suburban Chicago, soliciting friends and family for directed donations, or, in the ultimate in individualized blood donation, giving blood to themselves as an "autologous transfusion." Although not an option for the sickest patients or accident victims, for those patients able to plan ahead for anticipated blood needs, one's own blood was perceived as better, reducing the chance of rare immune incompatibility causing transfusion reactions and also avoiding blood-borne diseases potentially carried by the unknown donor. Autologous transfusion was considered by risk-adverse doctors and patients alike to be "the ideal form of blood transfusion."[143]

The emerging negative conception of the paid blood supplier of the postwar decades was reminiscent of the image of the unsavory turn-of-the-century wet nurse. She had been an "other" of a different class and ethnicity from her employers, morally inferior both in her often unwed motherhood and her willingness to abandon her own baby in order to earn enough to survive. Through public criticism of for-profit banks and paid donors, the paid donor was also described as morally suspect, often an alcoholic or drug abuser, poor, and dirty. From the medical perspective, the professional blood donor, like the wet nurse, was a necessary evil, a potential carrier of disease but also a willing supplier of a scarce resource. The medical profession continued to want what the professional donor helped to provide: banked blood as a potentially marketable commodity that they could access as needed and use for their patients.

When the British sociologist Titmuss claimed that all blood donation other than civic-minded voluntary gifting was morally flawed and socially corrupting, he was challenging not only the professional donor but the assumption of the American medical community and, under its influence, the American government, that all aspects of health care should be left to the market. The early criticism that Fantus, by calling his blood supply management system a "bank," was inappropriately "using such a commercial term," had been long forgotten in the elevation of free markets to a pillar of American democracy.[144] Despite the turn against the paid donor, the blood bank remained a popular idea because of the widespread belief that financial banks, and the markets they made possible, were good and necessary and appropriately imported through analogy into medical care in a modern capitalist economy. In his book *The Gift Relationship,* however, Titmuss rejected capitalism as the appropriate system through which to build not just a blood supply, but medical care itself. The attention Titmuss's book focused on the blood supply provided a chance to reexamine not only the paid donor but also the bedrock assumptions about body products as market commodities that had developed since the early twentieth century.

Better Blood through Better Capitalism

By 1971 both the lay public and the medical profession had ample reason to reject the professional donor and to long for a safer and more efficient blood supply. After almost thirty years of failed attempts to create an orderly national blood supply, the professional donor was a convenient scapegoat for all the frustrations arising out of the "chaotic" American system, as well as a socially acceptable way of excluding the contaminating other. The analogy between banks and bodies might have gone too far, inviting profiteering at the expensive of the public health. In this atmosphere *The Gift Relationship* quickly caught the attention of the American intelligentsia. The *New York Times* reported it as one of seven books of "special significance" for 1971.[145] *Newsweek* discussed it favorably, as did other general interest magazines.[146] Titmuss told Americans that their fears were true: reliance on paid blood suppliers in the United States was causing insufficient supplies, waste, and increased risk of hepatitis. His argument was made by comparison with the British health system, which relied entirely on unpaid donors and had, he argued, much less transfusion-transmitted hepatitis and blood wastage.

With Titmuss's assumptions about the correlation between dangerous paid donors and African American donors left unquestioned and unremarked, his book helped obscure the racial subtext of American fear of the professional donor by tying it to the earlier politics of the blood bank battles of the 1950s.[147] The AABB and the AMA had long linked payment by blood *recipients* to medical opposition to "socialized medicine." Now Titmuss linked the public concern with payment to blood *suppliers* to this same argument about the best way to pay for and allocate health care. Titmuss sought to use the failures of the American blood supply system to argue against the economic principle that markets allocate resources more efficiently than governments and to defend the postwar British welfare state. Comparing the U.S. system to the government-run, all-volunteer British blood system of the National Health Service, Titmuss indicted the U.S. blood system as both less efficient and more dangerous, a provocative challenge to the supporters of liberal capitalism. In essence, he argued that taking the banking metaphor seriously and treating blood as a business was the source of American problems, as he condemned both the metaphorical and the actual links between blood and cash. Just as the blood bank battles of the 1940s and 1950s had used blood as a proxy to argue the broader question of health care financing, Titmuss's book made the blood system the flashpoint for a critique of the intersection of market economics and public policy in the United States, emphasizing the different direction the United States was taking in the postwar period in contrast to the socialist governments of Great Britain and other former wartime allies. In addition to the ongoing academic and popular discussion Titmuss sparked about the role of government in modern liberal capitalist societies, his book intensified the ongoing criticism of the U.S. blood system.[148]

In Titmuss's view, cash for blood was not simply a matter of economics, an efficient but perhaps costly means of getting blood as needed; it was immoral and proof of a national failing. The failure of Americans to make the civic-minded wartime volunteer who had given blood as a personal gift into the basis of a postwar blood system, and the continued reliance of blood banks on the "martyr of the $5 deal," had caused two types of damaging results.[149] The American blood system was not functioning well as a business—as proven by its inefficiency and contamination—and blood banking had cheapened the American soul by its foundational assumption that U.S. citizens would donate blood only out of the rankest self-interest. Titmuss argued that altruism engendered altruism and that payments stifled altruism, breaking the "bonds of community."[150] Americans could not eliminate the paid donor because the paid donor was creating the very shortage he was designed to eliminate, discouraging Americans from giving their blood voluntarily by reducing the value of such a gift to dollars and cents.

With Titmuss's book drawing more public attention to the American blood supply, the blood system returned to the national political agenda. Spurred by the popular concern about paid donors and blood safety, the federal government intervened in blood policy for the first time since it had encouraged the Red Cross in its national schemes in the late 1940s. President Richard Nixon (1969–74), a cold warrior who had gained national prominence by joining the anticommunist baiting of the 1950s, called for the development of a federal blood policy.[151] The policy, which, as announced in 1973, called for a safe, efficient blood supply and created the American Blood Commission to implement this goal, led to yet another blood supply survey, stacks of conference proceedings, and the redesignation of the National Heart and Lung Institute as the National Heart, Lung and Blood Institute, adding blood to the priorities of government-funded medical research.[152] In addition to this executive branch effort, Congress introduced about forty bills addressing the blood supply between 1970 and 1972.[153]

What this federal attention did not generate was more federal control of the blood supply. Better capitalism, not socialism, was the American answer to Titmuss. Beginning in 1974 the National Heart, Lung and Blood Institute invited business school management experts and data-processing experts to annual conferences in order to talk to blood bankers about how to be better businesspeople using the most up-to-date management techniques.[154] Using expertise developed during the wartime administration of complex defense projects, scholars specializing in operations research and the application of management science to medical technology analyzed the "blood services complex."[155] In response to post-Titmuss criticisms of blood supply management, they offered a technocratic approach to blood banking.

The response of the AABB, as a self-regulating body, was far more significant than the government efforts. Consistent with its embrace of liberal capitalism, the Association agreed that the failures of the American blood supply were not due to reliance on market forces by its membership but were the result of the inability of medical societies, the Red Cross, and non-profit hospitals to establish and maintain blood banks as well-run business organizations. While its membership was no more interested in socialized medicine than it had been in the 1950s, the member banks saw the wisdom of responding to public fears and undercutting Titmuss's criticism. They could also strengthen the distinction between community banks and commercial banks by eliminating the perceived source of trouble: the paid donor. At a time when not all states had passed blood shield laws, such a move might also minimize the legal characterization of banked blood as a commercial product, meeting another goal of AABB members. Under Hemphill's leadership, in 1972 the AABB set 1975 as its target date for eliminating the use of paid donors by its members.[156]

The difficulty of this transition varied. In Stockton, where the paid donor was the mainstay of the blood supply, the community blood bank had to rethink its approach. It hired a director of donor recruitment and began to emphasize mobile unit collections over walk-ins, finding that while paid donors appeared when and where asked, it needed to make donation more convenient for unpaid voluntary donors. The Stockton bank proudly reported that its changeover was complete by July 1, 1974, in advance of the target date.[157] Other banks simply needed to eliminate their reliance on supplies from for-profit banks as a last resort in case of shortages. Without any federal intervention, after nearly three-quarters of a century, the professional whole blood donor was nearly gone by 1975, well before the Food and Drug Administration issued a regulation requiring blood collectors to label blood "paid" or "volunteer."[158] While banks continued to purchase some extremely rare blood types, less than 3 percent of whole blood came from paid suppliers by 1976.[159] Meanwhile plasma, no longer manufactured from whole blood but extracted directly from suppliers in the lengthy process of plasmapheresis, was still almost exclusively purchased from donors by the for-profit companies that had entered blood processing during the war. Plasma was generally not banked but rather was processed into the specialized blood products used to treat hemophilia and other medical conditions.[160]

Even with this rapid change in whole blood procurement, the significance of money in blood banking did not disappear. The raw material of blood banks might be donated rather than sold, but as blood bankers since Fantus well knew, to process and provide blood required money, and even without paid donors, keeping blood bank books balanced was a tricky business. Ironically the paid supplier was disappearing at about the same time as the two mainstays of the AABB, the local community blood bank and the replacement donor, were also disappearing.

By the 1960s some of the founding banks of the AABB had grown into regional blood organizations. Blood Service of Arizona, originally the Salt River Blood Bank serving the community of Phoenix, served six hundred hospitals across the southwestern states by 1963.[161] Blood Service and other similar organizations formed their own group, the Council of Community Blood Centers, in 1962 to discuss the issues of running regional centers. By 1974 Council members and Red Cross centers (which were also organized regionally rather than by county or municipality) collected over three-quarters of the nation's blood supply. Regional coordination of the blood supply had become the reality, even though national rationalization remained unachieved. Instead of arguing for local control, blood bankers began to talk about the "inexorable" replacement of hospital blood banks and community blood banks by regional blood centers.[162]

These new centers also had to learn to manage without replacement donors. Bottled blood had long been an accounting anomaly in hospital care, either under the Red Cross model as a "free" therapeutic or as the only item on a hospital bill that could be paid in kind. When Fantus set up a bank to save his patients out-of-pocket expenses for blood, he was creating a cost-saving solution unavailable for other life-saving therapies, like the antibiotics that became available during the 1940s.[163] By the late 1960s the way patients paid for hospital-based health care had shifted considerably. Banked blood charges were paid by the patient's insurance, not specialized blood assurance plans run by blood banks but the same insurance that covered other aspects of a hospital bill, either private hospitalization insurance or the new government programs, Medicaid and Medicare, established in 1965.[164] Once blood transfusion charges were covered by insurance plans, insured patients had no financial incentive to repay their blood "loans" in kind, and the currently healthy lost the incentive to give against future need. In order to maintain sufficient cash flow, community blood banks began to charge a hefty fee for "processing" blood rather than a smaller service fee and larger replacement fee. In these transitions, the differences between blood banks and Red Cross blood centers in procuring and providing blood faded. With all blood collected from unpaid donors and charged the same way by the hospital that provided the blood to patients, the "free or paid" battle over recipients appeared at an end, and the "gift" dominated the "commodity," as measured by compensation to suppliers.

The transition of the American blood supply to a nearly 100 percent unpaid donor model, however, did not represent the triumph of Titmuss's arguments about the gift relationship and the community-building ethos of socialized medicine. The medically led backlash in the 1960s and 1970s against the earlier claims that banked blood was a market commodity just like silver teaspoons had long-lasting consequences in the form of blood shield laws and the elimination of the professional donor. It did not, however, respond to Titmuss's broader critique or adopt the Red Cross view of blood as a public resource available to all on the basis of need. The medical profession adjusted its implementation of blood banking but maintained its opposition to socialized medicine and its adherence to the capitalist implications of the banking metaphor. The touting of unpaid blood donations as "gifts of life" overlay a complicated system of health care financing. Blood, like other medical therapeutics, was not free to patients. Reliance on the free market to allocate not just blood but most medical care resulted in great health care disparities, based on the employment and income of American citizens.

By replacing the midcentury public resource/private property debates about the allocation of medical therapeutics to patients with gift/commodity debates about compensation to donors, the new blood debates sidestepped questions about the allocation of profits from body products once they were collected, either by the Red Cross or blood banks, and about distributive justice in their use to treat the sick. This focus was the result of taking the banking metaphor seriously and the market backlash. In concentrating on the role of donors in the market for body products, Americans began to pay renewed attention to the benefits of fostering altruism, which had been consciously promoted in the wartime blood program, and to saving "martyrs of the $5 deal" from themselves, one of the early goals of the New York City donor registration system. While these developments were laudable, the effects of the market on recipients were neglected.

The backlash against tying blood, cash, and markets too closely together within the blood supply system was readily apparent in the demise of the professional donor and the blood shield laws. The consequences of that backlash were also felt in the law and policy of body products generally. Part of the pressure on the blood supply system in the postwar decades came from the new medical procedures that were making front-page news: organ transplants. Ruth Tucker received the first cadaveric kidney transplant in the United States in 1950, and by the 1960s doctors were also performing liver and heart transplants.[165] A new type of body product donor was needed: individuals willing to have their organs harvested after death. When the U.S. Senate held hearings on the proposed legislation to exempt nonprofit blood banks from the antitrust laws in 1964, both legislators and the witnesses were already looking ahead to this new form of body product and whether it too would be incorporated into commercial law.[166] By 1968 the National Conference of Commissioners on Uniform State Laws had finalized the Uniform Anatomical Gift Act, a model law eventually enacted in some form by thirty-eight states.[167] This Act was designed to make antemortem gifts of cadaveric organs legally recognized. The model law included a definition of *donor* that was very different from the first legal definition of a body product donor in 1930. In New York City's municipal regulation of blood donors, the "professional" donor was defined as one who "offers or gives his blood for transfusion purposes for a fee."[168] In 1968 an organ donor was "an individual who makes a gift of all or part of his body."[169] Many states further legally distinguished organs for transplants from goods for sale by expanding their blood shield laws to include organs and other body tissues as part of medical *services* that were outside the law of sales.[170]

The Uniform Anatomical Gift Act, while encouraging gifts, did not outlaw sales. Its drafters deliberately avoided discussing what they called the "profit motive" for premortem donations, while noting that existing laws in three states banned organ sales.[171] However, after one doctor announced his scheme to treat cadaveric organs as doctors before him had previously treated blood, creating a for-profit registry to broker donors and recipients, there was widespread outrage in the medical community.[172] In response, Congress passed the National Organ Transplant Act in 1984, which placed all organ exchanges in the United States on the gift side of the gift/commodity divide, making both the blood supply and the organ supply dependent on recruiting donors of the "gift of life."[173] The newly developed American fear of the paid donor profoundly affected the development of whole organ exchanges, both from deceased and living donors.

The banking metaphor, as part of how doctors, hospitals, and patients lived with the blood supply system in the mid-twentieth century, helped create both the market backlash and the long-lasting laws that continue to control blood and organ exchanges today. The banking metaphor has been powerful, and blood, as a ubiquitous feature of medical care, has been a powerful model for thinking about body products. This power, however, does not translate into inevitability in all body product exchanges. With little attention from the medical profession or legislators, other forms of body banks developed during the second half of the twentieth century, demonstrating the possibility of other approaches to body property.

5

Feminine Banks and the
Milk of Human Kindness

We don't charge and we don't pay. We don't believe a price can be put
on human milk.

—Milk bank administrator, 1981

In a well-to-do Chicago suburb in the early 1950s, a mother was searching
the neighborhoods for spare breast milk. Mrs. Jeanne Feagans had delivered her son prematurely at the Evanston Hospital in Evanston, Illinois.
E. Robbins Kimball, her pediatrician, recommended breast milk for her delicate infant, but like many mothers of premature babies, Feagans was unable
to produce any milk herself. Only about one-third of American mothers
initiated breastfeeding in the 1950s, but by actively promoting breastfeeding
among the mothers of his practice, Dr. Kimball had created a local anomaly. Two-thirds of the newborns among his patients were breastfed.[1] He
provided Feagans with the names of recently delivered women in his practice. Armed with a stock of rented electric breast pumps, she contacted
these women and asked if they would be willing to pump extra milk for her
child. A group of these mothers pumped three to four times a day after

nursing their own babies, and Feagans collected their milk daily and fed it to her son for six months. Her experience led her to help found the Evanston Premature Babies' Milk Bank, an institution that relied on female volunteers to collect milk from unpaid mothers and gave the milk free of charge to needy premature babies.[2]

While Feagans's quest was reminiscent of Dr. Fritz Talbot's street car journey through Boston in 1908 in search of a wet nurse, it reflected the new reality that Talbot and other pediatricians had helped to create. The solution to a lack of maternal milk for a needy baby in the 1950s was not a wet nurse but bottled human milk. When Feagans's baby was born, however, there was no mothers' milk station in Evanston, and for unknown reasons, she did not obtain milk from the station in nearby Chicago. Like most American mothers at midcentury, Feagans did not have a ready source of bottled breast milk available for purchase. In stark contrast to the postwar boom in blood banking, mothers' milk stations became much *less* common during the early Cold War period. While the stations persisted throughout World War II, with a reported twenty-four in existence in the United States in 1944, when the Evanston bank opened in 1955 it brought the total to only about seven. These numbers, showing a two-thirds decline in milk stations between 1944 and 1955, are necessarily approximate. Unlike blood banks, which were repeatedly surveyed in the postwar years, there were no formal surveys of milk stations. It is clear, however, based on press accounts and the efforts of people interested in milk collection who periodically did their best to locate existing institutions, that milk stations rapidly decreased in number in the first postwar decade.[3]

This decline was rapid, and it persisted, because by the late 1940s, and for much of the second half of the century, the medical profession did not see the need to continue its frustrating attempt to manage human milk as an infant food source, in either disembodied or maternal form. One pediatrician expressed the opinion of the majority of his colleagues in 1967 when he characterized bottle-feeding as "simple, safe, and almost uniformly successful."[4] Canned infant formulas, requiring only dilution with water, became available after 1950, making off-the-shelf commercial formulas easier to use.[5] Outside of Evanston, breastfeeding rates were at an all-time low. The one-third of mothers initiating breastfeeding nationwide in 1956 represented a drop from two-thirds in 1946, and the rate continued to fall throughout the late 1950s and 1960s, although it varied by geography and education level of

mothers.[6] More significantly for the fate of mothers' milk stations, this decline was no longer decried by the medical profession, as it had been at the
turn of the century. Instead artificial feeding was accepted as part of modern
medical practice that included a hospitalized, medicated birth. Technologies
and medical expertise had supplanted lay-led methods of both birth and infant feeding, to the near-universal acclaim of both doctors and mothers.[7]
While human blood was becoming nearly indispensable for cutting-edge
medicine, human milk was becoming dispensable and disfavored.

In the face of medical indifference, breast milk became a body product
"banked" by warm-hearted mothers, rather than by men of business, in a
feminized version of body banking that came to emphasize nature over
commerce. Like Talbot himself, who, spurred by his frustration in finding
wet nurses, founded first a wet nurse registry and then a human milk collection organization, Feagans took her own experience and generalized it,
making her solution available to other mothers by creating a milk bank in
her community. When planning a new institution to collect and distribute
bottled human milk, Feagans could draw upon the result of Talbot's efforts, that is, the long history of bottled human milk sold through mothers'
milk stations, as well as the newer idea of the blood bank and the wartime
national blood program as models for body product exchange. The bank
Feagans helped create in 1955 was an early example of what became the
dominant mode of postwar milk banking as mothers' milk stations closed:
a feminized, lay-led institution that emphasized peer-to-peer maternal
gifting, taking the blood bank as a model but adapting it in new ways. The
history of human milk banks during the postwar decades of tumult in
blood banking demonstrates the flexibility in American medical, legal,
and lay thought about bodies, markets, and medical care, even within the
banking metaphor. Continually marginalized by organized medicine, milk
banks persisted, maintained by the recurring enthusiasm of small groups
who ensured that at least one milk bank was always in operation, an unbro-
ken line extending from Talbot's Directory for Mother's Milk to the end of
the twentieth century and beyond.

Bureaus to Banks

The founders of the Evanston Premature Babies' Milk Bank drew upon the
banking metaphor made popular through blood supply management when

they organized their institution in 1955, choosing to call it a bank rather
than a station. In contrast, when Dr. Bernard Fantus developed the concept
of the blood bank in 1937 while working at Cook County Hospital, he had
paid no attention to the thriving mothers' milk station located elsewhere in
Chicago, where other medical personnel had been successfully collecting a
human body product for disembodied use since 1935.[8] Milk stations, in existence for almost thirty years by then, were organizations that *bought* human milk, and the purpose of the blood bank was to avoid the paid donor.
As hospitals scrambled to open blood banks in the late 1930s and early
1940s, the existing mothers' milk stations continued to operate as they always had, buying milk from mothers to dispense to babies. While the municipal milk station in Chicago continued to buy and sell milk through the
1960s, the widespread enthusiasm for the blood bank quickly surpassed
the earlier enthusiasm for milk stations, in Chicago and everywhere else.[9]
The number of blood banks skyrocketed, and the number of milk stations
dwindled.

Just as Fantus ignored milk stations in 1937, most milk station administrators had initially ignored his new term, *bank.* The power of the banking
metaphor to explain the management of body products beyond blood had
been immediately apparent to medical and lay people alike once they learned
about the new blood banks. For example, Pennsylvania doctors were discussing an "eye bank" by 1938.[10] The mothers' milk stations, however, already had their own successful metaphors. *Station* had been borrowed from
campaigns to distribute pure cow's milk to the urban poor, and the Chicago mothers' milk station would continue to use that term throughout its
existence.[11] In 1943 the American Academy of Pediatrics, headquartered in
Chicago, issued standards for the collection and distribution of disembodied human milk, the high-water mark of efforts by Talbot and other pediatricians to promote bottled milk as a medical therapeutic. The Academy,
like the Chicago station, ignored the possibilities of *bank* and instead used
the term *mothers' milk bureau,* with all its Progressive-era connotations of
public improvement agencies such as the Children's Welfare Bureau (which
administered mothers' milk stations in New York City) and municipal sani-
tation bureaus.[12] Like the stations distributing cow's milk, these organizations were run by cities or philanthropic organizations (including hospitals)
in the interests of improving the public health. The terms *bureau* and *station* maintained the focus on this medically directed goal rather than on
the treatment of human milk as a market commodity by buying and sell-

ing. Like Fantus, the early organizers of human milk exchange assumed that this new body product was property to be controlled by the medical profession for its own purposes. The prewar professional milk seller, although analogous to the professional blood donor in her engagement in a "profitable business," was engaged in a different sort of trade.[13] While the professional blood donor was an intrepid man of business engaged in a somewhat risky and uncomfortable job, the milk seller was a vulnerable woman recovering from childbirth, and facing another mouth to feed. She was thus a "deserving mother" who was herself an object of "charity," helped by her participation in this public improvement project.[14]

When the Academy issued its guidelines in 1943, there was no reason to think about the milk supply in banking terms. Fantus's accounting method, the crux of his blood bank, would not work for bottled milk because doctors could not solicit patients and their families to repay their use of body products in kind. The friends and family of a baby needing breast milk were almost certainly unable to donate breast milk themselves. Further, while the volume of blood withdrawn had become standardized at about a pint, and blood was transfused by the pint, facilitating credits and debits in the blood bank, babies did not drink milk in standardized amounts. Neither did donors produce milk in predictable amounts, as capacity to express milk varied among women and, for the same woman, from day to day. On the other hand, once doctors had recruited a milk donor, unlike a blood donor she could donate daily, in amounts ranging from two ounces to several quarts, and could continue to make such donations for months. At the Detroit Mothers Milk Bureau in the 1920s, the organizers had found several women able to supply three to four quarts daily and refused to employ any woman who could not produce at least sixteen ounces on her daily visit.[15] The administrators of the Mothers' Milk Bureau in Manhattan were grateful for Mrs. Mabel Caines Joell, who was able to regularly express more than a quart of milk per day beyond what she fed her own baby and was earning $44 per week selling her milk in 1946. Even though Joell might be able to continue to sell her milk for up to eighteen months, with most other donors at the New York bureau producing only about half her volume, the bank was experiencing a "galactic crisis," with "demand far ahead of supply."[16]

These swings in supply and demand could be managed in part because milk preservation technology was much more advanced than blood preservation technology. Although there was initially an assumption that freezing would destroy the value of milk, by the late 1930s researchers and doctors were convinced that frozen milk could be used interchangeably with fresh milk to feed babies.[17] As refrigeration technology improved, the ability to store milk long term greatly reduced any need to balance in-flows and out-flows in the short term. The blood bank was a refrigerator where citrated blood lasted only ten days and deteriorated with each passing day, but the milk stations used freezers.[18] Still, quick changes in supply and demand could tax even frozen inventory. Any baby relying on bottled milk needed multiple feedings per day, and increasing volumes as the baby grew. In 1945 a Los Angeles mothers' milk station was pleading for donors, facing the need to supply two babies, each of whom required thirty or more ounces a day. Because most women could not match Mrs. Joell and express a quart of excess milk daily, many donors were needed to keep up with this peak demand.[19] On the supply side, mothers "retired" as their babies grew and they stopped nursing. The nurse in charge of the Chicago milk station put out an urgent call for more lactating mothers in 1943, explaining, "Some days we give out more milk than we are able to take in and the problem has become acute."[20] Another milk bank administrator told her new volunteers that they must understand that "there is nothing at all regular about the number of donors or the numbers of babies using the milk."[21] The assembly-line processing of blood donors, so necessary to maintain perishable inventories, was neither required nor possible as part of managing the supply of human milk as a body product.

While milk station administrators and the doctors who ordered bottled human milk for patients wrestled with matching supply to demand, they did not wrestle with whether to pay donors. Just as in blood banking at midcentury, the paid milk supplier was not a perceived problem. Rather the medical personnel who ran milk stations, the milk providers, and the purchasing families were all comfortable with the cash flows surrounding the milk station. The assumption of both pediatricians and surgeons that they needed to pay body product suppliers in order to induce them to part with their harvestable fluid was strengthened in the case of breast milk by the wet nurse tradition, in which lactating women had long been paid for the service of providing milk. Since time immemorial, those who desired such services and could pay for them did so. If doctors wanted to arrange a wet nurse, or later, bottled milk for those who could not afford market rates, they did so in the same way they arranged for medical care for the poor generally, rationing out charity care, subsidized by the fees charged to the well-to-do or by government funds.[22] In Detroit the bureau aimed always to collect more milk than was needed by its private patients, that is, those who could pay. After distributing the milk to such patients, at a sliding scale from 10 to 30 cents per ounce, it sold milk to institutions at 8 cents per ounce and distributed any excess to charity cases free of charge.[23]

Despite the differences in obtaining and storing an inventory and in the type of patient need, there were parallels between the new blood banks and the older mothers' milk stations. Each was dedicated to the collection, processing, and distribution of a disembodied human fluid as a medical therapeutic. After the term *bank* became popular as applied to blood supply management, medical professionals gradually began to use it to describe human milk management systems as well. In 1941 a Chicago nurse used the term to explain to other nurses how her hospital collected and used human milk. Apparently relying on moral suasion of a captive pool of potential donors, the hospital asked each new mother to give without compensation a few times during her postpartum stay. The milk was frozen and kept on hand to feed premature babies without a maternal milk source.[24] The patients of the maternity ward were thus responsible for both deposits and withdrawals. Unlike in blood banks, however, there was no attempt to balance accounts, to offer credits, or to claim loan repayment obligations.

The informal designation of these institutions as banks was useful to catch the general public's attention as well. In 1942, when the four-year-old mothers' milk station in Milwaukee put out a call for milk, the *Chicago Tribune* headlined the story "Mothers' Milk Bank Dwindles in Milwaukee."[25] Similarly, although the Los Angeles Mothers' Milk Bureau, founded in 1925, still retained its designation as a bureau, a newspaper reporting on the bureau's call for donations in 1943 described an "acute shortage" at the "city milk bank" on the same page that it reported favorably on the national blood program, noting in its column on the military that "blood plasma . . . [is] saving countless thousands of men."[26] The nomenclature change not only took advantage of the increased public understanding of body product exchange created by the mass collection of blood during World War II but modernized the Progressive-era terminology of *bureaus* and *stations*. In 1944, in an article describing a hospital milk supply system to lay readers, the American Medical Association (AMA) used the headline "Milk Bank," a switch from its prewar praise of a "breast milk dairy."[27]

With the tag line "Deposit breast milk, draw interest in living babies," the author deftly applied the banking metaphor to this decades-old practice. The nurse was described as making a "withdrawal" as she removed milk from the freezer. In this article it was not just the terminology but the milk bank itself that was new. In a reordering of history, the article explained that the unnamed hospital "is in the banking business; it has a blood bank, a plasma bank—and now a bank of preserved breast milk."[28]

While preexisting stations and bureaus in Chicago and Los Angeles adopted the new terminology informally, institutions of human milk exchange founded after the war, like the Evanston Premature Babies' Milk Bank and the Mothers' Milk Bank of San Francisco, established in 1947, called themselves "banks." Most of these institutions, new and old, continued to operate as the mothers' milk stations always had. They did not engage in anything comparable to Fantus's careful accounting effort as he attempted to eliminate the professional donor by making the bank "more than a mere metaphor."[29] In the milk bank, the banking metaphor fit only loosely. Business as usual in human milk management meant paying donating mothers and charging by the ounce for the processed milk, often on a sliding fee scale as in Detroit, or sometimes fulfilling the charitable goals of the founders by using another source of funds to subsidize the bank and providing milk without charge. The Mothers' Milk Bank of Essex County, New Jersey, paid donating mothers 10 cents an ounce in 1953 and charged recipients based on their parents' ability to pay, up to 35 cents per ounce. The Mothers' Milk Bank of San Francisco also paid donating mothers but was able to give milk away without charge through the late 1960s, due to outside funds.[30]

Rather than a bank managing accounts for customers, the milk bank was more of a manufacturing facility that bought its raw material and sold its final product at a mark-up. This view of banked body products as manufactured commodities caused a great deal of legal trouble for blood banks beginning in the 1950s. There is no evidence of product liability law applied to milk banks during this period, however, in either the medical or legal literature or in published court cases. There are two likely causes for the failure of milk banks to encounter commercial law.

First, during the period in which commercial legal doctrines were becoming a problem for blood banks, there were very few milk banks in operation. Already in 1953 the director of the Essex County bank noted that "many older [banks] have ceased to exist," so that his bank shipped milk to New York and other surrounding states.[31] From seven in 1955 the total number had dropped to only three in 1968, when banks were open only in San Francisco, Evanston, and Wilmington, Delaware. With the extremely small number of bottles of milk changing hands, compared to the thousands of pints of blood being transfused, it is little wonder that few or no lawsuits were filed and that no doctors or lawyers spent time worrying about the issue. There was also no immunocompatibility issue with milk; mismatched blood could cause a serious reaction and death, but any mother's milk was acceptable to any baby. Malaria and hepatitis, diseases transmissible by blood, are not transmitted through breast milk, and the pasteurization and freezing of human milk also decreased the risk of disease transmission.[32] Although some viruses are transmissible through breast milk, until the AIDS epidemic the health risk from banked milk was largely limited to bacterial contamination issues caused in production, processing, or storage.[33] Still, as blood shield laws were passed, creating a national conversation about liability from body products, insurance companies took notice of the possible risks in milk banking. In 1977 the San Francisco Mothers' Milk Bank learned that its product liability insurance coverage would increase in price 700 percent. It first raised the price it charged for milk, and then closed the following year.[34]

Second, the milk bankers did not adopt the rhetoric of payment and markets that helped courts fit banked blood within the law of commercial sales. Women selling their milk had never been called "professional donors" or businesswomen. Instead they continued to be called "mothers," which they were. When the Chicago mothers' milk station turned to the press to advertise its urgent need for more suppliers, the administrator told the reporter that inventory was low because the station had "only 15 mothers at the present time."[35] More mothers were needed to solve the problem. Just as the prewar stations required donating mothers to prove that their own babies were healthy and well-fed, the postwar milk banks expected that each donor would be feeding her own baby. Her milk sales were ancillary to that maternal role. Wet nursing may have been an occupation, but selling bottled breast milk was a supplement to the primary role of mother. Unlike the "mercenary" wet nurse, she was not producing to sell, but selling extra as a way of helping other babies in addition to her own.[36] Thus by the 1940s the Chicago milk station sought mothers with "public spirit" to

sell their milk for 10 cents an ounce rather than mothers with private financial needs.[37]

In managing their woman-sourced body product, and unconstrained by
concern about legal liability, milk bankers did not follow either the blood
bankers' postwar embrace of market rhetoric or their later rejection of market concepts in body product management. Instead milk banks continued
to operate as milk stations had been operating, combining buying and selling with a gendered vision of caring and a medical mission of allocating
a therapeutic through a combination of market mechanisms and philanthropy. In the alternative vision of a body product promoted by milk bankers, banked milk was property that could be bought and sold to the mutual
benefit of buyer and seller, but it was also the "milk of human kindness."
This phrase had been used as early as 1848 to describe unpaid milk donation
to another woman's child, when William Thackeray thus referred to the
milk provided by a wet nurse who was left unpaid by her employers in his
novel *Vanity Fair*.[38] In the twentieth century, however, the "milk of human
kindness" was not the involuntary result of upper-class employers taking
advantage of a poor woman but milk flowing from a generous mother to a
grateful mother without any expectation of payment to the providing mother
and, increasingly, without any payment from the receiving mother.

The Milk of Human Kindness

Although the cash flows of milk banking remained largely the same as they
had been in the prewar mothers' milk stations, the postwar milk banks
gradually came to put more emphasis on "human kindness" as the motivation for suppliers. In the atmosphere of medical indifference toward breast
milk, the driving force behind founding and maintaining milk banks was
middle-class laywomen rather than harried urban doctors. These bankers,
who did not see themselves or their donors as being in business, eschewed
the language of the market, instead using the language of intimate relationships and uncompensated caring to explain the exchange of human milk as
a body product. In the surviving banks during the 1950s and 1960s, laywomen made both milk donating and milk bank administration an expression of their own femininity.

Like Feagans, these founding women of the postwar banks often had
direct experience with an infant who failed to thrive on artificial formula.

They tended to be from the higher socioeconomic classes, with the social capital and leisure time to devote to institution building. While they generally sought a medical director and the protection of a medical institution, the day-to-day operations of the milk banks were kept going by staffs of volunteer laywomen, usually in conjunction with one or two paid nurses.

The same sort of women, for the first time, might also be recruited as milk donors. As the hospital became the locus of modern medical care, it also served as a site of democratization of body product suppliers. Rather than a charitable institution where only the poor sought care, the hospital became the place where all socioeconomic classes received medical care and where nearly all women delivered their babies.[39] The postwar blood bankers, as they sought deposits from the friends and family of each patient, were thus recruiting from a broader swath of the American public than had the earlier professional donor registries. The milk banks too expanded their conception of appropriate suppliers. Even though the milk sellers of the 1920s and 1930s were generally married and better off than the early twentieth-century wet nurses, they had been recruited as milk sellers on the basis of financial need. That need might have led them to deliver their child in a hospital as a charity patient rather than at home with an attending physician, or led them to answer a newspaper advertisement seeking women willing to sell milk.[40] When milk banks recruited hospitalized postpartum women in the 1940s and 1950s, they were now reaching not only women who saw selling milk as a way to avoid the necessity of leaving their baby for paid employment outside the home but also women who could afford to be full-time mothers and housewives. Kimball, in explaining the Evanston Premature Babies' Milk Bank to his fellow pediatricians, noted that practically all the bank's donors were "mothers of private patients," that is, women who could afford to pay for their stay at his suburban hospital. These women delivered in the same hospital as "clinic patients," who received charity care. Like the private patients, if the clinic patients had received "careful prenatal care," they might also be recruited as donors.[41]

The San Francisco Mothers' Milk Bank also exemplified these trends in milk bank management and suppliers. Since 1917 the local branch of the American Association of University Women, an upper-middle-class women's voluntary organization, had managed an infant welfare clinic in the city. During World War II, however, the women found it impossible to keep the clinic in operation because of a shortage of medical personnel.[42] Upon the closing of the clinic, the women immediately redirected their efforts to the establishment of the second milk bank west of Chicago and opened the San Francisco bank in 1947. For the next thirty years an auxiliary of unpaid society women kept the bank going. They drove to collect milk, provided office assistance, and engaged in fund-raising activities such as gala balls and fashion shows, reported in the society pages of the newspapers in the wealthy San Francisco suburbs.[43] The founding bank president, Mrs. Walter C. Fell, worked diligently to coordinate the volunteers and the paid nurse and to maintain relations with local doctors.[44]

Similarly the Mothers' Milk Bank in Wilmington, Delaware, began in 1947 with the encouragement of a local pediatrician, Margaret Handy, who suggested the need for a source of human milk for hospitalized premature infants. Although Handy's support was important, the bank depended on the crucial support of a lay volunteer, Mrs. Margaret Trentman. Like Feagans, Trentman had delivered a baby prematurely and sought bottled human milk to feed her own child. Her solution had been to purchase milk from the Directory for Mother's Milk in Boston. Based on her personal experience and her membership in the Wilmington hospital's Junior Board—its organization of female volunteers—she persuaded the Board to sponsor a local milk bank, which would serve other babies like her own. The Board continued to support the bank for decades, like the San Francisco AAUW chapter, raising funds and supplying volunteers to keep the milk bank in operation.[45]

Some of these organizing women also acted as suppliers, and they recruited as donors other women like themselves who delivered in the same hospitals and shared the same pediatricians. This peer recruitment rejected the prewar model of treating milk sellers like the servile wet nurses they were replacing or like factory workers producing a product. Instead the milk suppliers encompassed both the social elite and more humble women who might be glad of some extra cash, linked by maternal status rather than socioeconomic status. The mothers' milk stations of the 1930s had almost uniformly required women to travel to the milk station to express their milk under supervision, a means of medical control over the product and an indication of suspicion that the women, like untrustworthy servants, might otherwise adulterate or dilute their milk. They also often were required to bring their own babies to a public authority for weighing or produce other proof that their own nursling was thriving in order to be permitted to sell their milk.

In contrast, the postwar milk supplier was allowed to express her milk at home, without any eyes upon her and without the elaborate preparations and costuming of the prewar stations. Each new Evanston donor was visited in her home by a lay volunteer, who brought a loaned electric breast pump and written instructions. Mothers were told to wash their arms and hands three times before washing their breasts and to avoid touching the inside of the sterile bottles brought to them daily.[46] How well they complied was up to them. The medical director of the Evanston bank described the donors as "being from the middle and upper social strata" and having generally "good hygienic habits."[47] The San Francisco Mothers' Milk Bank used a medical certificate from each donor's doctor as a replacement for the scrutiny of the station nurse.[48] The volunteers, who themselves would almost certainly have rejected the notion that they express milk under the watchful eye of a nurse, treated the suppliers as they expected to be treated and greatly minimized the power hierarchy that had existed in the prewar banks, where the male doctor and his nursing representatives exercised authority over the donating mothers. While volunteer visits to a home to collect milk provided some check that donors met middle-class standards of cleanliness, the watchful eye was more that of a neighbor than that of an agent of a male medical profession.

Even in the medically founded and controlled Essex County Mothers' Milk Bank (established in 1938), this shift occurred in the postwar decades. In the early years donors usually came to the bank to express their milk and receive their 10 cents per ounce payment. The women were those who "had to return to work almost immediately after their confinement" in order to earn money and often found that the money from selling their milk was sufficient to allow them to stay home with their own children.[49] With postwar prosperity, the doctors in charge found that more mothers expressed a willingness to donate their milk without compensation, to save "babies in distress." Their offers of free milk, however, were always refused; all mothers were paid, even if they disavowed a monetary motivation. But by 1953 these prosperous, generous mothers were allowed to express their milk at home and bring it in bottles to the bank. The supervising doctor noted that rather than spending their milk payments on necessities, these mothers were investing their earnings in savings bonds for their children.[50]

This shift in the providers' attitude toward payment reached beyond Essex County. The records of the San Francisco bank also show that women were surprised to receive checks for an act they had performed without any expectation of financial compensation.[51] Unlike the Essex bank, the San Francisco bank did allow suppliers to return their checks, giving them the ability to define their act as an altruistic gift. The Wilmington bank continued to pay its donors into the 1990s but found that most of its suppliers rejected its offer of 20 cents per ounce.[52] From a Progressive-era institution of class uplift, the milk bank was becoming an institution through which all the female participants—bankers and donors alike—could express their public spirit and motherly concern for infants at risk.

The group of upper-middle-class laywomen who founded the Evanston bank took this reconfiguration of the donor from a recipient of charity to a philanthropist to its logical conclusion and proudly described their bank as the first and only milk bank that did not pay its suppliers. Evanston had a long history of female civic activism, most prominently as the headquarters of the National Woman's Christian Temperance Union since the nineteenth century.[53] Evanston women had formed one of the earliest Junior League groups and became charter members of the Association of Junior Leagues of America when it was founded in 1924. The Junior League, an all-female voluntary organization that grew out of the settlement house movement, recruited young nonworking mothers and trained them in the organizational and fund-raising skills of civic improvement. The Evanston Junior Leaguers immediately set to work on infant welfare clinics, the same project that had engaged the San Francisco AAUW women.[54] Like most female civic activists at the turn of the twentieth century, the Evanston women assumed and enforced a class hierarchy. The reformers were, by and large, white, native-born, Protestant, middle-class women, concerned with ameliorating the conditions of the urban poor, who were often immigrants.[55] Their targets of reform came from the same population that filled the urban hospitals in the early decades of the twentieth century. The Junior League in Hartford, Connecticut, had been involved in founding a mothers' milk station in that city in the 1920s.[56] By midcentury the Junior League also took on projects that benefited a broader cross-section of the community, like the Milwaukee blood bank.[57]

Feagans was not only an energetic mother of a premature baby she was determined to feed mothers' milk; she was also a member of the Evanston

Junior League and, like her fellow members, a housewife without the need to work for wages and an experienced veteran of community projects.[58] Her doctor, Kimball, rather than searching for human milk himself as Talbot had done in 1908, facilitated Feagans's efforts to arrange matters herself. She asked her neighbors to provide their milk as an uncompensated gift to her and her son. After her organizational efforts paid off for her own child, she helped another local woman do the same for her premature infant.[59] Their personal experiences, coupled with their self-conceptions as community-oriented volunteers, led the two women to convince the Junior League of Evanston to found the milk bank in 1953. Feagans acted as the first chairwoman.[60]

The driving force behind the Evanston bank was thus the energy of laywomen, although they enlisted a pediatrician from Evanston Hospital, Alvah Newcomb, as a medical advisor and received the enthusiastic support of Kimball, who was credited in news stories decades later with founder status, although at the time he credited Feagans as the "initiating force."[61] Feagans's own experience shaped the organization and purposes of the bank. In the network she had created for her own son and her neighbor's child, both the mother of the recipient baby and the donating mothers were suburban women, delivered in the same hospital and patients of the same pediatrician. It is likely that they also shared racial and socioeconomic characteristics; that is, that they were white middle-class women, like the members of the Junior League whose photographs appeared in the community newspaper, the *Evanston Review*.[62] The Evanston Hospital Premature Babies' Milk Bank had a different target beneficiary than the infant welfare clinics previously established by the Junior League. The babies who received milk were defined by medical need based on low birth weight or other factors, without any class assumptions. They would receive milk free of charge. Even more significant, the target donor population was mothers from the "middle and upper strata," not the sort of women who in decades past would have become wet nurses. They were women of the same socioeconomic class as the organizing women. In this peer-to-peer context, Feagans evidently had not thought of paying the women who provided milk for her son (although she supplied the pumps so that they did not have any out-of-pocket expenses), and the milk bank copied her approach. The donating women were motivated by their own charitable impulses, by altruism and civic-mindedness, to become some of the first organized unpaid milk donors.

Evanston's unique model for organizing the transfer of human milk from one woman to another woman's baby received national attention after Kimball reported on the success of the project in 1955 to a meeting of the American Academy of Pediatrics and then published his report in the Academy's journal.[63] Popular interest was captured by the idea of stylishly dressed young housewives driving an "unusual milk route."[64] Newspaper readers as far away as Virginia learned about the daily routine of an "attractive, young Evanston, Ill., matron." After "her banker husband had caught his commuter train to Chicago's financial district" and she got her children safely off to day camp, she "finished her morning tasks." What she did next was what made this matron newsworthy: "Picking up a small pail with a lid on it, she hopped into the family's station wagon 'second' car to begin her milk run. Hers was the local Evanston route. Her stops are not to deliver milk, however, but to pick up precious mothers' milk for the United States' only free 'Preemies Milk Bank.'"[65] Her socioeconomic status firmly signaled by her "banker husband" and her possession of a second car, she was portrayed as fulfilling her domestic role of caring for husband and children first, and then engaging in this novel activity. In stories headlining the activities of such "debs" and "society girls," the new milk bank received attention across the United States.[66]

The actions of these Evanston housewives not only flowed from a tradition of middle-class female activism but also were embedded in the heightened domesticity of the early Cold War years that supported the actions of mothers volunteering as both milk bankers and donors. Evanston, like most other American suburbs in the 1950s, was the site of the enthusiastic enactment of a home-based family life with increased emphasis on white women's roles in child-rearing and homemaking. With the release of consumer demand at the end of wartime restrictions and the return of soldiers to home front employment, women were actively encouraged to drop any wage-earning activities they had assumed during the war and occupy themselves with husbands and children and with consumption for the home. The average age at marriage dropped, the average age at childbearing dropped, home ownership increased, and the suburbs were filled with families.[67] The Junior League, which explicitly encouraged mothers of young children to become involved, provided one of the few acceptable outlets for women

whose lack of paid employment underlined their husband's role as successful providers. Through volunteer activities, they could leave their homes,
meet other women, and participate in civic affairs.

As these "society girls" made their milk runs to single-family suburban
homes occupied by other young matrons, the idea that they would offer
cash to the donors they visited was as far from their minds as the idea that
they would be paid for their work in keeping the bank running. The children of both donors and bankers had all the creature comforts they needed,
courtesy of their employed fathers, and the donating mothers were giving
milk without payment in the same spirit that the bankers gave their time
without payment—as altruistic volunteers, caring for their community and
other women's children as an extension of their primary roles as mothers
and homemakers. They were mothers, not professional donors or wet nurses
looking for a "profitable business."

Participation in human milk collection and distribution, however, required readjustment of some aspects of the dominant narratives of Cold War
femininity and domesticity, even as the extension of women's unpaid labor
from their own homes and children to other women's homes and children
fit so well within the prevailing ideology of maternity. Outside of Evanston
the rates of breastfeeding continued to decline. The Evanston Junior Leaguers may have garnered so much publicity for their efforts in part because of
the oddity of attractive young matrons advocating the use of human milk,
with the implication that they nursed their own children. The heightened
emphasis on the role of middle-class white women as mothers in the postwar years did not, by and large, include any calls to reverse the century-long
trend away from maternal nursing. Instead mothering was to be combined with a new standard of housewifery and sexualized motherhood,
involving interior decoration, cleanliness, and feminine self-care and presentation that required increased time spent on housework, grooming, and
consumerism.[68]

Bottle-feeding fit better into the clean and orderly middle-class
household. Bottle-fed babies could go longer between feedings and could be
fed by someone else—an older sibling, household help, a grandmother—or
even feed themselves from a propped bottle. Bottle-feeding also allowed
women to present a more polished appearance, without regard for a baby's
access to the breast. Fashions in the 1950s were particularly "stiff," women's
clothes constituting a type of "armor" not well-suited to periodic nursing.[69]

The ideal feminine appearance emphasized an hour-glass figure, sculpted with girdles and brassieres, as the breast became increasingly sexualized in popular culture, a coding of the female body that existed only uncomfortably with the practice of breastfeeding.[70]

The cashless model of the milk bank that was tried in Evanston as a "community project" relying on the extension of women's maternal role required both a supply and a demand.[71] Evanston remained an anomaly with respect to both. Without lactating women to donate and doctors to suggest to the mothers of preemies and other sickly babies that breast milk might be helpful, there could be no milk banks. Even with volunteer labor and women motivated to donate free milk, the seven milk banks existing in 1958 could not survive the climate of medical indifference. The fate of the Evanston bank was indicative of national trends. In 1966 the Junior League turned the Evanston bank over to the hospital and the "milk runs" ceased.[72] The maternity nursing coordinator at Evanston Hospital in 1973 recalled that in the 1960s formula was preferred because it could be "precisely analyzed for its nutrient and caloric value."[73] In 1968 the San Francisco milk bank took an informal survey of local pediatricians, seeking their opinion about whether maintaining its service was useful. The responses were decidedly mixed. Some doctors agreed with one who felt that "it has been well-established that there really is no significant advantage to breastmilk in the normal, healthy infant" and that "artificially-prepared formulas will do the job, and do it well, in the majority of cases," even for "compromised infants," while others remained "staunch supporter[s]."[74]

In the late 1960s, when blood bankers were worried about convincing the American public that they provided services rather than sold goods, and Americans were beginning to mistrust the professional blood donor, the pressing problem in milk banking was not cash payments to suppliers but rather the demand from recipients. Banks that had offered payment for milk continued to do so, without criticism, but fewer and fewer doctors and parents were seeking banked breast milk. Milk banks had always relied on doctors to identify patients for their product, and at a time when human milk was considered so dispensable that breastfeeding was virtually ignored in the medical curriculum, the demand was disappearing.[75] The milk bank in Wilmington repeatedly reached out to pediatricians through the pages of professional journals in the 1960s, seeking to remind doctors that it supplied breast milk on request.[76] In San Francisco the bank served only twenty babies in 1966, and even after its outreach efforts the bank continued to serve comparatively few infants, for example, only ninety-five in 1971.[77] With the lack of demand, most milk banks closed. The Directory for Mother's Milk in Boston closed in 1962.[78] The Los Angeles bank closed sometime in 1960s.[79] When the San Francisco bank closed in 1978, the Evanston bank was also defunct, and of the three banks that had been in operation in 1968, only one remained, the bank in Wilmington.[80] The Wilmington mothers' milk bank would be the only postwar milk bank still in operation when a resurgence in milk banking began in the 1980s.

"Natural" versus "Commercial"

In the immediate postwar period, medical indifference had led to an emphasis on maternal kindness rather than money as the motivating factor for both milk bankers and their suppliers, even as money flows remained an assumed part of all formal milk banks other than the Evanston bank. As continuing medical indifference drove the closure of almost all milk banks in the 1960s and 1970s, the exchange of human milk as a body product continued in less formal ways, including ad hoc networks and amateur "kitchen milk banks." Without pressure from the medical profession to fit banked milk into broader discussions about financing health care, women chose to treat bottled human milk in the same way that the Red Cross treated banked blood. The Red Cross argued that blood should be a public resource available to all Americans as a matter of democratic citizenship, a gift of, by, and for the people, provided based on need, not buying power.[81] Increasingly, laywomen also treated bottled human milk as a special kind of inalienable property, that while potentially marketable, should not be bought or sold. Just as there should be free blood, there should be free milk. In the language of the debates sparked by the British sociologist Richard Titmuss in the 1970s, milk bankers believed that milk should be a gift, not a commodity.[82]

Since the mothers' milk stations of the 1910s, bottled milk had been allocated according to medically determined need, even as it was bought and sold. The perceived problem with buying and selling milk in the new world of body products framed by the gift/commodity dichotomy was that such transactions commodified motherhood. Seeking to separate motherhood from the marketplace, women came to believe that cash transactions involving

human milk were suspect. This suspicion was related to the contemporane-
ous focus on "bought blood" and the "paid donor" in the American blood
supply, but it was expressed differently. In milk banking, unlike in blood
banking, there was neither fear of legal liability to drive a distinction between product and service, nor a lingering fear of the diseased other in the
nonhierarchical world of similarly situated donors, bankers, and recipients.
Instead, in milk banking the gift/commodity dichotomy emerged as a separation of the "commercial" from the "natural." In this developing understanding, cow's milk–based infant foods, and even milk bottled under the
medicalized conditions of the traditional milk stations and formal milk
banks, were "commercial" and thus bad, while breastfeeding and breast
milk gifted from mother to mother without formal institutions were "natural" and therefore good.

Considering breast milk "natural" was not new, of course. Turn-of-the-
century doctors had called other infant feeding options "artificial foods."
But in the postwar decades considering natural breastfeeding superior to
bottle feeding was a minority view. It was the few women who chose to
breastfeed during the decades when breastfeeding rates remained below 20
percent who emphasized the natural aspects of breast milk as a source of
benefit to mother and baby. In 1956 a group of housewives in the western
Chicago suburb of Franklin Park founded La Leche League, a laywomen's
organization to provide support for breastfeeding mothers.[83] The League
encouraged breastfeeding as the "womanly art" that was "an integral part
of good mothering."[84] In advice that went far beyond the mechanics of successful infant nursing, the League founders emphasized woman-directed
"natural" mothering over the medically directed "scientific" mothering that
had been popular in the prewar decades. Breastfeeding was part of "real
mothering" that meant leaving "charts and rules and schedules" behind
and letting the housework slip while putting the baby first.[85]

The League aligned itself with the natural childbirth movement of the
1950s by sponsoring a public lecture by Grantly Dick-Read, a British doctor
and author, as its first fund-raiser. Dick-Read's book, *Childbirth without
Fear,* had been published in the United States in 1944 but reached best-
seller status in the 1950s.[86] Its growing popularity spoke to the same narrative emphasized by the League and adopted by the later milk bankers: that
women should and could be more in control of mothering, beginning in
the delivery room. According to Dick-Read and the League, motherhood

was a crucial role for women, and they were naturally equipped with the skills to handle it. He advocated "natural" childbirth, without medications, forceps, or surgical interventions.[87]

The womanly art of breastfeeding was also something women could do naturally, without medical interference. The League explained to expectant mothers, "You will be able to nurse your baby. You can because you want to."[88] The League founders emphasized breastfeeding as a "natural art," a "normal function" that had been "happily" performed by mothers "since the time of Eve." The "simple, beautiful, natural way" of feeding a child through breastfeeding was juxtaposed against the "refrigeration, sterilization, and the rubber company" that intervened between a mother and her formula-fed baby, creating a "hard complicated way" of feeding.[89] Not only was breastfeeding natural rather than artificial, and woman-directed rather than doctor-directed, but it made women better mothers. The League worked from the premise that "breastfeeding is an integral part of good mothering," a reflection of a deep, intimate connection between mother and baby that would help the mother "become a more real, more loving person." The League collected testimonials about the benefits of breastfeeding to the mother. One mother nursing her fifth child after bottle-feeding the previous four reported, "I am amazed at the difference in me. . . . It is a feeling of growth and development. . . . I feel as if I have finally arrived."[90]

By 1964 there were over 150 active La Leche League groups in the United States, each providing peer-to-peer support for new mothers, and the League had sold over forty thousand copies of its lay guide, *The Womanly Art of Breastfeeding*.[91] Group members and readers were offered an alternative vision of Cold War domesticity, replacing keeping-up-with-the-Joneses consumerism with child-centered authenticity. In *The Womanly Art* the League urged women to reject the notion that a perfectly cleaned and decorated house was more important than well-nurtured children. Its authors advocated substituting fresh fruit for "home-baked goodies every night" as a way of saving time for mothering. They recommended against "going all out for cleaning" when the baby was napping, instead spending that time with older children. They told readers that a "spotless house" was not so important and urged them, "Resign yourself to living a more easy-going kind of life."[92] The League also taught women simple techniques to adjust and modify their clothing to permit easy and inconspicuous public nursing.[93] The League mother lived in a differently arranged house and wore different clothes than the "attractive young matrons" with their children at day camp, whose interest in breast milk was waning by the mid-1960s. With their valorization of natural mothering and the links they drew between breast milk and maternal love, League members were a reserve of milk that could be tapped during the 1960s and 1970s, when there were few formal milk banks; they were a feminine version of the "giant blood bank" of the "living American public."[94]

This reserve could be life-saving. While milk banks often provided milk for premature babies, occasionally mothers of full-term babies, happy to let their milk supply dry up and bottle-feed, were chagrined to find that their child simply did not thrive on any formula due to allergies or other medical complications. In this period mothers of such children often turned to bankless milk distribution arrangements, rendering the mother-to-mother model of the postwar banks still more informal by eliminating the supporting medical institution and avoiding all hierarchy. Parents made appeals for their particular infant, leading to the creation of a temporary and informal donor network to serve that child, often involving the participation of La Leche League members. Such ad hoc practices, linking a local group of mothers with an infant in need, were not new. For example, when a premature infant was born in Prairie Grove, Arkansas, in 1950, whose mother then died, a radio appeal brought forth sufficient donors to keep the child alive, and the local county child welfare director coordinated what the local media called a "milk bank" for that infant, with the local Red Cross chapter helping to transport donors, just as other Red Cross chapters transported blood donors.[95] In an era when bottle-feeding was nearly universal, however, such networks might have to draw upon a much wider geographic area, unless, like Feagans, the parents could find an usually high local concentration of nursing mothers.

In 1968 it was Ricky Madson of Spokane, Washington, whose need for human milk led to newspaper stories across the country, often illustrated with a photograph of Ricky's mother holding him and feeding him donated milk from a bottle. The appeal raised a combination of donations from the Mothers' Milk Bank of San Francisco, La Leche League members in Portland, Oregon, and individual women in Oregon, Washington, Idaho, and British Columbia.[96] The American Red Cross stepped in with transportation assistance, paying for an airlift of bottled milk from the San Francisco bank to Washington.[97] Baby girl Jennifer Weekes of Boise, Idaho, was the subject of similar national concern in 1970; she was fed on milk from mothers in Idaho, California, Utah, Nevada, Arizona, Colorado, Wyoming, and Oregon collected after multiple local press appeals, as well as supplies flown in from the Wilmington Mothers' Milk Bank in Delaware.[98] Such press appeals were evidently quite successful. In 1970 the Stanford University Hospital reportedly received five hundred calls within two hours when it publicized its need for donor milk for two baby boys whose ongoing need for milk was taxing the local supply.[99]

Another local network was established for "Little Linda" from Burlington, Wisconsin, photographed as a beaming infant sitting next to her stuffed rabbit. Wisconsin newspaper readers learned that Linda Holmberg, at age nine months, "is literally being kept alive by the milk of human kindness," largely through the generosity of mothers from the Madison branch of La Leche League. Linda was consuming sixty ounces of donated milk a day and was expected to continue receiving only mothers' milk for another nine months. A Madison La Leche League group leader and mother of four was driving weekly rounds to collect milk from members and then storing it in her freezer until Linda's policeman father drove to Madison to collect the milk.[100]

The mothers and children portrayed in these stories were invariably white, and while the reporters frequently mentioned the parents' financial difficulties in meeting their child's medical expenses, the mothers were photographed in their own homes, looking clean and neatly dressed.[101] These were not the urban poor but nuclear families with stay-at-home mothers and wage-earning father-providers. The fathers were often mentioned by occupation but never photographed. The women who supplied milk through such ad hoc networks were described as part of similar households. Six women were named as ongoing donors to Linda, and the existence of over twenty-five others was mentioned. All were described as married nursing mothers, willing to share their enthusiasm for breastfeeding by helping out in this emergency.[102] The "milk of human kindness" flowed from like to like in a network of mothers with common values, not a charity but a gift, without any payment changing hands.

The milk of human kindness flowed in the formal milk banks as well, as the bankers and donors enacted maternal femininity, gifting their time and their milk. As a Chicago newspaper explained, when the Evanston milk bank was seeking to build up an inventory again in 1973 in response to the demands of fragile quintuplets and triplets in the Chicago area, the bank was searching for "nursing mothers, with more than enough for their own babies' needs, to contribute to the mothers milk bank." In return the bank promised that "mothers who are content that they are giving their babies the best start in life now can have the added satisfaction of helping give other babies a chance for a better life, perhaps even a chance for life itself."[103] The continuation of payments to milk donors by banks elsewhere may not have raised eyebrows because of the strong sense that even mothers who accepted the small checks—which had become less significant as the price paid for milk remained unchanged since the 1930s—also were giving "other babies a chance for a better life," motivated by maternal kindness more than by money.

While there was no controversy in the 1960s and 1970s about payments to milk donors, there was controversy about the relationship between banked milk and the market. Unlike the focus on the paid blood seller during this period, the issue in milk banking was payments from recipients to the banks. In the newspaper reports of ad hoc milk donation networks, the only women in financial need were the mothers of recipient babies, whose families were being stressed by the cost of buying banked milk. In the traditional milk banks that bought and sold milk, the supplying mothers may have been giving gifts and receiving intangible rewards along with the money they received, but the parents who were seeking human milk for their children saw the formal milk banks as selling a commodity that carried a significant price tag. In place of the earlier question, "How much money will it take to motivate milk sellers?," the question now asked was "How are milk banks justified in charging for this gift?"[104]

Like the freestanding community blood banks that emphasized "paid blood" in the 1940s and 1950s, the milk banks faced the problem of obtaining both sufficient funding and sufficient body product to remain in operation. The blood banks found that their solution, a requirement that recipients take responsibility to repay blood debts, caused problems with recipients who then sued them for product liability. Milk banks similarly found that their solution, an emphasis on feminine gifting that helped recruit donors and reduce cash outlay, also angered the population they sought to serve. To charge for banked milk was to commodify a maternal gift, and by implication to commodify motherhood, making "natural" infant food a commercial product.

It was extremely difficult for any bank to sustain the model first promoted in Evanston, in which no donors were paid and no recipients were charged. While milk bankers may have preferred that their bottles be given out free of charge, just like Feagans had received free milk from her neighbors, milk banks, like blood banks, had overhead expenses in salaries and equipment, even with their heavily volunteer labor force. Refrigeration, pasteurization, real estate, and supplies all cost money. While the prewar mothers' milk stations had matter-of-factly charged a per ounce price, which was seen as replacing the salary families would have paid a wet nurse, charging recipient families began to seem increasingly immoral in the 1960s and 1970s. As the landscape of financing medical care changed, with more patients having private insurance that covered blood charges, the position of milk banks on the periphery of medical care caused milk to be excluded from conventional ways of billing and paying for therapies. Instead, as if they were buying cow's milk at the grocery store, families were asked to pay out of pocket. Worse yet, instead of a few pints of blood, babies might need banked milk daily for months, racking up significant debts.

As the difference to patient pocketbooks between banked milk and banked blood widened, the price of banked milk increased in two ways. First, over time the first generation of postwar milk banks found themselves less able to rely on philanthropy to subsidize their operations and began to charge, either for the first time, as the San Francisco Mothers' Milk Bank did in the late 1960s, or at higher rates. By the early 1970s the San Francisco milk bank, which had originally been subsidized and had not charged for milk, was charging 80 cents an ounce, a rate that meant a bill of $120 per week to feed a three-month-old infant. One young mother of a baby suffering from a life-threatening intestinal disorder told the press that she simply could not afford to buy milk at that price. Instead she sought donations from La Leche League members and other women in California, one of whom arrived at her front door in Fresno and pulled two small bottles of still-warm breast milk from her purse, a direct woman-to-woman offering.[105]

Second, as the milk banks became more scarce, those that remained found themselves petitioned for milk by families across the country, necessitating high costs of transport that they largely sought to pass on to the recipients, unless the Red Cross or another organization stepped in to help.

The Wilmington bank, for example, was charging about $225 for monthly shipments of milk to Boise for Jennifer Weekes in 1970.[106] In newspaper accounts about sick children and their desperate families, the nonprofit, volunteer-dependent banks were often referred to as "commercial," and their fees were described as prohibitive for working-class families seeking a long-term feeding solution for a child, creating "economic hardship" of "tragic proportions."[107] An Ohio mother described relying on La Leche League donors until her allergic child was eight months old, and then being "forced" to buy milk from the Wilmington milk bank at a cost of 10 cents an ounce, plus $30 for each shipment.[108]

Unlike blood donors, who could not control the service and processing charges that the recipient of their blood might be asked to pay, milk donors could circumvent the formal institutions of exchange and give a direct, uncompensated gift, mother to mother. With the use of human milk already largely outside of the medical system, informal milk exchange further demedicalized human milk in a way not possible with blood exchange and separated it from the marketplace, two shifts making it more "natural" and less commercial and scientific. As blood banks sought to become more businesslike in the 1970s, transitioning from paid and replacement donors to uncompensated donors and relying on insurance reimbursement for hefty processing payments to balance their books, milk banks reinforced the noncommercial quality of their body product, not just as a matter of production but also in its dispersal.

This retreat from commerce was evident in a reinvention of milk banking during the 1970s, which hastened the disappearance of the paid milk seller and further separated milk banking from any market exchange and from organized medicine. In the year before the San Francisco milk bank closed, it received requests for advice about starting a bank from nine cities.[109] Between 1973 and 1982 the number of milk banks nationwide increased from approximately four to twenty-seven. The new banks included Milk for Life and the Human Milk Bank in New York; Milk Ltd. in Wilmette, Illinois; the Eastern Pennsylvania Milk Bank; the Worcester Milk Bank in Massachusetts; and the Honolulu Milk Bank in Hawaii.[110] While the banks in San Francisco and Wilmington continued to pay donors, these new banks followed the unpaid donor model pioneered in Evanston. This model was motivated by a combination of the peer-to-peer ethos that rendered it unthinkable to offer payment to donors; the lack of resources of the new banks, who had trouble making ends meet even with unpaid donors; and a new emphasis on keeping banked milk noncommercial.

The new banks increased their emphasis on the feminine rewards of milk donation. Lois Arnold, later a milk bank administrator, described her experience of unpaid donation to the Honolulu Milk Bank in the 1980s as "the ultimate in being female." Echoing the La Leche League literature from the 1960s, she claimed breastfeeding one's child created for many women a feeling "of triumph and enormous power." "The body is working the way it should, we are expressing our femininity in the most elemental of ways, and we are investing our whole self in a parenting and nurturing role." Arnold linked this affirmation of her femininity and maternity not just to breastfeeding her own child but to donating milk. Donating allowed her to multiply this "triumphant feeling as a reward when there are no monetary rewards to be had" for mothering one's own child.[111] Arnold's feelings of female empowerment were shared by other milk donors, like Patricia May of Schenectady, New York, who explained in 1982 that she had a "motherly instinct" for the recipient babies, which led her to donate to a local milk bank.[112] The milk of human kindness was a gift that benefited both supplier and recipient, heightening the donor's successful fulfillment of her maternal role.

Just as the context for blood banking had shifted between the immediate postwar period and the 1970s, the context for milk banking had also changed. In the 1950s the "milk runs" of well-to-do Evanston mothers fit the idealized role of the housewife and civic volunteer, but by the time Arnold and May were giving, that role had been sharply questioned. The heightened domesticity of the early Cold War years led not only to the quiet critique of standards of housekeeping and child rearing by the housewives who formed La Leche League but also to a much sharper, broader critique of gender roles by other white, middle-class women, famously given voice by the publication in 1963 of Betty Friedan's *The Feminine Mystique*.[113] The women's liberation movement that followed included a reexamination of the postwar emphasis on full-time mothering. Perhaps most significant for milk banks, the women's health movement, arising out of feminist activism, made a concerted attempt to reconfigure the doctor-patient relationship in order to overthrow the patriarchal hierarchy its theorists identified between male doctors and female patients, particularly with regard to reproductive health care. The participants in the women's health movement

often came out of New Left politics. They broadened their existing suspicion of the military-industrial complex to include what was coming to be
called the "medical-industrial complex" and were engaged in a critique of
industrial capitalism and patriarchy that made their emphasis on lay practice
and collective modes of organization a key political value.[114] The women's
health clinics they formed shared a strong emphasis on lay services, with
women caring for each other as peers, and a rejection of dependence on
medical professionals. This trend included lay midwives, lay abortionists,
and lay birth control counseling, as well as an emphasis on home remedies
and self-care, such as yogurt douches and menstrual extraction.[115]

In this context claiming breast milk as natural and noncommercial acquired political significance. The minority discourse of breastfeeding as a
significant act of mothering that had helped sustain milk banks in the suburbs of the 1950s became radicalized when framed by a critique of patriarchy and male medical control. Breast milk, like breastfeeding, was natural
and woman-controlled, as La Leche League had noted. These characteristics, which in the philosophy of La Leche League had supported a sex-
differentiated household with a stay-at-mother focused on her children,
could also be subversive, and the League struggled to define its attitude toward "liberated" women who wanted both to work outside the home and to
breastfeed.[116] To breastfeed was to challenge the corporate infant formula
manufacturers and the medical-industrial complex. Breast milk required
neither doctors nor corporations to produce. At a time when the countercultural back-to-the-land movement supported buying and eating "natural" foods as a political act, breast milk was the ultimate in homemade
food.[117] And as activists organized a boycott of Nestlé Foods, accusing the
multinational corporation of killing babies in the developing world by marketing infant formula to mothers who lacked access to clean water, breast
milk was also the natural, free antidote to this attempt to make money by
replacing maternal feeding with a consumer product.[118] Even in the American
suburbs, breast milk, like the information and services shared in women's
health clinics, was something one woman could offer to another without a
medical mediator or participation in a commercial market.

Under the influence of these political movements and the shifting ter-
rain of health care delivery, the milk bank was reconceptualized. The bank
had begun as an analogy to a quintessentially capitalist institution, the financial bank. While the analogy had never been strong with respect to

milk banks, they, like the mothers' milk stations, had been institutions within capitalism in which a woman's body product was anonymized and made into something with a market value, that is, into a fungible commodity. In the 1970s and 1980s the milk bank was rethought as an anticapitalist institution of women's power in which an intimate act was extended to strangers to save them from reliance on the cold, impersonal world of the market represented by artificial feeding choices. The gift was superior to the commodity, just as the natural was superior to the commercial.

This new bank was what more traditional milk banks called the "kitchen milk bank."[119] Using the self-help ethos of the women's health movement, women saw a need and filled it, using the resources at hand. Driven by their own experiences with an infant who required breast milk or their belief that breast milk provided advantages to any baby, women collected milk in their own homes for dispersal to other women's babies on request. Like Feagans, these women looked beyond ad hoc collection for one needy baby, such as little Linda, and imagined an ongoing institution to meet needs as they arose. But instead of turning to a civic organization, like the Junior League, and working to create a hospital-based institution, as Feagans had in 1953, these women simply did it themselves. While Feagans had been able to draw on her experience as a Junior Leaguer in organizing community projects, these milk bank founders might draw upon their paid employment experience as lactation consultants, another job category that had gained support from the women's health movement, or as nurses.[120] In the absence of any legal regulation of milk banking, they were free to collect and store milk in their own freezers and pass it out to those who asked, generally without any money changing hands or any medical involvement.

Two women who had experienced their own children being unable to tolerate cow's milk formulas established such a bank in Mt. Vernon, Ohio. The women, one of whom was a registered nurse, took the collected milk to one local hospital for sterilization and to another hospital for a bacterial count, and then stored it in a home freezer.[121] They, not doctors, maintained ownership of this body product and had complete freedom to distribute it. A Kansas City milk bank founded in the early 1980s had a similar origin and location in the founder's basement freezer. Using the term *bank* to bolster her argument that a milk bank was "just as important as a blood bank," the founding mother also separated her organization and the property she was creating from the marketplace: "We don't charge and we don't pay. We don't believe a price can be put on human milk."[122] In a city that had housed a mothers' milk station in the interwar years where milk was bought and sold, she chose a new model for the exchange of bottled milk.[123]

While it is impossible to get an accurate count of kitchen milk banks, which were informal and local, one milk bank administrator has estimated that by the early 1980s there were about thirty milk banks in the United States, mostly kitchen-based, and another twenty-seven in Canada.[124] These numbers may have exceeded the number of milk stations at the height of their medical popularity in the mid-1940s. Despite their use of the *bank* term, these banks were much less like the blood banks than like the Red Cross blood collection system, albeit with a gendered twist, making milk's magic available for all in the way the Red Cross had set out in 1948 to make "blood's magic available for all."[125] Lacking the careful accounting of credits and debits borrowed from financial banks, these home-based systems of exchange were more like a way of passing along secondhand baby clothing and equipment, a traditional means of connecting networks of mothers to save new mothers money and allow surpluses in some homes to be used in others. By the 1970s milk banks were collecting and dispensing bottled milk as gifts from and to mothers, without medical intervention, cash payments, or legal oversight.

Professional Milk without Professional Donors

Initially the trend toward kitchen milk banking went unnoticed by the medical profession, so much so that even while these banks were opening across the country, the Committee of Nutrition of the American Academy of Pediatrics claimed in 1980 that milk banks "stopped operating in North America shortly after World War II."[126] Soon, however, this explosion of body banking outside of medical control came to the attention of both the administrators of the few hospital-based milk banks and the medical profession. They began a campaign against the excessive domestication of this body product, with an attempt to reposition bottled milk and milk banks back within medical control. With the blood bank remaining the dominant model for body product management, doctors, government regulators, and a new generation of milk bankers strove to remake the milk bank in the image of the blood bank.

When the blood supply was under discussion by doctors and in the popular press in the 1970s, it was the paid donor who was suspected of disease. At the same time, with respect to the milk supply, doctors argued that *unpaid* donors gifting milk outside of formal banks were the source of possible infection. In 1973 a doctor affiliated with the San Francisco Mothers' Milk Bank warned the pediatrician treating baby Brian Bedrosian, whose parents were relying on the "milk of human kindness" donated informally by multiple mothers to feed their son, that such unregulated donations from unscreened women could include contaminated milk from failures in collection and storage and diseased milk from an infectious donating mother. Brian's mother told a local reporter that she was faced with either using a freezer full of possibly dangerous milk or paying the costs of banked milk.[127] The safe, "commercial" milk had been purchased from suppliers by the San Francisco bank; the potentially diseased milk was the natural gift. As the medical profession began to reconsider the medical virtues of human milk and to take steps to reassert control over this body product that it had ceded to laywomen activists, doctors and formal milk bank administrators sought to adjust this dichotomy, so that milk as a body product better aligned with blood as a body product. Like blood banks after 1975, milk banks under medical control would become the source of safe, gifted milk. To accomplish this alignment, milk bankers would need both to bolster the medically controlled formal milk banks, popularly disliked as "commercial," and jettison the paid milk seller, just as blood banks had eliminated the professional blood donor.

This project received some support from a return of medical attention to the possibilities of bottled breast milk. In 1975 the federal Office of Maternal and Child Health held a workshop to consider the benefits and risks of feeding human milk to premature infants, generating sufficient enthusiasm for human milk that a follow-up workshop was held in 1976 specifically to discuss possible guidelines for the collection, processing, and storage of human milk for the first time since the American Academy of Pediatrics had issued its standards for mothers' milk bureaus in 1943.[128] The first workshop brought together pediatricians from the Academy with representatives of other medical specialties and from public health. No laywoman from any milk bank was present, nor were any of the female nurses who ran the remaining hospital-based banks. The participating doctors were struck anew by their inability to control and to know human milk the way they controlled and understood cow's milk formulas. "A recurrent theme through-out the workshop was the lack of uniform composition of human milk."[129] Just as doctors had realized fifty years earlier, the participants noted that milk varied from woman to woman and from feeding to feeding by the same woman. Further, the doctors wrestled with the ways collection, pro-cessing, and storage altered milk, creating new categories, just as blood processing and storage had created new bloods. Fresh milk and stored milk were biochemically different, and the method of collection and storage made a difference, as well as the method of processing (some form of heat treatment) if processing was used. It also seemed relevant to categorize dis-embodied stored milk from an infant's own mother differently from disem-bodied milk from another woman.[130]

After considering potential hazards, the participants concluded that it was "safe" to feed human milk to premature infants, with the possible ex-ception of fresh unprocessed milk from a woman other than the baby's bio-logical mother. Questions remained, though, about the nutritional ade-quacy of human milk. More research was needed. Guidelines were also needed. Medically directed standardization would return these institutions to medical control.[131] If all milk banks were medically controlled, a pedia-trician, like the one treating baby Brian, could arrange for the provision of safe banked milk and help patients and their parents avoid unsafe informal milk exchanges.

When the workshop reconvened the following year, specifically to con-sider milk banking guidelines, the participant list had changed only slightly. The male director of pediatrics from the Wilmington (Delaware) Medical Center, site of the only persisting hospital milk bank, attended, but not the female milk bank administrator. Also present were representatives from three of the largest infant formula manufacturers, whose commercial prod-ucts offered uniform composition.[132] The participants recommended that milk bank guidelines require a detailed history of every donor, including the infant's own mother, in order to support "meticulous screening of do-nors" as an "essential feature." They debated the relative merits of "fresh human milk"—which they defined as milk stored in a refrigerator for no more than twenty-four hours without freezing or heat-treating—and fro-zen. They recommended that any milk not used within twenty-four hours be frozen in "small containers impervious to air and with as little head space as possible." Advocating for storage at −20°C or lower for no more than three months, the workshop participants "pointed out that temperatures of 'frost-free' home freezers . . . do not remain consistently" at such temperatures.[133] The checklist they created proposed a model of the milk bank that was hospital-based, supplied by medically selected donors who could express their milk at home, following appropriate instructions for collection and storage, and then transport their milk to the hospital for safety testing, treatment, nutritional analysis, and long-term storage.[134] These guidelines, if given the force of law as regulations, would have eliminated the "kitchen milk bank" and returned milk banking to formal medical control.

Despite this medical consensus, no such guidelines were prepared under the auspices of the government or of organized medicine. Instead, in a move analogous to the formation of the American Association of Blood Banks (AABB), almost a decade later a group of laywomen took matters into their own hands. In 1985 personnel from at least twelve milk banks, representing about two-thirds of all North American milk banks existing at that time, called their own meeting in Washington, D.C. to found a professional organization of milk banks, the Human Milk Banking Association of North America (HMBANA).[135]

A primary goal of the new organization was to develop standard milk bank procedures to ensure the quality and safety of disembodied milk, that is, to generate the guidelines that organized medicine, under the sponsorship of the federal government, had failed to create. Like the AABB blood banks, the HMBANA banks sought to self-regulate. The Association published the first edition of these guidelines in 1990 and has issued multiple revised versions.[136] The AABB initially self-regulated in order to support its blood clearinghouse, to allow better exchange of supplies and more efficient use of a resource, and, later, to quell public worries about blood safety. The milk bankers had a different goal: to move bottled human milk back into the medical mainstream, a goal that would both stabilize demand and help with cash-flow problems.

At its second meeting, in 1986, the new milk banking association created a list of its "top ten" goals. These included persuading the American Academy of Pediatrics to sponsor a third workshop on milk banking and to appoint an ad hoc committee on milk banking, as well as persuading insurance companies to reimburse banked milk as a medical expense.[137] These goals were related. Better acceptance of banked milk by organized medicine would assist the incorporation of this body product into the American health care financing system. Insurance coverage would solve the problem of "commercial milk" by making payment less of a burden on the families of recipients and allowing banked milk to join banked blood as property that was transferred for compensation without being sold, as part of medical services. While the Denver Mothers' Milk Bank, formed in 1985, tried to negate any implication of commerce by stating that it did not charge for milk itself but rather charged a $1 per ounce processing fee, all milk bank administrators in attendance at the meeting discussed funding as a problem. Two administrators made a formal presentation to their colleagues on funding sources, noting that the per ounce fees their banks charged did not cover their costs and that they looked to grants, hospital support, and fundraisers, such as bake sales and stroller-a-thons, to raise needed additional funds.[138]

To gain both medical acceptance and insurance coverage for their product, HMBANA focused on safety and standardization in its first guidelines, creating a product that could serve "the specific needs of individuals for whom human milk is prescribed by physicians" by meeting consistent standards for donor screening, bacterial counts, and processing—that is, by being a fungible commodity.[139] Referencing the AABB blood bank guidelines, HMBANA wrote guidelines requiring donor testing for syphilis, HIV, and hepatitis B, and later expanded them to include hepatitis C and HTLV, in each case following the lead of blood banks, even though there was no evidence that hepatitis B or C was transmissible through breast milk.[140] Human milk as a body product was to mimic blood as a body product. Medical acceptance of banked milk as a therapeutic ordered by prescription would open the door to paying for milk just like paying for banked blood, that is, through insurance. In addition to its published guidelines, the milk banking association also sought medical acceptance for its body product by encouraging research into human milk as a therapeutic and, unsuccessfully, by seeking federal regulation for milk banking.[141]

As part of this process of seeking medical acceptance, the HMBANA banks sought to remake their product into what milk bankers began calling "donor breast milk." Although the government committee meetings in the 1970s had not even considered the paid donor as a threat to bottled milk, by 1985 milk banks had decided to eliminate her. Blood banks kept their product pure by eliminating the paid donor; milk banks would do the same.

Donor breast milk was a phrase intended to place a new emphasis on the unpaid nature of the supply. In its first guidelines for *donor milk banks*, and since, HMBANA has advocated for uncompensated milk donation.[142]

By the late 1980s the fear of disease transmission through body products had escalated significantly, enhancing the spillover effect of the fear of the paid donor from blood to milk. Shortly after the medical community identified the first known case of AIDS transmission through a blood transfusion, the cause of AIDS was identified as the virus now known as HIV, and HIV was found in human milk.[143] In 1985 the first case of transmission of HIV via breast milk was reported in the medical literature.[144] Mothers' milk, for so long seen as safe and full of "kindness" and largely absolved of the turn-of-the-century fears of character transmission, had become, like transfused blood, potentially fatal. Just as the world of blood banking was convulsed by the AIDS epidemic, AIDS caused a cataclysm in the much smaller world of milk banking.[145]

The boom in milk banking of the 1970s and early 1980s came to an abrupt end. Most banks lacked the financial resources necessary to screen milk for HIV and to heat-treat the milk to kill the virus. Instead they ceased operation. By 1986 a Texas mother who had been operating a milk bank out of her home since 1981 had ceased to recruit donors and recipients and was down to providing milk to one child rather than five at one time.[146] The amount of milk dispensed by all U.S. banks dropped 30 percent in three years, from 260,000 ounces in 1986 to 177,000 ounces in 1989.[147] Prescriptions for human milk from formal milk banks dropped as doctors calculated that the risk of HIV transmission outweighed the benefits of using human milk.[148] By the time the new milk banking association published its first guidelines in 1990, about half of the nation's milk banks had closed.[149]

Although it was the informal kitchen milk banks that had never paid donors that had the fewest resources to screen out HIV-positive milk, this crisis only strengthened the rejection of the paid milk seller. In 1996 the executive director of the milk banking association had stern words for women who sought compensation for their milk, detailing arguments differentiating bought milk as inferior:

Purchasing milk could have harmful consequences. First, infants whose mothers would sell their milk might be deprived of their own birthright to that milk. Second, mothers might be tempted to adulterate milk with either cow's milk or water to increase the volume and thus the amount earned by the "donor." Third, milk banks might inadvertently purchase adulterated milk and recipient infants could suffer either from inadequate nutrition or allergic reaction to bovine proteins.[150]

These same concerns, of course, had led to different solutions in the prewar mothers' milk stations. While the organizing doctors assumed that monetary compensation was necessary to maintain a supply, payment underscored the subservience of the lower-class mothers and allowed the stations to impose surveillance to preclude such dangers. Mothers had to donate on site, submitting to inspection of both themselves and their infants. It was the loss of control over donor bodies that created the potential problems. By the 1990s, when only a few banks were open, banks were accepting donations by mail of frozen milk, which precluded even the loose surveillance that banks such as the San Francisco Mothers' Milk Bank had maintained over their paid donors by visiting their homes for milk retrieval. In the same article, the director of the milk banking association explained that the "ideal donor" was the mother of a young, thriving infant who was willing to express her "excess" milk daily, motivated by her gratitude for her own healthy infant and the ability to affirm herself as a mother "by a life-giving action" of donating a "precious gift."[151] The milk of human kindness now could not be sold, or its purity would be threatened.

The consequences of continuing to borrow both the banking metaphor and blood banking practices in order to manage the breast milk supply have included both the intended consequence of increased medical acceptance and the unintended consequence of a new type of milk bank. The increased medical acceptance of banked milk at the turn of twenty-first century is reflected in a new boom in milk banking. Milk banks opened in Indiana, Michigan, Ohio, Texas, and Massachusetts since 2000 have followed HMBANA guidelines and have joined the association as donor milk banks, collecting milk from uncompensated suppliers. By 2013 there were thirteen HMBANA-accredited banks in the United States and four more planned.[152]

The unintended consequence is a for-profit business that takes advantage of the gift/commodity dichotomy and the public acceptance of body banks to maximize shareholder profits. The HMBANA banks, like their predecessor banks and the mothers' milk stations, and like the community blood banks the medical profession prefers, are nonprofit organizations. Rather than treating milk as property tradable in markets solely to satisfy individual preferences, they treat milk as a form of civic property, property that should be distributed to the neediest first, even if compensable by insurance. At the second milk bank association meeting, the member banks discussed how they established ownership of milk and how they decided allocation of milk when potential recipients exceeded the supply. The Denver Mothers' Milk Bank asked all donors to sign a form acknowledging that donor milk became the property of the bank, allowing the bank to make allocation decisions. How banks made those decisions differed. At the University of Kentucky bank, the smallest infant was given priority, while milk bank administrators at the San Jose, California, bank asked the prescribing physician to confer with the bank's medical advisor to decide which baby had priority.[153] In the twenty-first century HMBANA banks have been joined by a network of milk banks established by a for-profit company, Prolacta Bioscience, that follows a market property model, selling bottled milk for the benefit of its shareholders.[154]

Using language very similar to the nonprofit banks, Prolacta on its website and through its network of milk banks with names like Helping Hands and Milkin' Mamas solicits unpaid donations of milk from mothers "to help save the lives of the most fragile infants."[155] This maternal gift is rewarded, like milk donated to HMBANA milk banks, by the knowledge that the donor is nurturing other children as she nurtures her own. What she may not realize, now that milk banks are no longer seen as commercial but as equivalent to blood banks in serving the community by managing gifts of life, is that her donation to Prolacta is processed into patent-protected human milk–based infant formulas and sold to hospitals like infant formulas from other for-profit companies.[156]

This new form of commercial milk leverages the fear of the professional donor and the half-century of the feminine maternal donor providing the milk of human kindness as part of its business model, using donor human milk as the basis of a profitable business. Unlike during the Depression, however, the transformation of milk into therapeutic merchandise is not a "profitable business" for "healthy mothers."[157] In the twenty-first century healthy mothers give without payment as raw material suppliers, and the profitable business is profitable for investors. Prolacta's leadership is obligated by the rules of corporate governance to prioritize shareholder return. Unlike HMBANA milk banks, it is not free to treat the milk it buys as civic property to manage for the public good. Instead Prolacta's business model separates the production of human milk as a body product from its distribution, just as the for-profit blood banks in Kansas City separated blood collection from the medical ethic of providing care to the needy. The hospitals that buy its body product, like the hospitals that bought blood from the Kansas City banks, decide who receives it and how much they pay.

While Prolacta thus follows the model of earlier for-profit body product providers, like commercial blood donor agencies and for-profit blood banks, it is unlike these earlier for-profit organizations in that it does not pay its suppliers. Just like an organ donor, a woman who donates milk to a Prolacta milk bank is providing a needed body product into a supply chain along which all participants except the supplier are reimbursed, many at a profit. While the National Organ Transplant Act prohibits payment to organ donors, such as the family of Anna Kasper, whose face transformed Connie Culp, there is no law that prohibits Prolacta, or any milk bank, from paying for human milk. It is the gift/commodity dichotomy, that inaccurate understanding of body products that resulted from the banking metaphor and the backlash against it, that supports Prolacta's business model. All banked milk is a commodity in that it is a fungible product that can be bought and sold, whether or not the supplier is reimbursed and whether or not it is ultimately bought by the recipient. But because Americans have come to understand body products from uncompensated suppliers as good and safe gifts, and body products from compensated suppliers as bad and unsafe commodities, both the public and the medical community have come to prefer body products in the former category, supplied without compensation. Since the 1970s with respect to blood, and since the 1990s with respect to milk and organs, Americans have been told that the only way to have a safe supply of such body products is for civic-minded Americans to donate them, without payment.

In blood banking the blood supply has been separated into gifted whole blood, collected by nonprofit organizations, and sold plasma, collected by for-profit manufacturers of blood products that continue to use money to incentivize people to submit to plasmapheresis. In milk banking the distaste for commodifying motherhood by offering payment for a natural maternal gift that reflects the feminine kindness of the supplying mother and the desire to keep breast milk separate from commercial products sold in markets has allowed even a for-profit manufacturer such as Prolacta to solicit the raw material for its business as the milk of human kindness, the gift of which is its own reward. The gendered version of the body product seller as "mother" rather than "businessperson" has been so successful that unlike for-profit blood banks or blood product manufacturers, Prolacta has not needed to ask itself "what price would have to be paid for the milk in order to secure it."[158] The answer, it appears, is nothing at all. This situation is startling both in comparison to the history of blood banking, in which equally profit-minded businessmen have always compensated their suppliers, and in comparison to the most prominent body product sourced solely from men: sperm.

6

Buying Dad from the
Sperm Bank

Earn up to $1200.00/month!
Purchase 5 vials and receive 1 year of FREE storage!

—California Cryobank, 2013

"Earn up to $1200.00/month!" This enticing message to potential do-
nors is part of online advertising for one of the largest sperm banks in the
United States in the twenty-first century, California Cryobank. In addition
to locations adjacent to the University of California in Los Angeles and
Stanford University, it has an East Coast office "conveniently located within
walking distance of the Harvard University and MIT campuses."[1] This dollar amount is the first item on the list of reasons to donate.[2] Potential egg
donors visiting the website for the Center for Human Reproduction, a fertility center based in New York City that boasts clients from all across the
world, learn that they might be able to earn $8,000 for an egg retrieval cycle,
although they need to scroll through multiple paragraphs before the monetary figure appears.[3] In the world of assisted reproduction, gamete sales are

big business, and most sperm banks and egg donor agencies are for-profit entities, buying and selling sperm and eggs via the Internet at a brisk rate.[4] Unlike Prolacta Bioscience, the for-profit infant formula manufacturer that uses breast milk as its key ingredient, these body product brokers do not rely on human kindness alone to motivate their suppliers; they offer cash.

Given the strong fear of the professional donor that developed in the United States in the late 1960s, which led first to the elimination of professional blood donors, then to federal laws banning organ sales, and finally, in the 1990s, to the end of eighty years of buying human milk, why are gamete donors paid? The answer lies in the unique history of sperm banks.

If there is a "father of sperm banking," it is Jerome K. Sherman, who has been honored for his pioneering work in cryopreservation that made the frozen sperm bank possible.[5] As a young graduate student in zoology, Sherman developed the first successful protocol to freeze and thaw human semen while preserving the viability of the sperm. With physician collaborators, Sherman created the first frozen sperm bank at the University of Iowa in 1953.[6] While milk stations and blood banks were established by doctors eager to improve the use of body products as medical therapeutics, and therefore motivated to solve supply management problems, the key technology for sperm banking was developed by a scientist, not a doctor. At midcentury doctors were not pushing for a better way of managing a supply of human semen, and consequently it took decades for Sherman's innovation to become a routine part of fertility medicine.

Sperm banks, long spurned by a medical profession that preferred fresh semen for artificial insemination, developed a for-profit business model that focused on recruiting patients as customers rather than on serving doctors. As part of their focus on selling banked sperm to patients, sperm banks have used donor differentiation as a key marketing tool. Milk banks and blood banks replaced the known donor—the wet nurse, living with her employers, and the supplier of a person-to-person blood transfusion, whose body was visible to the patient—with anonymized bottles of fungible product. Sperm banks have done the reverse, replacing anonymous donors, whose personal details were carefully guarded by the doctor, with increasingly individuated body products, providing so many details to prospective parents that they can now choose to match or replace almost any characteristic of the intended parents, from race and religion to coffee-drinking habits.[7] This surfeit of information has eliminated the fear of an unknown and therefore potentially contaminating other and allowed reliance on the professional donor of banked sperm. In an alternative narrative of body banking that has largely ignored the gift/commodity dichotomy, sperm banks have established and maintained the professional semen seller as a taken-for-granted part of assisted reproduction. The legacy of body banking, however, still influences gamete exchange. The gendered differences in egg and sperm selling apparent in the way donors are paid and are encouraged to think about their body product sales track the gendered history of professional donors, reflecting the same differences that separated male blood sellers from female milk sellers and that have permitted Prolacta to obtain donations of its chief raw ingredient.[8]

Human Sperm as a Body Product

Although doctors were not interested in sperm banks for much of the twentieth century, they were interested in human semen. What are commonly called "sperm banks" are, to be more precise, "semen banks," in that they collect, process, and store semen, a body fluid that is composed of only 2 to 5 percent sperm.[9] At the turn of the twentieth century, as some doctors were working to use disembodied blood and milk to treat patients, and in the process creating the gendered "professional donor," other doctors were involved in the same process with human semen. Doctors seeking to cure involuntary childlessness used disembodied semen to perform artificial insemination. This technique involved the use of instruments to place semen in the reproductive tract of the intended mother in order to facilitate conception. Just as there was little demand for a blood supply until blood transfusion became workable, until artificial insemination became reliably successful, there was not much demand for disembodied semen. Further, there was an additional hurdle to be overcome before doctors sought semen donors. Unlike the pioneer users of donated milk and blood, who believed that sickly babies and hemorrhaging patients desperately needed a body product from a third party, doctors treating involuntary childlessness assumed that almost any woman seeking to conceive had a ready supply of semen on hand from her husband. For semen to become a body product subject to exchange between strangers, two steps were needed. Doctors had to learn to make artificial insemination successful by learning more about human reproduction. They also had to decide that some childlessness was best treated by insemination with nonhusband semen, what became known as donor insemination.

Like blood transfusion, artificial insemination, earlier called "artificial impregnation" or "instrumental impregnation," was a possibility that had long fascinated doctors.[10] In 1866 an American doctor with a strong interest in curing infertility, J. Marion Sims, published reports of his fifty-five attempts at the artificial insemination of six women. After his efforts resulted in only one pregnancy, he gave up on the technique.[11] Sims, who had been a member of a wealthy slave-owning family in the antebellum South, controversially honed his expertise in gynecological surgery on slave women.[12] In 1853 he moved north and established a women's hospital in New York City, where his reported cases of artificial insemination involved free white women, both charity and private patients.[13] When he abandoned artificial insemination, he did so in favor of surgical solutions for infertility, which continued to be the treatment preferred by American doctors for decades, despite success rates nearly as poor as those Sims reported for artificial insemination.[14] Other American doctors persisted, however, and one enterprising medical man even sold an "impregnating syringe" by mail order for home use.[15] In 1912 one of the few female gynecologists, Dr. Eliza Mosher, advocated artificial insemination as both "proper" and "peculiarly adapted to women in medicine." She reviewed the medical literature on attempts made since Sims and explained the "technic" she used in her Brooklyn practice.[16] Dr. Frank Davis, an Oklahoma practitioner, published a treatise in 1917 titled *Impotency, Sterility and Artificial Impregnation* in which he explained that he provided couples with instruments and instructions to perform the technique themselves.[17] Artificial insemination got a significant boost into the mainstream of medical discussion when the newly elected president of the American Gynecological Society, Dr. Robert Latou Dickinson, used his inaugural speech in 1920 to urge his fellow gynecologists to study and pool their experience with "artificial impregnation," a technique he had been using since at least 1890.[18]

Dickinson, like his colleagues, was aware that artificial insemination could be performed using nonhusband semen. Since the nineteenth century, the medical profession had recognized that sometimes the only solution was to bring in the "hired man."[19] Such an approach made many, if not most, doctors profoundly uncomfortable. While a few argued, using an early modern understanding of conception, that semen was simply the "trigger" that initiated embryonic development, rendering its source unimportant, most other doctors disagreed.[20] Introducing a third party between husband and wife in order to produce a child went against centuries of effort by the church and the state to establish clear lines of paternity. Sexual intercourse between a married woman and a man not her husband was adultery, a crime and a violation of Judeo-Christian religious teachings. As early as 1897 the Catholic Church went on record as opposing any form of artificial impregnation.[21] Further, adultery by a wife was absolute grounds for divorce in most states at the turn of the twentieth century.[22] Artificial insemination by donor was condemned as simply adultery by doctor.[23] When in 1909 a doctor published an account of a successful donor insemination he claimed to have witnessed while a medical student in 1884, his letter provoked a firestorm of critical letters from his fellow physicians.[24]

When Dickinson gave his presidential address in 1920, he was able to achieve much better success with artificial insemination than Sims, because the medical understanding of ovulation had improved, allowing a more accurate prediction of the optimum time to inseminate. He also knew that Sims and his contemporaries had been wrong in their assumption that virtually all childlessness was caused by female sterility.[25] Dickinson admitted that when he attempted insemination using semen from a husband who lacked ample "quick travelers," he generally failed to produce a conception.[26] If doctors were going to "cure" barren wives married to infertile husbands, no amount of husband sperm would help. Donor insemination was virtually the only medical treatment for male infertility; the only other choice was adoption.[27]

Even Dickinson, who was willing to take provocative stances throughout his career—for example, challenging his colleagues in his presidential address to face up to their exclusion of women from their profession and supporting the campaign to legalize contraception—glossed over insemination by donor. He obliquely mentioned the possibility by suggesting that artificial impregnation had "enormous potentialities of betterment of the race."[28] Not only could donor insemination solve the private grief of a childless couple, but it also permitted the deliberate choice of a biological father. The possibility and consequences of *selection* separated semen as a body product from other body products. Once doctors began to contemplate using donor semen to treat involuntary childlessness, supply became a problem, as it was for other body products. Choosing the source, however, became uniquely daunting, with what Dickinson and his well-educated audience would have understood as high-stakes benefits and risks.

In 1920 Dickinson's audience would have recognized that in referring to racial "betterment," he was suggesting that artificial insemination could be used to support eugenics, the planned breeding of humans to improve desired characteristics. At this time many elite Americans believed that such characteristics abounded in people like themselves, educated, well-to-do people of northern European ancestry and Protestant religious beliefs, but were less common or absent in people from almost anywhere else and those holding different religious beliefs. President Theodore Roosevelt and other prominent men worried about "race suicide," caused by the decreased fertility of white elites. During the 1920s eugenics advocates sought to increase "the birth-rate of the superior" through exhortation to white middle-class women to bear more children and "fitter family" contests and to discourage reproduction by the "unfit," advocating the forced sterilization of those perceived to be defective. When the "fit" reproduced, it was important to avoid racial dilution and promote racial betterment.[29] To achieve these goals, eugenicists supported antimiscegenation laws and immigration restrictions, as well as laws permitting involuntary sterilization.[30]

The eugenic implications of artificial insemination were clear. Any semen sample with sufficient "quick travelers" could induce pregnancy, giving a child to the childless, but to preserve and improve the race, careful donor selection was needed. Dickinson himself believed that all aspects of reproduction, including birth control and sterilization, should be used to improve the race.[31] He advocated sterilization of women who were "idiots, epileptic, hopelessly insane, or incurably criminal."[32] His published articles do not reveal how he incorporated his eugenic beliefs into his practice of artificial insemination, although he almost certainly avoided using men who were "idiots, epileptic, hopelessly insane, or incurably criminal" as semen donors. He, like every practitioner of donor insemination, had to decide which other characteristics he found relevant in donor selection. Eugenics theory also required doctors to think carefully about whom they aided to reproduce by this technique. Davis, the Oklahoma doctor who promoted do-it-yourself artificial insemination for his patients, was the former superintendent of the Oklahoma State Hospital for the Feeble-Minded, an institution designed to isolate the unfit in a state that would authorize the involuntary sterilization of "mental defectives" in 1931. Davis was very concerned with "race suicide"; his book advocating artificial insemination and his private practice were designed to encourage the right sort of Americans to overcome their involuntary childlessness.[33]

Even when American doctors were unwilling to discuss donor insemination openly, the dual possibilities it offered—a cure for involuntary childlessness and a superior race—piqued public discussions in the 1930s. In 1932 British novelist Aldous Huxley published his futuristic vision of humankind, *Brave New World,* which incorporated human breeding by artificial insemination.[34] In 1934 a German physician, Hermann Rohleder, published an English translation of his history of artificial insemination, which described its use in the United States and Europe up to that time, including the possibility of donor insemination.[35] That same year *Scientific American,* a magazine aimed at lay readers, published the results of a survey of two hundred urban physicians. In response to in-person queries by the reporter, eighteen doctors admitted using artificial insemination with donor sperm to impregnate women, with nine succeeding in initiating pregnancy. Based on the survey, the author estimated that perhaps as many as 150 "test tube babies" were being born each year in the United States.[36] The author reported that this technique permitted "babies by scientific selection" and was "one of the most significant eugenic developments in the history of man." He suggested that "racial improvement" might be achieved through organizations in each city with "a staff of selected donors in order that women who want motherhood from selected sources might obtain it. The occasional contribution from a dozen men of excellent mental and physical development and of good stock would provide all the sperm an entire city would require."[37]

Just two months later the subject reached a broader audience when local newspapers across the United States published pictures of Mrs. Lillian Lauricella of Long Island, New York, holding her twin baby girls, described as the "blessed" results of artificial insemination.[38] Lauricella's doctor, Frances Seymour, broke the medical silence and described her success in impregnating multiple women in the previous two years. Americans thus learned that "13 babies in N.Y. have test tube as father."[39] While the Lauricella babies were reportedly the result of artificial insemination using Mr. Lauricella's sperm, it was the "eugenic babies" that sparked the most interest, that is, those conceived using donor sperm.[40] Seymour was a staunch advocate of the eugenic use of donor insemination, working within the National Research Foundation for the Eugenic Alleviation of Sterility, along with her husband and collaborator, the doctor and lawyer Alfred Koerner. According to the report of an Oregon doctor who admired her eugenic principles, Seymour required "a minimum I.Q. of 120 in all receptive mothers, and . . . [required] prospective parents [to] take out an educational insurance policy" to ensure that their eugenic child was appropriately educated.[41] She was also willing to inseminate unmarried "businesswomen" who were not seeking a cure for the sterility of their husbands but simply wanted a eugenic baby. Later she suggested a similar approach to repopulate war-devastated parts of Europe after significant numbers of young men had been killed in World War II.[42]

For the first time a doctor described how she organized professional semen donors. Seymour told the press that she picked the sperm donors from a hospital blood donor registry, confirmed their excellent health, and then had the men hospitalized until the artificial insemination was successful, keeping them available as needed. For their willingness to submit to this period of confinement and to provide semen upon request, she reportedly paid the men $100 to $150.[43] Seymour thus used men already disciplined to professional donation to create a reliable source of semen for purchase. Like the *Scientific American* author and other doctors who would discuss donor insemination in the future, she also borrowed the term *donor* from the professional blood donor to describe the supplier of this new body product who received a cash payment.

Seymour's bold statements and ambitious insemination program made many of her medical colleagues uneasy. Most doctors preferred not to discuss artificial insemination, particularly donor insemination. Immediately after the Lauricella story broke, the New York Academy of Medicine released a statement declaring that artificial insemination was "rarely" a solution to childlessness, and reporters writing follow-up stories found many doctors unwilling to discuss donor insemination, although one Chicago physician admitted to the media that he too assisted married couples with donor insemination.[44] Despite this attempt to dampen public enthusiasm, these news reports of successful pregnancies encouraged childless couples to seek medical help, and the persistent might find a willing practitioner. The husband and wife team Drs. Abraham and Hannah Stone, who staffed the Marriage Consultation Center in New York City, would refer couples to doctors who were willing to perform donor insemination if the husband signed a document indicating his consent to this procedure to preserve the "mutual happiness" of the couple and the "well-being" of his wife.[45] They also made information about the technique available to all Americans through their lay guide to sex and marriage, first published in 1935.[46] A survey taken in 1947 of the membership of the newly established professional organization of fertility specialists, the American Society for the Study of Sterility (today the American Society for Reproductive Medicine), found that more than half of the seventy respondents offered donor insemination.[47]

These American doctors, like Seymour, assumed that it was the responsibility of the doctor to choose and manage semen donors, which they each did privately, through individual transactions. This medically directed approach to donor selection was not required. The German physician Rohleder, who, despite his willingness to publish a history of artificial insemination, was ambivalent about donor insemination, suggested in his book that the husband of the woman to be inseminated find the donor, preferring to avoid physician responsibility for this crucial choice.[48] In the United States, however, those physicians who publicly addressed the topic felt that complete physician control over the donor selection process was crucial.[49]

While it is impossible to know how each American doctor approached donor selection, one New York City practitioner, Dr. Abner Weisman, published guidelines for donor selection first in a clinical manual in 1941 and then in a medical journal in 1942, describing his own practice.[50] His approach was not strictly eugenic but carefully considered the personality and physical characteristics of the donor. After stressing the need for no one but the doctor to know the identity of the donor, and the related obligation of the couple to rely completely on the doctor's selection of a donor, he listed a series of factors for consideration. In order to ensure the safety and efficacy of the procedure, as predicted from donor health and fertility, he preferred to use men who already had children, and he required blood tests and urinalysis, a Wassermann test for syphilis, and a satisfactory health history. As a crude genetic screen to ensure the robustness of the child, the health history should include information about the health and longevity of the donor's relatives. Once these issues were considered, nearly half the factors listed by Weisman had nothing to do with creating a healthy or superior child. Instead they were designed to promote the secrecy of the child's origins. For this reason, the character of the donor mattered. Weisman sought to avoid "sly, shrewd, [and] cunning" men who might seek to circumvent

the wall of secrecy between donor and recipient or to supply substitute semen; instead he looked to recruit "honest, upright and reputable" men who
could follow the rules and maintain the desired noninterest in their biological offspring for the rest of their lives.[51]

Doctors worried about donors and recipients catching glimpses of each
other in the lobby or waiting room or lurking outside the building to watch
people exit, attempting to learn the hidden identity of the other half of this
strange dyad.[52] In the 1950s Dr. Sophia Kleegman, a New York City practitioner who learned artificial insemination from Dickinson, relied on a taxi
service to deliver fresh semen from her donors to her office, keeping the
donor away from the place of insemination altogether.[53] Other doctors recommended directing donors and recipients to separate entrances (usually it
was the donor who was asked to use the back door), prescribing set times
for donors to appear, an hour or two before the intended recipients were
scheduled for insemination, or using a separate location in a large office
building for specimen collection so that no interested person, watching the
doctor's office, could guess the identity of donors.[54]

The physical characteristics of the donor were also important, *not* for
purposes of breeding the fittest child but in order to make it difficult to
detect the donor's contribution to the parent-child relationship. The donor
should match the husband as much as possible in weight, height, coloring, and
blood type, as well as in race and religion. Weisman preferred the "medical
and scientific world" as a source of men with the appropriate humanitarian
impulses and cooperative spirit, although he also expected to compensate
donors.[55] Without the burden of a hospital stay that Seymour had imposed
on her donors, in 1948 semen sellers were reportedly paid $10 per specimen
in Baltimore and $35 per specimen in New York City.[56]

By the 1940s doctors such as Weisman had taken two initial steps to
make semen into a body product. First, they had optimized the use of semen as a medical therapeutic in artificial insemination. Although the technique could be frustrating, with Dickinson reporting in 1920 that his patients frequently gave up before he could perform the recommended six
trials, improved knowledge of human reproduction continued to make it
more reliable. Practitioners in the 1940s claimed success rates from 50 to 85
percent if patients were willing to submit to three to six treatments per
month for several months. Second, besides improving their success rates
with "quick travelers" from any source, doctors were also quietly seeking

and using professional donors, with one estimate of over three thousand donor children born by 1947.[57] But while blood banks were proliferating and milk stations were converting into milk banks, the semen supply remained profoundly unorganized.

In part the lack of organization was due to the limits of knowledge: no one had yet learned how to make semen shelf-stable. Doctors believed that semen needed to be kept at body temperature once produced and should be used within one to two hours.[58] Dickinson described in 1920 how he expected a husband providing semen for the insemination of his wife to produce "a friction specimen about an hour before the appointed time" and to keep it "warm but not hot, under a warm water bag or in a thermos bottle."[59] Semen was not the first such perishable body product, however. The medical profession by midcentury had decades of experience with blood donor registries, designed to facilitate access to screened, cooperative donors who would appear in a timely fashion. Despite the apparent advantages to busy practitioners from such a registry, the doctors who were using semen as a body product resisted such organization. Popular press reports in 1938 that Dr. Ivy Pelzman at Georgetown University School of Medicine was planning or maintaining a sperm donor registry caused Pelzman and Georgetown administrators great distress. Pelzman explained that the press had taken out of context a casual aside he made in a speech to alumni and that what the press called a "gene register" neither existed nor was planned.[60]

Not only did doctors refrain from forming such organizations themselves, as pediatricians and surgeons had done for milk and blood, but they resisted an attempt by an entrepreneurial group in New York City to do so. In 1947 a group of students reportedly made the following announcement: "We offer semen drawn from healthy and investigated professional donors. Suitable types for your patients' specifications. Active specimens guaranteed and delivered daily. Confidential service, office hours 5.30 to 7.00 pm."[61] Rather than supporting such a service, which offered the ability to choose donors to meet "patients' specifications," the doctors successfully urged the City of New York to augment its municipal regulation of body product agencies to include "Regulations Governing the Providing of Seminal Fluid for Artificial Human Insemination." Under the regulations, semen used for artificial insemination needed to be examined and tested, as did the donors—requirements that precluded such a service in the absence of medical supervision.[62] Rather than centralize such supervision, doctors

continued their individualized approach to donor recruitment and management out of the public eye.

While Pelzman's distress about the false report of his planned "fathers
corps" was undoubtedly due in part to his association with a Catholic institution and the strong Catholic stance against artificial insemination of any
type, in 1947 there may have been uneasiness within the broader medical
community about such agencies because of the strong association between
organizing the semen supply and eugenics.[63] By the late 1940s eugenics had
fallen from favor in American public discourse, tainted by the Nazi atroci-
ties performed in the name of racial purity.[64] A large part of the medical
opposition to sperm donor registries, however, probably stemmed from the
same cause that kept most doctors from discussing donor insemination at
all: a firm conviction that the practice of donor insemination needed to remain profoundly secret. Doctors who performed the technique not only
kept quiet themselves but also enjoined their patients from ever mention-
ing, even within their own families, the origins of their donor children.[65]
This emphasis on secrecy was based in part on the belief that making the
knowledge public would harm both the child and the parents psychologi-
cally, as the child might feel rejected, the sterile husband might feel humili-
ated, and the wife might be condemned as an adulteress.[66] Even Seymour,
willing to discuss her use of the technique, believed that if a donor child
were to learn of his or her origins, "an inferiority complex would be set up
with a root that psychoanalysis could not destroy and the child's maladjust-
ment to society would result."[67] But the need for secrecy also stemmed from
the fear of distressing legal consequences if a donor child's true paternity
were known.

While there had been a presumption at common law that a child born to
a married woman was the offspring of her husband, in many states that
presumption could be overcome by proof of a husband's infertility.[68] If such
children were legally the offspring of their donor father, then in the event of
divorce or death, such children would be ineligible for support or inheri-
tance from their supposed father, and the unknown donor father might be
responsible for child support.[69] Still more troubling, a sterile father might
be able to use the child to prove his wife's adultery, thus enabling him to
divorce her. In 1921 a Canadian judge had stated in a divorce case that donor insemination might be grounds for divorce. This case was frequently
discussed by medical practitioners and legal scholars who considered the

legal status of donor insemination, and while there were no published U.S. court decisions on the topic before 1945, the few legal scholars who analyzed the issue were pessimistic about the ability to create a legally accepted family through secret donor insemination.[70]

To doctors who justified their performance of the legally suspect technique based on the belief that they were bringing great happiness to desperate couples, the idea that exposure would destroy the very families they were creating mandated profound and permanent secrecy. Dr. Alan Guttmacher, a staunch advocate of physician-controlled donor insemination and a founding member of the American Society for the Study of Sterility, reiterated in two published articles, "A successful artificial insemination is one of the most satisfying of all medical experiences. It would require a petrified heart not to warm to the scene of a sterile father doting on his two children, who, according to the neighbors, resemble him very closely."[71] Guttmacher also published a response in the medical journal *Human Fertility* to a reprinted legal article concluding that donor insemination had the same legal effect as female adultery resulting in pregnancy. He called this analysis "balderdash" and vigorously defended donor insemination as a practice that ought to produce legitimate children of the intended father.[72] Until the legal status was clear, however, human semen as a body product had to remain completely invisible, sourced from what *Newsweek* called "ghost fathers" who faded away even before the procedure was performed.[73] Guttmacher therefore advocated keeping no records of the procedure.[74]

The continuing legal cloud over donor insemination discouraged not only record keeping by inseminating doctors but also the creation of any institution that would make the practice more visible. By the 1950s, however, the opposition of doctors to sperm registries or banks was also the result of the banking metaphor itself and its association with free market principles through the ongoing blood bank battles. Kleegman, Dickinson's former student who had been practicing donor insemination since 1930, considered donor selection and recruitment an "arduous task." Almost alone among the practitioners who were willing to discuss the technique publicly, Kleegman repeatedly suggested to her fellow practitioners that they adopt a blood bank model for donor management.[75] Like pediatricians seeking a reliable breast milk supply and surgeons wanting to transfuse blood quickly, Kleegman thought outsourcing body product management would allow doctors to serve their patients more efficiently. Her proposals gained no acceptance.

When Kleegman reportedly proposed at the First World Congress of the Society for the Study of Sterility in 1953 that semen banking should be organized like blood banking, with a central, medically controlled institution to manage donors and collection in each city, her colleagues rejected her proposal and the analogy.[76] They knew that blood banks considered each pint of blood to be equivalent, differentiated only by blood group and Rh factor. Blood donor selection screened for health but not for personality or hair color. The doctors believed that every donor insemination needed individual handling and therefore that semen should not be banked like blood, because semen was *not* a fungible fluid. Semen from one healthy donor was never equivalent to the next specimen. Guttmacher had previously urged that "artificial insemination must always be completely individualized, it should never be an assembly-line kind of medical treatment." He reiterated this criticism in 1958, specifically rejecting the idea that the sperm donor should be like the "professional blood donor."[77] The problem was not payment of donors but standardization of donors. The professional semen donor needed to be anonymous but highly particularized. The doctors who used disembodied semen in their practices did not want a readily available supply if such a supply meant giving up the exercise of medical judgment that Weisman had described in his donor selection guidelines. The process of donor selection might be arduous, but most doctors were convinced that its careful performance by educated medical men was what was keeping this controversial practice possible.

At least in theory, the medical profession claimed to agree with Guttmacher and accept an obligation to use professional expertise to select donors. According to a Dutch medical student who conducted an investigation into American artificial insemination practices in the mid-1950s, however, "the donor selection procedure [was] not all that it should be."[78] While most practitioners did consider some or all of the characteristics Weisman had emphasized, especially focusing on the need to find a donor who resembled the husband and was of the same race, according to this foreign observer, the process of donor selection generally came down to finding willing medical students and hospital staff.[79] There was simply not a donor pool sufficient to allow much selection. Like Weisman, who felt that men from the "medical and scientific world" were the best candidates, the inseminating doctors must have comforted themselves with the belief that by using medical men, they were always choosing intelligent, well-educated men who would be likely to report their own health and their family health history accurately and would cooperate with the timing of the procedure. While a sperm registry might increase available inventory, and thus the ability to exercise medical judgment in donor selection, doctors of the 1950s preferred to select donors as they had since the early twentieth century. Sperm remained a body product bought fresh from individually recruited suppliers and used immediately by the collecting doctor. The responsibility of recipients was not to balance a bank account but, once they paid their bill, to do their best to forget that any body product had been used in their treatment.

Banking Sperm

The young Iowa graduate student Jerome Sherman was motivated to disturb this gentlemen's agreement among doctors to keep the sperm supply informal, secret, and under strict medical control because of the public and enthusiastic discussion of sperm among animal husbandry specialists. In the postwar decade this group was openly and eagerly focused on making nonhuman semen into a body product that could be easily accessed on demand, shipped over distances, and preserved for more than a few hours after its initial production. Even in 1920, when explaining his use of artificial insemination to his fellow gynecologists, Dickinson had noted that the effectiveness of the treatment had been proven by "our successful and scientific brother the veterinarian."[80] Artificial insemination in domestic animals was increasingly common after 1930. One early advocate declared, "No other new practice in the field of animal husbandry has been welcomed with so much approval throughout most of the world as artificial insemination."[81] With no legal impediments or social qualms to halt its spread, the practice became widely used in dairy cattle in the United States, and by 1938 an organized institution of cattle semen exchange, "Cooperative Artificial Breeding Association No. 1," was operating.[82]

Animal husbandry specialists were not only performing artificial insemination at ever-increasing rates but also were experimenting with ways to increase the shelf life of semen. In his *Spermatozoa and Sterility,* published in 1941, human artificial insemination practitioner Weisman considered the possibility of what he considered true "test tube babies": babies born using sperm that had been stored in a special solution to extend its extracorporeal life. Just as researchers had been experimenting with "stored blood," he was aware that in animal husbandry, glucose solutions were added to fresh semen, allowing the sperm to survive as long as twenty-one days when refrigerated. Weisman saw no need for what he called "stock semen" in his work with patients, however. His goal was to avoid diluting the sperm and to use a specimen as quickly as possible to maximize the chance of conception.[83] Farmers had no such qualms about stored semen, and by 1945 about 75 percent of American dairy farmers used artificial insemination with "stock semen" to breed their cows. In the twenty years after World War II, the average milk yield per dairy cow in the United States jumped 65 percent, an improvement in the stock attributed to improved breeding through artificial insemination.[84] In a field in which prize stud bulls and horses had long been valued as breeding stock, there was ample motivation to overcome the three-week limitation on the use of collected semen. Semen from a champion animal could retain value long after the animal's death if it could be successfully frozen and later thawed for use, while retaining its ability to initiate a pregnancy.

While research on freezing and thawing sperm had begun in the nineteenth century, prompting an Italian experimenter to speculate about storing frozen human sperm in 1866, it was not until 1949 that a group of British animal husbandry researchers reported that glycerol could successfully protect sperm motility during temperature changes.[85] The use of glycerol was the breakthrough that transformed frozen sperm into a clinically useful substance.[86] One of the British researchers told the press in 1951 that "what is true for animals is also true for men."[87]

At the University of Iowa, Sherman, who had begun his doctoral studies in 1949 and had a part-time job freeze-drying tissue specimens in the urology department, was intrigued by this breakthrough in preserving the vitality of tissue during freezing and thawing. He was not a doctor or a medical student; he was a scientist confronted with a challenge. Could he freeze, or perhaps even freeze-dry, human sperm and preserve viability? Adapting the British methods and using his own semen in after-hours experiments, Sherman was soon able to achieve 67 percent survival rates of human spermatozoa after freezing and thawing, at least as measured by motility.[88] The ultimate test would be insemination.

The University of Iowa medical center, like many up-and-coming medical centers across the United States, had opened a fertility clinic in 1952. During the postwar baby boom, childless couples had become even more eager to seek medical help. The Iowa clinic was staffed by a urologist and a gynecologist and sought to examine the fertility of both husband and wife. If the husband produced low numbers of viable sperm but the wife was apparently fertile, the clinic doctors might offer to perform artificial insemination.[89] Sherman collaborated with the clinic urologist, Raymond Bunge, to collect semen from clinic patients and freeze it for later use in treatment. The clinic gynecologist, William Keettel, performed the inseminations.[90] In 1953 Bunge and Sherman announced the first human conceptions using frozen sperm in *Nature,* the same internationally renowned scientific journal in which the British researchers had announced their glycerol results in nonhuman animals.[91]

Bunge and Sherman immediately recognized that the ability to store sperm indefinitely in a frozen state made sperm banks possible.[92] Not only might this technical innovation ease the problem of donor recruitment and management, but the eugenic possibilities of artificial insemination were now within reach in new ways. In private correspondence, Bunge mused about the "tremendous implications" of the ability to preserve the sperm of "great men," speculating that "perhaps a race of superior individuals can be ultimately expected."[93] As the Iowa newspaper that broke the story screamed in its front-page headline, "fatherhood after death" was now a possibility.[94] Any man's sperm could be used for perhaps years after collection, and with the ability to ship frozen sperm, women and their doctors could request semen from anywhere. Nobel Prize–winning geneticist Hermann Muller, a professor at Indiana University who had been advocating the planned breeding of humans for years, even suggested that men long dead should be preferred as semen donors.[95] Once their lives had ended, it would be easy to assess whether they were in fact superior men whose genes should be preferentially used to create the next generation.

To the surprise and frustration of the Iowa researchers, however, the new technology of cryopreservation was not sufficient to overcome medical resistance to organized supplies of semen. Although freezers at the University of Iowa, the University of Arkansas—where Sherman soon began his long faculty career—and scattered other institutions served as informal sperm banks, these collections were privately maintained and controlled by individual doctors or small groups of doctors for their own patients.[96] The collections were private in that only the collecting doctor(s) had access, and also private in that they were not discussed in print. Unlike the explosion of

Dr. Jerome K. Sherman with his sperm bank at the University of Arkansas, 1969. *Courtesy of the University of Arkansas Medical Sciences Library Historical Research Center, Little Rock, AR.*

blood banking that occurred after Chicago physician Bernard Fantus publicized his new method of managing a hospital blood supply to the medical profession in 1937, or the rapid opening of mothers' milk stations in cities across the United States in the 1920s after Dr. Fritz Talbot wrote up his success in collecting milk for Boston Floating Hospital patients, there was no public embrace of sperm banks by the medical community. The early dream of sperm banks in each city to serve the needs of hard-pressed doctors like Kleegman and of parents seeking "babies by scientific selection" remained unfulfilled.

This medical reluctance reflected the continuing strong social and legal opposition to the practice of donor insemination, opposition that kept Bunge and Sherman from the professional acclaim they had anticipated for their feat of human reproduction. After negative public reaction to the Iowa "test tube babies," the American Society for the Study of Sterility canceled its annual prize competition for the best research paper rather than grant the prize to Bunge and Sherman.[97] Only a few years earlier, in 1949, a Minnesota legislator, believing that the uncertain legal status of the practice should be corrected, had introduced three alternative bills on artificial insemination: one banning the practice, one allowing artificial insemination only of married women with their husband's sperm, and the third allowing both the use of husband sperm and donor sperm. Even though he had not endorsed donor insemination, he found himself and his family the target of "personal abuse" so extreme that reportedly his children could not venture out onto the streets. Lobbying against the bills was "terrific," he noted some years later. He received "hundreds of vicious, anonymous phone calls" and had to hire extra staff to deal with the correspondence.[98] In Ohio in 1955 another legislator proposed to criminalize donor insemination and to declare all children so born to be illegitimate.[99]

None of these bills passed, leaving the legal issues surrounding donor insemination up to individual judges presiding over custody cases involving donor children. By the 1950s these cases were occurring every few years, both in the United States and in Europe. Major U.S. newspapers avidly reported on such cases.[100] One such case began in Chicago in 1954 when Mrs. Mary Doornbos sought to divorce her husband of eight years, George, alleging habitual drunkenness. The contested issue became their son, David. Mary sought sole custody, as well as child support and alimony.[101] Her attorney soon asked the court to rule that David was the child of Mary only and that George had "no claim, right or interest in" the boy because he was conceived through donor insemination.[102] George responded that donor insemination was "without sanction of moral or natural law" and that not only was Mary guilty of adultery, but the physician who performed the technique was also guilty, having "no right to inject semen into [her] body . . . any more than he has the right to take the life of any human being."[103] The dispute, as well as George's insistence that the physician be identified and criminally charged, caught the public's attention from coast to coast.[104] George was subsequently forced to admit that he had been diagnosed as sterile and had consented to the insemination, which occurred in his presence, but the judge still agreed with him. Judge Gibson E. Gorman issued a formal ruling that donor insemination, even with husband consent, was "contrary to public policy and good morals," and therefore David was an illegitimate child and George was not liable for child support.[105] The state of Illinois sought to intervene, fearing that untold thousands of children had just been made bastards and might end up dependent on the public purse, without any man liable for their support, since their donor father could never be identified.[106] After intervention by the state was denied on technical grounds, the legal dispute petered out without a higher court ruling, but the national conversation the case sparked continued.[107]

The plight of parents and children facing the legal destruction of the family they thought they had created elicited both sympathy and condemnation. In 1955 the *Women's Home Companion* ran a generally favorable article about "happy homes" created by donor insemination, and it was reprinted in condensed form in the *Reader's Digest,* further disseminating its message of hope for the infertile.[108] Another popular magazine, *Coronet,* published an anonymous firsthand account of a woman happily parenting two donor children and undergoing donor insemination for a third time.[109] An article in *McCall's,* however, while citing a doctor who claimed that donor insemination was "as legal as a blood transfusion," painted a more ambivalent picture of the process as creating "synthetic triangles" in a "shadowy realm" where men wonder "if they are cuckolds or stepfathers" and donors show "signs of uneasiness."[110]

Other reports were much more harsh. In an exposé published in the *Chicago Tribune* in 1958 entitled "The Tragedy of Test Tube Babies," the journalist warned, "The American public is being duped on one of the most serious and controversial issues in the history of medical science." The article was illustrated by a couple and baby shown in silhouette, hiding in the shadows, with the caption "The possibility of later resentment on the part of the husband is very great." The author claimed, "The preponderance of medical, legal and religious opinion is overwhelmingly against the use of AID [artificial insemination by donor]."[111]

Still, the demand for donor insemination from childless couples increased, as each article in the popular press led some to quietly seek out the technique. New York practitioner Kleegman saw an increase in her practice from eight couples in the eight years between 1931 and 1939 to 150 couples in the five years between 1954 and 1959.[112] After Bunge and Sherman published their results, she corresponded with Bunge, interested in the possibilities of frozen sperm.[113] In 1963 she reiterated her suggestion of sperm banks and attempted to address the concerns of her colleagues by arguing that a sperm bank could be operated by professionals trained in psychology and genetics whose expertise might enhance the delicate task of donor selection.[114]

While Kleegman's colleagues remained indifferent to sperm banks, by the 1960s lay opinion about artificial insemination was continuing to shift, becoming more positive. Sherman was back in the national news after he announced more pregnancies resulting from frozen and thawed sperm, using an improved freezing technique.[115] *Parade Magazine* published an admiring two-page spread in 1964 with a photograph of the "modest, grey-eyed, brilliant" young biologist discussing the possible uses of freezing sperm to allow men to reproduce posthumously or in their advanced years and to permit couples to pick from a catalogue of donors. Sherman suggested that five to ten sperm banks throughout the country could meet the needs of doctors and patients.[116] In 1965 numerous newspapers also published a feature titled "Babies to Order," which explained donor insemination and the potential of sperm banks, quoting from Nobel laureate Muller.[117]

Americans wishing to learn more about artificial insemination after reading one of these popular accounts could for the first time buy a lay guidebook to the practice, published in 1964 by a long-time Pittsburgh practitioner, Dr. Wilfred Finegold. He described donor insemination in great detail as a "desirable means of overcoming childlessness," and his volume was sufficiently successful that the publisher issued a second printing in 1972.[118] By 1976, when Finegold revised the book, he claimed that "in the last decade artificial insemination ha[d] arrived," as shown by the "popularity, approval and demand" for the procedure.[119] A practitioner in Tennessee agreed that patient requests for donor insemination had been "dramatically increasing," making it a "major technique" at the Vanderbilt University infertility clinic by 1975.[120]

Despite this public interest in donor insemination and Kleegman's efforts to create medical support for organizing the sperm supply, medical opposition to frozen sperm banks remained. Sherman, a continual advocate for sperm banks, admitted that as of 1973, the "requisite demand for clinical application" of frozen semen was still lacking.[121] The new technology had been developed and introduced by two men outside of fertility medicine; Sherman was a biologist without a medical degree, and Bunge, although associated with the just-opened university fertility clinic in Iowa, had previously focused his research on cancer of the urinary system and did not continue in reproductive medicine much beyond his collaboration with Sherman, which ended when the younger man graduated.[122] To those actively engaged in donor insemination, frozen sperm was a technology they had neither sought nor particularly wished to use as part of their medical practice. Medically controlled donor selection and sperm banks continued to seem incompatible to doctors.

Despite this lack of clinical demand, the first public sperm banks opened in 1971. These were not the sperm banks that Muller had been envisioning, maintaining an inventory as a centralized public resource to allow easy access to superior donors. They were also not community versions of the existing informal private banks that would allow busy doctors like Kleegman to outsource donor recruitment the way that community blood banks fulfilled that task for hospitals. To certain entrepreneurs, cryopreservation of human semen was a market opportunity, just as for-profit blood banking had been a market opportunity in Kansas City. The first public sperm banks were for-profit enterprises targeting a particular consumer in need of banking services: the soon-to-be infertile man. They were public in comparison to the existing informal sperm banks in that they courted public attention and sought to do business with anyone interested, but they were privately held.

Unlike the organizers of the first milk banks and blood banks, the sperm bankers were not interested in creating a reliable supply of a body product as a medical therapeutic or in any form of buying or gifting semen. Like the technology to freeze and thaw human semen, the first formal institutions to manage human semen as a body product arose alongside, but outside, of fertility medicine. Instead of transforming raw semen into a body product for sale to patients, they sold the service of freezing and storing human sperm as a form of "fertility insurance" for the depositor. This was not insurance of the type blood banks offered, in which members gained a credit from a deposit to be used in case of future need, but rather a safe deposit box model of insurance. In the event of future need, the depositor would withdraw not a credit but the actual semen he had provided earlier, which had remained his personal and private property throughout its custody in the bank. When Genetic Laboratories opened in St. Paul, Minnesota, as the first such bank, its organizers, a scientist with expertise in cryobiology and a local doctor, saw their primary market as men planning vasectomies, who would bank their semen before the sterilization procedure, just in case of a later change of heart, keeping their "fatherhood on ice."[123]

A few years before the British sociologist Richard Titmuss sparked national debate by publishing *The Gift Relationship,* a book that unfavorably compared the American blood supply to the British blood supply, another book had generated significant public interest in the United States: *The Population Bomb*. This book predicted world disaster unless human population growth was radically checked.[124] With a new social and political emphasis on broad access to birth control and the need for small families, vasectomy became an increasingly popular procedure. Although obtaining reliable figures was difficult, as there were no reporting requirements for this simple surgery, some estimated that the number of men undergoing vasectomy jumped from about 100,000 in 1969 to about 750,000 in 1971.[125] Whether the number was 750,000 or three million, as another journalist reported, with increasing concerns about population pressure, more visible advocacy of intentional childlessness as a desirable lifestyle choice, and a sexual revolution condoning nonmarital sexual relations, there was a new trend, "the sterilization of the American male."[126] Businessmen seeking to cash in on this trend through cryobanking pointed out that men facing possible involuntary loss of fertility, by chemotherapy or hazardous employment, could also purchase this new form of fertility insurance by becoming depositors.

Genetic Laboratories and its competitors were not interested in facilitating any exchange of frozen semen, even though they were helping patients make their semen into property capable of being traded in markets. Unlike the doctors who had established milk banks and blood banks so that they could treat disembodied body products as their own property, to be distributed according to their rules and at their discretion, the sperm bank administrators, even those who were doctors, were not interested in any property rights. "We don't want to be in the position of owning semen and controlling who gets it," stated Dr. Robert Ersak, medical director of Genetic Laboratories' Minnesota facility. Men paid $50 a visit to produce a specimen, which might fill as many as twelve vials. Then they paid an annual storage fee to maintain this "insurance."[127]

With favorable news reports, such as one titled "Vasectomies Breed Banks," these new banks courted and received a great deal of publicity, as they sought to create a market for their services.[128] Within a year Genetic Laboratories was storing the sperm of about one hundred men in their suburban Minnesota offices, including sperm from men who lived in New York and California.[129] The company quickly opened four more branches and gained a competitor, Idant Corporation, which opened first in New

York City and then expanded into suburban Baltimore. Idant planned to open in twenty more cities domestically and then open overseas branches.[130] Idant's president was a lawyer turned businessman, although, like Genetic Laboratories, he hired medical directors to supervise his banks. At Idant $180 bought a depositor three deposits and ten years of storage.[131] By 1973 a third commercial bank had opened, the Chartered International Cryobank in San Francisco.[132] Another competitor that opened later in the 1970s, Michigan Sperm Bank, issued a customer brochure with a list of "common questions about semen banks and frozen semen." In the answers, the bank administrators explained that prevasectomy storage was the "most common reason" to preserve semen and detailed the "great lengths" taken to ensure that a specimen was correctly labeled and tracked, so that each depositor was certain to receive his own sperm upon withdrawal.[133] These consumer-oriented banks existed alongside about nine other private sperm banks, located within university medical centers or organized by doctors in private practice. The noncommercial banks primarily stored semen purchased from professional donors for use in donor insemination as a supplement to the collection of fresh semen by doctors, although they also banked semen from husbands for insemination of their wives and occasionally stored semen for their vasectomy patients.[134]

Although their business model was very different from that of blood banking, like milk bankers, the new sperm bankers sought to use the term *bank* and the familiar practices of blood banking to increase public and medical acceptance. In 1976 the sperm bankers formed the American Association of Tissue Banks, which, like the American Association of Blood Banks (AABB) and the later-founded Human Milk Banking Association of North America, assisted the exchange of information among members and promoted self-regulation.[135] Sherman was a charter member of the tissue bank association and drafted the first standards used by the association to certify its members.[136] Despite the ready adoption of the *bank* term, these commercial institutions were unlike either Fantus's original blood bank or the blood banks and milk banks in existence during the 1970s, because of their safe deposit box model of operation. The primary business of these sperm banks was maintaining frozen semen as inalienable property, neither bought nor sold. This approach to body product ownership and exchange was not analogous to the retreat from the market by kitchen milk banks that proudly "didn't charge" and "didn't pay," nor to the promise of Red

Cross blood centers to manage blood as a public resource for all citizens. The sperm banks did not promote donation from those who could give in order to provide for those in need. Rather than seeking to maintain their product on the gift side of the gift/commodity divide, sperm banks sought to preserve frozen sperm as the private property of its supplier, a "personal resource," as blood had been in the minds of AABB members through most of the postwar era. There was no question of "personal responsibility," however, which drove replacement donors to repay blood loans or to purchase a blood credit plan with a donation to provide for future need. Sperm bank deposits came from men who could afford the luxury of keeping their "fatherhood on ice," just in case of a later change of plans.

Underlying all these differences separating the new sperm banks from other body banks was the lack of clinical demand, which made sperm bankers indifferent to the questions of allocation and payment for medical treatment that had significantly shaped blood banks through the postwar decades and was driving kitchen milk bankers to avoid all commercialism. The new public sperm banks were unquestionably capitalist institutions. Created by investors to make a profit, the sperm banks had no need to push the banking metaphor to extremes to maintain inventories through debt collection, nor to resist any appearance of links to the market by emphasizing the naturalness of their product. To the extent that these businesses relied on the banking metaphor at all, it was through their promise to keep stored semen as safe as money in the bank, promising to have viable sperm ready to return to customers on demand.

Although the for-profit sperm banks were created neither to meet clinical demand nor to serve the desire of their founders to treat patients, they did court medical approval. An early sperm bank founder described how he published articles and visited hospitals, being "academic" in his effort to build his business.[137] To get paying customers through the door, he and his banking colleagues looked to urologists who performed vasectomies as a source of referrals. Some urologists were willing to endorse sperm banks and, in doing so, emphasized the aspect of their management they found most like the familiar blood bank: medical control. "A successful semen bank should be kept within the medical community and handled by only the medical profession. Frozen semen should be only given to doctors. Otherwise we may wind up on the road to madness." So said a speaker at the First National Conference on Vasectomy in 1971.[138] The "madness" that worried him was patient-directed use of frozen semen, perhaps in pursuit of eugenic dreams of superior children. He may have been troubled by a news report that one early customer of Genetic Laboratories was a "prominent businessman" who was so committed to maintaining his genetic legacy that he sought to bank his sperm so that in the event his son proved sterile, his son's wife could be inseminated with her father-in-law's sperm.[139] Before the advent of for-profit sperm banks to facilitate such planning, doctors had been able to deny such requests by insisting on their medical prerogative to pick a donor of fresh semen unknown to the intended parents. Fine-gold, in his lay guide to artificial insemination, included a description of how he indignantly denied a similar request in his own practice, in which a man was demanding that Finegold use his sperm to impregnate his daughter-in-law.[140]

Even with limited medical endorsement, the new sperm bankers found that they had overestimated consumer demand. The expected customers from "the sterilization of the American male" did not materialize. Although the director of Genetic Laboratories' New York office boasted two months after opening that "business [was] booming," by 1976, Idant and Genetic Laboratories were closing branches, having lost money.[141] One prominent fertility clinic director estimated that even when cryopreservation was offered for free, fewer than 1 percent of vasectomy patients were interested in the service.[142]

The problem was not only the limited pool of men planning sterilization procedures who were willing to buy "fertility insurance" from a bank but the limits of cryopreservation as a technology. The arrival of the first commercial sperm banks finally prompted a robust discussion of sperm storage in the medical literature. While Sherman continued to insist that thawed frozen sperm was viable, safe, and usable up to ten years after collection, it did not result in pregnancies as often as fresh semen.[143] Since treatment with frozen semen had begun in the 1950s, the pregnancy rates with frozen-thawed sperm had never been as high as with fresh specimens. At the University of Iowa, where doctors had hoped to use the technique to create concentrated samples from subfertile men in order to perform husband insemination more successfully, the clinic quietly dropped the use of frozen sperm by 1954, after finding that conception rates were much lower than with fresh sperm.[144] Twenty years later matters had not improved. Two Philadelphia doctors who maintained a private sperm bank reported increasing loss of viability with length of storage and recommended against relying on sperm banking as insurance in the case of vasectomy.[145] Their work led an author in the new field of vasectomy counseling to conclude in 1977, "Current sperm-banking techniques for man have proved to be undependable."[146] Even the Michigan Sperm Bank warned its potential customers, "There can be no guarantee that you will be able to father a child using the semen you have preserved," in part because the bank "cannot guarantee the long term fertilizing capacity of your frozen semen."[147] The American Public Health Association and the National Medical Committee of Planned Parenthood issued public statements skeptical of sperm banking as a means of preserving one's own fertility.[148] The initial burst of medical enthusiasm among urologists was hard to sustain as they read published reports from their colleagues such one titled "Frozen Sperm—A Poor Form of Fertility Insurance." The article, published in 1979, described two men who were seeking vasectomy reversals, a very difficult procedure, after their frozen sperm, stored for five or six years, failed to produce pregnancy in their new wives, with whom they now wished to have a child.[149]

Even Finegold, who maintained a private frozen sperm bank starting in 1969 in order to increase the options available to his patients, reported that he always preferred fresh sperm.[150] Similarly Dr. Edward Tyler in Los Angeles, who had been greatly interested in the Iowa research in the 1950s and maintained a private sperm bank until his death in 1973, primarily used fresh sperm.[151] A survey of doctors most involved in donor insemination in 1977 found that while about one-third of them used frozen semen sometimes, only about half of those used it more than 10 percent of the time.[152] The demand for frozen sperm as a solution for involuntary childlessness remained very small.

As doctors gained experience with frozen sperm, they encountered a seemingly insoluble problem: like human milk, sperm differed. Only about one-third of semen samples maintained 40 percent or greater sperm motility after freeze-thawing.[153] Men in the other two-thirds of the population, even if fertile by all other measures, were likely to find that their semen sample, once thawed, did not contain sufficient viable sperm for successful insemination. Given this technical limitation, selling semen storage services was not a sustainable business model. With an inadequate pool of potential customers and little medical support, for-profit sperm banks floundered in the 1970s. What saved these businesses was a willingness by sperm bankers to drop their reluctance to own frozen semen and to profit from buying and selling this body product. In the 1980s and 1990s sperm banks took over management of the professional donor from doctors but maintained two crucial aspects of their original business model: profit maximization and prioritization of the patient as the primary customer.

Sperm Banking, the Third Wave

In the last years of the twentieth century, sperm bankers reinvented their business as marketers of goods to women rather than providers of services to men. This new model of the sperm bank, familiar today through institutions that promise $1,200 per month to professional donors and offer online catalogues of potential "dads," treats frozen semen as a highly marketable body product.[154] To take advantage of the "FREE storage" California Cryobank offered would-be parents in 2013, customers needed to buy five vials of frozen semen, at a minimum price of $550 per vial.[155] Each donor is paid up to $100 per specimen, which usually yields multiple vials, a markup by the bank that can reach 2,000 percent.[156] The transition required attitudinal shifts by both bankers and doctors. Without appearing to endorse discredited eugenics approaches, sperm bankers needed to rethink their position regarding the unique possibilities of selection when marketing semen as a body product, as they came to rely on popular eugenic conceptions.[157] Treating semen as inseminating doctors long had—as anonymous but not fungible—could be a way to attract customers. Banked semen could be market property that was less like "carrots or silver teaspoons," mass produced and interchangeable, and more like fine wine or artisanal cheese, a product valued for the unique qualities of its producer, although available in standardized units. Selection is what frozen sperm banks could offer patients, and like farmers willing to pay for prize bull semen, patients might be willing to pay for preferred characteristics.

Implementing this new business model, however, required the cooperation of the same doctors who had been long resistant to sperm banks, the fertility specialists who performed artificial insemination. The medical profession was adamant that donor insemination was a medical procedure, to be performed by doctors. The participation of a doctor did the cultural work of transforming what some considered a variation of adultery into a treatment for infertility, that is, "sin into therapy."[158] As states began to pass laws to legitimate children conceived through donor insemination in the 1960s, these laws enshrined the role of the physician. Georgia, the first state to pass such a law, in 1964, required artificial insemination to be performed by a licensed physician in order for the resulting child to be the legitimate offspring of his or her intended father.[159] In addition, both spouses had to consent in writing to the procedure.[160] The requirement of physician involvement, as well as consent of the husband, was made part of a model state law, the Uniform Parentage Act, in 1973, which included a short provision on artificial insemination as part of its broader rewrite of the law of legitimacy.[161] By the mid-1980s about half of all states had laws legitimating such children.[162] To maintain medical approval of their businesses and to comply with state laws, sperm banks released sperm only on a doctor's order to a doctor's office. As long as patient choice was "madness" and donor selection was the preserve of medical expertise, the banks would be limited to marketing themselves to the unreceptive medical community.

The sperm banks were able to make the transition to direct-to-consumer semen marketing in the 1980s because they were not alone in pressuring individual doctors to relinquish their gatekeeping role in donor selection. Additional pressure came from new and shifting elements within fertility medicine. The AIDS crisis and the discovery of the HIV virus as the cause of this lethal contagious disease profoundly impacted all body banks. The effect on sperm banks, however, was the opposite of the effect on milk banks and blood banks. Instead of depressing demand, AIDS *increased* demand for frozen banked sperm.[163] Medical researchers confirmed the transmission of HIV through artificial insemination in 1985.[164] Although the chance of pregnancy increased by using fresh sperm, so did the chance of infection. Holding frozen sperm in quarantine, followed by retesting of the donor for HIV some months later, greatly diminished the risk that the patient would contract this fatal incurable disease. By 1987 fewer than one-quarter of doctors performing donor insemination relied exclusively on fresh sperm, a sharp decline from the two-thirds who did so in 1977.[165] This switch was made at the urging of the American Fertility Society (formerly the American Society for the Study of Sterility and now the American Society for Reproductive Medicine), which revised its guidelines to recommend against the use of fresh sperm. The best practice became the use of frozen sperm after a six-month quarantine and retesting of the donor.[166] Just as had occurred in milk banking, the proprietors of small, private sperm banks found that the need to manage the risk of HIV transmission increased the costs of banking, causing many doctors to close their banks and rely on commercial banks instead. The total number of banks dropped from one hundred in 1989 to twenty-eight in 2001.[167] After years of medical indifference toward frozen semen as a medical therapeutic, AIDS transformed semen into a body product that *required* a bank for a safe exchange. At the same time Americans were learning to fear banked blood as disease-ridden, the transformation of the sperm bank from long-term self-storage to disease-preventing institution of anonymized body product exchange was completed. At last clinical demand was reaching levels that could sustain sperm banks as businesses.

Patient demand was also continuing to increase. With each passing decade, couples were more likely to seek medical help for fertility problems. In 1974 a self-help organization for involuntarily childless couples, Resolve, began to provide a public forum for information sharing about the formerly highly secret problem of infertility.[168] Even when sperm banks were marketing themselves as storage facilities, newspaper stories often mentioned their potential use in aiding childless couples, and banks found such couples knocking on their doors. Most commercial banks did buy some sperm for use in donor insemination, but with the private medically run banks still in operation, they found few takers.[169]

Some of the increased demand came from a new population seeking to use artificial insemination to create families, a population that found itself largely unable to access banked sperm, as long as banks released semen only to doctors. The same social movements that supported the kitchen milk banks of the 1970s—the women's liberation and women's health movements—also supported a movement by women without male partners to take charge of their reproduction through artificial insemination. As the gay liberation movement emboldened more lesbians to embrace motherhood, laywomen developed and publicized ways of collecting and using sperm for self-insemination. Under the physician-controlled model of artificial insemination, these women had long been excluded from access to the technique. Despite Seymour's use of donor insemination for the benefit of unmarried businesswomen in the 1930s, most doctors refused to inseminate any unmarried woman. In the 1964 edition of his lay guide, Finegold had described an unmarried woman seeking donor insemination as a psychiatric patient, whose "instability" was manifested by her unnatural desire for the procedure.[170] At a time when lesbians were considered unfit mothers of children conceived by any method, their desire to use donor insemination to create alternative families was not recognized as justification for the use of a technique designed to combat biological infertility.[171]

Yet these women persisted. They asked friends for semen donations or used paid go-betweens to arrange anonymous fresh donations.[172] In 1979 two unpartnered women published anonymous first-person accounts of their successful self-inseminations, with practical advice for the benefit of other women, in the pointedly titled *Woman Controlled Conception*.[173] By 1984 the classic text of the women's health movement, *Our Bodies, Ourselves,* had been updated to include a two-page description of donor insemination as a simple technology "we can do . . . at home."[174] Women were told that they could use sperm from any male who was willing to masturbate into a clean jar and, within an hour, to make the semen available to the intended mother, who could self-inseminate using an eye-dropper or a turkey baster. While the do-it-yourself turkey baster approach was cheaper and avoided medical scrutiny, it also exposed these women to risks, even before the advent of the HIV virus. The new laws designed to make the husband of an inseminated woman the father of her child gave no protection to unmarried women, especially if they did not have the insemination performed by a physician. A known donor could assert his parental rights at any time and use the law to destroy the intended father-free family structure. American family law was predicated on assigning a father to each child, who would be responsible for child support.[175] Fully anonymized banked sperm and physician insemination would provide more legal protection to these vulnerable families. Feminist women's health clinics in Vermont and Los Angeles, themselves products of the women's health movement, helped unmarried women access sperm from commercial banks in the 1970s and 1980s. Another group of women's health activists went even further in 1980, founding the only nonprofit sperm bank, the Sperm Bank of Northern California, in order to improve all women's access to donor sperm.[176] By 1985 this new group of potential sperm bank consumers had their own lay guide to artificial insemination, *Having a Baby without a Man,* coauthored by a female gynecologist who had worked with a progressive community health clinic that served many gay and lesbian patients. Along with directions for using fresh semen and for self-inseminating, the book included information about finding sperm banks and the particular legal and emotional issues faced by single women and lesbian couples seeking to conceive a child.[177]

The two main demographic groups seeking donor insemination—involuntarily childless heterosexual couples and women without male partners—both found improved ways of accessing and using banked sperm in the late twentieth-century boom in assisted reproduction. In 1978 heterosexual childless couples wishing for their own biological child found new hope in Louise Brown, a new type of "test tube baby" born in England.[178] She was conceived in the laboratory through the fertilization of her mother's egg by her father's sperm. Her arrival, proof of the possibilities of this new technique, called in vitro fertilization, or IVF, created the medical excitement that Bunge's and Sherman's test tube babies had not. American doctors raced to open private clinics to offer IVF.[179]

In the IVF-induced boom in reproductive services, the long-standing practice of artificial insemination became part of what has become known as the "assisted reproductive industry," in which fertility clinics offer a growing array of assisted reproduction services, including IVF using donor sperm or donor eggs, ovarian stimulation, surrogacy, and embryo donation.[180] With little or no insurance coverage for such treatments in the United States, such baby-making treatments became medical care available to those who could afford to pay, with allocation of fertility medicine largely left to the invisible hand of the market. Americans quickly learned to consider themselves consumers in this market, in which they shopped not only for gametes but for wombs, conception rates, and doctors willing to treat them regardless of many of the criteria fertility specialists had formerly used to screen out patients: marital status, sexual orientation, physical disability, and age.[181] An early lay guide to this new world of reproductive choice was written not by a doctor but by a lawyer, who termed her book "a consumer's guide."[182] Buying sperm became normalized within this larger reproductive services complex, and in the 1980s sperm banks began the transition from selling sperm to doctors to selling sperm directly to would-be parents. In 1987 five out of fifteen banks surveyed sold sperm directly to would-be parents as well as to doctors.[183]

As sperm banks built inventories of frozen semen from which doctors and their fertility patients could choose, they tracked the same sorts of characteristics that doctors long had claimed to use to select the appropriate donor: health history, personality, hair color, eye color, race, and religion.[184]

Selection was the distinguishing feature of semen as a body product, and it was selection that the frozen sperm banks could offer. When fresh semen was being used, it was a struggle to maintain a handful of willing donors, greatly limiting the choice of donor for any recipient. While doctors were anxious to maintain control of the entire process and to limit recipient knowledge of donors to prevent any breach of the veil of secrecy between donor and recipient, surely part of the reason they kept potential parents out of donor choice was the embarrassingly small selection.

Before the 1980s medical use of frozen sperm had not changed the medical role in donor choice. In 1977 over 90 percent of the inseminating doctors surveyed did not allow recipients to select their own donors, regardless of whether they used fresh or frozen sperm.[185] It was the doctors who chose which vials of frozen sperm to purchase from a sperm bank and use for each patient. Since doctors were used to limited options, it is not surprising that a sperm bank director during the 1970s felt that having semen from ten donors on hand was plenty.[186] Once sperm banks transitioned to purchasing semen from donors as the major part of their business, however, a bank could build up a breadth and depth of inventory. Not only could they collect from more individuals, but they could also store enough sperm from one donor to allow for repeated inseminations using the same donor sperm, either for multiple attempts by one couple or for a subsequent pregnancy, producing two full-sibling donor children. By the mid-1980s a California bank had twenty-five donors in its inventory.[187]

With more options, the parameters of donor selection changed. The ability to choose sperm from an inventory large enough to contain more than one medium-size blond made it possible to consider factors beyond the early criteria of safety, efficacy, cooperation, and the roughest type of physical match. Not only did it take longer to review more inventory, but if more than secrecy was at issue and personal preference could come into play, how was the decision best suited to the doctor? Although doctors were the gatekeepers, it was the intended patients who were drawn to the opportunity to make more fine-grained selections. What the doctors did with the new possibilities of selection was up to them. The director of International Cryogenics, the corporate owner of the Michigan Sperm Bank, explained that the organization collected information about donor grade point average, profession, and educational background and that would-be mothers had access "to as much information about the donor as her physician want[ed] her to have."[188] Women in California who wanted more control sought out the Repository for Germinal Choice. This unique sperm bank was explicitly eugenic in its aims, founded in 1980 to promote reproduction using sperm from the most elite men, preferentially Nobel laureates. The Repository was willing to provide the detailed information it collected on its allegedly superior donors to patients.[189] Another early sperm bank director whose more traditional bank predated the transition to direct-to-patient sales explained what he imagined began to happen in doctor's offices: "Physicians really didn't want to study donor catalogs. . . . But as time went along, women probably said, 'Can I see that donor catalog?' And physicians said, Yeah, sure, fifteen less seconds that I have to spend with you. Take it home with you and spend all the time you want."[190] In 1990 a doctor who performed donor inseminations at the University of Michigan fertility clinic explained that the clinic bought sperm from the International Cryogenics bank. Patients were allowed to choose their donor from "about 25 vials" the clinic kept on hand, identified by "physical characteristics, ethnic and racial backgrounds, professional status, blood type, and sometimes hobbies" of the donors.[191]

In response to these changes, by the late 1980s commercial sperm banks began writing their catalogues in ways that were "patient friendly," replacing technical language with language that "somebody with at least a high school education could make sense of."[192] By 2001 three sperm banks offered more than one hundred donors from which to choose, and with patients able to order sperm delivered anywhere in the country, they could access specimens from about 1,200 donors.[193] The possibilities would continue to increase, with individual banks by the early twenty-first century offering hundreds of donors in online catalogues.[194] In these for-profit businesses, sperm banks compete on the basis of making more and more information about donors available—at a price. Would-be parents can buy extended biographies, voice recordings, baby pictures, and handwriting samples to help them pick "the perfect sperm donor."[195] They can choose between attempting to match the intended father or selecting a "dream daddy" who has characteristics they would like to have in a child, whether curly hair or a liking for coffee.[196] Rather than fungible market commodities, the therapeutic merchandise provided by sperm banks are highly individuated frozen semen ampoules tied to a cluster of preferred donor traits. In sperm banking, folk beliefs, expressed as popular eugenics, are not discouraged as unscientific and disruptive to the flows of inventory through body banks but are encouraged through the free market.

The sperm bank undoubtedly has eugenic aspects. For example, certain banks refuse to buy sperm from short men. The height minimum for would-be donors to California Cyrobank is 5′9″.[197] This decision, however, is not driven by the bankers' belief that taller men should preferentially reproduce but by what they perceive market demand to be, as expressed through multiple individual preferences—"short" sperm does not sell.[198] Semen as free market property is subversive of the eugenics that Hermann Muller and Frances Seymour dreamed about in the 1930s when they thought of organized semen supplies as a tool for improving the human race. The for-profit world of sperm banking has facilitated the allocation of banked sperm through the free market, without regard for any normative vision about who should reproduce. Despite those early eugenics dreams, banked sperm is not civic property, created and exchanged for the greater good. Instead it is simply market property, bought from suppliers and sold to users at whatever price the market will bear. Rather than the dominant model used in early blood banks and most milk banks, in which medical gatekeeping ensured the ability of some patients without sufficient means to access a body product, albeit access that depended on a definition of need determined by bank administrators and doctors, sperm bank administrators have stayed out of the determination of need and rely solely on market allocation. The market property model means that those without funds are shut out, but those who can pay can buy this body product, no longer constrained by the medical view of donor insemination as a treatment for carefully selected married couples composed of an infertile man and a fertile woman.

Doctors and patients alike have come to embrace this model of the professional semen donor as a convenient source of a desired commodity that is bought by banks and sold directly to users without medical control over allocation. Like other products, banked sperm can be purchased with a credit card and comes with limited warranties and return policies.[199] Even the nonprofit Sperm Bank of Northern California has adopted similar business practices to serve its goal of making banked semen available to underserved populations and uses market pricing to differentiate its "identity-release" donors. Men who agree that their biological donor children can have access to their identity once the children turn eighteen years old are paid more for their semen, and women pay more for this rarer sperm prod-uct.[200] In a market in which it sometimes appears that "demand knows no limit," sperm as market property has created choice to meet that insatiable demand.[201] Would-be parents have more choices, and more would-be par-ents can enter the market as long as they can pay market prices.

Human Eggs as Market Property

As egg donation became possible in the 1980s, doctors and patients have embraced the professional egg (oocyte) seller alongside the professional se-men seller. She too exists within the assisted reproductive industry in which patients act as consumers and are willing to pay for particularizing infor-mation that allows them to be selective in the gametes they use to build a family. Although eggs are not yet often banked, like sperm banks, for-profit egg donor agencies compete on the basis of providing selection to patient-customers, allowing them to pick and choose among donors and even, at some agencies, to meet them in person before a "match," that is, a directed donation, is finalized.[202] Patients choose, patients pay, and doctors perform. The $8,000 offered to egg donors by the for-profit Center for Human Reproduction is the fee that a donor may receive at the conclusion of one cycle of egg retrieval, although the fee is individually negotiated between each donor-recipient pair. Once accepted into the program and "matched" with a customer, the donor will undergo hormone treatments to synchro-nize her reproductive cycle with the intended mother and to hyperstimulate her ovaries to release many eggs at once. In a carefully timed procedure, the eggs are surgically harvested from the donor, then fertilized in vitro with sperm of the intended parents' choice. Some of the resulting embryos will be implanted into the intended mother or a surrogate. After the egg retrieval, no matter how many eggs are harvested, the donor will receive her contracted-for fee.[203]

Although sperm and egg donors are both portrayed as highly individual-ized to patients and are paid for their body products, there are considerable differences in how egg donation and sperm donation are structured. As so-ciologist Rene Almeling has demonstrated in her study of early twenty-first-century gamete donation, sperm donation is treated by banks and donors alike as a job, for which the donors are paid on a piece-rate, per specimen basis. In contrast, egg donation is framed, even in donor recruitment materials that specify a four-figure compensation fee, as a gift from the donor to the recipient.[204] On the Center for Human Reproduction website page providing information for potential egg donors, the money offered is not visible unless the viewer scrolls down, past the text telling her that donors are "special women" who can help couples experiencing "significant emotional and financial strain" to build a family.[205]

Pointing out that this difference is not mandated by the biological differences in the process of harvesting male and female gametes, Almeling has argued that gamete donation in the early twentieth-first century thus reproduces the gift/commodity dichotomy dominant in American thinking about body products in a gendered way. While both male and female gametes are market commodities within the assisted reproduction industry, sperm donation is framed as a business relationship while egg donation is framed as a gift relationship.[206] A historical perspective demonstrates that this version of the dichotomy in the assisted reproduction industry owes less to fear of the other and the association of taint and disease with cash that helped drive paid donation out of other types of body product exchange, and more to the long history of gendering the professional donor. No matter how the payments are structured and how direct the relationship between donor and recipient, when the donor body is male, he has been a "professional," and when the donor body is female, she has been a nurturing mother or potential mother.

Contemporary egg donation, which is explained by participants as a compensated gift exchange, is very like blood donation in the early decades of the twentieth century, when the professional blood donor first emerged. Like today's donor of fresh eggs, the blood donor needed to be available in coordination with the patient's need. Donating by direct transfusion was a surgical procedure that involved pain and danger to the donor. The fee paid was high, reflecting that danger, and was generally independent of the amount of body product harvested, which was usually unknowable. Recipient and donor met each other, and after a successful transfusion, the recipient might reward the donor with an additional gift to show his or her gratitude.[207] Yet despite the intimacy of the transaction and its nurturing life-saving aspect, and given the option of using either men or women as donors, the medical profession deliberately framed the professional blood donor role as a masculine job. Like egg harvesting is today, direct blood donation could have been framed as a compensated gift, but it was not. The professional blood donor was a "man of business," "providing bread and butter for the family table" by donating as often as forty times a year, fortified by a "scientific diet of blood-producing foods."[208] From the very beginning of the use of body products in medicine, when given a choice, doctors preferred men as paid suppliers and used the rhetoric of employment to recruit them and reinforce the appropriateness of their behavior.

Like egg donor agencies, the doctors who formed mothers' milk stations, on the other hand, had no choice but to recruit female suppliers. As they developed these institutions, they chose to structure milk selling much more like sperm donation today. Expressing milk is a self-manipulation that does not require medical assistance, but like sperm donors, milk sellers were asked to come to the facility to make their donation and then paid by the ounce rather than by the visit. Once recruited, milk sellers, like sperm donors, were encouraged to give regularly. Like sperm donors, milk sellers never saw the recipients of their body product. Yet even though milk selling replaced the recognized occupation of wet nurse, and though such structuring of the donation process as "piece work" fits well in employment rhetoric, once the term *wet nurse* was dropped, milk sellers were never called "professional donors" by doctors or milk station administrators, nor "businesswomen." They were called "mothers." Even milk sales by poor women, who were assumed to be motivated by the cash payment, were framed as a "double charity," as the mother was not only helping "sick babies" but also supporting "herself and [her own] child."[209] Female donation was so tied to maternal gifting that by the time egg donation became a possibility in the late 1980s, payment for milk selling was disappearing altogether, as banked milk became "donor milk," collected only from uncompensated, warmhearted mothers. This gendered construction has been so strong that Prolacta Bioscience has been able to supply its need for breast milk as the raw material for its patented infant formula using unpaid donors, whose reward has been the knowledge that their body product is helping needy babies. Women donate body products for love and men donate for money.

It is not surprising, then, that there has been considerable sociocultural reluctance to leave compensation for egg donation to the market. Some egg donations are uncompensated, unpaid gifts by family or friends. Without compensation, however, there were severe shortages as demand for IVF with donated eggs increased through the 1990s.[210] Just as money was used to establish adequate supplies of blood and milk, money has been used to increase the supply of eggs. While professional blood donors were paid at market rates when blood donation was invasive and dangerous, however, the invasive and dangerous nature of egg donation has been used to justify a cap on fees, as set forth in the American Society for Reproductive Medicine guidelines, to keep women from accepting medical risk due to financial motivation.[211] The professional blood seller could proudly prove his virility and support his family by donating forty times a year, but young women are kept from supporting even themselves, let alone a family, through sales of this feminine body product. Instead grateful recipients are encouraged to send expensive jewelry and thank-you notes to their hospitalized donor while she is recovering from the egg-harvesting procedure.[212] She can accept gratitude but not too much cash.

By choosing to consider gamete donation through a gendered version of the gift/commodity dichotomy, Americans have extended the consequences of the past history of body banking to the different trajectories of the semen donor and the egg donor, even as the sperm bank itself proves the flexibility of the banking metaphor. Contrary to Fantus's original admonition, the sperm bank adopted the term *bank* as a mere metaphor, a quick way of communicating to the public that, as blood banks did with blood, sperm banks collected, stored, and dispensed sperm as a medical product. Unlike the blood bank, however, the sperm bank does not transform a body product into abstract credits that flow from suppliers to recipients without regard to the source of the product. Neither doctors nor patients have "accounts" that they need to keep balanced. The sperm bank is not just like a financial bank. But the sperm bank is also unlike the late twentieth-century milk banks, which rejected not only any need to operate just like financial banks but all possible ties to the market, attempting to treat milk as a good without price, that was neither bought nor sold, even as it was exchanged as a fungible commodity, provided by any mother for the benefit of any baby. In different ways, milk bankers and blood bankers came to embrace the gift/commodity dichotomy during the second half of the twentieth century, replacing an earlier civic property view of their body product as something sold by suppliers and distributed through medically controlled markets, with a view of their product as inalienable market property, kept pure and safe by the elimination of the paid supplier.

In contrast, sperm stored in the for-profit banks that came to dominate the landscape of sperm banking after 1970 has never been civic property. As institutions that arose despite medical demand rather than because of it, sperm banks have always treated sperm as market property. With their increasing success in meeting consumer demand for donor selection and differentiation, their role in reducing the risk of disease transmission, and American willingness to let the market allocate reproductive health services, they have continued to do so. The professional semen seller and the later-arising egg seller, however, who are the suppliers of the market properties these banks distribute, were created by doctors attempting to meet patient demand. These roles replicate the gendered history of body product supply developed over the twentieth century as the for-profit banks and brokers use ways of describing and managing sellers originating with doctors in the 1920s and reinforced for decades thereafter. The power of the banking metaphor is evident even in these for-profit institutions that lack any features of financial banks, as their managers rely on what Americans have learned about body product exchange through the body bank. The history of the sperm bank and the professional gamete donor illustrates an alternative narrative of body banking as well as the continuing power of the banking metaphor to shape the exchange of even unbanked body products, such as human eggs.

Beyond the Body Bank

I am a mother who is health conscious, drug free, non-smoker, non-drinker, physically fit, and educated. . . . Each bag has 5–8 oz. [of frozen milk] depending how much was pumped during that session. . . . I'm selling it for $10/oz.

—"Healthy Breast Milk for Sale," Craigslist, November, 2013

Throughout much of the twentieth century, the body bank was the dominant means of exchanging body products. What came to be called "banks" have had an outsize influence on how we have come to understand such exchanges in law and society. In the twenty-first century, as doctors further expand the frontiers of what can be taken from one body to treat another, they continue to rely on the original body bank, the blood bank, to enable their surgical feats of derring-do. And as face transplant recipient Connie Culp smiles with what was formerly Anna Kasper's mouth, one of increasing numbers who are learning to use new faces and new limbs transferred from strangers, the body bank undergirds not only the demanding surgical procedures but the way that Culp, Kasper's family, and those of us who follow news reports think about transplantation and body product donation.[1] The bank, more than a mere metaphor, shapes our assumptions about how such property transfer occurs, even as body product exchange moves beyond the bank.

Just as in the first decades of the twentieth century, it is the body products that medical science has not yet learned how to store and bank, such as eggs, faces, hands, and lungs, that are at the cutting edge of medical care. History, however, is not so much repeating itself as continuing in a trajectory established by the first transformations of body parts into body products and the first attempts to rationalize body product supplies. During the first decades of body product exchange and through the earliest formal institutions for such exchange, mothers' milk stations and blood donor registries, we learned to accept and rely upon the "professional donor." That oxymoronic and usually masculine character blended professionalism, with its implication of service to society, with both the language of uncompensated gifting ("donor") and payment. Americans retained the ambivalent attitude about cash and body products expressed in the phrase *professional donor,* as we, guided by Dr. Bernard Fantus and his colleagues seeking to manage hospital blood supplies, learned to think about body products like money in a financial bank. Body banks were more than a mere metaphor in their similarity to financial institutions, but they were also banks that took donations. Blood could be accounted for just like silver teaspoons, but it also could be a precious and personal gift of life. That ambivalence has continued to the present, filtered through nearly a century of experience with body banking.

Since the 1940s, as body banks became omnipresent in American medicine, legal and popular attitudes toward body product exchange have been mixed and changing. They reflect a medical profession unable to resolve its own conflicting commitments to health care access and to individual responsibility to pay for medical services. The peacetime Red Cross blood program, treating blood as a public resource, was initially welcomed by organized medicine. As the American Medical Association grew more hostile toward the Red Cross program, the American Association of Blood Banks told the public that the program would undermine capitalism and destroy our blood supply and pushed for a "paid blood" system in which the similarity between financial banks and blood banks was emphasized. The legal conclusion that pints of paid blood were commercial goods, like teaspoons or cars, caused a medically led backlash against a market-based approach, creating blood shield laws that removed the buying and selling of banked blood—and ultimately other body products—from the reach of commercial law. In the early twenty-first century, many states have expanded their blood shield laws to include other banked products, such as sperm.[2] The same retreat from the market led to the downfall of the professional donor, who became stigmatized as a source of disease, disguising a continuing fear of the other as a body product supplier. It also led to a legal division between selling and gifting the most significant new body products of the late twentieth century, organs for transplant, through a federal law banning selling by suppliers. Ironically Fantus's metaphor of treating body products like money in the bank ultimately led to a strict separation between cash and many body products, including blood and organs, as a means of resolving that original ambivalence about mixing commerce, bodies, and medicine.

The history of body banking, however, also reveals other ways in which that ambivalence has been mitigated, if perhaps never fully resolved. In the shadow of medical indifference, late twentieth-century milk banks and sperm banks demonstrated the elasticity and power of the banking metaphor by taking opposite paths to become part of contemporary health care. For decades milk banks attempted to deny the link between their body product and the market implied by the term *bank*, instead considering banked milk a feminine gift that offered a natural alternative to commercial infant formulas, even if supplying mothers were paid by the ounce. As milk banks mimicked blood banks by eliminating the paid donor, women were told that their compensation lay in affirmation of their maternity, a gendered reward threatened when mothers sought payment for their milk. Sperm banks, slow to develop even after the technology of freezing and thawing sperm was first created, have become successful for-profit businesses relying on the masculine professional donor as a supplier, embracing the free market to allocate their inventory of frozen, and therefore safer AIDS-free semen among patient-consumers.

The end result of these choices in body product banking is that body products now exist in two very distinct legal regimes. Organs, including bone marrow, are subject to a strict federal law prohibiting sales and establishing a particular procurement and distribution system, the National Organ Transplantation Act.[3] They are to be given for love but not for money. In contrast, gametes and breast milk can be bought and sold freely in almost all states without any legal regulation at all.[4] Blood, although subject to stricter federal controls since the AIDS crisis and exempted from commercial law through state blood shield statutes, can still be legally sold, although whole blood is usually collected from uncompensated donors, and only blood plasma is regularly purchased.[5] Body products are either pure market property, able to be traded in markets without medical or legal oversight, or legally inalienable property, considered appropriate only for gift exchange. The gift/commodity dichotomy is entrenched in law, with the only options being free market sales or unpaid donations.

New Frontiers

The current limited approach to body product exchange is in contrast to a wide variety of exchanges used by body bankers over the past century. Body banks have relied on both love and money, in differing proportions, depending on the time period and the body product at issue. While assuming a relationship among bodies, markets, and money, the banking metaphor has proved flexible in implementation. Further, as is readily apparent in the twenty-first century, body banks are only one way to exchange body products. Before there were body banks, body products were bought and sold, and also given out of personal love and civic-minded altruism. Even with body products that are bankable, such as milk and sperm, such extrabank exchanges persisted throughout the twentieth century, and they continue to the present.

Even as formal milk banks relying on uncompensated donors are opening in more locations across the United States, there are websites devoted to "milksharing" on which parents and lactating women can arrange direct exchanges of expressed breast milk, versions of the ad hoc milk donation networks for the Internet age.[6] Entrepreneurial women can use Craigslist, the online version of newspaper advertisements, to advertise their high-quality breast milk, or rely on Only the Breast, an online "community for moms to sell, buy and donate natural breast milk."[7] One nineteen-year-old college student earned enough from milk sales at $2 per ounce through the community to buy a laptop and her wedding dress, and a blogger estimated in 2013 that selling excess breast milk might allow a woman to earn $21,000 over the course of a year.[8] Women can choose to consider excess breast milk a handy way to earn extra money, as well as a precious maternal gift. Parents with cash, who lack a maternal source of breast milk, can obtain breast milk without any medical intervention, even if their infant is not premature or otherwise medically needy. If parents prefer to meet their milk seller and have more opportunity to keep her under surveillance, wet nursing is also making a comeback.[9]

Similarly formal sperm banks coexist alongside a secondary market in "leftover" sperm. Parents or would-be parents seek to recoup the high cost of gametes by selling unneeded vials to other would-be parents. The secondary market offers both a chance to buy gametes for less than sperm bank prices and a way of accessing sperm supplied by a particular donor, whose inventory is sold out at the bank.[10] Parents often value the option of having donor children who share the same biological father. Sperm, like breast milk, can also be donated, person to person, without payment. Even though would-be parents seeking to parent outside of heterosexual marriage now have improved access to banked gametes, some continue to make their own arrangements of directed sperm donation, which may or may not involve payment to the donor. Such arrangements can allow women to use gay donors (excluded from accredited sperm banks) or to include negotiated donor involvement in the planned child's life.[11]

Such person-to-person direct exchanges also occur in organ donation. In addition to the illegal black market and an international gray market that circumvent the American legal prohibition of organ sales, there are legally permissible person-to-person organ donations arranged outside of organ procurement agencies, as desperate patients take to the Internet to search for a stranger willing to become a living kidney donor.[12] While federal law forbids people from allowing their organs to be harvested for money or from accepting money in exchange for a promise of organs after death, uncompensated submission to living kidney donation is permissible. Patients lingering on the organ procurement lists set up Facebook pages, seeking a way to jump the queue by enticing a directed donor through the social media network.[13] Living Donors Online facilitates such Internet searches by providing message boards for those seeking organs and those contemplating living donation to a needy stranger.[14] In the black market it is those with the most money who can buy organs; in the world of uncompensated living donors, organs go to those who are Internet-savvy, can tell a compelling story, attract the most Facebook "likes," or perhaps are just lucky.

The desperately ill, like reproductive consumers and mothers committed to breast milk as the best infant food, are finding informal and extralegal ways to treat body products as personal property and as commodities. Both banked and nonbanked body products are being traded briskly, both through formal organizations and in private exchanges. Suppliers can choose compensated and uncompensated ways of transferring their gifts of life. In many cases, whether or not compensation to the seller is involved, the allocation of these valuable commodities is deeply flawed. The challenge for the twenty-first century is not how to define or reform the body bank, the medical frontier of the previous era, but rather how to move beyond the body bank and the legal straitjacket that is its legacy to focus on the ends of body product exchange rather than the means. We need to think about how to appropriately regulate body products as a type of property currently exchanged in many ways for many purposes.

History Lessons

Meeting this challenge is a complex task, and sociologists, legal scholars, and other theorists have already begun to set aside the fruitless debate between sales and gifts and move beyond the legal division of "service" or "product" to contemplate alternatives.[15] Understanding the history of body products through the body bank offers a few simple lessons to inform this ongoing work. Each of the following propositions is grounded in historical experience, yet because of the gift/commodity dichotomy has been either rejected or ignored in American law, medicine, and society. It is time to examine them anew. Body products are property. Body products are appropriately civic property. Markets in body products can be harnessed to serve communal goals. The professional donor can be a safe and respected supplier of body products.

In the first decades of the twentieth century, the claim that body products were property once taken from a supplying body and stabilized into a storable form went without saying. Without recourse to legal niceties, doctors simply treated these new therapeutics as property, that is, as material objects they had the right to buy, sell, distribute, and otherwise control. Medical ownership was assumed, as was the right of the supplier to receive money in exchange for the act of disembodiment, an act that created this new piece of property. Dr. Bertram Bernheim, buying blood from "rovers" in the boardinghouses of Baltimore for transfusion into his civilian patients, or using blood bled from lightly wounded troops in World War I, never doubted that the disembodied blood was his to control.[16] This assumption was shared by suppliers, such as the mothers who sold their milk to stations in the 1930s and gave their excess milk to the Evanston bank in the 1950s. Their gift or sale was the transfer of ownership.

In the absence of legal regulation, Americans today continue to treat disembodied body products as the property, first, of suppliers, who assume their right to sell or give them away, and then of the subsequent possessor, who has the right to use, resell, or donate such products. Just as nursing mothers assume they can sell their milk at whatever price the market will bear, and families of the desperately ill assume others can give their loved one a kidney, we treat body products as property and assign initial property rights to the supplying body. Having purchased the body product or received it as a gift, the possessor, whether a sperm bank selling vials of sperm or a patient looking to recoup some of her out-of-pocket costs for IVF, assumes that he or she has full ownership rights that will allow him or her to use the product, destroy it, or transfer possession of it.

One perverse result of the blood bank battles and the resulting market backlash, however, has been a line of legal reasoning that denies property interests in body products. The blood shield statutes of the 1960s began this process by declaring banked blood not a "good" but part of a service. Because it could not be a market property without subjecting the medical profession to product liability doctrines, it was not property at all. The increasing tendency in American law over the twentieth century to understand all property as market property has inclined courts to deny property status to body products. Only by declaring them nonproperty, it is assumed, can body products be protected from the invisible hand of the market. This protection is needed to prevent links between bodies and cash, rendered suspect by the late twentieth-century fear of the professional donor and presumed to threaten human dignity by putting price tags on body parts.[17] This legal denial of what doctors and patients involved in body product exchange had long assumed has neither prevented such links, nor price tags on body parts. What it has done is to promote a loss of supplier control over disembodied body products as well as over any profits that come from their commercialization.

A disembodied body product, as nonproperty, can become trash or an unclaimed thing, *res nullius* in the law, and therefore available to be picked up and claimed by a medical researcher who sees value in it. Following this reasoning, the Supreme Court of California in 1990 confirmed that a patented cell line developed from a patient's tissue belonged to the doctor who chose to experiment with the tissue rather than to the patient who unwittingly and repeatedly supplied blood and other samples for the doctor's commercializable discovery.[18] The uncompensated taking of Mr. John Moore's body products was not a theft, because they were not his property. By denying property status to the excised tissue, the court denied Moore the legal power to exclude others from its use without his permission. This denial of property rights in order to protect the pricelessness of the human body resulted in the transfer of any and all resulting profits to those who used the nonproperty without any obligation to compensate the supplying body.[19] Under this same reasoning, medical schools that are the recipient of gifted cadavers for research purposes are free to resell the bodies, in whole or in parts, although under the Uniform Anatomical Gift Act, a premortem decision to sell one's body is not legally enforceable.[20] The family of Anna Kasper, who donated her body to be used as a source of body products, was precluded from compensation. If Kasper had made the decision before death to become an organ donor, she also could receive nothing. Yet each other participant in the chain of effort that led to Connie Culp's new face was entitled to reimbursement—the hospital, the doctors, the physical therapists, even the staff of any nonprofit organ procurement organization involved in the multiple donations from Kasper's body. All are making a living, and in the case of transplant surgeons a very good living, from their work facilitating body part exchanges, and Culp, or her insurance company, is expected to pay them. Only the supplier of the body products is left uncompensated, prevented by law from profiting from the act of creating what becomes valuable property.

There are good reasons for this prohibition. We do not want families of the recently deceased to feel pressured by financial need to make a transfer they otherwise would not. We also do not want living donors to damage their own health by selling body products.[21] There are other ways to achieve these goals, however, than by excluding body products in the possession of their suppliers from the legal category of property. In contrast to this developing set of legal doctrines, the history of body banks is a long history of treating body products as property. It provides a reminder that arguing about whether body products should be included within the legal definition of property separates law from the lived reality of body product exchange. This history also demonstrates that treating body products as property does

not inevitably lead to the creation of unrestrained markets or to the devalu-
ation and exploitation of body product suppliers. The prevalence of the
professional donor in the 1930s did not deter the philanthropic from enrolling in blood donor leagues, promising to give without pay for those who
could not afford professional donors. While offering money for blood at
midcentury did attract the economically marginal and for-profit middle-
men who may have taken advantage of some donors, it also attracted car-
loads of rural Minnesotans, who chose to sell their blood to buy a new
church organ. The suppliers chose their own interpretation of their actions rather than inevitably falling into a scenario of exploitation. For some,
blood selling was seen as preferable and more protective of a sense of dignity and self-worth than panhandling for survival. For the church members, blood selling became a way of contributing to their community. Paid
blood donors remained subjects of commodification—choosing to commodify a part of themselves by allowing the harvesting of a body product—
rather than objects of commodification, becoming themselves a form of
property.[22]

Refusing to incorporate material sourced from the human body within
property law is a crude and ineffective bulwark against possible harms that
are real but not inevitable. It is also important to learn from this history,
however, that the original solution that helped militate against the possible
harm of supplier exploitation during the first decades of body banking is no
longer reliable. In the first years after disembodied milk, blood, and semen
were created as body products, the medical profession was able to exercise
tight control over these new body products, monitoring sellers and the distribution of such products in a way that provided at least rough assurance
that such exchanges were protective of the human dignity of both suppliers
and recipients. That control no longer exists. In the twenty-first century, the
laws of property should be used as a starting point from which to regulate
the various forms of body property and their market exchanges, taking into
account not only the medical goals for such therapeutics but the perceptions of suppliers and users.

Such regulation should be based on the founding assumption of body
banks: that body products, as property, are civic property. They were created as property to be used instrumentally to promote a particular form of
social order that involves communal considerations beyond the sum of individual preferences. The impulse to deny property rights in body products

has stemmed from the limiting belief that market property is the only possible type of property. The history of body banks underscores the strength of this belief, part of the general dominance of market talk in American law and society in the second half of the twentieth century. The term *bank* helped to create and maintain this perspective. Yet the history of body banks also demonstrates that the primary users of body products, medical professionals, long maintained a separation between general market goods and the therapeutic merchandise they sought in order to provide the most efficient and effective treatment for patients.

Even when the administrator of the Blood Bank of Hawaii explained that her institution managed blood just like "silver teaspoons or carrots," and Bernice Hemphill, the "mother of blood banking," labored to increase the ways blood banking mimicked financial banking, these participants also maintained a sense that their product was different.[23] Yes, donors might sell their blood to the bank, and patients who received blood needed to take responsibility and pay for it. But the blood bank was *not* just another business. According to Hemphill, "it rate[d] up there with fire, police, trauma service," that is, with organizations designed to pool resources to provide a community benefit, available to whoever needed help, whenever they needed help.[24] Community blood banks, like Hemphill's Irwin Memorial in San Francisco, were nonprofit organizations managing their inventory with the goal of maintaining stocks of all blood types in each local hospital so that any patient could receive a blood transfusion whenever his or her doctor believed it advisable. Unlike purveyors of spoons or carrots, they were not trying to sell as many units as possible or to maximize the sales prices but to meet local needs at the lowest possible cost.

The idea that health care should be allocated to those who need it rather than only, or preferentially, those who can buy it remains a powerful strand within the American medical community, although this normative vision, and the best means of implementing it, remain highly contested in American politics.[25] Taking a civic property approach to body product exchange requires considering the use and allocation of body products, in addition to payments and pricing. Fantus's initial goal in establishing the first blood bank in 1937 is a useful, if perhaps insufficient, starting point. He was trying to create a communal resource of safe stored blood, available at reasonable prices to all in need. Doctors who came before and after him accepted allowing suppliers to profit from body product sales, and even tolerated for-profit intermediaries, so long as profit-making did not become profiteering at the expense of safety and availability.

The current legal regime, with its focus on avoiding paid exchanges, may avoid some, although not all, types of profiteering, but it has not met adequate levels of safety and availability. The National Organ Transplantation Act has helped keep organs scarce, and created injustices in organ allocation.[26] In addition, the blood shield laws removed legal incentives for blood bankers to guard against dangers in the blood supply. The same blood shield laws that kept blood banks and hospitals from liability for hepatitis transmission in the 1960s and 1970s shielded the blood supply management system from liability for HIV infections, arguably slowing the adoption of steps to reduce the risk of transfusion-acquired AIDS.[27] Treating body products as a form of civic property that might also be market commodities refocuses attention from the means of exchange, paid or unpaid, to its ends. From a civic property perspective, the ends include not just the satisfaction of each individual supplier and recipient but also the communal effect of many such exchanges. The law of product liability is one way of regulating individual market exchanges to serve the communal goal of safe body products. Product liability law is based upon the utilitarian principle that requiring those most able to avoid harm to compensate individual victims for serious harms will, over time, decrease the number of such victims by encouraging all reasonable efforts to prevent such harms from occurring again. Allowing a harmed recipient of bad blood to sue for a defective product thus promotes the social good of safer blood, which might outweigh the social ill of treating either hospitals or blood sellers as manufacturers of a product.

Treating body products as civic property requires thinking about the effects on patients rather than single-mindedly focusing on the compensation received by sellers. The civic property tradition also acknowledges that markets can be harnessed in support of the normative vision such property is intended to promote. This idea is not new in American thought, and indeed is present even in the philosophy of the most ardent free market advocates, insofar as they believe that the invisible hand of the market will create the greatest good for the greatest number. The choice is not between market and nonmarket but between a free market and the almost infinite variations on a free market that are possible. Reviewing the history of body banking from a civic property perspective reveals repeated examples of market exchanges used to increase the availability and desired qualities of body products. On the supply side, doctors and the organizations they created used money to induce suppliers to allow harvesting of their body products in order to ensure adequate supplies. When Dr. Raymond Hoobler experimented with how much money he needed to offer new mothers in New York City for their breast milk, he was creating a new market. He and others experimented with per ounce and per visit payments.[28] In the world of blood transfusions, doctors also tried different pricing schemes in addition to payments based on volume or per bleeding, offering reimbursement of taxi fare to get donors to the bedside quickly and, in the days before donor registries, offering payments to those who traveled to the hospital and had their blood typed but were found unsuitable as donors.[29] In cities across the United States, payments for pain and risk, for time and inconvenience, and for the body product itself were offered and accepted in multiple individual exchanges. These exchanges created local markets in which prices stabilized at levels donors were willing to accept and at which doctors believed gave them access to the quantity, quality, and ready availability of a body product they needed.

In addition to ensuring a supply, payments for body products also bought medical control. Paid blood donors in New York City were required by municipal regulation to have Wassermann tests every six months for syphilis and to submit to physical inspection. When Blood for Britain began, doctors realized that unpaid donors would not accept a similar level of medical surveillance and relied instead on information provided by donors that they were free from syphilis. History repeated itself in the early days of the AIDS crisis, when friends and family of a patient might be asked to provide a directed donation to avoid a transfusion of possibly unsafe banked blood—but might be unwilling to acknowledge their own risky behavior that made their blood potentially hazardous.[30] Twenty-first-century milk bankers fear that payment to milk donors would encourage mothers to dilute their offerings, but payment in the twentieth century was contingent on expressing the milk under the scrutiny of a nurse and other donors, making such deception impossible. Twenty-first-century sperm banks use payment to induce donors to produce semen on site, ensuring its rapid processing and the inability of one man to sell another man's sperm. Payment is also conditioned on producing an acceptable sample, that is, with a minimum concentration of viable sperm. Such production is possible only through sexual abstinence, so sperm banks are using donor payments to encourage donors to exercise the self-discipline needed to maintain body product quality, leverage that milk banks have forgone.[31]

Markets have also been used to manage the demand side in the service of communal goals. Early milk station administrators used a sliding scale in their sale of bottled breast milk to parents in order to allocate milk to the neediest babies, without regard to ability to pay. They charged some patients over market rates in order to charge others under market rates. They manipulated individual transactions in order to keep the average price as low as possible. In the competition among for-profit sperm banks for customers, pricing strategies have been used to improve consumer choice. In addition to competing on quality and per vial price, sperm banks have developed differentiated pricing structures that allow parents to buy additional information about their donor child's biological father, from voice recordings to baby pictures. There are thus more options available to would-be parents to glean information about a sperm donor and at least some ability for them to purchase sperm at different price points.

The variability in the historic relationship among body products, suppliers, and recipients in markets offers lessons for resolving contemporary questions of allocation and justice. In order to manage body products in a way that promotes the goal of increasing accessibility of these medical therapeutics while promoting safety, history suggests the value of expanding attention from the presence or absence of cash transactions to the result of such transactions. If we allow body products to be legally recognized as property that we seek to regulate as civic property, there is a range of questions to ask beyond whether the seller is paid: Is there a profit being made? How much, and by whom? Who is selling? Is a price floor needed to protect sellers? Who is buying? Is a price ceiling needed to protect buyers? How are the body products, once collected and prepared for use, being allocated? To the highest bidder? Through the application of medical expertise to determine need? By a priority system established through a democratic process? Is there a resale market? Because each type of body product exists in its own market, these questions will have different answers. Each body product market can be considered and regulated independently, to optimize the public benefits.

Finally, if we consider the possibility that cash exchanges with suppliers, as well as with recipients, may serve communal goals, then we need to consider how the professional donor can be a part of a body product supply system that is safe, equitable, and respectful. One of the most striking aspects of the history of body banking is the fall from grace of the professional donor. For decades the professional donor was the mainstay of the blood and milk supply, as those body products were bought from sellers and sold to patients through medical intermediaries. In the case of blood, the uncompensated Red Cross donor coexisted with the replacement donor and the paid donor. To donors themselves, giving for love and giving for money has not been an either/or situation.[32] Nor do the two donation categories necessarily correlate with the absence and presence of disease. The continuing reliance of sperm banks and egg brokers on professional donors provides current proof of the long-standing historical truth that the professional donor is not inevitably diseased, dangerous, or exploited. At the same time, current practices also confirm the historical tendency of Americans to gender the professional donor male and to treat female body product sellers differently. With an awareness of this tendency, and using the data collected by researchers, legal regulations can promote the respectful treatment of all body product sellers by ensuring equity of treatment by sex as well as by race, class, and sexual orientation, other categories that historically have been used to discriminate among suppliers.

Implementing these history lessons is not an easy task. Even the medical profession, which for most of the twentieth century was a relatively small and homogeneous group, could not sustain agreement for long on whether blood should be a public resource or private property or whether a commitment to local, medical control superseded the efficiencies to be gained by reliance on a national, nonmedical organization to create a safe blood supply. In replacing the broad brush of the gift/commodity dichotomy with more useful distinctions among body products and markets, any new regulations should reflect the perspectives not only of doctors but also of recipients and body product suppliers. The rewards from moving beyond the gift/commodity dichotomy and thinking about the power of property in the body as enhancing communal goals, however, are potentially great.

At various points in their history, body banks have served the original goal of the first blood bank: to keep life-enhancing medical technologies and care accessible to all. In the twenty-first century, body products can continue to support that goal. The creation of property does not require its abandonment to the free market. Nor does owning property, and even exchanging it in markets, preclude the type of relations between people linked by bonds of generosity and gratitude. Our century of experience with body banks points the way for using body products as the private basis for promoting the public good, in ways that can be independent of the bank and may include markets. We can use law to choose consciously among different types of body product management organizations. Some body products might be best collected and allocated by democratizing institutions that increase access to a needed medical therapeutic to all those who could benefit by such treatment. Other body products may be successfully managed by laissez-faire institutions of capitalism that facilitate the transfer of medical therapeutics to those willing to pay. The extent to which we regulate a body product market should reflect the body product itself, those who supply it, and those who use it. To Fantus's normative vision, arising out of his commitment to the medical profession, we can add another normative vision of the role of property in American society, arising out of law and political philosophy: "Property rights serve human values. They are recognized to that end and are limited by it."[33] Property in the human body has been created through the efforts of doctors and scientists to serve human values and can and should be recognized in law as both serving and limited by human values.

NOTES

ACKNOWLEDGMENTS

INDEX

Notes

INTRODUCTION

Epigraph: Bernard Fantus, ed., "The Therapy of the Cook County Hospital," *Journal of the American Medical Association* 109 (July 10, 1937): 128.

1. Marilynn Marchione, "Face Transplant Recipient Reveals New Look," *Boston Globe,* May 6, 2009; Jennifer Thomas, "Face Transplant Patient Can Smell, Taste, Breathe Normally," *Consumer Health News,* Nov. 17, 2009; "Face Transplant Reunion Donor's Family Meets Recipient," *Good Morning America,* ABC News, Dec. 21, 2010; and Donna Dickenson, *Body Shopping: The Economy Fuelled by Flesh and Blood* (Oxford, UK: Oneworld, 2008), 137.

2. Leslie A. Zebrowitz, *Reading Faces: Windows to the Soul?* (Boulder, CO: Westview Press, 1997), 2.

3. Susan E. Lederer, *Flesh and Blood: Organ Transplantation and Blood Transfusion in Twentieth-Century America* (Oxford: Oxford University Press, 2008), 3–20; and "Face Transplant Reunion."

4. Lederer, *Flesh and Blood,* 23, 165–84; Lesley A. Sharp, *Strange Harvest: Organ Transplants, Denatured Bodies, and the Transformed Self* (Berkeley: University of California Press, 2006), 49–51; and Renée C. Fox and Judith P. Swazey, *Spare Parts: Organ Replacement in American Society* (New York: Oxford University Press, 1992), 9.

5. Scott Carney, *The Red Market: On the Trail of the World's Organ Brokers, Bone Thieves, Blood Farmers, and Child Traffickers* (New York: William Morrow, 2011); Dickenson, *Body Shopping;* and Lori Andrews and Dorothy Nelkin, *Body Bazaar: The Market for Human Tissue in the Biotechnology Age* (New York: Crown, 2001).

6. Diane Suchetka, "Lakewood Woman was Donor for the First Near-Total Face Transplant in the United States," *Cleveland Plain Dealer*, December 20, 2010, http://blog.cleveland.com/health_impact/print.html?entry=/2010/12/lakewood _family_goes_public_wi.html.

7. U.S. Department of Health and Human Services, *The 2011 National Blood Collection and Utilization Survey Report* (Washington, DC: DHHS, 2013), 15.

8. Michele Goodwin, *Black Markets: The Supply and Demand of Body Parts* (New York: Cambridge University Press, 2006), 6–7 and throughout; and Arthur L. Caplan, "Obtaining and Allocating Organs for Transplantation," in *Human Organ Transplantation: Societal, Medical-Legal, Regulatory, and Reimbursement Issues,* edited by Dale H. Cowan, Jo Ann Kantorowitz, Jay Moskowitz, and Peter H. Rheinstein (Chicago: Health Administration Press, 1987), 5–17.

9. 42 U.S.C. §274e(a)(Dec. 21, 2007), first enacted as Pub L. 98-507, Title III, §301, Oct. 19, 1984.

10. Goodwin, *Black Markets,* 7.

11. Brief of Appellants, 7, Flynn v. Holder, Case No. 10-55643, U.S. Court of Appeals for the Ninth Circuit (filed Sept. 1, 2010).

12. Brief of Appellants at 7.

13. Flynn v. Holder, 684 F.3d 852, amending 665 F.3d 1048 (9th Cir. 2011).

14. M. L. P. van der Hoorn et al., "Clinical and Immunologic Aspects of Egg Donation Pregnancies: A Systematic Review," *Human Reproduction Update* 16 (2010): 704–12.

15. American Society for Reproductive Medicine Ethics Committee, "Financial Incentives in Recruitment of AR Egg Providers," *Fertility and Sterility* 82, Supp. 1 (2004): S240–S244 (issued by committee in 2000) and American Society for Reproductive Medicine Ethics Committee, "Financial Compensation of Oocyte Donors," *Fertility and Sterility* 88 (2007): 305; and Kamakahi v. American Society for Reproductive Medicine, et al., C 11-01781-SBA (N.D. Cal.)(filed Apr. 12, 2011) and Levy v. American Society of Reproductive Medicine, et al., C 11-03803-SBA (N.D. Cal.)(filed Aug. 2, 2011), consolidated as a single class action lawsuit (Order, Mar. 14, 2012, 2012 WL 892163).

16. Goodwin, *Black Markets,* 11–13, 14–16; and Nancy Scheper-Hughes, "Commodity Fetishism in Organs Trafficking," *Body & Society* 7 (2001): 31–62.

17. James A. Tobey, "A New Foster Mother," *Hygeia* 7 (Nov. 1929): 1110.

18. George Lakoff and Mark Johnson, *Metaphors We Live By* (1980; Chicago: University of Chicago Press, 2003), title, 3.

19. Fantus, "Therapy of the Cook County Hospital," 128.

20. Ibid.

21. Niall Ferguson, *The Ascent of Money: A Financial History of the World* (New York: Penguin Press, 2008), 9–11; Benjamin J. Klebaner, *American Commercial*

Banking: A History (Boston: Twayne Publishers, 1990), 5, 138–42; James Willard Hurst, *A Legal History of Money in the United States, 1774–1970* (Lincoln: University of Nebraska Press, 1973), 77–78; and Milton Esbitt, "Bank Portfolios and Bank Failures during the Great Depression: Chicago," *Journal of Economic History* 46 (June 1986): 455.

22. Janet Golden, *A Social History of Wet Nursing in America: From Breast to Bottle* (1996; Columbus: Ohio State University Press, 2001), 151–53; Jacqueline H. Wolf, *Don't Kill Your Baby: Public Health and the Decline of Breastfeeding in the Nineteenth and Twentieth Centuries* (Columbus: Ohio State University Press, 2001), 132–57; Valerie Fildes, *Wet Nursing: A History from Antiquity to the Present* (New York: Basil Blackwell, 1988), 19–20, 73, 141; and Jacqueline H. Wolf, " 'Mercenary Hirelings' or 'a Great Blessing'? Doctors' and Mothers' Conflicted Perceptions of Wet Nurses and the Ramifications of Infant Feeding in Chicago, 1871–1961," *Journal of Social History* 33 (1999): 97–120.

23. Lederer, *Flesh and Blood*, 107–64; Thomas A. Gugliemo, " 'Red Cross, Double Cross': Race and America's World War II–Era Blood Donor Service," *Journal of American History* 97 (2010): 63–90; Michael G. Kenny, "A Question of Blood, Race and Politics," *Journal of the History of Medicine and the Allied Sciences* 61 (2006): 456–91; and Jeffrey A. Bennett, *Banning Queer Blood: Rhetorics of Citizenship, Contagion and Resistance* (Tuscaloosa: University of Alabama Press, 2009).

24. Goodwin, *Black Markets*, 22–23.

25. Elizabeth H. Schirmer, "The County Blood Bank," *County Intern*, Apr. 1943, 5.

26. Viviana A. Zelizer, *The Social Meaning of Money: Pin Money, Paychecks, Poor Relief, and Other Currencies* (New York: Basic Books, 1994); and Viviana A. Zelizer, *Pricing the Priceless Child: The Changing Social Value of Children* (New York: Basic Books, 1985).

27. Rene Almeling, *Sex Cells: The Medical Market for Eggs and Sperm* (Berkeley: University of California Press, 2011); and Kieran J. Healy, *Last Best Gifts: Altruism and the Market for Human Blood and Organs* (Chicago: University of Chicago Press, 2006).

28. Almeling, *Sex Cells*, 112–13, 125–29.

29. Judges 16:17–30; Mary K. Gayne, "Illicit Wig-making in Eighteenth-Century Paris," *Eighteenth-Century Studies* 38 (2004): 119; and Anson Rabinbach, *The Human Motor: Energy, Fatigue, and the Origins of Modernity* (New York: Basic Books, 1990), 1–3 and generally.

30. Françoise Héritier-Augé, "Semen and Blood: Some Ancient Theories Concerning Their Genesis and Relationship," in *Fragments for a History of the Human Body*, edited by Michel Feher (New York: Zone Books, 1989), 3:159.

31. Holly Tucker, *Blood Work: A Tale of Medicine and Murder in the Scientific Revolution* (New York: Norton, 2011), 18; and John Harley Warner, *The Therapeutic*

Perspective: Medical Practice, Knowledge, and Identity in America, 1820–1885 (Cambridge, MA: Harvard University Press, 1986), 85–86.

32. Laura S. Underkuffler, *The Idea of Property: Its Meaning and Power* (New York: Oxford University Press, 2003), 12–13; Gregory Alexander, *Commodity and Propriety: Competing Visions of Property in American Legal Thought, 1776–1970* (Chicago: University of Chicago Press, 1997), 1; and Stephen R. Munzer, *A Theory of Property* (New York: Cambridge University Press, 1990), 15–16.

33. Alexander, *Commodity and Propriety*, 1, 5.

34. Ibid., 1.

35. Ibid., 6, 384–85. Alexander uses *market property* and *civic property* interchangeably with his preferred terms, *property-as-commodity* and *property-as-propriety* (1–3).

36. Ibid., 2.

37. Alexander, *Commodity and Propriety*, generally, and 379–84.

38. Margaret Jane Radin, *Contested Commodities* (Cambridge, MA: Harvard University Press, 1997), 6–8, 13–14, 79–101. See also Margaret Jane Radin, "Market-Inalienability," *Harvard Law Review* 100 (June 1987): 1859–70.

39. Paul Starr, *The Social Transformation of American Medicine* (New York: Basic Books, 1982), 235–36, 280.

1. Bankable Bodies and the Professional Donor

Epigraph: Louis Schwartz, "Full-Blooded Donors," *Hygeia*, Dec. 1930, 1109.

1. Albert Nelson Marquis, ed., *Who's Who in New England,* 2d ed. (Chicago: A. N. Marquis, 1916), 1048; Howard Markel, "For the Welfare of Children: The Origins of the Relationship between U.S. Public Health Workers and Pediatricians," in *Formative Years: Children's Health in the United States, 1880–2000,* edited by Alexandra Minna Stern and Howard Markel (Ann Arbor: University of Michigan Press, 2002), 48; and Sydney A. Halpern, *American Pediatrics: The Social Dynamics of Professionalism, 1880–1980* (Berkeley: University of California Press, 1988), 1–2, 35.

2. Janet Golden, *A Social History of Wet Nursing in America: From Breast to Bottle* (1996; Columbus: Ohio State University Press, 2001); and Valerie A. Fildes, *Wet Nursing: A History from Antiquity to the Present* (New York: Basil Blackwell, 1988).

3. Golden, *Social History of Wet Nursing,* 140, 142–43, 147–51, 155; Jacqueline H. Wolf, *Don't Kill Your Baby: Public Health and the Decline of Breastfeeding in the Nineteenth and Twentieth Centuries* (Columbus: Ohio State University Press, 2001), 132–57; and Jacqueline H. Wolf, " 'Mercenary Hirelings' or 'a Great Blessing'? Doctors' and Mothers' Conflicted Perceptions of Wet Nurses and the Ramifications of Infant Feeding in Chicago, 1871–1961," *Journal of Social History* 33 (Fall 1999): 97–120.

4. Fritz B. Talbot, "An Organization for Supplying Human Milk," *New England Journal of Medicine* 199 (Sept. 27, 1928): 610.

5. Samuel W. Lambert, "Melaena Neonatorum with Report of a Case Cured by Transfusion," *Medical Record* 73 (1908): 885–87; and Richard E. Rosenfield, "Early Twentieth Century Origins of Modern Blood Transfusion Therapy," *Mount Sinai Journal of Medicine* 41 (1974): 627.

6. George Crile, "The Technique of Direct Transfusion of Blood," *Annals of Surgery* 46 (Sept. 1907): 329–32.

7. Susan D. Lederer, *Flesh and Blood: Organ Transplantation and Blood Transfusion in Twentieth-Century America* (New York: Oxford University Press, 2008), 32–33, 39–48; and Peter C. English, *Shock, Physiological Surgery, and George Washington Crile: Medical Innovation in the Progressive Era* (Westport, CT: Greenwood Press, 1980), 100–101.

8. Lambert, "Melaena Neonatorum," 885–87.

9. For example, Genevieve Grandcourt, "The New Method of Blood Transfusion," *Harper's Weekly* 55 (Feb. 4, 1911): 28; Reuben Ottenberg, "Reminiscences of the History of Blood Transfusion," *Journal of the Mount Sinai Hospital* 4 (Nov.–Dec. 1937): 264; and Douglas P. Starr, *Blood: An Epic History of Medicine and Commerce* (New York: Knopf, 1998), 31.

10. Lambert, "Melaena Neonatorum," 885; and Lederer, *Flesh and Blood,* 20.

11. George Washington Crile, *George Crile: An Autobiography,* edited by Grace Crile (Philadelphia: Lippincott, 1947), 1:166.

12. Holly Tucker, *Blood Work: A Tale of Medicine and Murder in the Scientific Revolution* (New York: Norton, 2011), xviii–xix, and generally; Lederer, *Flesh and Blood,* 33–39; Pete Moore, *Blood and Justice: The Seventeenth-Century Parisian Doctor Who Made Blood Transfusion History* (Chichester, England: John Wiley & Sons, 2003); and Starr, *Blood,* 3–16. Cf. the use of paid donors for skin grafts. Lederer, *Flesh and Blood,* 3–31.

13. Wolf, *Don't Kill,* 9–41.

14. Golden, *Social History of Wet Nursing,* 136–40.

15. Thomas E. Cone, *History of American Pediatrics* (Boston: Little, Brown, 1979), 63.

16. Rima D. Apple, *Mothers and Medicine: A Social History of Infant Feeding, 1890–1950* (Madison: University of Wisconsin Press, 1987), 8–11; and Harvey Levenstein, " 'Best for Babies' or 'Preventable Infanticide'? The Controversy over Artificial Feeding of Infants in America, 1880–1920," *Journal of American History* 70 (June 1983): 77–78.

17. William H. Davis, "Statistical Comparison of the Mortality of Breast-Fed and Bottle-Fed Infants," *American Journal of Diseases of Children* 5 (1913): 234.

18. Statistics collected by the Boston Board of Health for 1893, quoted in the *Boston Floating Hospital Annual Report for 1900* and in "Historical Sketch," 6, both

as reported in "Notes for The History of Floating Hospital for Infants and Children," Sept. 15, 1988, 3, D3 fH #369, New England Medical Center Archives, Hirsh Health Sciences Library, Tufts University, Boston, MA.

19. Davis, "Statistical Comparison," 238–39; Samuel H. Preston and Michael R. Haines, *Fatal Years: Child Mortality in Late Nineteenth-Century America* (Princeton, NJ: Princeton University Press, 1991), 16, 27; Gretchen A. Condran and Harold R. Lentzner, "Early Death: Mortality among Children in New York, Chicago, and New Orleans," *Journal of Interdisciplinary History* 34 (Winter 2004): 315–54; and Robert V. Wells, "The Mortality Transition in Schenectady, New York, 1880–1930," *Social Science History* 19 (Autumn 1995): 402, 410.

20. Rima D. Apple, *Perfect Motherhood: Science and Childrearing in America* (New Brunswick, NJ: Rutgers University Press, 2006), 2, 40–41; Wolf, *Don't Kill,* 158–85; Levenstein, "'Best for Babies,'" 83–84; and Richard A. Meckel, *Save the Babies: American Public Health Reform and the Prevention of Infant Mortality, 1850–1929* (Baltimore: Johns Hopkins University Press, 1990), 92–158.

21. Wolf, *Don't Kill,* 42–73; Meckel, *Save the Babies,* 62–91; and Apple, *Mothers and Medicine,* 57–60.

22. Apple, *Mothers and Medicine,* 24–31, 60, 62–67; and Wolf, *Don't Kill,* 82–86, 93–94, 172–75.

23. Advertisement, *Boston Medical and Surgical Journal* 159 (Oct. 1, 1908): 16.

24. J. P. Sedgwick, "Establishment, Maintenance, and Reinstitution of Breast Feeding," *Journal of the American Medical Association* 64 (Aug. 11, 1917): 417–18; J. P. Sedgwick and E. C. Fleischner, "Breast Feeding in the Reduction of Infant Mortality," *American Journal of Public Health* 11 (Feb. 1921): 153–57; and J. P. Sedgwick, "A Preliminary Report of the Study of Breast Feeding in Minneapolis," *American Journal of Diseases of Children* 21 (1921): 455–64.

25. "Notes for The History of Floating Hospital for Infants and Children," 29.

26. Wolf, *Don't Kill,* 1.

27. Mathilda Carlson, "Breast Feeding in Private Practice under Ideal Conditions," *Archives of Pediatrics* 38 (1921): 570.

28. Icie G. Macy and Julia Outhouse, "Breast Milk—A Variable Food," *Journal of the American Dietetic Association* 4 (1928): 9–14; and Fritz B. Talbot, "A Summary of Present Knowledge of Human Milk," *American Journal of Diseases of Children* 7 (1914): 452–54, 456–63.

29. Fritz B. Talbot and Richard M. Smith, *The Latest Facts about Breast-Feeding* (n.p.: Advisory Committee on Maternal and Infant Hygiene, 1922), 2; Sedgwick and Fleischner, "Breast Feeding," 156; and Fritz B. Talbot, "Two Methods of Obtaining Milk for Hospital Use," *Boston Medical and Surgical Journal* 164 (Mar. 2, 1911): 305.

30. Jacqueline H. Wolf, "The Social and Medical Construction of Lactation Pathology," *Women and Health* 30 (2000): 96–100; and Levenstein, "'Best for Babies,'" 88–89.

31. Davis, "Statistical Comparison," 234 (citing Holt); and Halpern, *American Pediatrics,* 62.

32. John Zahorsky, "The Pathology of Human Milk," *St. Louis Courier of Medicine* 23 (1900): 38–41; and N. O. Pearce, "Review of Recent Literature on the New-Born," *American Journal of Diseases of Children* 18 (1919): 51.

33. James A. Tobey, "A New Foster-Mother," *Hygeia,* Nov. 1929, 1110.

34. Golden, *Social History of Wet Nursing,* 98–113.

35. Ibid., 54–55, 70–72; and Fildes, *Wet Nursing,* 18–20, 29, 39, 70–74.

36. Francis P. Denny, "The Use of Human Milk in Typhoid Fever to Increase the Bacteriolytic Power of the Blood," *Boston Medical and Surgical Journal* 158 (Apr. 1908): 627.

37. Ibid., 627, 630; Golden, *Social History of Wet Nursing,* 194.

38. Golden, *Social History of Wet Nursing,* 184–89; and Janet Golden, "From Wet Nurse Directory to Milk Bank: The Delivery of Human Milk in Boston, 1909–1927," *Bulletin of the History of Medicine* 62 (Winter 1988): 589–605. For similar efforts in Chicago, see Wolf, *Don't Kill,* 147.

39. For example, in the June 26, 1913, issue of the *Boston Medical and Surgical Journal* 168, 25, sixteen such nurses' directories were listed, with dates of establishment ranging from 1890 to 1909. See also Susan M. Reverby, *Ordered to Care: The Dilemma of American Nursing, 1850–1945* (New York: Cambridge University Press, 1987), 97, 101–4.

40. Fritz B. Talbot, "Directory for Wet Nurses," *Boston Medical and Surgical Journal* 162 (Feb. 24, 1910): 255; Talbot, "Two Methods," 304; and George R. Bedinger, "The Wet Nurse Directory of Boston," *Transactions of the American Association for the Study and Prevention of Infant Mortality* 6 (1915): 252–54.

41. Talbot, "Directory for Wet Nurses," *Boston Medical and Surgical Journal.* For example, in *Boston Medical and Surgical Journal* 191 (Oct. 23, 1924): xiii (advertising section).

42. Bedinger, "The Wet Nurse Directory," 252.

43. Talbot, "Organization for Supplying Human Milk," 610.

44. Fritz B. Talbot, "A Directory for Wet-Nurses: Its Experiences for Twelve Months," *Journal of the American Medical Association* 56 (June 10, 1911): 1715–17; Talbot, "Two Methods"; and Golden, *Social History of Wet Nursing,* 184–89.

45. Talbot, "Directory for Wet Nurses," *Boston Medical and Surgical Journal* 162 (Feb. 24, 1910): 255; and Bedinger, "Wet Nurse Directory," 253.

46. "Report of the Infants' Hospital," *Boston Medical and Surgical Journal* 172 (May 27, 1915): 798.

47. John Lovett Morse, "Directory for Wet Nurses," *Boston Medical and Surgical Journal* 179 (Aug. 8, 1918): 218.

48. Cone, *History of American Pediatrics,* 69–70, 99; Preston and Haines, *Fatal Years,* 13; Charles E. Rosenberg, *The Care of Strangers: The Rise of America's Hospital*

System (New York: Basic Books, 1987), 114; and Alexandra Minna Stern and Howard Markel, "Introduction," in Stern and Markel, *Formative Years*, 3.

49. Talbot, "Two Methods," 305; Lewis A. Scheuer and Jessie E. Duncan, "A Method of Preserving Breast Milk: A Study of Its Clinical Application," *American Journal of Diseases of Children* 51 (1936): 250; and Golden, *Social History of Wet Nursing*, 84, 90, 95, 102–7.

50. Talbot, "Organization for Supplying Human Milk," 610; and Talbot, "Two Methods," 304 (using the earlier name, Massachusetts Infant Asylum).

51. Talbot, "Two Methods," 304–5.

52. Julius Hays Hess, *Premature and Congenitally Diseased Infants* (New York: Lea & Febiger, 1922), 120–23; and Fildes, *Wet Nursing*, 256–63.

53. Isaac A. Abt, "The Technic of Wetnurse Management in Institutions," *Journal of the American Medical Association* 69 (Aug. 11, 1917): 418–20; Isaac A. Abt, "Human Milking Machine," *Transactions of the American Pediatric Society* 33 (1921): 344–46; and Isaac A. Abt, "Some Further Observations on the Electric Breast Pump," *Transactions of the American Pediatric Society* 35 (1923): 23.

54. George Washington Crile, *Hemorrhage and Transfusion: An Experimental and Clinical Research* (New York: Appleton & Co., 1909), 159, 300–301; and Rene Almeling, *Sex Cells: The Medical Market for Eggs and Sperm* (Los Angeles: University of California Press, 2011), 12.

55. George M. Dorrance and Nate Ginsburg, "Transfusion: History, Development, Present Status and Technique of Operation," *New York Medical Journal* 87 (May 16, 1908): 943.

56. Roy D. McClure and George Robert Dunn, "Transfusion of Blood: History, Methods, Dangers, Preliminary Tests, Present Status," *Bulletin of the Johns Hopkins Hospital* (Mar. 1917), 99; and Maxwell M. Wintrobe, "Milestones on the Path of Progress," in *Blood, Pure and Eloquent: A Story of Discovery, of People, and of Ideas,* edited by Maxwell M. Wintrobe (New York: McGraw Hill, 1980), 2–6.

57. G. A. Lindeboom, "The Story of a Blood Transfusion to a Pope," *Journal of the History of Medicine* 9 (1954): 455–59; and N. S. R. Maluf, "History of Blood Transfusion," *Journal of the History of Medicine* 9 (1954): 59.

58. Tucker, *Blood Work*, 204–5, 210–11; Moore, *Blood and Justice*, 36–52, 67–77, 97–98, 105–6, 204–5; A. D. Farr, "The First Human Blood Transfusion," *Medical History* 24 (1980): 143–62; A. Rupert Hall and Marie Boas Hall, "The First Human Blood Transfusion: Priority Disputes," *Medical History* 24 (1980): 461–65; and Maluf, "History of Blood Transfusion," 61–67.

59. Lederer, *Flesh and Blood,* 34–35; and Maluf, "History of Blood Transfusion," 69–70.

60. Tucker, *Blood Work*, 31–33.

61. Ibid., 9–11.

62. Kim Pelis, "Blood Clots: The Nineteenth-Century Debate over the Substance and Meaning of Transfusion in Britain," *Annals of Science* 54 (1997): 331–66; and Lederer, *Flesh and Blood*, 35–36.

63. For example, James Blundell, "Experiments on the Transfusion of Blood by the Syringe," *Medico-Chirurgical Transactions* 9 (1818): 56–92; "Physiological Experiment," *Lancet* 1 (Feb. 22, 1824): 258; "Another Successful Case of Transfusion," *Lancet* 5 (Oct. 8, 1825): 111–12; J. Howell, "Successful Case of Transfusion," *Lancet* 9 (Feb. 9, 1828): 698–99; and James Blundell, "Observations on Transfusion of Blood," *Lancet* 12 (June 13, 1829): 321–24.

64. James Blundell, *The Principles and Practice of Obstetricy as at Present Taught* (Washington, DC: Duff Green, 1834), 424–26.

65. Blundell, *Principles and Practice*, 349.

66. W. B. Drinkard, "History and Statistics of the Operation of Transfusion of Blood," *Richmond and Louisville Medical Journal* 13 (1872): 20; Lederer, *Flesh and Blood*, 36–39; William H. Schneider, "Blood Transfusion in Peace and War, 1900–1918," *Social History of Medicine* 10 (Apr. 1997): 108; Paul J. Schmidt, "Blood Transfusion in the South before the War between the States," *Southern Medical Journal* 72 (Dec. 1979): 1587–89; and James. P. Morris, "An American First: Blood Transfusion in New Orleans in the 1850s," *Louisiana History* 16 (Autumn 1975): 342.

67. "The Transfusion of Blood," *Harper's Weekly*, July 4, 1874, 569–70 (supplement).

68. William S. Halsted, "Refusion in the Treatment of Carbonic Oxide Poisoning," *Annals of Anatomy and Surgery* 9 (Jan. 1884): 7–21.

69. "Transfusion of Blood," 569. See also Louis K. Diamond, "A History of Blood Transfusion," in Wintrobe, *Blood, Pure and Eloquent*, 661–75.

70. Crile, *George Crile*, 1:166. See also Ottenberg, "Reminiscences," 268.

71. Bertram M. Bernheim, *Adventure in Blood Transfusion* (New York: Smith & Durrell, 1942), 13–17.

72. Alexander S. Wiener, *Blood Groups and Blood Transfusion*, 1st ed. (Springfield, IL: Charles C. Thomas, 1935), 41; Bernheim, *Adventure*, 90–91, 102–4; and Ottenberg, "Reminiscences," 269.

73. "Karl Landsteiner, 1868–1943," *Journal of Immunology* 48 (1944): 1–16; and Paul Speiser and Ferdinand G. Smekal, *Karl Landsteiner: The Discoverer of the Blood-Groups and a Pioneer in the Field of Immunology—Biography of a Nobel Prize Winner of the Vienna Medical School*, trans. Richard Rickett (Vienna: Verlag Bruder Holliuek, 1975).

74. Stanhope Bayne-Jones, "Dr. Karl Landsteiner, Nobel Prize Laureate in Medicine, 1930," *Science* 73 (June 5, 1931): 600; and Karl Landsteiner, "On Agglutination of Normal Human Blood," trans. A. L. Kappus, *Transfusion* 1 (Jan.–Feb. 1961): 5–8 (reprint).

75. Louis K. Diamond, "The Story of Blood Groups," in Wintrobe, *Blood, Pure and Eloquent,* 692–93; and Lederer, *Flesh and Blood,* 144–45.

76. William C. Boyd, "Blood Groups," *Tabulae Biologicae* 17 (1939): 148–235; Lederer, *Flesh and Blood,* 143–64; Michael G. Kenny, "A Question of Blood, Race and Politics," *Journal of the History of Medicine and the Allied Sciences* 61 (2006): 456–91; William H. Schneider, "The History of Research on Blood Group Genetics: Initial Discovery and Diffusion," *History and Philosophy of the Life Sciences* 18 (1996): 277–303; and William H. Schneider, "Blood Group Research in Great Britain, France, and the United States between the World Wars," *Yearbook of Physical Anthropology* 38 (1995): 87–114.

77. Crile, *Hemorrhage and Transfusion,* 323–34. See also Bernheim, *Adventure,* xxxii–xxxiv; and Lederer, *Flesh and Blood,* 145–46.

78. Arthur H. Aufses Jr. and Barbara J. Niss, *The House of Noble Deeds: The Mount Sinai Hospital, 1852–2002* (New York: New York University Press, 2002), 74.

79. Ottenberg, "Reminiscences," 266; and Schneider, "Blood Transfusion in Peace and War," 111–12.

80. McClure and Dunn, "Transfusion of Blood," 103; and Bernheim, *Adventure,* xxxi–xxxviii.

81. Bernheim, *Adventure,* xxvii.

82. Ibid., 78.

83. Ibid., 44, 156.

84. Blundell, "Experiments on the Transfusion of Blood by the Syringe"; Bernheim, *Adventure,* 116–18; and Schneider, "Blood Transfusion in Peace and War," 108–9.

85. Edward Lindeman, "Blood Transfusion by the Syringe Cannula System," *Journal of American Medical Association* 63 (Oct. 31, 1914): 1545.

86. Richard Lewisohn, "A New and Greatly Simplified Method of Blood Transfusion," *Medical Record* 87 (Jan. 23, 1915): 141; and Wiener, *Blood Groups,* 1st ed., 42.

87. McClure and Dunn, "Transfusion of Blood," 102.

88. Bernheim, *Adventure,* 118.

89. L. Agote, "Nueva Procidimento para la Transfusion de Sangre," *Anales del Instituto Modelo de Clínica Médica* 1 (1915): 25 (Buenos Aires); A. Hustin, "Principe d'une Nouvelle Methode de Transfusion Muqueuse," *Journal Médical de Bruxelles* 12 (1914): 436–39 (Brussels); Richard Weil, "Sodium Citrate in the Transfusion of Blood," *Journal of the American Medical Association* 64 (Jan. 30, 1915): 425–26 (New York); and Lewisohn, "New and Greatly Simplified Method," 141–42 (New York).

90. Weil, "Sodium Citrate," 425.

91. Bernheim, *Adventure,* 140.

92. Lewisohn, "New and Greatly Simplified Method," 141; and Schneider, "Blood Transfusion in Peace and War," 118–20.

93. Bernheim, *Adventure,* xvi.

94. McClure and Dunn, "Transfusion of Blood," 103.

95. Ibid.; Lindeman, "Blood Transfusion," 1542–44; Crile, *George Crile,* 1:177; and English, *Shock, Physiological Surgery,* 104.

96. The following discussion of the Floating Hospital draws upon the *Annual Reports of the Floating Hospital,* from the collection of the Francis A. Countway Library of Medicine, Harvard Medical School, Boston, MA, and the following histories: Margery Ilana Miller, "The Boston Floating Hospital, 1894–1927 and Beyond: A Vessel of Science and Social Concern," B.A. thesis, Harvard University, 1996; Joan Ead Keefe, "The Genesis of a Community Health Center: The Boston Dispensary 1796, the Boston Floating Hospital 1894, Tufts Medical School 1894," M.L.A. thesis, Harvard University, 1999; "Notes for The History of Floating Hospital for Infants and Children"; and Paul W. Beaven, "A History of the Boston Floating Hospital," *Pediatrics* 19 (1957): 629–38. See also Golden, *Social History of Wet Nursing,* 184–89, 199; Kara W. Swanson, "Human Milk as Technology and Technologies of Human Milk: Medical Imaginings in the Early 20th Century United States," *Women's Studies Quarterly* 37 (2009): 21; Golden, "From Wet Nurse Directory"; and Janet Golden, "From Commodity to Gift: Gender, Class, and the Meaning of Breast Milk in the Twentieth Century," *Historian* 59 (Fall 1996): 75–87.

97. Miller, "Boston Floating Hospital," 14–17, 19.

98. Beaven, "History of the Boston Floating Hospital," 634, citing the Annual Report for 1900; and *Seventeenth Annual Report of the Boston Floating Hospital, Season of 1910,* June 1911, 10.

99. Talbot, "Two Methods," 305.

100. *Seventeenth Annual Report,* 12.

101. Talbot, "Two Methods," 305.

102. *Seventeenth Annual Report,* 12.

103. Morse, "Directory for Wet Nurses," 218; and Bedinger, "Wet Nurse Directory," 253.

104. Talbot, "Organization for Supplying Human Milk," 610.

105. Ibid., 611.

106. B. Raymond Hoobler, "An Experiment in the Collection of Human Milk for Hospital and Dispensary Uses," *Archives of Pediatrics* 31 (1914): 171–73; Henry Dwight Chapin, "Operation of a Breast Milk Dairy," *Journal of the American Medical Association* 81 (July 21, 1923): 200–202; Henry Dwight Chapin, "The Production and Handling of Human Milk," *Journal of the American Medical Association* 87 (Oct. 23, 1926): 1364; and B. Raymond Hoobler, "Human Milk: Its Commercial Production and Distribution," *Journal of the American Medical Association* 84 (Jan. 17, 1925): 165–66.

107. Tobey, "New Foster-Mother," 1112.

108. Katherine Jones, "The Mothers Milk Bureau of Detroit," *Public Health Nurse,* Mar. 1928, 142–43.

109. Tobey, "New Foster-Mother," 1110.

110. Jones, "Mothers Milk Bureau," 142.

111. Mary D. Blankenhorn, "A Breast Milk Dairy," *Hygeia,* May 1933, 411.

112. Chapin, "Production and Handling," 1364. See also photograph of expression cubicles in the Mother's Milk Bureau of Detroit in Tobey, "New Foster-Mother," 1111.

113. Chapin, "Production and Handling," 1364.

114. Shirley W. Wynne, "Preserving Mothers' Milk," *Parents' Magazine,* Aug. 1937, 73.

115. Mary Katherine Herwick, "A Mother's Milk Station," *American Journal of Nursing* 33 (1933): 454.

116. "Saving Lives with Mothers' Milk," *Hygeia,* May 1940, 425–28.

117. "Preserving Human Milk: An Interview with Helen F. Leighty," *Trained Nurse and Hospital Review,* Sept. 1939, 233.

118. Tobey, "A New Foster-Mother," 1110.

119. Ibid., 1110–11.

120. Talbot, "Directory for Wet Nurses," *Boston Medical and Surgical Journal* 162 (Feb. 24, 1910): 255.

121. Bedinger, "Wet Nurse Directory," 254.

122. Talbot, "Organization for Supplying Human Milk," 610.

123. Hoobler, "Experiment in Human Milk," 172–73.

124. Hoobler, "Human Milk," 166; and Chapin, "Production and Handling," 1364.

125. Susan B. Carter et al., eds., *Historical Statistics of the United States,* millennial ed. (New York: Cambridge University Press, 2006), 2: 265, 273 (data for 1925).

126. Tobey, "A New Foster-Mother," 1112.

127. "Saving Lives with Mothers' Milk," 425.

128. "Doctor Describes Quintuplets' Birth," *New York Times,* Aug. 30, 1934; and "Saving Lives with Mother's Milk," 425.

129. Tobey, "New Foster-Mother," 1110; and Blankenhorn, "Breast Milk Dairy," 412.

130. Jones, "Mothers Milk Bureau," 142–43.

131. B. Raymond Hoobler, "The Production, Collection and Distribution of Human Milk: Retrospect and Prospect," *Journal of the American Medical Association* 88 (June 4, 1927): 1787; and Hoobler, "Human Milk," 165.

132. Swanson, "Human Milk as Technology," 29–32.

133. Hoobler, "Experiment in Human Milk," 172.

134. Bernheim, *Adventure,* 8.

135. Ottenberg, "Reminiscences," 266; and Bernheim, *Adventure,* 68–69.

136. Bernheim, *Adventure,* 19, 85. See also Wiener, *Blood Groups,* 1st ed., 69.

137. Bernheim, *Adventure,* 86.

138. Ibid., 76–78.

139. Ibid., 79–81.

140. Ibid., 121–22.

141. Ibid., 84.

142. Ibid.

143. Ibid., 89.

144. Crile, *Hemorrhage and Transfusion,* 300; and Lederer, *Flesh and Blood,* 45–46, 52, 83–84.

145. Bernheim, *Adventure,* 87–88. See also Lederer, *Flesh and Blood,* 82.

146. "Bill to Pay Donors," *Journal of the American Medical Association* 87 (Aug. 7, 1926): 423; and "The Price to Be Paid for Blood Transfusions," *Boston Medical and Surgical Journal* 196 (Feb. 10, 1927): 251.

147. "Earning a Living by Letting Blood," newspaper clipping in possession of author, paper name and exact date missing.

148. "Has Donated 23 1–2 Gallons of Blood," *Chronicle-Telegram* (Elyria, OH), May 29, 1929.

149. "Earning a Living by Letting Blood"; "Man Eats Onions to Give Blood in 59 Transfusions," *Oakland (CA) Tribune,* Mar. 28, 1924.

150. "Shedding Blood for an Education," *Youth's Companion,* Nov. 26, 1925; and Lederer, *Flesh and Blood,* 82.

151. "Earning a Living by Letting Blood."

152. Herbert G. Harlan, "This Business of Selling Blood," *Hygeia,* May, 1929, 470–74; and Schwartz, "Full-Blooded Donors," *Hygeia,* Dec. 1930, 1109.

153. Harlan, "Business of Selling Blood," 470.

154. Schwartz, "Full-Blooded Donors," 1109. For the career of one nominally unpaid but near-professional female blood donor in the late 1930s, see Lederer, *Flesh and Blood,* 85–87.

155. Harlan, "Business of Selling Blood," 470.

156. Ibid., 474.

157. Lederer, *Flesh and Blood,* 51–55.

158. Harlan, "Business of Selling Blood," 470–71.

159. Noah Fabricant and Leo M. Zimmerman, "The Cry for Blood," *Hygeia,* Oct. 1939, 884.

160. Bernheim, *Adventure,* 129.

161. Herbert Z. Griffin and Samuel F. Haines, "A Review of a Group of Professional Donors," *Journal of the American Medical Association* 81 (Aug. 18, 1923): 532.

162. Ibid., 533.

163. Philip Levine and Eugene M. Katzin, "A Survey of Blood Transfusion in America," *Journal of the American Medical Association* 110 (Apr. 16, 1938): 1245.

164. DeWitt Stetten, "The Blood Transfusion Betterment Association of New York City," *Journal of the American Medical Association* 110 (Apr. 16, 1938): 1248.

165. Fabricant and Zimmerman, "Cry for Blood," 884.

166. Stetten, "Blood Transfusion Betterment Association," 1249; and E. H. L. Corwin, "Blood Transfusions and Donors," *Bulletin of the American Hospital Association,* July 1930, 117–18.

167. Stetten, "Blood Transfusion Betterment Association," 1249.

168. E. H. L. Corwin, "Community Control of Professional Blood Donors," *New York State Journal of Medicine* 35 (1935): 317.

169. Corwin, "Blood Transfusions," 121; and Stetten, "Blood Transfusion Betterment Association," 1250.

170. Corwin, "Blood Transfusions," 118. By 1938 the BTBA was planning the creation of a small list of women donors for "special needs," such as transfusions of children and nuns. Stetten, "Blood Transfusion Betterment Association," 1249.

171. Stetten, "Blood Transfusion Betterment Association," 1248; and Fabricant and Zimmerman, "Cry for Blood," 884.

172. Corwin, "Blood Transfusions," 118.

173. Stetten, "Blood Transfusion Betterment Association," 1249.

174. Ibid., 1250.

175. Levine and Katzin, "Survey of Blood Transfusion," 1245.

176. Corwin, "Blood Transfusions," 118; and New York Sanitary Code Sec. 108 (adopted Nov. 21, 1930 and amended Mar. 14, 1939), reproduced in Fritz Schiff and William C. Boyd, *Blood Grouping Technic: A Manual* (New York: Interscience, 1942), 115. See also Public Health Law of 1909 §24-a, as amended by L. 1930, c. 326, and repealed by NY CLS Public Health §5002 (1953).

177. Levine and Katzin, "Survey of Blood Transfusion," 1249.

178. Charles V. Nemo, "I Sell Blood," *American Mercury* 31 (Feb. 1934): 194.

179. J. C. Furnas, "Blood from a Stranger," *Saturday Evening Post,* Aug. 20, 1938, 9, 32.

180. Nemo, "I Sell Blood," 194–98.

181. Corwin, "Blood Transfusion," 117.

182. Stetten, "Blood Transfusion Betterment Association," 1251.

183. Ottenberg, "Reminiscences," 270.

184. Levine and Katzin, "Survey of Blood Transfusion," 1245.

185. L. W. Diggs and A. J. Keith, "Problems in Blood Banking," *American Journal of Clinical Pathology* 9 (1939): 591.

186. Thomas Hale Ham, "Transfusion Therapy," *New England Journal of Medicine* 223 (Aug. 29, 1940): 332.

2. Banks That Take Donations

Epigraph: Bernard Fantus, "Cook County's Blood Bank," *Modern Hospital* 50 (Jan. 1938): 57.

1. The details of Fantus's life are drawn from Hugh A. Mcguigan, "Dr. Bernard Fantus (1874–1940)," *Illini Scope,* May 1940, 9; D. J. Davis, "Bernard

Fantus, M.D. 1874–1940," *County Intern,* June 1940, 1; John G. Raffensperger and Louis D. Boshes, eds., *The Old Lady on Harrison Street: Cook County Hospital, 1833–1995* (New York: P. Lang, 1997), 91; and "Dr. Bernard Fantus: A Life of Kindness Guided by Intelligence," address given by Edwin H. Wilson, minister of the Third Unitarian Church of Chicago, at the funeral of Dr. Bernard Fantus on April 16, 1940, Box 1 2002-199, Bernard Fantus Papers, University of Chicago Archives (hereafter Fantus Papers).

2. Raffensperger and Boshes, *Old Lady on Harrison Street,* 129–34, 159–66.

3. Elizabeth H. Schirmer, "The County Blood Bank," *County Intern,* Apr. 1943, 7.

4. Fantus, "Cook County's Blood Bank," 57.

5. Ibid.

6. Paul W. Emerson and Washington Platt, "The Preservation of Human Milk. VI. A Preliminary Note on the Freezing Process," *Journal of Pediatrics* 2 (1933): 472–77; Mary L. Watson, "Our Frozen Milk Bank," *American Journal of Nursing* 41 (June 1941): 672–74; and Kara W. Swanson, "Human Milk as Technology and Technologies of Human Milk: Medical Imaginings in the Early 20th Century United States," *Women's Studies Quarterly* 37 (2009): 29–30.

7. Karl A. Meyer, "The History of the Cook County Hospital Blood Bank," *Quarterly Bulletin of Northwestern University Medical School* 23 (Fall 1949): 318–19.

8. Roy D. McClure and George Robert Dunn, "Transfusion of Blood: History, Methods, Dangers, Preliminary Tests, Present Status," *Bulletin of the Johns Hopkins Hospital* 23 (Mar. 1917): 102.

9. Bertram M. Bernheim, *Adventure in Blood Transfusion* (New York: Smith & Durrell, 1942), 147.

10. Peyton Rous and J. R. Turner, "The Preservation of Living Red Blood Cells in Vitro: I. Methods of Preservation," *Journal of Experimental Medicine* 23 (Sept. 1916): 219–37; and Peyton Rous and J. R. Turner, "The Preservation of Living Red Cells in Vitro: II. The Transfusion of Kept Cells," *Journal of Experimental Medicine* 23 (Sept. 1916): 239–48.

11. C. L. Hoag, "The World's First Blood Banker—Oswald Hope Robertson," *Bulletin of the American Association of Blood Banks* 11 (1958): 95–97.

12. Oswald H. Robertson, "Transfusion with Preserved Red Blood Cells," *British Medical Journal* 1 (June 22, 1918): 691–95; and Kim Pelis, "Taking Credit: The Canadian Army Medical Corps and the British Conversion to Blood Transfusion in WWI," *Journal of the History of Medicine* 56 (2001): 243–44.

13. Bernheim, *Adventure,* 163; George Washington Crile, *George Crile: An Autobiography,* edited by Grace Crile (Philadelphia: Lippincott, 1947), 1:281; Peter C. English, *Shock, Physiological Surgery, and George Washington Crile: Medical Innovation in the Progressive Era* (Westport, CT: Greenwood Press, 1980), 195–99;

and William H. Schneider, "Blood Transfusion in Peace and War, 1900–1918," *Social History of Medicine* 10 (Apr. 1997): 117–18.

14. Bernheim, *Adventure,* 165.

15. Schneider, "Blood Transfusion in Peace and War," 125.

16. Bernheim, *Adventure,* 165; and Douglas B. Kendrick, *Blood Program in World War II (Supplemented by Experiences in the Korean War)* (Washington, DC: Office of the Surgeon General, Department of the Army, 1989), 9.

17. Bernheim, *Adventure,* 168–69.

18. Schneider, "Blood Transfusion in Peace and War," 119.

19. Arlie V. Bock, "The Use and Abuse of Blood Transfusion," *New England Journal of Medicine* 215 (Sept. 3, 1936): 421–25; and Bernard Fantus, ed., "The Therapy of the Cook County Hospital: Blood Preservation," *Journal of the American Medical Association* 109 (July 10, 1937): 130.

20. William H. Schneider, "Blood Transfusion between the Wars," *Journal of the History of Medicine* 58 (Apr. 2003): 192–93; and Schneider, "Blood Transfusion in Peace and War," 118.

21. J. S. Lundy, R. M. Tovell, and E. B. Tuohy, "Annual Report for 1935 of the Section on Anesthesia: Including Data on Blood Transfusion," *Proceedings of the Staff Meetings of the Mayo Clinic* 11 (July 1, 1936): 432, copy in MHU-0676: Subject Files, Blood Bank Folder, Mayo Clinic Historical Unit, Rochester, MN.

22. J. C. Furnas, "Blood from a Stranger," *Saturday Evening Post,* Aug. 20, 1938, 34.

23. Schneider, "Blood Transfusion between the Wars," 21.

24. R. Lewisohn and N. Rosenthal, "Prevention of Chills Following Transfusion of Citrated Blood," *Journal of the American Medical Association* 100 (Feb. 18, 1933): 466–69; Bernheim, *Adventure,* 142–46; Reuben Ottenberg, "Reminiscences of the History of Blood Transfusion," *Journal of the Mount Sinai Hospital* 4 (Nov.–Dec. 1937): 270; and Schneider, "Blood Transfusion between the Wars," 211.

25. Lillian Larson, "Blood Transfusions—Indirect," *Modern Hospital* 48 (June 1937): 85–86.

26. Fantus, "Cook County's Blood Bank," 57.

27. Karl A. Meyer, Leonard H. Weissman, and J. Lester Wilkey, "Blood Bank Service," *Hospitals* 12 (Dec. 1938): 79; M. Telischi, "Evolution of Cook County Hospital Blood Bank," *Transfusion* 14 (1974): 623–24; and Charles Richard Drew, " 'Banked Blood': A Study in Blood Preservation," D.M.S. thesis, Columbia University, 1938, 65–74.

28. Telischi, "Evolution of Cook County Hospital Blood Bank," 623–24.

29. Fantus, "Cook County's Blood Bank," 48.

30. Schirmer, "The County Blood Bank," 5; and Meyer, "The History of the Cook County Hospital Blood Bank," 319–20.

31. See, for example, S. Breanndan Moore, "A Brief History of the Early Years of Blood Transfusion at the Mayo Clinic: The First Blood Bank in the United States (1935)," *Transfusion Medicine Reviews* 19 (July 2005): 241–44.

32. F. Duran Jorda, "The Barcelona Blood-Transfusion Service," *Lancet* 233 (Apr. 1, 1939): 773–75; Nicholas Coni, *Medicine and Warfare: Spain, 1936–1939* (New York: Routledge, 2008), 69–80; and Schneider, "Blood Transfusion between the Wars," 211–12n55.

33. Larson, "Blood Transfusions—Indirect;" and Fantus, "Therapy of the Cook County Hospital: Blood Preservation," 128–31.

34. Bernard Fantus, "Therapy of the Cook County Hospital," *Bulletin C,* May 1937, 1, copy in Box 1 2002-199, Fantus Papers and reprinted in revised form as Fantus, "Therapy of the Cook County Hospital: Blood Preservation."

35. Schirmer, "The County Blood Bank," 5.

36. Fantus, "Therapy of the Cook County Hospital," *Bulletin C,* 1.

37. Fantus, "Therapy of the Cook County Hospital: Blood Preservation."

38. Bernard Fantus, ed., "The Therapy of the Cook County Hospital," *Journal of the American Medical Association* 111 (July 23, 1938): 320.

39. Fantus, "Cook County's Blood Bank," 58.

40. Ibid., 57.

41. Fantus, "Therapy of the Cook County Hospital," *Bulletin C,* 1.

42. Ibid., 2.

43. Ibid.; and Elizabeth H. Schirmer, "Blood Banking," *American Journal of Nursing* 39 (June 1939): 610.

44. Fantus, "Therapy of the Cook County Hospital," *Bulletin C,* 1.

45. Fantus, "Therapy of the Cook County Hospital: Blood Preservation," 129–30.

46. Fantus, "Cook County's Blood Bank," 58 fig. 3.

47. Ibid., 57–58.

48. Meyer, "History of the Cook County Hospital Blood Bank," 318.

49. Schirmer, "The County Blood Bank," 5. See also Telischi, "Evolution of Cook County Hospital Blood Bank," 625 (estimating $1.00 in late 1930s).

50. Telischi, "Evolution of Cook County Hospital Blood Bank," 624–25.

51. Schirmer, "The County Blood Bank," 5.

52. Meyer et al., "Blood Bank Service"; and Schirmer, "Blood Banking," 609–13.

53. Frank E. Barton and Thomas M. Hearne, "The Use of Placental Blood for Transfusion," *Journal of the American Medical Association* 113 (Oct. 14, 1939): 1475.

54. O. A. Brines, "The Blood Bank in a Charity or City-County Hospital," *Proceedings of Blood Bank Institute,* Dallas, TX, Nov. 17–19, 1947, 46.

55. Newton Evans, "The Use of the 'Blood Bank' in Transfusions," *California and Western Medicine* 55 (July 1941): 14–16; and C. S. White and J. J. Weinstein,

"The Management of a Blood Bank," *Southern Medicine and Surgery* 101 (Oct. 1939): 479–81.

56. Alexander S. Wiener, *Blood Groups and Blood Transfusion,* 2d ed. (Springfield, IL: Charles C. Thomas, 1939), 76.

57. Fantus, "Therapy of the Cook County Hospital," *Bulletin C,* 1; and Fantus, "Therapy of the Cook County Hospital: Blood Preservation," 131.

58. L. W. Diggs and A. J. Keith, "Problems in Blood Banking," *American Journal of Clinical Pathology* 9 (1939): 596–97.

59. Ibid., 592, 597.

60. Ibid., 597.

61. Ibid., 591.

62. Ibid., 603.

63. Mark M. Ravitch, "The Blood Bank of the Johns Hopkins Hospital," *Journal of the American Medical Association* 115 (July 20, 1940): 171.

64. Ibid., 172.

65. Wiener, *Blood Groups and Blood Transfusion,* 2d ed., 53.

66. Blood Transfusion Association, *Report of the Blood Transfusion Association Concerning the Project for Supplying Blood Plasma for England* (New York: Blood Transfusion Association, 1941), 108–10.

67. Drew, "'Banked Blood'"; Charles E. Wynes, *Charles Richard Drew: The Man and the Myth* (Urbana: University of Illinois Press, 1988), 41–43; and Spencie Love, *One Blood: The Death and Resurrection of Charles R. Drew* (Chapel Hill: University of North Carolina Press, 1996), 120–21, 124–25.

68. "Illinois Civilian Blood Bank," *Journal of the American Medical Association* 119 (Aug. 15, 1942): 1378; "Blood Banks," *Journal of the American Medical Association* 119 (July 18, 1942): 956; and "Blood Banks in West Virginia," *Journal of the American Medical Association* 119 (July 4, 1942): 802.

69. Robert A. Kilduffe and Michael DeBakey, *The Blood Bank and the Technique and Therapeutics of Transfusions* (St. Louis: C.V. Mosby, 1942), 197.

70. Furnas, "Blood From a Stranger," 34.

71. Noah Fabricant and Leo M. Zimmerman, "Cry for Blood," *Hygeia,* Oct. 1939, 936.

72. Charles S. Cameron and L. Kraeer Ferguson, "The Organization and Technique of the Blood Bank at the Philadelphia General Hospital," *Surgery* 5 (1939): 238–39.

73. Kilduffe and DeBakey, *Blood Bank,* 199–200.

74. William Cronon, *Nature's Metropolis: Chicago and the Great West* (New York: Norton, 1991), 111–17.

75. Fabricant and Zimmerman, "Cry for Blood," 937.

76. Cronon, *Nature's Metropolis,* 111–17.

77. Fantus, "The Therapy at Cook County Hospital," 318.

78. Ibid., 317–18.

79. Furnas, "Blood From a Stranger," 9; Thomas A. Guglielmo, "'Red Cross, Double Cross': Race and America's World War II–Era Blood Donor Service," *Journal of American History* 97 (2010): 65.

80. E. H. L. Corwin, "Blood Transfusions and Donors," *Bulletin of the American Hospital Association,* July 1930, 118; and DeWitt Stetten, "The Blood Transfusion Betterment Association of New York City," *Journal of the American Medical Association* 110 (Apr. 16, 1938): 1249.

81. Drew, "'Banked Blood,'" unpaginated material between pages 215 and 216.

82. Diggs and Keith, "Problems in Blood Banking," 596.

83. Ravitch, "Blood Bank of Johns Hopkins Hospital," 171.

84. DeWitt K. Burnham, "History of the Irwin Memorial Blood Bank of the San Francisco County Medical Society," in *Starting and Operating a Blood Bank: Seven Articles,* edited by Bureau of Medical Research, Committee on Blood Banks, American Medical Association, Bulletin No. 82 (Chicago: American Medical Association, 1951), 27–28; and Bernice Hemphill, *The Mother of Blood Banking: Irwin Memorial Blood Bank and the American Association of Blood Banks, 1944–1994,* interviewed by Germaine LaBerge (Berkeley, CA: Regional Oral History Office, Bancroft Library, University of California, 1998), 131.

85. Kilduffe and DeBakey, *Blood Bank,* 262.

86. Janet Golden, *A Social History of Wet Nursing in America: From Breast to Bottle* (1996; Columbus: Ohio State University Press, 2001), 26; Katherine Jones, "The Mothers Milk Bureau of Detroit," *Public Health Nurse,* Mar. 1928, 142; and B. Raymond Hoobler, "The Production, Collection and Distribution of Human Milk: Retrospect and Prospect," *Journal of the American Medical Association* 88 (June 4, 1927): 1788.

87. "Galactic Crisis," *Time,* June 24, 1946.

88. Susan D. Lederer, *Flesh and Blood: Organ Transplantation and Blood Transfusion in Twentieth-Century America* (New York: Oxford University Press, 2008), 108, 111–12.

89. Furnas, "Blood From a Stranger," 36.

90. Kilduffe and DeBakey, *Blood Bank,* 197; and C. A. Pons, "The Blood Donor Registry as a Substitute for the Blood Bank," *American Journal of Clinical Pathology* 9 (1939): 588.

91. Pons, "Blood Donor Registry," 589.

92. Furnas, "Blood From a Stranger," 8; William DeKleine, "Red Cross Blood Transfusion Projects," *Journal of the American Medical Association* 111 (Dec. 3, 1938): 2101–3; Foster Rhea Dulles, *The American Red Cross: A History* (New York: Harper & Bros., 1950), 415; and Lederer, *Flesh and Blood,* 84–85.

93. Arthur John Collinson, "The Legion of Blood Donors!," *Hygeia,* Mar. 1940, 236–37.

94. James N. Miller, "Giant Blood Bank," *Hygeia,* Feb. 1941, 107–9, 119.

95. Earl S. Taylor, "Procurement of Blood for the Armed Forces," *Journal of the American Medical Association* 120 (Sept. 12, 1942): 119.

96. G. Canby Robinson, *American Red Cross Blood Donor Service During World War II: Its Organization and Operation,* ARC Report No. 1267 (Washington, DC: American National Red Cross, July 1946), 33–45; and Kendrick, *Blood Program,* 122–23.

97. Blood Transfusion Association, *Report of the Blood Transfusion Association,* 3; DeWitt Stetten, "The Blood Plasma for Great Britain Project," *Bulletin of the New York Academy of Medicine* 17 (Jan. 1941): 27; and Schneider, "Blood Transfusion between the Wars," 218.

98. John Scudder, Charles R. Drew, Dorothy R. Corcoran, and David C. Bull, "Studies in Blood Preservation," *Journal of the American Medical Association* 112 (June 3, 1939): 2263–71; and Charles R. Drew, Katherine Edsall, and John Scudder, "Studies in Blood Preservation," *Journal of Laboratory and Clinical Medicine* 24 (Dec. 1939): 239–45.

99. T. Gaillard Thomas, "The Intravenous Injection of Milk as a Substitute for the Transfusion of Blood," *New York Medical Journal* 27 (1878): 449–65; John H. Brinton, "The Transfusion of Blood and the Intravenous Injection of Milk," *Medical Record* 14 (1878): 344–47; Joseph C. Hutchinson, "Transfusion of Blood (Aveling's Method); and Transfusion of Milk," *Medical and Surgical Reporter* 40 (1879): 230–31.

100. Schneider, "Blood Transfusion in Peace and War," 114.

101. Kendrick, *Blood Program,* 267–68.

102. Ibid., 270.

103. Ibid., 13; and Stetten, "Blood Plasma," 27.

104. Kendrick, *Blood Program,* 13.

105. Stetten, "Blood Plasma," 27–28.

106. Earl S. Taylor, "Blood Procurement for the Army and Navy," *Journal of the American Medical Association* 117 (Dec. 20, 1941): 2123; and Stetten, "Blood Plasma," 29.

107. Stetten, "Blood Plasma," 36.

108. Ibid., 33.

109. Ibid., 34; and Love, *One Blood,* 155–60.

110. Stetten, "Blood Plasma," 32–33; and Kendrick, *Blood Program,* 14.

111. Stetten, "Blood Plasma," 33; and Schneider, "Blood Transfusion between the Wars," 220.

112. Robinson, *American Red Cross,* 6.

113. Kendrick, *Blood Program,* 371n1.

114. Robinson, *American Red Cross,* 62; and Kendrick, *Blood Program,* 265.

115. Robinson, *American Red Cross,* 62; and Kendrick, *Blood Program,* 325, 339–50, 355.

116. Kendrick, *Blood Program*, 50, 54, 208, 213, 222–25, 395, 422.

117. Charles H. Ellis Jr. and Robert E. S. Thompson, "Your Blood Goes to War," *Saturday Evening Post*, May 2, 1942, 44, 47; and Schneider, "Blood Transfusion between the Wars," 208, 220n81.

118. Robinson, *American Red Cross*, 1.

119. Miller, "Giant Blood Bank," 109.

120. Kendrick, *Blood Program*, 233.

121. Blood Transfusion Association, *Report of the Blood Transfusion Association.* This report had two parts, a "narrative account" (1–34) and the "medical report" (35–121), the latter of which was credited to Drew.

122. Kendrick, *Blood Program*, 36.

123. Blood Transfusion Association, *Report of the Blood Transfusion Association*, 14.

124. Kendrick, *Blood Program*, 119 (paraphrasing Robinson, *American Red Cross*, 33).

125. "The Red Cross Donor Service," *Hygeia*, Feb. 1943, 108–9, 156.

126. "Red Cross Blood Shipments Near 5000 a Week," *Daily Boston Globe*, Dec. 22, 1942.

127. Robinson, *American Red Cross*, 53.

128. Harold Putnam, "Victory Forum: Champion Blood Donors," *Daily Boston Globe*, Oct. 9, 1942.

129. Donita Ferguson, "My Blood Is in the War," *Reader's Digest*, Feb. 1943, 35–37 (reprinted from *Vogue*, Jan. 15, 1943).

130. Robinson, *American Red Cross*, 27; and Kendrick, *Blood Program*, 145.

131. Kendrick, *Blood Program*, 120.

132. Ibid., 120, 152–53.

133. Ibid., 280.

134. Ibid., 14; but see Ferguson, "My Blood Is in the War," 35.

135. Stetten, "Blood Plasma," 37; and New York State Sanitary Code Sec. 105, no. 14.

136. "Red Cross Deplores 'Absenteeism' on Blood Donors' Front," *Daily Boston Globe*, Apr. 18, 1943.

137. Blood Transfusion Association, *Report of the Blood Transfusion Association*, 6, 9–10.

138. Ibid., 14.

139. Ibid., 42.

140. Rosemary Stevens, *In Sickness and in Wealth: American Hospitals in the Twentieth Century* (New York: Basic Books, 1989), 105.

141. DeKleine, "Red Cross Blood," 2102.

142. Blood Transfusion Association, *Report of the Blood Transfusion Association*, 16–17; and Kendrick, *Blood Program*, 148.

143. Blood Transfusion Association, *Report of the Blood Transfusion Association*, 42.

144. Kendrick, *Blood Program*, 139; and Robinson, *American Red Cross*, 46.

145. Blood Transfusion Association, *Report of the Blood Transfusion Association*, 30.

146. Kendrick, *Blood Program*, 139–40.

147. Ibid.; Guglielmo, "'Red Cross, Double Cross'"; Lederer, *Flesh and Blood*, 116–35; Phillip McGuire, "Judge William Henry Hastie and Military Hemophobia, 1940–1943," *Journal of the Afro-American Historical and Genealogical Society* 4 (1983): 127–35; Phillip McGuire, "Judge Hastie, World War II, and the Army's Fear of Black Blood," *Review of Afro American Issues and Culture* 1 (1979): 134–51; and Love, *One Blood*, 141, 155–60, 194–97.

148. Kendrick, *Blood Program*, 145.

149. Ibid., 145–48.

150. Ferguson, "My Blood Is in the War," 36.

151. Kendrick, *Blood Program*, 121; and Sarah E. Chinn, *Technology and the Logic of American Racism: A Cultural History of the Body as Evidence* (London: Continuum, 2000), 98–105.

152. Kendrick, *Blood Program*, 128.

153. Ibid.

154. Robinson, *American Red Cross*, 85.

155. Robert Trumbull, "Two Surgeons Win Praise of Wounded," *New York Times*, Mar. 13, 1945 (subtitled "Names of Girl Blood Donors Are Treasured and GIs Promise to Look Them Up at Home"); and "Blood Donor, Recipient Meet," *New York Times*, Mar. 27, 1945.

156. Stephen Pemberton, *The Bleeding Disease: Hemophilia and the Unintended Consequences of Medical Progress* (Baltimore: Johns Hopkins University Press, 2011), 94–95, 170–72; Angela N. H. Creager, "Producing Molecular Therapeutics from Human Blood: Edwin Cohn's Wartime Enterprise," in *Molecularizing Biology and Medicine: New Practices and Alliances, 1910s–1970s*, edited by Soraya de Chadarevian and Harmke Kamminga (Amsterdam: Harwood Academic, 1998), 107–38; Angela N. H. Creager, "Biotechnology and Blood: Edwin Cohn's Plasma Fractionation Project, 1940–1953," in *Biotechnology and the Rise of the Molecular Sciences*, edited by Arnold Thackray (Philadelphia: University of Pennsylvania Press, 1998), 39–62; and Angela N. H. Creager, "'What Blood Told Dr. Cohn': World War II, Plasma Fractionation, and the Growth of Human Blood Research," *Studies in the History and Philosophy of Biology and the Biomedical Sciences* 30 (1999): 380–82.

157. Kendrick, *Blood Program*, 600.

3. BLOOD BATTLES IN THE COLD WAR

Epigraph: "Red Cross Blood Banks," *Journal of the Medical Society of New Jersey* 45 (August 1948): 417 (quoting House of Delegates resolution).

1. Bernice Hemphill, *The Mother of Blood Banking: Irwin Memorial Blood Bank and the American Association of Blood Banks, 1944–1994*, interviewed by

Germaine LaBerge (Berkeley: Regional Oral History Office, Bancroft Library, University of California, 1998), title, 12, 23–24, 26–33, 72.

2. Ibid., 53.

3. Herbert A. Perkins, introduction to Hemphill, *Mother of Blood Banking*, i–ii; and Hemphill, *Mother of Blood Banking*, 74–76, 134.

4. Perkins, introduction, i; and James N. Miller, "Giant Blood Bank," *Hygeia*, Feb. 1941, 107–9, 119.

5. Paul Starr, *The Social Transformation of American Medicine* (New York: Basic Books, 1982), 280.

6. Douglas B. Kendrick, *Blood Program in World War II (Supplemented by Experiences in the Korean War)* (Washington, DC: Office of the Surgeon General, Department of the Army, 1964), 548.

7. Jane Stafford, "Blood against the Atom Bomb," *Science News-Letter* 54 (July 3, 1948): 10.

8. Ibid.

9. State Department of Public Health, *Report on Blood Services in California* (n.p.: Senate of the State of California, 1947), 7.

10. M. G. Evans, "The Battle of the Blood Banks," *Medical Economics*, Feb. 1949, 56.

11. Basil O'Connor, "Dedication Address," given Jan. 12, 1948, Rochester, New York, printed as American Red Cross publication 1709, no page numbers; and American Association of Blood Banks, "Blood: A Personal Resource," Sept. 20, 1976 (copy in Hemphill, *Mother of Blood Banking*, 426).

12. Donald E. Brown, "Basic Problem in Blood Banks: Free or Pay," *Modern Hospital* 84 (May 1955): 51–56.

13. Bernard Fantus, ed., "The Therapy of the Cook County Hospital: Blood Preservation," *Journal of the American Medical Association* 109 (July 10, 1937): 128.

14. Joint Blood Council, *The Nation's Blood Transfusion Facilities and Services* (Washington, DC: Joint Blood Council, 1960), 7; Frank G. Dickinson and Everett L. Welker, *Second Survey of Blood Banks: A Report to the Committee on Blood Banks*, Bureau of Medical Economic Research, American Medical Association, Bulletin No. 83 (Chicago: American Medical Association, 1951), 1; and Louanne Kennedy, "Community Blood Banking in the United States from 1937–1975: Organizational Formation, Transformation and Reform in a Climate of Competing Ideologies," Ph.D. dissertation, New York University, 1978, 58, 77 (Table 1).

15. Robert A. Kilduffe and Michael DeBakey, *The Blood Bank and the Technique and Therapeutics of Transfusions* (St. Louis: C. V. Mosby, 1942), 231.

16. Rosemary Stevens, *In Sickness and in Wealth: American Hospitals in the Twentieth Century* (New York: Basic Books, 1989), 230.

17. Helen B. Crews, "Small Hospital Blood Bank," *American Journal of Nursing* 55 (Mar. 1955): 320.

18. Ibid., 320–23.

19. Joint Blood Council, *Nation's Blood Transfusion*, 4.

20. Ibid.

21. Ibid., 7.

22. Carl Schlicke, *Spokane and the Inland Empire Blood Bank: A History* (Fairfield, WA: Ye Galleon Press, n.d.), 15–16.

23. Joint Blood Council, *Nation's Blood Transfusion*, 7.

24. DeWitt K. Burnham, "History of the Irwin Memorial Blood Bank of the San Francisco County Medical Society," in *Starting and Operating a Blood Bank: Seven Articles*, edited by Bureau of Medical Research, Committee on Blood Banks, American Medical Association, Bulletin No. 82 (Chicago: American Medical Association, 1951), 27–28.

25. For example, Miller, "Giant Blood Bank"; and Donita Ferguson, "My Blood Is in the War," *Reader's Digest*, Feb. 1943, 35 (reprinted from *Vogue*, Jan. 15, 1943).

26. Foster Rhea Dulles, *The American Red Cross: A History* (New York: Harper & Bros., 1950), 527.

27. U.S. Office of Defense Mobilization, *National Blood Program Publicity Manual* (Washington, DC: Executive Office of the President, [1952]), ii, 2.

28. National Research Council, *Bulletin, Blood and Blood Derivatives* (1948), 21.

29. Dulles, *American Red Cross*, 518.

30. Kendrick, *Blood Program*, 727.

31. O'Connor, "Dedication Address."

32. Ibid.

33. George B. Dowling, "Red Cross Blood Program," *Virginia Medical Monthly*, Oct. 1948, 498.

34. Ibid.; G. B. Dowling, "The Red Cross Blood Program," *Military Surgeon*, Aug. 1948, 94–96; and George B. Dowling, "The Implications in a Blood Program," *American Biology Teacher*, Mar. 1949, 66–70.

35. Alton L. Blakeslee, *Blood's Magic for All*, Public Affairs Pamphlet No. 145 (New York: Public Affairs Committee, 1948), 27, 31.

36. Stafford, "Blood against the Atom Bomb"; Jane Stafford, "Regional Centers for Blood," *Science News-Letter* 54 (July 10, 1948): 26–28; and Jane Stafford, "Blood Wards Off Disease," *Science News-Letter* 54 (July 17, 1948): 42–44.

37. Stafford, "Regional Centers for Blood," 26–28.

38. Gunnar Gundersen, "Objectives and Activities of AMA Committee on Blood," *Proceedings of Conference on Blood and Blood Banking*, Chicago, IL, Dec. 11–12, 1964, 3.

39. Alton L. Blakeslee, "The Gift of Miracles," *Hygeia*, Nov. 1948, 794.

40. Marcia Gray Doty, *Delta Blood Bank, 1954–1986* (Stockton, CA: Delta Blood Bank, 1986), 1.

41. Doty, *Delta Blood Bank,* 4–5, 7–8.

42. R. M. Harlow, "Red Cross Blood Bank Plan Draws Medical Fire," *Medical Economics,* Mar. 1948, 143–44.

43. National Research Council, Committee on Blood and Blood Derivatives, "Present Status National Blood Program American Red Cross," Appendix A to Minutes of First Meeting, Mar. 8, 1948, *Bulletin, Blood and Blood Derivatives* (1948): 31; and Ross T. McIntire and George W. Hervey, "Collection and Distribution of Blood by the American National Red Cross," in Bureau of Medical Research, *Starting and Operating a Blood Bank,* 21.

44. Kendrick, *Blood Program,* 717–810; and Frank R. Camp Jr., Nicolas F. Conte, and Jerry R. Brewer, *Military Blood Banking 1941–1973: Lessons Learned Applicable to Civil Disasters and Other Considerations* (Fort Knox, KY: U.S. Army Medical Research Laboratory, Blood Bank Center, 1973), 3–5, 12–15, 15–21.

45. Louis K. Diamond, "The History of Blood Banking," *Proceedings of Conference on Blood and Blood Banking,* Chicago, IL, Dec. 11–12, 1964, 9.

46. Kennedy, "Community Blood Banking," 290–91.

47. Starr, *Social Transformation,* 235–36, 280.

48. W. Lee Hart, "Greetings from Southwestern Medical College," *Proceedings of Blood Bank Institute,* Dallas, TX, Nov. 17–19, 1948, 7.

49. Harlow, "Red Cross Blood Bank," 145; and "Summary of Business Session, Wed., Nov. 19, 1948," *Proceedings of Blood Bank Institute,* Dallas, TX, Nov. 17–19, 1948, 176.

50. Julius W. Davenport Jr., "Blood Transfusion in Louisiana," *New Orleans Medical and Surgical Journal,* Nov. 1949, 264–65.

51. McIntire and Hervey, "Collection and Distribution of Blood," 19, 19n3.

52. Starr, *Social Transformation,* 235–449; and "The Blood Business," *Time,* Nov. 30, 1962.

53. Starr, *Social Transformation,* 354.

54. Patricia Spain Ward, "United States versus American Medical Association, et al.: The Medical Antitrust Case of 1938–1943," *American Studies* 30 (1989): 123–53.

55. Stevens, *In Sickness and in Wealth,* 203.

56. Starr, *Social Transformation,* 259–60, 335.

57. Stevens, *In Sickness and in Wealth,* 182–89, 228, 258–59; and Starr, *Social Transformation,* 295–98, 306–10.

58. Davenport, "Blood Transfusion in Louisiana," 264; and Brown, "Basic Problem," 51.

59. Hemphill, *Mother of Blood Banking,* 73.

60. Julius W. Davenport Jr., "Blood Bank Administration," *Proceedings of Blood Bank Institute,* Dallas, TX, Nov. 17–19, 1948, 126.

61. Ibid.

62. Evans, "Battle of the Blood Banks."

63. Davenport, "Blood Bank Administration," 124.

64. Davenport, "Blood Transfusion," 259.

65. Ibid., 260.

66. Lester J. Unger, "The Blood Bank Service of the New York Post-Graduate Medical School and Hospital," *Proceedings of Blood Bank Institute,* Dallas, TX, Nov. 17–19, 1948, 109–10.

67. Ibid., 104.

68. Richard H. Rovere, *Senator Joseph McCarthy* (1956; Berkeley: University of California Press, 1996), 3; and Thomas A. Reeves, *The Life and Times of Joe McCarthy: A Biography* (Lanham, MD: Madison Books, 1997), 207–15.

69. Joint Blood Council, *Nation's Blood Transfusion,* 4.

70. Harlow, "Red Cross Blood Bank," 143.

71. "Red Cross Blood Banks," 416–17.

72. Kennedy, "Community Blood Banking," 394–95.

73. "Red Cross Blood Banks," 417; and Evans, "Battle of the Blood Banks," 56 (quoting resolution using slightly different wording).

74. Davenport, "Blood Transfusion," 264.

75. McIntire and Hervey, "Collection and Distribution of Blood," 22.

76. O. A. Brines, "The Blood Bank in a Charity or City-County Hospital," *Proceedings of Blood Bank Institute,* Dallas, TX, Nov. 17–19, 1948, 47–48.

77. Dickinson and Welker, *Second Survey of Blood Banks,* 1.

78. Bureau of Medical Economic Research, American Medical Association, "Miscellaneous Publication M-49" (Chicago: American Medical Association, 1951), 1–3.

79. Ibid., 4–5.

80. Ibid., 2.

81. Ibid., 8.

82. Gundersen, "Objectives and Activities," 4–5; and Diamond, "History of Blood Banking," 14–15.

83. Joint Blood Council, *Nation's Blood Transfusion,* 22.

84. Regulation of Biological Products, 42 U.S.C. §262, et. seq. (as of July 31, 2009); and Establishment, Regulation, and Product Listing for Manufacturers of Human Blood and Blood Products, 21 C.F.R. §607, et seq. (as of July 28, 2009).

85. Joint Blood Council, *Nation's Blood Transfusion,* 22.

86. Paul C. Rapp, *The Gift of Life: A Fifty Year History of Central Florida Volunteers Donating* (Orlando: Central Florida Blood Bank, 1991), 6; and Richard A. Martin, *Jacksonville's Silent Service: A History of the Jacksonville Blood Bank and Florida-Georgia Blood Alliance, 1942–1992* (Jacksonville, FL: Centurion Press, 1992), 18–19.

87. State Department of Public Health, *Report on Blood Services in California,* 24 (appendix, Table IX); Martin, *Jacksonville's Silent Service,* 18–19, 78–82; and Dickinson and Welker, *Second Survey of Blood Banks,* 30.

88. Robert Starr, "Blood Transfusion and Blood Banks," M.D. thesis, University of Wisconsin, 1950, 38–44.

89. Melvin E. Koons, "The Status of North Dakota's Plasma Program," *Journal-Lancet,* Apr. 1948, 136.

90. Dickinson and Welker, *Second Survey of Blood Banks,* 31.

91. Frank E. Barton and Thomas M. Hearne, "The Use of Placental Blood for Transfusion," *Journal of the American Medical Association* 113 (Oct. 14, 1939): 1476; and Charles C. Lund, "Medical Sponsorship and Supervision: The Massachusetts Regional Blood Program of the American National Red Cross," *Proceedings of Conference on Blood and Blood Banking,* Chicago, IL, Dec. 11–12, 1964, 39.

92. "Red Cross Blood Shipments Near 5000 Pints a Week," *Daily Boston Globe,* Dec. 22, 1942; John G. Harris, "Modern Paul Revere Gets 1500 Donors to Blood Bank Here," *Daily Boston Globe,* Feb. 24, 1943; and "Boston Blood Used in 5 Days Overseas; Col. Kendrick Says," *Daily Boston Globe,* Nov. 3, 1944.

93. Lund, "Medical Sponsorship and Supervision," 39, 42; and Starr, "Blood Transfusion and Blood Banks," 42–44.

94. Lund, "Medical Sponsorship and Supervision," 44; National Research Council, *Bulletin, Blood and Blood Derivatives* (1948), 18; and American National Red Cross, *Hospitals Served by the Red Cross Blood Program and Usage of Blood and Derivatives Distributed 1957–58* (n.p.: American National Red Cross, n.d.).

95. Lund, "Medical Sponsorship and Supervision," 39–40.

96. Ibid., 41; and Dickinson and Welker, *Second Survey of Blood Banks,* 35.

97. State Department of Public Health, *Report on Blood Bank Services,* 4–5, 11, 13.

98. Ibid., 7.

99. Ibid., 5, 16; and C. Y. Gates, "Medical Sponsorship and Supervision," *Proceedings of Conference on Blood and Blood Banking,* Chicago, IL, Dec. 11–12, 1964, 29.

100. Cal. Health & Safety Code §1601 (enacted 1963).

101. Dickinson and Welker, *Second Survey of Blood Banks,* 31.

102. I. J. Brightman, "Plan for State-wide Distribution of Blood and Blood Derivatives—Organization," *New York State Medical Journal* 47 (Feb. 1, 1947): 264–65.

103. Unger, "Blood Bank Service," 101–2, 104.

104. Dickinson and Welker, *Second Survey of Blood Banks,* 30.

105. Committee on Public Health, "Human Blood in New York City: A Report of Its Procurement, Distribution and Utilization, Summaries and Conclusions," *Bulletin of the New York Academy of Medicine* 34 (June 1958): 408.

106. Ibid., 409–10; and Joint Blood Council, *Nation's Blood Transfusion,* 28.

107. Aaron Kellner, "Automation," *Proceedings of Conference on Blood and Blood Banking,* Chicago, IL, Dec. 11–12, 1964, 18, 20.

108. Brown, "Basic Problem," 51.

109. Fantus, "Therapy of the Cook County Hospital," 128.

110. Elizabeth H. Schirmer, "The County Blood Bank," *County Intern,* Apr. 1943, 7; Robert G. Boyd, "The Bank Depends upon Its Friends," *Modern Hospital* 72 (May 1949): 70; and Schlicke, *Spokane and Inland Empire Blood Bank,* 22.

111. Stephen Pemberton, *The Bleeding Disease: Hemophilia and the Unintended Consequences of Medical Progress* (Baltimore: Johns Hopkins University Press, 2011), 120–23; Schlicke, *Spokane and Inland Empire Blood Bank,* 37; and Hemphill, *Mother of Blood Banking,* 178.

112. Schlicke, *Spokane and the Inland Empire Blood Bank,* 18.

113. Ibid., 19–20.

114. Ibid., 22.

115. Bernice M. Hemphill, "Reserve Funds, Insurance Plans and Administrative Policies," *Proceedings of Blood Bank Institute,* Dallas, TX, Nov. 17–19, 1947, 81–85; W. Quinn Jordan, "Blood Assurance Plans," *Proceedings of Conference on Blood and Blood Banking,* Chicago, IL, Dec. 11–12, 1964, 93; Hemphill, *Mother of Blood Banking,* 64; and Rapp, *Gift of Life,* 22.

116. Jordan, "Blood Assurance Plans," 97; and Kennedy, "Community Blood Banking," 191.

117. Doty, *Delta Blood Bank,* 27.

118. Bernice M. Hemphill, "National Clearinghouse Program of the American Association of Blood Banks," *Proceedings of Conference on Blood and Blood Banking,* Chicago, IL, Dec. 11–12, 1964, 77.

119. Hemphill, *Mother of Blood Banking,* 101, 104.

120. Hemphill, "National Clearinghouse Program," 75.

121. Hemphill, *Mother of Blood Banking,* 104–105; "Blood Bank Plan Voted at Convention," *Washington Post and Times Herald,* Sept. 15, 1954; and AABB, "Blood: A Personal Resource. A Position Paper," Sept. 20, 1976 (copy included in Hemphill, *Mother of Blood Banking,* 431), 1.

122. E. R. Jennings, "Standards, Inspection, Accreditation Programs of American Association of Blood Banks," *Proceedings of Conference on Blood and Blood Banking,* Chicago, IL, Dec. 11–12, 1964, 109–11.

123. Hemphill, *Mother of Blood Banking,* 104–5.

124. Doty, *Delta Blood Bank,* 19.

125. Hemphill, *Mother of Blood Banking,* 129; and Kennedy, "Community Blood Banking," 147, 169–73.

126. Leon E. Mermod and Hazel Bond, "The Blood Bank of Hawaii," *Proceedings of Blood Bank Institute,* Dallas, TX, Nov. 17–19, 1948, 30.

127. Marion R. Rymer, "The History and Function of the Belle Bonfils Memorial Blood Bank," *Proceedings of Blood Bank Institute,* Dallas, TX, Nov. 17–19, 1948, 54–56.

128. Editorial, "Why Don't More Women Give Blood?," *Saturday Evening Post,* June 7, 1952, 12; and Joint Blood Council, *Nation's Blood Transfusion,* 5.

129. Peter L. Twohig, " 'Local Girls' and 'Lab Boys': Gender, Skill and Medical Laboratories in Nova Scotia in the 1920s and 1930s," *Acadiensis* 31 (Fall 2001): 68–69, 72–73, and generally; and Ellen More, *Restoring the Balance: Women Physicians and the Profession of Medicine, 1850–1995* (Cambridge, MA: Harvard University Press, 1999), 5.

130. Hemphill, *Mother of Blood Banking,* 154.

131. Ibid., 280.

132. Interview with Betty Carley, in Hemphill, *Mother of Blood Banking,* 364.

133. Hemphill, "Reserve Funds, Insurance Plans, and Administrative Policies," 84; and Burnham, "History of the Irwin Memorial Blood Bank," 31.

134. "Blood Bank Society Is Organized," *Mayovox,* June 20, 1964; and "Blood Bank Society Elects," *Mayovox,* Dec. 4, 1964. Copies in MHU-0676: Subject Files, Blood Bank Folder, Mayo Clinic Historical Unit, Rochester, MN.

135. Martin, *Jacksonville's Silent Service,* 236.

136. Helen Bates, *Jacksonville Journal,* Apr. 6, 1960, as quoted in Martin, *Jacksonville's Silent Service,* 214.

137. Patricia McCormack, "Women Are Out for Your Blood," *Chicago Daily Defender,* Mar. 2, 1965.

138. Robert Wiedrich, "It's a Pleasure, Almost, to Give Blood at U. of C.: Pretty Nurses Sidetrack Fears of Donors," *Chicago Daily Tribune,* Apr. 12, 1951.

139. Raymond L. White, "Welcome," *Proceedings of Conference on Blood and Blood Banking,* Chicago, IL, Dec. 11–12, 1964, 1.

140. J. Richard Czajkowski, "Central Typing and Crossmatching Functions of the King County Central Blood Bank," *Proceedings of Conference on Blood and Blood Banking,* Chicago, IL, Dec. 11–12, 1964, 25 (emphasis added).

141. Richard E. Dice, "Paid Donor Programs," *Proceedings of Conference on Blood and Blood Banking,* Chicago, IL, Dec. 11–12, 1964, 72.

142. Pemberton, *The Bleeding Disease,* 120–23.

143. Robert M. Greendyke and Jane C. Corner, *Introduction to Blood Banking,* (Flushing, NY: Medical Examination, 1970), unpaginated introduction.

144. Schlicke, *Spokane and the Inland Empire Blood Bank,* 37.

145. Hemphill, *Mother of Blood Banking,* 178.

146. Joint Blood Council, *Nation's Blood Transfusion,* 44.

147. Hemphill, "National Clearinghouse Program," 77.

148. Bernice Hemphill, preface to AABB, "Blood: A Personal Resource. A Position Paper," Sept. 20, 1976 (copy included in Hemphill, *Mother of Blood Banking,* 431).

149. AABB, "Blood: A Personal Resource."

150. National Heart and Lung Institute, *Supply and Use of the Nation's Blood Resource,* Blood Resource Studies, vol. 1, DHEW Publication No. (NIH) 73-417 (June 30, 1972) (Bethesda, MD: U.S. Department of Health, Education, and Welfare, Public Health Service/National Institutes of Health, National Heart and Lung Institute, National Blood Resource Program, n.d.), 13.

4. MARKET BACKLASH

Epigraph: Richard M. Titmuss, *The Gift Relationship: From Human Blood to Social Policy,* edited by Ann Oakley and John Ashton, expanded ed. (1970; New York: New Press, 1997), 58–59 (first U.S. edition, Pantheon Books, 1971).

1. Ibid., 59.

2. Donald E. Brown, "Basic Problem in Blood Banks: Free or Pay," *Modern Hospital* 84 (May 1955): 51.

3. Bernard Fantus, "Therapy of the Cook County Hospital," *Bulletin C,* May 1937, 1, copy in Box 1 2002-199, Fantus Papers and reprinted in revised form as Bernard Fantus, ed., "The Therapy of the Cook County Hospital: Blood Preservation," *Journal of the American Medical Association* 109 (July 10, 1937): 128–31.

4. American Law Institute, *Restatement of the Law, Second: Torts* (St. Paul, MN: American Law Institute Publishers, 1965), §402A(1); and Patricia Kussman, "Validity, Application, and Construction of Blood Shield Statutes," *American Law Reports: Cases and Annotations,* 5th ed. (Rochester, NY: Lawyers Cooperative, 2000), 75: 229, §§1[a], 2[a].

5. Titmuss, *Gift Relationship,* 58–59.

6. Olcott D. Smith, "The Tort Liability of Charitable Institutions," *Connecticut Bar Journal* 12 (July 1938): 214–15; and Kenneth Allen De Ville, *Medical Malpractice in Nineteenth-Century America: Origins and Legacy* (New York: New York University Press, 1990), 210–15.

7. Standiford v. Cantrell, 87 Cal. App. 736, 739–40, 262 P. 800, 801–2 (1922). Estimates of values in 2013 dollars based on the Bureau of Labor Statistics Consumer Price Index.

8. Jeter v. Davis, 127 S.E. 898, 898–99, 901 (Ga. App. 1925).

9. "Jury Awards Big Verdict," *Reno Evening Gazette,* Nov. 30, 1933; "$75,000 Suit in Death of Blood Donor," *Oakland Tribune,* May 23, 1933; and "Blood Donor and Woman Patient Die in Hospital," *Oakland Tribune,* May 13, 1933.

10. "Blood Transfusions—Medicolegal Responsibilities," *Journal of the American Medical Association* 163 (Jan. 26, 1957): 283.

11. Phillip Levine and Eugene M. Katzin, "A Survey of Blood Transfusion in America," *Journal of the American Medical Association* 110 (Apr. 16, 1938): 1247–48.

12. Neal C. Hogan, *Unhealed Wounds: Medical Malpractice in the Twentieth Century* (New York: LFB Scholarly Publishing, 2003), xi, 33.

13. DeWitt Stetten, "The Blood Transfusion Betterment Association of New York City," *Journal of the American Medical Association* 110 (Apr. 16, 1938): 1249; and E. H. L. Corwin, "Blood Transfusions and Donors," *Bulletin of the American Hospital Association,* July 1930, 117–18.

14. Frank W. Dickinson, "Letter of Transmittal," in *Starting and Operating a Blood Bank: Seven Articles,* edited by Bureau of Economic Medical Research, Committee on Blood Banks, American Medical Association, Bulletin No. 82 (Chicago: American Medical Association, 1951), 1, 2.

15. Committee on Medicolegal Problems, "Medicolegal Aspects of Blood Transfusion," *Journal of the American Medical Association* 151 (Apr. 18, 1953): 1437.

16. Frank W. Hartman, "The Henry Ford Hospital Blood Bank," in Bureau of Economic Medical Research, *Starting and Operating a Blood Bank,* 3, 8.

17. James A. Thomas, "Blood Transfusion Liability," *Cleveland-Marshall Law Review* 10 (1961): 473.

18. Necolayff v. Genesee Hospital, 270 A.D. 648, 649–52, 61 N.Y.S.2d 832, 833–36 (1946). See also Berg v. New York Society for the Relief of the Ruptured and Crippled, 154 N.Y.S.2d 455, 1 N.Y.2d 499 (1956).

19. Mississippi Baptist Hospital v. Holmes, 214 Miss. 906, 913, 55 So.2d 142, 143–44 (1951); and National Homeopathic Hospital v. Phillips, 181 F.2d. 293, 293–94 (D.C. Cir. 1950).

20. Brown v. Shannon West Texas Memorial Hospital, 222 S.W.2d 248 (Tex. Civ.App. 1949); Parker v. State, 105 N.Y.S.2d. 735 (1951); and "Blood Transfusions—Medicolegal Responsibilities," 283, 284, 287.

21. G. Edward White, *Tort Law in America: An Intellectual History,* expanded ed. (New York: Oxford University Press, 2003), 168–71.

22. *Restatement of the Law, Second,* §402A.

23. Perlmutter v. Beth David Hospital, 308 N.Y. 100, 103 (1954).

24. Perlmutter v. Beth David Hospital, 128 N.Y.S.2d 176, 177 (1953), aff'd without opinion, 283 A.D. 789 (1954).

25. *Perlmutter,* 308 N.Y. at 104.

26. *Id.*

27. *Id.* at 106.

28. *Id.*

29. *Id.* at 110–11.

30. James A. Tobey, "A New Foster-Mother," *Hygeia,* Nov. 1929, 1110.

31. Lester J. Unger, "The Blood Bank Service of the New York Post-Graduate Medical School and Hospital," *Proceedings of the Blood Bank Institute,* Dallas, TX, Nov. 17–19, 1948, 109–10.

32. Jan R. McTavish, *Pain and Profits: The History of the Headache and Its Remedies in America* (New Brunswick, NJ: Rutgers University Press, 2004), 112.

33. Committee on Medicolegal Problems, "Medicolegal Aspects of Blood Transfusion," 1435–43.

34. California Health and Safety Code §1623 (1955), recodified as §1606 in 1963.

35. "Blood Transfusions—Medicolegal Responsibilities," 286.

36. Cunningham v. MacNeal Memorial Hospital, 47 Ill.2d 443, 449–50 (1970).

37. Gerald D. Roth, "Sales," *New York University Law Review* 29 (Dec. 1954): 1585.

38. "Blood Transfusions—Medicolegal Responsibilities," 286.

39. *Cunningham*, 47 Ill. 2d at 457.

40. Russell v. Community Blood Bank, Inc., 185 So.2d 749, 752–53 (Fla.App. 1966), rev'd on other grounds, Community Blood Bank, Inc. v. Russell, 196 So.2d 115 (Fla. 1967).

41. Reilly v. King County Central Blood Bank, 6 Wash.App. 172, 175 (1971).

42. Sidney N. Zipser, "Liability for Negligence in Blood Transfusions," *Federation of Insurance Counsel Quarterly* 16 (Spring 1966): 9.

43. "The Blood Business," *Time*, Nov. 30, 1962.

44. Bernice M. Hemphill, "National Clearinghouse Program of the American Association of Blood Banks," *Proceedings of Conference on Blood and Blood Banking*, Chicago, IL, Dec. 11–12, 1964, 77.

45. In the Matter of Community Blood Bank of the Kansas City Area, Inc., 70 F.T.C. 728, 1966 WL 88193, *7 (1966)(emphasis added).

46. R. M. Harlow, "Red Cross Blood Bank Plan Draws Medical Fire," *Medical Economics*, Mar. 1948, 145.

47. Louanne Kennedy, "Community Blood Banking in the United States from 1937–1975: Organizational Formation, Transformation and Reform in a Climate of Competing Ideologies," Ph.D. dissertation, New York University, 1978, 58–59, 67, 77 (Table 1).

48. *In the Matter of Community Blood Bank*, 1966 WL 88193 at *21–22, 31–33.

49. *Id.* at *20, 33.

50. *Id.* at *34–37.

51. Donald L. Beschle, "Doing Well, Doing Good and Doing Both: A Framework for the Analysis of Noncommercial Boycotts under the Antitrust Laws," *Saint Louis University Law Journal* 30 (Mar. 1986): 396–98.

52. *In the Matter of Community Blood Bank*, 1966 WL 88193.

53. *Id.* at *24.

54. *Id.* at *34.

55. *Id.* at *24, 29.

56. *Id.* at *25.

57. *Id.* at *118.

58. "Blood Business"; and "Blood Traffic," *Time,* Feb. 9, 1962.

59. "Recent Decisions," *Virginia Law Review* 55 (1969): 1147–48; and Beschle, "Doing Well," 396–98.

60. Community Blood Bank of Kansas City Area, Inc. v. Federal Trade Commission, 405 F.2d 1011, 1022 (8th Cir. 1969).

61. Warren E. Whyte, "Federal Trade Commission versus the Community Blood Bank of Kansas City, et al.," *Proceedings of Conference on Blood and Blood Banking,* Chicago, IL, Dec. 11–12, 1964, 152–56.

62. Carl Schlicke, *Spokane and the Inland Empire Blood Bank: A History* (Fairfield, WA: Ye Galleon Press, n.d.), 43; and *Community Blood Bank,* 405 F. 2d at 1011.

63. *In the Matter of Community Blood Bank,* 1966 WL 88193, *81.

64. J. S. Lundy, Annual Report, Section on Anesthesia, 1944, MHU-0002, Subject Files, Blood Bank Folder, Mayo Clinic Historical Unit, Rochester, MN.

65. Brown, "Basic Problem in Blood Banks," 54 (emphasis added).

66. *In the Matter of Community Blood Bank,* 1966 WL 88193, *66.

67. American Association of Blood Banks, "Statement of Principles of Blood Procurement," Oct. 30, 1962, copy included in Addendum to Memorandum to Assembly Members on the Committee on Public Health, California State Legislature, dated Mar. 25, 1966, A/C Public Health, AB 333, 1963, California State Archives, Sacramento, CA (hereinafter Memorandum to Assembly Members).

68. Memorandum to Assembly Members, 2.

69. Testimony of Mrs. Bernice Hemphill, Hearings before Subcommittee on Antitrust and Monopoly of the Committee of the Judiciary, U.S. Senate, 88th Cong., 2d Sess., Aug. 18, 1964 (Washington, DC: U.S. Government Printing Office, 1964), 34.

70. *In the Matter of Community Blood Bank,* 1966 WL 88193, *81.

71. Testimony of Dr. Rosser L. Mainwaring, Hearings before Subcommittee on Antitrust and Monopoly of the Committee of the Judiciary, U.S. Senate, 88th Cong., 2d Sess., Aug. 18, 1964 (Washington, DC: U.S. Government Printing Office, 1964), 5, 12.

72. *In the Matter of Community Blood Bank,* 1966 WL 88193, *80.

73. Testimony of Dr. Francis Coleman, Hearings before Subcommittee on Antitrust and Monopoly of the Committee of the Judiciary, U.S. Senate, 88th Cong., 2d Sess., Aug. 19, 1964 (Washington, DC: U.S. Government Printing Office, 1964), 86–87.

74. IRS General Counsel Memorandum 23310, A-37321 (July 6, 1942); Bridget J. Crawford, "Our Bodies, Our (Tax) Selves," *Virginia Tax Review* 31 (2011–12): 717–18; and Susan E. Lederer, *Flesh and Blood: Organ Transplantation and Blood Transfusion in Twentieth-Century America* (New York: Oxford University Press, 2008), 94–95.

75. Hoffman v. Misericordia Hospital of Philadelphia, 1969 WL 11075, 6 UCC Rep.Serv. 779 (Pa.Com.Pl. July 16, 1969); and Hoffman v. Misericordia Hospital of Philadelphia, 439 Pa. 501, 507, 267 A.2d 867, 870 (1970) (quoting *Russell,* 185 So.2d at 752).

76. Reuben A. Kessel, "Transfused Blood, Serum Hepatitis, and the Coase Theorem," *Journal of Law and Economics* 17 (1974): 277, 277n51; and Marc A. Franklin, "Tort Liability for Hepatitis: An Analysis and a Proposal," *Stanford Law Review* 24 (1971–72): 475n205.

77. Draft copy of Health and Welfare Agency Bill Analysis (Bill No. A.B. 333), addressed to Winslow Christian, Administrator, Health and Welfare Agency, dated Feb. 28, 1963, A/C Public Health, AB 333, 1963, California State Archives; and California Health & Safety Code §§1600.4, 1606 (Stat. 1963, ch.1055, June 29, 1963).

78. Pub. Act No. 77–184, §3 (1971), codified as 745 Ill. Comp. Stat. Ann. 40/2 (2013); Act No. 9 of 1972 (House Bill 1266), codified as 42 Pa. Cons. Stat. Ann. §8333 (2013); and Franklin, "Tort Liability," 475n205.

79. Heirs of Fruge v. Blood Services, 365 F.Supp. 1344, 1350 n. 3 (W.D. La. 1973).

80. Titmuss, *The Gift Relationship,* 125; and Marcel Mauss, *The Gift: Forms and Functions of Exchange in Archaic Societies,* translated by Ian Cunnison (1954; New York: Norton, 1967).

81. Titmuss, *The Gift Relationship,* 129–41.

82. Testimony of Dr. Sam T. Gibson, Hearings before Subcommittee on Antitrust and Monopoly of the Committee of the Judiciary, U.S. Senate, 88th Cong., 2d Sess., Aug. 19, 1964 (Washington, DC: U.S. Government Printing Office, 1964), 63.

83. Douglas Starr, *Blood: An Epic History of Medicine and Commerce* (1998; New York: Perennial, 2002), 252, 263.

84. William H. Schneider, "Introduction" to Special Issue: The First Genetic Marker, *History and Philosophy of the Life Sciences* 18 (1996): 273–76; Keith Wailoo, "Genetic Marker of Segregation: Sickle Cell Anemia, Thalassemia, and Racial Ideology in American Medical Writing 1920–1950," *History and Philosophy of the Life Sciences* 18 (1996): 305–20; Keith Wailoo, *Drawing Blood: Technology and Disease Identity in Twentieth-Century America* (Baltimore: Johns Hopkins University Press, 1997), 138–51; Keith Wailoo, *Dying in the City of the Blues: Sickle Cell Anemia and the Politics of Race and Health* (Chapel Hill: University of North Carolina Press, 2001), 78–79, 89–90, 143–50; and Daniel J. Sharfstein, "Crossing the Color Line: Racial Migration and the One-Drop Rule, 1600–1860," *Minnesota Law Review* 91 (2007): 592–656.

85. Thomas A. Guglielmo, " 'Red Cross, Double Cross': Race and America's World War II–Era Blood Donor Service," *Journal of American History* 97 (2010): 63–90; Spencie Love, *One Blood: The Death and Resurrection of Charles R. Drew*

(Chapel Hill: University of North Carolina Press, 1996), 141, 155–60, 194–97; and Lederer, *Flesh and Blood*, 116–35.

86. Foster Rhea Dulles, *The American Red Cross: A History* (New York: Harper & Bros., 1950), 5.

87. George B. Dowling, "Red Cross Blood Program," *Virginia Medical Monthly,* Oct. 1948, 498.

88. Guglielmo, " 'Red Cross, Double Cross,' " 82.

89. *National Blood Program: Publicity Manual* (Washington, DC: Office of Defense Mobilization, 1952), 21.

90. Michael G. Kenny, "A Question of Blood, Race and Politics," *Journal of the History of Medicine and the Allied Sciences* 61 (2006): 456–91; and Lederer, *Flesh and Blood*, 123–29.

91. American Association of Blood Banks, *Technical Methods and Procedures of the American Association of Blood Banks,* revised ed. (Minneapolis: Burgess, 1956), 3, 64–67.

92. Julius W. Davenport Jr., "Blood Transfusion in Louisiana," *New Orleans Medical and Surgical Journal,* Nov. 1949, 261.

93. Hospital Telegram from Adriani to Sister Alphonse, Director, Sisters' Division (undated), Box 75, Folder 10; Blood Bank Directives (undated), 3, Box 75, Folder 9; and Hospital Telegram from Adriani to "All Concerned" dated Jan. 12, 1962, Box 75, Folder 9, Papers of John Adriani, MS C 452, National Library of Medicine Archives, Bethesda, MD.

94. Kenny, "Question of Blood," 470; and Lederer, *Flesh and Blood*, 129–35.

95. Charles A. Reynard, "Segregation," *Louisiana Law Review* 19 (1958–59): 123–24.

96. Hospital Telegram from Adriani to "All Concerned," dated Jan. 12, 1962.

97. "Hospitals Told to Desegregate Blood Supplies," *Los Angeles Times,* May 14, 1967; and Morton Mintz, "La. Hospitals Segregate Blood While Receiving Federal Funds," *Washington Post,* July 6, 1969.

98. Guglielmo, " 'Red Cross, Double Cross,' " 66; Wailoo, *Drawing Blood,* 134–61; and Lederer, *Flesh and Blood*, 115–16.

99. Testimony of Mrs. Bernice Hemphill, 35.

100. Hartman, "The Henry Ford Hospital Blood Bank," 5–7; and Testimony of Dr. John W. Rebuck, Hearings before Subcommittee on Antitrust and Monopoly of the Committee of the Judiciary, U.S. Senate, 88th Cong., 2d Sess., Aug. 18, 1964 (Washington, DC: U.S. Government Printing Office, 1964), 55.

101. I. S. Ravdin and Brooke Roberts, "The Blood Bank at the Hospital of the University of Pennsylvania," in Bureau of Economic Medical Research, *Starting and Operating a Blood Bank,* 15.

102. Tibor J. Greenwalt, "The Junior League Blood Center of Milwaukee," in Bureau of Economic Medical Research, *Starting and Operating a Blood Bank,* 36.

103. Joint Blood Council, *The Nation's Blood Transfusion Facilities and Services* (Washington, DC: Joint Blood Council, 1960), 27.

104. Ibid., 28.

105. Kenneth McCracken, "Clinic Seeks Blood Donors to Meet Rising Demands," *Post-Bulletin* (Rochester, MN), Mar. 4, 1971, clipping in MHU-0676: Subject Files, Blood Bank Folder, Mayo Clinic Historical Unit.

106. Harold Severson, "Town & Country Scene," *Post-Bulletin* (Rochester, MN), May 16, 1975, clipping in MHU-0676: Subject Files, Blood Bank Folder, Mayo Clinic Historical Unit.

107. "Smooth-Functioning Clinic Blood Bank Moves Quarters," *Mayovox* 2 (Feb. 17, 1951): 1, copy in Blood Bank Folder, Mayo Clinic Historical Unit.

108. *Perlmutter*, 308 N.Y. at 103, 123 N.E.2d at 793; and "Recent Decisions," *Duquesne Law Review* 9 (1970–71): 288.

109. King County Central Blood Bank v. United Biologic Corp., 1 Wash. App. 968, 465 P.2d 690 (1970).

110. Morris Kaplan, "More Hospitals Warned on Blood," *New York Times,* Nov. 2, 1961; and "Blood Traffic."

111. "3 Indicted in Jersey in Blood Bank Case," *New York Times,* July 3, 1963.

112. "City Hunt Locates Malaria Suspect," *New York Times,* Apr. 18, 1963; and Charles L. West, "Donor of Diseased Blood Hunted amid Bowery's Nameless Derelicts," *Washington Post,* Apr. 22, 1963.

113. F. H. Wright, "Accidental Transmission of Malaria through the Injection of Whole Blood," *Journal of Pediatrics* 12 (Mar. 1938): 327; and Robert A. Kilduffe and Michael DeBakey, *The Blood Bank and the Technique and Therapeutics of Transfusions* (St. Louis: C. V. Mosby, 1942), 507.

114. G. F. Grady, ed., "Incidence, Mortality and Prevention of Post-Transfusion Hepatitis," Special Report of the Committee on Plasma and Plasma Substitutes, Division of Medical Sciences, National Academy of Sciences (Washington, DC: National Research Council, 1965), 3.

115. American Association of Blood Banks, *Technical Methods,* 62.

116. Calvin M. Kunin, "Serum Hepatitis from Whole Blood: Incidence and Relation to Source of Blood," *American Journal of the Medical Sciences* 237 (1959): 293.

117. John B. Alsever, "The Blood Bank and Homologous Serum Jaundice: A Review of Medicolegal Considerations," *New England Journal of Medicine* 261 (Aug 20, 1958): 383.

118. "Routine Testing in Blood Banks for HAA," *HSMHA Health Reports* 86 (Nov. 1971): 973–74.

119. Charles E. Rosenberg, *The Cholera Years: The United States in 1832, 1849 and 1866,* expanded ed. (Chicago: University of Chicago Press, 1987), 6–7, 120, 133–50; Naomi Rogers, *Dirt and Disease: Polio before FDR* (New Brunswick, NJ: Rutgers University Press, 1992), 4–5, 145–64; and Nancy Tomes, *The Gospel of Germs: Men,*

Women, and the Microbe in American Life (Cambridge, MA: Harvard University Press, 1998), 24–25, 57–62.

120. Kunin, "Serum Hepatitis from Whole Blood," 293.

121. Ibid., 298.

122. Richard E. Dice, "Paid Donor Programs," *Proceedings of Conference on Blood and Blood Banking*, Chicago, IL, Dec. 11–12, 1964, 71.

123. Testimony of W. Quinn Jordan, Hearings before Subcommittee on Antitrust and Monopoly of the Committee of the Judiciary, U.S. Senate, 88th Cong., 2d Sess., Aug. 19, 1964 (Washington, DC: U.S. Government Printing Office, 1964), 74, 76.

124. Rennie Taylor, "Hepatitis Is Traced to Professional Blood Donor," *Fresno (CA) Bee*, Apr. 17, 1959; and "Best Blood Is Given by Pros, Group Is Told," *Chicago Daily Tribune*, Nov. 6, 1959.

125. "Report of the Commission on Clinical Laboratories, Blood Banks, and Blood Bank Depositories to the 74th General Assembly," State of Illinois, Mar. 1, 1965, 7.

126. "Nightmare: Alcoholic in Jail," *Chicago Tribune*, Jan. 12, 1964.

127. "Blood Bank Frees Donor of Cost," *Chicago Tribune*, July 17, 1966; and "Aurora Blood Co-op Stocks Premium Vintage," *Chicago Tribune*, Oct. 5, 1969.

128. Lloyd General, "Blood Money: It May Mean a Meal to a Down-and-Outer or a Life for Desperately-Ill Patient," *Chicago Defender*, Jan. 12, 1963.

129. Marcia Gray Doty, *Delta Blood Bank, 1954–1986* (Stockton, CA: Delta Blood Bank, 1986), 27.

130. John Reynolds, "Foto Facts," *Cedar Rapids (IA) Gazette*, July 23, 1953.

131. "Cash Blood Banks Thriving in City," *New York Times*, Nov. 12, 1968.

132. Harry Nelson, "Increase in Hepatitis after Transfusions Plagues Experts," *Los Angeles Times*, Oct. 13, 1968.

133. Lawrence Galton, "6,000,000 Pints of Blood Is Not Enough," *New York Times*, Mar. 29, 1964; and "Critical Blood Shortage Hits Nation's Blood Banks," *Los Angeles Times*, Dec. 31, 1968.

134. "Wastage of Blood in Storage Placed at Nearly a Third," *New York Times*, Apr. 1, 1967.

135. "Blood Business," 40.

136. Ibid.; William F. Longgood, "Bowery Bums Can Get $5 If They Pass Health Test," *New York World-Telegram* (undated clipping included in Addendum to Memorandum to Assembly Members); and General, "Blood Money."

137. Lester David, "Whose Blood Was That?," *Science and Mechanics*, Nov. 1963, text reprinted in Hearings before Subcommittee on Antitrust and Monopoly of the Committee of the Judiciary, U.S. Senate, 88th Cong., 2d Sess., Aug. 18–20, 1964 (Washington, DC: U.S. Government Printing Office, 1964), 165.

138. Jackson v. Muhlenberg Hospital, 53 N.J. 138, 139–40, 249 A.2d 65, 66 (1969).

139. *Jackson*, 53 N.J. at 141–43, 249 A.2d at 67–68.

140. "2 Democrats Urge Blood-Buying Curb," *New York Times,* Aug. 1, 1967.

141. Illinois Blood Bank Act (proposed) §801(c), Annex VI to "Report of the Commission on Clinical Laboratories, Blood Banks, and Blood Bank Depositories to the 74th General Assembly," State of Illinois, Mar. 1, 1965, 9.

142. Letters in opposition from Hyland Laboratories (dated Feb. 7, 1963) and Community Blood and Plasma Service, Inc. (dated Feb. 22, 1963), Legislative History File, A/C Public Health, AB 333, 1963, California State Archives.

143. Neva M. Abelson, *Topics in Blood Banking* (Philadelphia: Lea & Febinger, 1974), 17.

144. Elizabeth H. Schirmer, "The County Blood Bank," *County Intern,* Apr. 1943, 5.

145. "Seven Books of Special Significance Published in 1971," *New York Times* (book review section), Dec. 5, 1971.

146. Paul A. Samuelson, "Blood," *Newsweek,* Sept. 13, 1971, 94; Nathan Glazer, "Blood—Review Essay," *Public Interest,* Summer 1971, 86–94; and Clark C. Havinghurst, "Trafficking in Human Blood: Titmuss (1970) and Products Liability," *Journal of Law and Contemporary Problems* 17 (2009): 1n.2, 2n.5.

147. Michele Goodwin, *Black Markets: The Supply and Demand of Body Parts* (New York: Cambridge University Press, 2006), 7–8.

148. See, for example, Kenneth J. Arrow, "Gifts and Exchanges," *Philosophy and Public Affairs* 1 (Summer 1972): 343–62; Robert M. Solow, "Blood and Thunder," *Yale Law Review* 80 (1970–71): 1696–1711; Kessel, "Transfused Blood"; and Edmund S. Phelps, ed., *Altruism, Morality, and Economic Theory* (New York: Russell Sage Foundation, 1975).

149. Dice, "Paid Donor Programs," 70.

150. Titmuss, *The Gift Relationship,* 264.

151. Roger Morris, *Richard Milhous Nixon: The Rise of an American Politician* (New York: Henry Holt, 1990), 313–14, 317–20, 342–508.

152. Richard A. Knox, "White House's Health Plans Big on Scope, Short on Detail," *Boston Globe,* July 15, 1973; and Report to the Secretary, Department of Health, Education and Welfare, "Problems in Carrying Out the National Blood Policy," HRD-77-150 B-4641631(2), Mar. 7, 1978, 1–3.

153. Kennedy, "Community Blood Banking," 412.

154. Scott Swisher, ed., *The Logistics of Blood Transfusion Therapy Symposia Proceedings,* vol. 1 (Bethesda, MD: U.S. Department of Health, Education and Welfare, Public Health Service, National Institutes of Health, 1978); Joseph C. Fratatoni and Anthony A. Rene, eds., *The Management and Logistics of Blood Banking, Conference Proceedings,* vol. 2, DHEW Publication No. (NIH) 78-1471 (Bethesda, MD: U.S. Department of Health, Education and Welfare, Public Health Service, National Institutes of Health, 1977); Anthony A. Rene and Robert E. Huitt, eds., *The Management and Logistics of Blood Banking, Conference*

Proceedings, vol. 3, NIH Publication No. 79-1602 (Bethesda, MD: U.S. Department of Health, Education and Welfare, Public Health Service, National Institutes of Health, 1979); Robert C. Hubbell and Robert E. Huitt, eds., *The Management of Logistics of Blood Banking, Conference Proceedings,* vol. 4, NIH Publication No. 81-2021 (Bethesda, MD: U.S. Department of Health and Human Services, Public Health Service, National Institutes of Health, 1980); and Robert C. Hubbell, ed., *The Management and Logistics of Blood Banking, Conference Proceedings,* vol. 5, NIH Publication No. 82-2332 (Bethesda, MD: U.S. Department of Health and Human Services, Public Health Service, National Institutes of Health, 1981).

155. See, for example, C. Carl Pegels and Andrew E. Jelmert, "An Evaluation of Blood-Inventory Policies: A Markov Chain Application," *Operations Research* 18 (Nov.–Dec. 1970): 1087–98; and Alvin W. Drake, Stan N. Finkelstein, and Harvey M. Sapolsky, *The American Blood Supply* (Cambridge, MA: MIT Press, 1982), xi and generally. Starr, *Blood,* 250 (using term "blood-services complex").

156. Bernice Hemphill, *The Mother of Blood Banking: Irwin Memorial Blood Bank and the American Association of Blood Banks, 1944–1994,* interviewed by Germaine LaBerge (Berkeley: Regional Oral History Office, Bancroft Library, University of California, 1998), 123.

157. Doty, *Delta Blood Bank,* 42–44.

158. Starr, *Blood,* 257.

159. Hemphill, *Mother of Blood Banking,* 124; and "Oversight on Implementation of National Blood Policy, 1979," Hearing before the Subcommittee on Health and Scientific Research of the Committee on Labor and Human Resources, U.S. Senate, 96th Cong., 1st sess., June 7, 1979, 2.

160. Starr, *Blood,* 240, 258–60; and Stephen Pemberton, *The Bleeding Disease: Hemophilia and the Unintended Consequences of Medical Progress* (Baltimore: Johns Hopkins University Press, 2011), 169–83.

161. Kennedy, "Community Blood Banking," 144–48, 167–73, 187–94.

162. Richard H. Aster, "The Physician as a Director of a Regional Blood Program," in Fratatoni and Rene, *The Management and Logistics of Blood Banking, Conference Proceedings,* 2:239.

163. John Parascandola, "The Introduction of Antibiotics into Therapeutics," in *Sickness and Health in America: Readings in the History of Medicine and Public Health,* edited by Judith Walzer Leavitt and Ronald L. Numbers, 3rd ed. revised (Madison: University of Wisconsin Press, 1997), 108–9 (reprinted from Yosio Kawakita, Shizu Sakai, and Yasuo Otsuka, eds., *History of Therapy: Proceedings of the 10th International Symposium on the Comparative History of Medicine—East and West* (Tokyo: Ishiyaku EuroAmerica, 1990), 261–81).

164. Social Security Amendments of 1965, Public Law 97, 89th Cong., 1st sess. (July 30, 1965); and Rosemary Stevens, *In Sickness and in Wealth: American Hospitals in the Twentieth Century* (New York: Basic Books, 1989), 256–83.

165. Renée C. Fox and Judith P. Swazey, *The Courage to Fail: A Social View of Organ Transplants and Dialysis,* 2d ed. (Chicago: University of Chicago Press, 1978), 42; and Renée C. Fox and Judith P. Swazey, *Spare Parts: Organ Replacement in American Society* (New York: Oxford University Press, 1992), 9.

166. Hearings before Subcommittee on Antitrust and Monopoly of the Committee of the Judiciary, U.S. Senate, 88th Cong., 2d Sess., Aug. 18–20, 1964 (Washington, DC: U.S. Government Printing Office, 1964), 4, 84, 91–92.

167. Uniform Law Commission, *Legislative Fact Sheet—Anatomical Gift (1968),* http://www.uniformlaws.org/LegislativeFactSheet.aspx?title=Anatomical%20Gift %20%281968%29, last viewed Nov. 25, 2013.

168. New York Sanitary Code Sec. 108 (adopted Nov. 21, 1930 and amended Mar. 14, 1939), reproduced in Fritz Schiff and William C. Boyd, *Blood Grouping Technic: A Manual* (New York: Interscience, 1942), 115.

169. National Conference of Commissioners on Uniform State Laws, Uniform Anatomical Gift Act (1968), §1(c).

170. "Text of State Statutes Concerning Blood Transfusions and Organ Transplantations," Appendix E to *Human Organ Transplantation: Societal, Medical-Legal, Regulatory, and Reimbursement Issues,* edited by Dale H. Cowan, Jo Ann Kantorowitz, Jay Moskowitz, and Peter H. Rheinstein (Ann Arbor, MI: Health Administration Press, 1987), 416–32; and Richard E. Nolan and Whitney L. Schmidt, "Products Liability and Artificial and Human Organ Transplantation— A Legal Overview," in Cowan et al., *Human Organ Transplantation,* 137–58.

171. Uniform Anatomical Gift Act, §3, Comment.

172. Note, "Regulating the Sale of Human Organs," *Virginia Law Review* 71 (Sept. 1985): 1021–22; and Lederer, *Flesh and Blood,* 98–99.

173. 1984 Pub.L. 98-507, approved Oct. 19, 1984, codified as 42 U.S.C. §274e.

5. Feminine Banks and the Milk of Human Kindness

Epigraph: Robert Macy, "Women Start First Breast Milk Bank," *Gettysburg (PA) Times,* Mar. 5, 1981.

1. Herman F. Meyer, "Breast Feeding in the United States: Extent and Possible Trend," *Pediatrics* 22 (1958): 119; and Joan Beck, "Milk Bank," *Chicago Daily Tribune,* July 22, 1956.

2. E. Robbins Kimball et al., "The Breast Milk Bank as a Community Project," *Pediatrics* 16 (1955): 264–65, 269.

3. Richard E. Craiglow, "Milk Bank," *Hygeia,* May 1944, 362; "Chicago Junior League Has Premature Baby Aid Program," *Progress-Index* (Petersburg–Colonial Heights, VA), Nov. 27, 1955; and Notes dated Sept. 18, 1944, Box 1, Folder 2, American Association of University Women Archives, California Historical Society, San Francisco, CA (hereinafter AAUW Archives).

4. Lee Forrest Hill, "Infant Feeding: Historical and Current," *Pediatric Clinics of North America* 14 (Feb. 1967): 262.

5. Thomas E. Cone Jr., *200 Years of Feeding Infants in America* (Columbus, OH: Ross Laboratories, 1976), 87.

6. Katherine Bain, "The Incidence of Breast Feeding in Hospitals in the United States," *Pediatrics* 2 (1948): 319; and Herman F. Meyer, "Breast Feeding in the United States: Report of a 1966 Survey with Comparable 1946 and 1956 Data," *Clinical Pediatrics* 7 (Dec. 1968): 709.

7. Judith W. Leavitt, *Brought to Bed: Childbearing in America, 1750–1950* (New York: Oxford University Press, 1986), generally and 173; Judith W. Leavitt, "'Science' Enters the Birthing Room: Obstetrics in America since the Eighteenth Century," *Journal of American History* 70 (Sept. 1983): 295–99; and Richard W. Wertz and Dorothy C. Wertz, *Lying-in: A History of Childbirth in America,* expanded ed. (New Haven, CT: Yale University Press, 1989), 133–77.

8. Samuel L. Andelman, "A Municipal Milk Bank for Premature, Immature, and Sick Infants," *Bulletin of Maternal and Infant Health* 9 (1962): 26; Jacqueline H. Wolf, *Don't Kill Your Baby: Public Health and the Decline of Breastfeeding in the Nineteenth and Twentieth Centuries* (Columbus: Ohio State University Press, 2001), 153–54; and personal communication with Jacqueline H. Wolf, July 31, 2013.

9. Andelman, "Municipal Milk Bank," 26–27; and "Mothers' Milk Donors Sought," *Chicago Daily Defender,* Mar. 7, 1961. Cf. Wolf, *Don't Kill,* 154.

10. Susan E. Lederer, *Flesh and Blood: Organ Transplantation and Blood Transfusion in Twentieth-Century America* (New York: Oxford University Press, 2008), 92.

11. Andelman, "Municipal Milk Bank," 26.

12. Committee on Mothers' Milk, American Academy of Pediatrics, "Recommended Standards for the Operation of Mothers' Milk Bureaus," *Journal of Pediatrics* 23 (1943): 112–28.

13. James A. Tobey, "A New Foster-Mother," *Hygeia,* Nov. 1929, 1111.

14. B. Raymond Hoobler, "An Experiment in the Collection of Human Milk for Hospital and Dispensary Uses," *Archives of Pediatrics* 31 (1914): 173.

15. B. Raymond Hoobler, "The Production, Collection and Distribution of Human Milk: Retrospect and Prospect," *Journal of the American Medical Association* 88 (June 4, 1927): 1787; and B. Raymond Hoobler, "Human Milk: Its Commercial Production and Distribution," *Journal of the American Medical Association* 84 (Jan. 17, 1925): 166.

16. "Galactic Crisis," *Time,* June 24, 1946.

17. Mary L. Watson, "Our Frozen Milk Bank," *American Journal of Nursing* 41 (1941): 674; and Kara W. Swanson, "Human Milk as Technology and Technologies of Human Milk: Medical Imaginings in the Early 20th Century United States," *Women's Studies Quarterly* 37 (2009): 21.

18. Bernard Fantus, "Cook County's Blood Bank," *Modern Hospital* 50 (1938): 58.

19. "Mother's Milk Bank Pleads for Donations," *Los Angeles Times*, Sept. 16, 1945.

20. "Mothers' Milk Supply Drops; Aid Is Sought," *Chicago Daily Tribune*, Aug. 20, 1943.

21. Orientation for New Auxiliary Members, 2, Nov. 24, 1952, Box 2, Folder 36, AAUW Archives.

22. Charles E. Rosenberg, *The Care of Strangers: The Rise of America's Hospital System* (New York: Basic Books, 1987), 338–41; and Rosemary Stevens, *In Sickness and in Wealth: American Hospitals in the Twentieth Century* (New York: Basic Books, 1989), 10–11, 233–34.

23. Hoobler, "Human Milk," 166.

24. Watson, "Our Frozen Milk Bank," 672–74.

25. *Chicago Tribune*, Dec. 8, 1942.

26. "Milk for Baby" and "Soldiers," *The News* (Van Nuys, CA), Oct. 22, 1943. See also "Mother's Milk Bank Pleads for Donations," *Los Angeles Times*, Sept. 16, 1945.

27. Craiglow, "Milk Bank," 354; and Mary D. Blankenhorn, "A Breast Milk Dairy," *Hygeia*, May 1933, 411.

28. Craiglow, "Milk Bank," 354.

29. Bernard Fantus, ed., "The Therapy of the Cook County Hospital: Blood Preservation," *Journal of the American Medical Association* 109 (July 10, 1937): 128.

30. Harrold A. Murray, "The Mothers' Milk Bank of Essex County," *Journal of the Medical Society of New Jersey* 50 (1953): 401; and *The Mothers' Milk Bank, Inc.: Origins and History* (San Rafael, CA: Academic Therapy Publications, 1974), 13, Box 1, Folder 1, AAUW Archives (copy corrected by hand to change date on which the bank began to charge for milk from 1969 to 1970).

31. Murray, "Mothers' Milk Bank," 401.

32. Ruth A. Lawrence and Robert M. Lawrence, *Breastfeeding: A Guide for the Medical Profession*, 6th ed. (Philadelphia: Elsevier Mosby, 2005), 660–67, 683; Susanne Polywka et al., "Low Risk of Vertical Transmission of Hepatitis C by Breast Milk," *Clinical Infectious Diseases* 29 (Nov. 1999): 1328; and Jenny Pronczuk et al., "Global Perspectives in Breast Milk Contamination: Infectious and Toxic Hazards," *Environmental Health Perspectives*, 110 (June 2002): A349–50.

33. Polywka et al., "Low Risk," 1328; and Lawrence and Lawrence, *Breastfeeding*, 649, 653, 672.

34. Board of Directors meeting minutes, Mar. 15, 1977, Box 1, Folder 6, AAUW Archives.

35. "Mothers' Milk Supply Drops."

36. Jacqueline H. Wolf, " 'Mercenary Hirelings' or 'a Great Blessing'? Doctors' and Mothers' Conflicted Perceptions of Wet Nurses and the Ramifications of Infant Feeding in Chicago, 1871–1961," *Journal of Social History* 33 (1999): 106 (quoting Chicago doctor).

37. "Mothers' Milk Supply Drops."

38. William Makepeace Thackeray, *Vanity Fair: A Novel without a Hero,* edited by Geoffrey Tillotson and Kathleen Tillotson (1884; Boston: Houghton Mifflin, 1963), 356.

39. Wertz and Wertz, *Lying-in,* 133; and Stevens, *In Sickness and in Wealth,* 105–8.

40. Hoobler, "Production, Collection and Distribution," 1787; and Hoobler, "Human Milk," 166.

41. Kimball et al., "Breast Milk Bank," 265.

42. *Mothers' Milk Bank, Inc.,* 10–11.

43. " 'Wendy Elise' Coming to Marin to Raise Funds for Milk Bank," *Independent-Journal* (San Rafael, CA), Dec. 6, 1951; "Fashion Cast Announced," *San Mateo (CA) Times,* Jan. 15, 1954; and "Style Show to Aid Milk Bank," *Oakland (CA) Tribune,* Jan. 2, 1955.

44. Correspondence files, AAUW Archives.

45. Elizabeth R. Langerak and Lois D. W. Arnold, "The Mothers' Milk Bank of Wilmington, Delaware: History and Highlights," *Journal of Human Lactation* 7 (1991): 197.

46. Kimball et al., "Breast Milk Bank," 265–66.

47. Ibid., 265, starred footnote.

48. *Mothers' Milk Bank, Inc.,* 13.

49. Murray, "Mothers' Milk Bank," 402.

50. Ibid.

51. Letter of Feb. 2, 1970 from Ryann Abell (Mrs. William C.) to Mrs. Fell, Box 1, Folder 11, AAUW Archives.

52. Langerak and Arnold, "Mothers' Milk Bank," 198.

53. Margery Blair Perkins, *Evanstoniana: The History of Evanston and Its Architecture,* compiled and edited by Barbara J. Buchbinder-Green (Evanston, IL: Evanston Historical Society, 1984); and Agnes Dubbs Hays, *Heritage of Dedication: One Hundred Years of the National Woman's Christian Temperance Union, 1874–1974* (Evanston, IL: Signal Press, 1973), 20.

54. "Our History," Junior League of Evanston–North Shore, http://jle-ns.org /history/, last viewed Nov. 11, 2013; and Arlene Kaplan Daniels, *Invisible Careers: Women Civic Leaders from the Volunteer World* (Chicago: University of Chicago Press, 1988), 25–26, 28.

55. Mhyra S. Minnis, "Cleavage in Women's Organizations: A Reflection of the Social Structure of a City," *American Sociological Review* 18 (1953): 51.

56. Lois D. W. Arnold, "Donor Human Milk Banking: Creating Public Health Policy in the 21st Century," Ph.D. dissertation, Union Institute and University, 2005, 174.

57. Tibor J. Greenwalt, "The Junior League Blood Center of Milwaukee," in *Starting and Operating a Blood Bank: Seven Articles,* edited by Bureau of Economic Medical Research, Committee on Blood Banks, American Medical Association, Bulletin No. 82 (Chicago: American Medical Association, 1951), 33–40.

58. Mrs. David G. Feagans, "Volunteer Vistas," *Evanston (IL) Review,* Jan. 16, 1958.

59. Beck, "Milk Bank."

60. "League Invited to Exhibit Milk Bank at AMA Meeting," *Evanston Review* (May 26, 1955) (clipping from the Junior League files of the Evanston History Center, Evanston, IL).

61. "Death Notice: Ernest Robbins Kimball, M.D.," *New York Times,* Jan. 1, 2003; "Saving Lives Is This Bank's Interest," *Chicago Tribune,* Feb. 10, 1973; and Kimball et al., "Breast Milk Bank," 269.

62. "The Fifties," Junior League scrapbook, 13; Feagans, "Volunteer Vistas"; "Junior League Wins Citations," May 26, 1955 (no publication name given); "Doctors, Donors Attend Premiere of Junior League Milk Bank Movie," June 12, 1958 (no publication name given); and "Junior League's Milk Bank Filmed for Public Service," *Evanston Review* (May 26, 1955), all from the Junior League files of the Evanston History Center, Evanston, IL.

63. Kimball et al., "Breast Milk Bank."

64. Frank Carey, "Evanston Debs Conduct Unusual Milk Route," *Progress* (Clearfield, Curwensville, Philipsburg, PA), Oct. 5, 1955.

65. "Chicago Junior League Has Premature Baby Aid Program."

66. Frank Carey, "Junior League Runs Route for Breast Milk Bank for the Premature," *Greeley (CO) Tribune,* Oct. 6, 1955; "Society Girls Running Free 'Milk Bank,' " *Times-Bulletin* (Van Wert, OH), Oct. 14, 1955; Carey, "Evanston Debs"; and Frank Carey, "League Aids 'Preems' by Milk Route," *Long Beach (CA) Press-Telegram,* Oct. 3, 1955.

67. Elaine Tyler May, *Homeward Bound: American Families in the Cold War Era* (New York: Basic Books, 1988), 3–8, and generally; Lizabeth Cohen, *A Consumers' Republic: The Politics of Mass Consumption in Postwar America* (New York: Knopf, 2003), 113, 144–48, 278; Elaine Tyler May, *Barren in the Promised Land: Childless Americans and the Pursuit of Happiness* (New York: Basic Books, 1995), 127–40; and Margaret Marsh and Wanda Ronner, *The Empty Cradle: Infertility in America from Colonial Times to the Present* (Baltimore: Johns Hopkins University Press, 1996), 183–86.

68. Cohen, *Consumers' Republic,* 194–96, 278–83; Ruth Rosen, *The World Split Open: How the Modern Women's Movement Changed America* (New York: Penguin

Books, 2001), 14; and Ruth Schwartz Cowan, *More Work for Mother: The Ironies of Household Technology from the Open Hearth to the Microwave* (New York: Basic Books, 1983), 196–201.

69. Brett Harvey, *The Fifties: A Women's Oral History* (New York: HarperPerennial, 1993), xi.

70. Marilyn Yalom, *A History of the Breast* (New York: Ballantine Books, 1997), 136–38, 177–78.

71. Kimball et al., "Breast Milk Bank."

72. "Helping Preemies Stay Alive," *Herald* (Chicago, IL), Apr. 18, 1973.

73. Ruth Moss, "Saving Lives Is This Bank's Interest," *Chicago Tribune,* Feb. 10, 1973.

74. Assorted letters dated 1968 (quoted from Dr. Faber and Dr. Leonards), Box 1, Folder 1, AAUW Archives. See also "Report into Continued Need for MBB Services," Box 2, Folder 50, AAUW Archives.

75. Lucy R. Waletzky, preface to *Symposium on Human Lactation,* edited by Lucy R. Waletzky, Arlington, VA, Oct. 7–8, 1976, DHEW Publication No. (HSA) 79–5107 (Rockville, MD: U.S. Department of Health, Education, and Welfare, Public Health Service/Health Services Administration, Bureau of Community Health Services, 1979), n.p.

76. Margaret Handy, Letter to Editor, "Mothers' Milk Bank at the Delaware Hospital," *Pediatrics* 33 (1964): 468; and News and Announcements, "Human Milk Available," *Pediatrics* 43 (1969): 477.

77. Nurse's Annual Report for 1971, Box 2, Folder 35, AAUW Archives.

78. Janet Golden, "From Wet Nurse Directory to Milk Bank: The Delivery of Human Milk in Boston, 1909–1927," *Bulletin of the History of Medicine* 62 (1988): 604.

79. Letter of Mrs. Walter C. Fell to Mr. Clifford Lander, Nov. 27, 1967, Box 1, Folder 13, AAUW Archives.

80. Susan Giller, "Wilmington's Milk Bank Saves Babies Everywhere," *Delaware County (PA) Daily Times,* Aug. 30, 1972.

81. George B. Dowling, "Red Cross Blood Program," *Virginia Medical Monthly,* Oct. 1948, 498.

82. Richard M. Titmuss, *The Gift Relationship: From Human Blood to Social Policy,* edited by Ann Oakley and John Ashton, expanded ed. (1970; New York: New Press, 1997). Cf. Janet Golden, "From Commodity to Gift: Gender, Class, and the Meaning of Breast Milk in the Twentieth Century," *Historian* 59 (Sept. 1996): 75–87.

83. Kaye Lowman, *The LLLove Story* (Franklin Park, IL: La Leche League International, 1978); Mary Ann Cahill, *Seven Voices, One Dream* (Schaumburg, IL: La Leche League International, 2001); Jule DeJager Ward, *La Leche League: At the Crossroads of Medicine, Feminism, and Religion* (Chapel Hill: University of North

Carolina Press, 2000); and Lynn Y. Weiner, "Reconstructing Motherhood: The La Leche League in Postwar America," *Journal of American History* 80 (1994): 1357–81.

84. La Leche League, *The Womanly Art of Breastfeeding*, 2d ed. (Franklin Park IL: La Leche League International, 1963), title, 10.

85. Ibid., 15–18; and Rima Apple, *Perfect Motherhood: Science and Childrearing in America* (New Brunswick, NJ: Rutgers University Press, 2006), 2, 40–41, and generally.

86. Grantly Dick-Read, *Childbirth without Fear: The Principles and Practice of Natural Childbirth* (New York: Harper & Bros., 1944); Cahill, *Seven Voices*, 71–73; and Margarete Sandelowski, *Pain, Pleasure and American Childbirth: From the Twilight Sleep to the Read Method, 1914–1960* (Westport, CT: Greenwood Press, 1985), 86, 91.

87. Sandelowski, *Pain, Pleasure*, 85–92; Wertz and Wertz, *Lying-in*, 178–200; and Jacqueline H. Wolf, *Deliver Me from Pain: Anesthesia and Birth in America* (Baltimore: Johns Hopkins University Press, 2009), 139–41, 151–63.

88. La Leche League, *Womanly Art of Breastfeeding*, 4.

89. Ibid., viii, 4–5, 12.

90. Ibid., 10–13.

91. Weiner, "Reconstructing Motherhood," 1363.

92. La Leche League, *Womanly Art of Breastfeeding*, 17–18.

93. Ibid., 23–24. See also Weiner, "Reconstructing Motherhood," 1372–73.

94. James N. Miller, "Giant Blood Bank," *Hygeia*, Feb. 1941, 107; and Jane Stafford, "Blood against the Atom Bomb," *Science News-Letter* 54 (July 3, 1948): 10.

95. "Generosity of Women Who Gave Milk after Death of Mother Apparently Saving Life of Tiny Premature Boy at Prairie Grove," *Northwest Arkansas Times*, May 23, 1950.

96. "Nation Rallies to Baby Milk Call," *Fresno (CA) Bee*, May 17, 1968; "Human Milk Bank Supplies Food to Ailing Infant," *Daily Review* (Hayward, CA), May 17, 1968; "Moms Give for Richard," *Independent–Press Telegram* (Long Beach, CA), May 17, 1968; and "Little Ricky Gets Account," *Morning Herald* (Hagerstown, MD), May 17, 1968. Note that Ricky's last name is given as "Mabson" in some stories ("Nation Rallies").

97. "Mothers' Milk from Freezer," *Oakland (CA) Tribune*, May 17, 1968.

98. "Child Needs Human Milk," *Post-Register* (Idaho Falls, ID), Oct. 6, 1970; and "Milk Pours In to Save Baby Girl," *Independent* (Long Beach, CA), Aug. 11, 1970.

99. "500 Women Offer Milk for Sick Tots," *Independent* (Long Beach, CA), Nov. 11, 1970.

100. Lea Andresen, "Mothers' Milk Keeps Little Linda Alive," *Wisconsin State Journal*, Apr. 20, 1969.

101. "Feeding Problem," *Fresno (CA) Bee*, Oct. 12, 1970; and "Moms Give for Richard."

102. Andresen, "Mothers' Milk Keeps Little Linda Alive."

103. "Donors Needed," *Chicago Tribune,* Feb. 10, 1973.

104. Hoobler, "An Experiment in the Collection of Human Milk," 172.

105. Jim Boren, "Milk of Human Kindness: Others Give So That Baby May Live," *Fresno (CA) Bee,* July 20, 1972.

106. "Idaho Mothers Give Milk to Allergic Baby," *Chicago Tribune,* Aug. 10, 1970.

107. Jim Boren, "A New Threat for Brian: Milk Supply May Be Unsafe," *Fresno (CA) Bee,* Aug. 24, 1972.

108. Shirley Vandeberg, "First in the State: Mt. Vernon Mothers Start Milk Bank," *Mansfield (OH) News Journal,* Feb. 14, 1973.

109. Nurse's Annual Report for 1977, Box 2, Folder 35, AAUW Archives.

110. Arnold, "Donor Human Milk Banking," 185, citing M. T. Asquith, *Organizing a Distributing Human Milk Bank: Human Milk Banking Protocols and Procedures* (San Jose, CA: Institute for Medical Research, 1982).

111. Arnold, "Donor Human Milk Banking," 13–14.

112. Erik Kriss and Thomas Heath, "Milk for Life: Group of 'Jet-Age Wet Nurses' Distributes Mother's Milk to Babies with Special Needs," *Post-Standard (NY),* Oct. 12, 1982.

113. Betty Friedan, *The Feminine Mystique* (1963; New York: Norton, 2001).

114. Michelle Murphy, *Seizing the Means of Reproduction: Entanglements of Feminism, Health, and Technoscience* (Durham, NC: Duke University Press, 2012), 5; Sandra Morgen, *Into Our Own Hands: The Women's Health Movement in the United States, 1969–1990* (New Brunswick, NJ: Rutgers University, 2002), 3–10, 18–19, 22–26; and Sheryl Burt Ruzek, *The Women's Health Movement: Feminist Alternatives to Medical Control* (New York: Praeger, 1978), generally.

115. Wendy Kline, *Bodies of Knowledge: Sexuality, Reproduction, and Women's Health in the Second Wave* (Chicago: University of Chicago, 2010), 135–36; Laura Kaplan, *The Story of Jane: The Legendary Underground Abortion Service* (New York: Pantheon Books, 1995); and Murphy, *Seizing the Means of Reproduction,* 150–63.

116. Weiner, "Reconstructing Motherhood," 1374–75, 1378–80.

117. Ryan H. Edgington, "'Be Receptive to the Good Earth': Health, Nature and Labor in Countercultural Back-to-the-Land Settlements," *Agricultural History* 82 (Summer 2008): 281–82, 291.

118. Derrick B. Jelliffe and E. F. Patrice Jelliffe, *Human Milk in the Modern World: Psychosocial, Nutritional, and Economic Significance* (Oxford: Oxford University Press, 1978), 211–99, 320–34; and "Nestle Boycott Victory, 1977–1984," *off our backs* 14 (Apr. 1984): 7.

119. Arnold, "Donor Milk Banking," 185.

120. "Nurse Starts Milk Bank," *Alton (IL) Telegraph,* Mar. 4, 1985.

121. Vandeberg, "First in the State."

122. Macy, "Women Start First Breast Milk Bank."

123. "A Fairy Palace the Origin of Mothers' Milk Station," *Kansas City Star,* Mar. 1, 1933; and Mary Katherine Herwick, "A Mother's Milk Station," *American Journal of Nursing* 33 (1933): 454.

124. Frances Jones, "History of North American Donor Milk Banking: One Hundred Years of Progress," *Journal of Human Lactation* 19 (Aug. 2003), 315. See also Kriss and Heath, "Milk for Life."

125. Alton L. Blakeslee, *Blood's Magic for All,* Public Affairs Pamphlet No. 145 (New York: Public Affairs Committee, 1948).

126. Committee on Nutrition, American Academy of Pediatrics, "Human Milk Banking," *Pediatrics* 65 (Apr. 1980): 854–57, 854.

127. Boren, "New Threat."

128. Samuel J. Fomon, "Human Milk in Premature Infant Feeding: Report of a Second Workshop," *American Journal of Public Health* 67 (1977): 361.

129. "Human Milk in Premature Infant Feeding: Summary of a Workshop," *Pediatrics* 57 (1976): 741, 742–43.

130. Ibid., 741–42.

131. Ibid., 742–43.

132. Fomon, "Report of a Second Workshop," 361–63.

133. Ibid., 361–62.

134. Ibid.

135. *Human Milk Banking Association of North America Newsletter* 1 (Spring 1987): 1 (private collection of Lois D. W. Arnold, copy in author's possession); and Arnold, "Donor Milk Banking," 190.

136. Lois D. W. Arnold and Mary Rose Tully, *Guidelines for the Establishment and Operation of a Donor Human Milk Bank* (n.p.: Human Milk Banking Association of North America, 1990); and Arnold, "Donor Milk Banking," 192.

137. *Human Milk Banking Association of North America Newsletter* 1, 5–6; and Arnold, "Donor Milk Banking," 190.

138. Maria Teresa Asquith and Miriam Erickson, "Sources of Funds for Milk Banks," presentation at Human Milk Banking Association of North America meeting, Oct. 17, 1986, Denver, notes prepared by Mary-Margaret Coates, 1–3 (private collection of Lois D. W. Arnold, copy in author's possession).

139. Arnold and Tully, *Guidelines,* 2.

140. Ibid., 11; and Centers for Disease Control and Prevention, "Hepatitis B and C, Diseases and Conditions, Breastfeeding," http://www.cdc.gov/breastfeeding /disease/hepatitis.htm, last viewed Mar. 23, 2013.

141. Lois D. W. Arnold and Maria Asquith, "The Evolution of Services in Modern Human Milk Banking," *Journal of Human Lactation* 7 (1991): 87; and Patricia Wen, "Breast-Milk Banks Push for More Federal Oversight," *Boston Globe,* Oct. 24, 2002.

142. Arnold and Tully, *Guidelines.*

143. Margaret K. Davis, "The Role of Human Milk in Human Immunodeficiency Virus Infection," in *Breastfeeding, Nutrition, Infection, and Infant Growth in Developed and Emerging Countries,* edited by Stephanie A. Atkinson, Lars A. Hanson, and Rajit K. Chandra (St. Johns, Newfoundland, Canada: ARTS Biomedical, 1990), 154.

144. J. B. Ziegler et al., "Postnatal Transmission of AIDS-Associated Retrovirus from Mother to Infant," *Lancet* 1 (1985): 896–98.

145. Douglas P. Starr, *Blood: An Epic History of Medicine and Commerce* (New York: Knopf, 1998), 266–78, 292–300, 315–27, 335–44.

146. Bruce Nichols, "Threat of AIDS Poses Problems for Milk Banks," *Dallas Morning News,* Aug. 17, 1986.

147. Lois D. W. Arnold, "The Statistical State of Human Milk Banking and What the Future Holds," *Journal of Human Lactation* 7 (Mar. 1991): 25.

148. L. A. Chung, "Fear of AIDS Closes Many Milk Banks," *San Francisco Chronicle,* Aug. 4, 1990.

149. Arnold, "The Statistical State of Human Milk Banking."

150. Lois D. W. Arnold and Lauraine Lockhart Borman, "What Are the Characteristics of the Ideal Human Milk Donor?," *Journal of Human Lactation* 12 (1996): 143–44.

151. Ibid., 144.

152. HMBANA, "Existing HMBANA Milk Bank Locations," https://www.hmbana.org/existing-hmbana-milk-bank-locations, and "Developing and Mentoring Banks," https://www.hmbana.org/developing-hmbana-milk-bank-locations, last viewed Oct. 10, 2013.

153. Miriam Erickson and Lois Arnold, "Ethical Decisions in Milk Banking," presentation at Human Milk Banking Association of North America meeting, Oct. 17, 1986, Denver, notes prepared by Mary-Margaret Coates, 4 (private collection of Lois D. W. Arnold, copy in author's possession).

154. Jennifer Huget, "Others' Milk; Entrepreneur Plans Network of Breast Milk Banks," *Washington Post,* Sept. 1, 2001; Denise Gallene, "Coming to a Store Near You: Mothers' Milk," *Los Angeles Times,* Sept. 25, 2005; Blythe Bernhard, "Breast Milk Clinic Confronts Criticisms: Ethics of Company Looking to Profit from the Sale of Human Breast Milk Are Questioned," *Orange County (CA) Register,* Aug. 5, 2005; and PR newswire, "National Milk Bank Now Accepting Donations Nationwide—Now Mothers Can Donate Regardless of Their Location," Dec. 5, 2005.

155. Prolacta, http://www.prolacta.com/find-a-milk-bank; and http://www.milkbanking.net, last viewed Apr. 11, 2013.

156. "Compositions of Human Lipids and Methods of Making and Using Same," U.S. Patent Number 8,377,445 B2, issued Feb. 19, 2013.

157. Tobey, "A New Foster-Mother," 1110–11.

158. Hoobler, "An Experiment in the Collection of Human Milk," 171.

6. Buying Dad from the Sperm Bank

Epigraph: California Cryobank, http://www.spermbank.com/newdonors/index. cfm?ID=4, and http://www.cryobank.com/Services/Pricing/, last viewed Oct. 10, 2013.

1. California Cryobank, http://www.spermbank.com/newdonors/index.cfm ?ID=12, last viewed Mar. 13, 2013. California Cryobank also has a deposit location in New York City. See http://www.spermbank.com/newdonors/index.cfm?ID=11, last viewed Mar. 13, 2013.

2. California Cryobank, http://www.spermbank.com/newdonors/index.cfm ?ID=4, last viewed Oct. 10, 2013.

3. Center for Human Reproduction, http://www.centerforhumanreprod.com/ and https://www.centerforhumanreprod.com/egg_donor_expect.html, last viewed Mar. 13, 2013.

4. Rene Almeling, *Sex Cells: The Medical Market in Eggs and Sperm* (Berkeley: University of California Press, 2011); Debora L. Spar, *The Baby Business: How Money, Science and Politics Drive the Commerce of Conception* (Boston: Harvard Business School Press, 2006); and Cynthia R. Daniels, *Exposing Men: The Science and Politics of Male Reproduction* (Oxford: Oxford University Press, 2006), 73–108.

5. University of Iowa Alumni Association, http://www.iowalum.com/daa /sherman.cfm, last viewed Nov. 13, 2013.

6. Kara W. Swanson, "The Birth of the Sperm Bank," *Annals of Iowa* 71 (Summer 2012): 241.

7. Diane M. Tober, "Semen as Gift, Semen as Goods: Reproductive Workers and the Market in Altruism," *Body and Society* 7 (2001): 137, 139.

8. Almeling, *Sex Cells,* generally.

9. Lisa Jean Moore, *Sperm Counts: Overcome by Man's Most Precious Fluid* (New York: New York University Press, 2007), 5.

10. Robert L. Dickinson, "Artificial Impregnation: Essays in Tubal Insemination," *Transactions of the American Gynecological Society* 45 (1920): 141; and Robert L. Dickinson, "Suggestions for a Program for American Gynecology," *Transactions of the American Gynecological Society* 45 (1920): 6.

11. J. Marion Sims, *Clinical Notes on Uterine Surgery: With Special Reference to the Management of the Sterile Condition* (New York: Wood, 1866), 369.

12. D. Ojanuga, "The Medical Ethics of the 'Father of Gynaecology,' Dr. J. Marion Sims," *Journal of Medical Ethics* 19 (1993): 28–31; and L. L. Wall, "The Medical Ethics of Dr. J. Marion Sims: A Fresh Look at the Historical Record," *Journal of Medical Ethics* 32 (2006): 346–50.

13. Deborah Kuhn McGregor, *Sexual Surgery and the Origins of Gynecology: J. Marion Sims, His Hospital, and His Patients* (New York: Garland, 1990), 1–2, 257–58, 273–74; and Randi Hutter Epstein, *Get Me Out: A History of Childbirth from the Garden of Eden to the Sperm Bank* (New York: Norton, 2010), 35–48.

14. Margaret Marsh and Wanda Ronner, *The Empty Cradle: Infertility in America from Colonial Times to the Present* (Baltimore: Johns Hopkins University Press, 1996), 81, 101–5.

15. Eliza M. Mosher, "Instrumental Impregnation," *Woman's Medical Journal* 22 (Oct. 1912), 224–25; and Marsh and Ronner, *Empty Cradle*, 69–70.

16. Mosher, "Instrumental Impregnation," 223; and Ellen S. More, *Restoring the Balance: Women Physicians and the Profession of Medicine, 1850–1995* (Cambridge, MA: Harvard University Press, 1999), 47–49, 55, 96.

17. Frank P. Davis, *Impotency, Sterility, and Artificial Impregnation* (St. Louis, MO: C. V. Mosby, 1917), 104–5.

18. Dickinson, "Suggestions for a Program for American Gynecology," 6–7; and Sophia J. Kleegman, "Practical and Ethical Aspects of Artificial Insemination," *Advances in Sex Research* 1 (Oct. 1963): 114.

19. A. D. Hard, "Artificial Impregnation," *Medical World* 27 (Apr. 1909): 163.

20. Ibid.; and John Farley, *Gametes and Spores: Ideas about Sexual Reproduction, 1750–1914* (Baltimore: Johns Hopkins University Press, 1982), 17–20, 29.

21. Glanville Williams, *The Sanctity of Life and the Criminal Law* (New York: Knopf, 1966) (revised and expanded from the 15th Annual James S. Carpentier Series, Columbia University School of Law, Apr. 1956), 129.

22. Lawrence M. Friedman, "Rights of Passage: Divorce Law in Historical Perspective," *Oregon Law Review* 63 (1984): 653.

23. Williams, *Sanctity of Life*, 124.

24. Hard, "Artificial Impregnation"; A. T. Gregoire and Robert C. Mayer, "The Impregnators," *Fertility and Sterility* 16 (1965): 132–33; Anne Lockhart Needham, "Artificial Insemination and the Emergence of Medical Authority in Twentieth Century America," B.A. thesis, Harvard University, 1988, 17–20, 21–22, 24–34; and Elaine Tyler May, *Barren in the Promised Land: Childless Americans and the Pursuit of Happiness* (New York: Basic Books, 1995), 65–69.

25. Hermann Rohleder, *Test Tube Babies: A History of the Artificial Impregnation of Human Beings* (New York: Panurge Press, 1934), xii–xiv; and May, *Barren in the Promised Land*, 43–44.

26. Dickinson, "Artificial Impregnation," 147–48.

27. Abner I. Weisman, "Studies on Human Artificial Insemination," *Transactions of the Conference on Sterility and Infertility* 2 (1946): 126.

28. Dickinson, "Suggestions for a Program," 6, 10–11; Merriley Borell, "Biologists and the Promotion of Birth Control Research, 1918–1938," *Journal of the History of Biology* 20 (1987): 64–73; and Wendy Kline, *Building a Better Race:*

Gender, Sexuality, and Eugenics from the Turn of the Century to the Baby Boom (Berkeley: University of California Press, 2001), 66–67, 132–34.

29. Paul Poponoe and Roswell Hill Johnson, *Applied Eugenics* (New York: Macmillan, 1920): 255; May, *Barren in the Promised Land,* 61–93; Daniel J. Kevles, *In the Name of Eugenics: Genetics and the Uses of Human Heredity* (Harvard University Press, 1995), 72–76; Marsh and Ronner, *Empty Cradle,* 113–14; Kline, *Building a Better Race,* 11–12 and generally; and Cynthia R. Daniels and Janet Golden, "Procreative Compounds: Popular Eugenics, Artificial Insemination and the Rise of the American Sperm Banking Industry," *Journal of Social History* 38 (2004): 5, 6–7, 9–11.

30. Kevles, *In the Name of Eugenics,* 96–100.

31. Kline, *Building a Better Race,* 66–67.

32. Dickinson, "Suggestions for a Program," 6.

33. 35 Okl.St.Ann. §§ 141–146 (1931); and Davis, *Impotency, Sterility,* 8, 76–83.

34. Aldous Huxley, *Brave New World* (London: Chatto and Windus, 1932).

35. Rohleder, *Test Tube Babies,* 165–78.

36. John Harvey Caldwell, "Babies by Scientific Selection," *Scientific American* 150 (Mar. 1934), 124.

37. Ibid., 125.

38. " 'Synthetic' Babies Born to 12 Mothers," *New York Times,* May 1, 1934; "13 Babies in N.Y. Have Test Tube as Father," *Chicago Daily Tribune,* May 1, 1934; "Parents of 'Test Tube' Twins Reveal Eugenic Baby Practice," *Washington Post,* May 1, 1934; "Laboratory Twins Born to Couple on Long Island," *Los Angeles Times,* May 1, 1934; "Birth of 'Test Tube' Twins Reveals 'Lab Baby' Technique," *Billings (MT) Gazette,* May 1, 1934; and " 'Ghost' Fathers: Children Provided for the Childless," *Newsweek,* May 12, 1934, 16.

39. "13 Babies in N.Y."

40. "Laboratory Twins"; and "13 Babies in N.Y." Cf. Marsh and Ronner, *Empty Cradle,* 163.

41. Grant S. Beardsley, "Artificial Cross Insemination," *Western Journal of Surgery, Obstetrics and Gynecology* 48 (Feb. 1940): 94.

42. "13 Babies in N.Y."; Martin Richards, "Artificial Insemination and Eugenics: Celibate Motherhood, Euteliegenesis, and Germinal Choice," *Studies in the History and Philosophy of Biology and Biomedical Sciences* 39 (2008): 211, 217; and Marsh and Ronner, *Empty Cradle,* 167.

43. "13 Babies in N.Y."

44. "Academy Statement on 'Test Tube Babies,'" *New York Times,* May 10, 1934; and " 'Test Tube Babies' Began Long Ago, Check Up Shows," *Los Angeles Times,* May 2, 1934.

45. " 'Ghost' Fathers," 16.

46. Hannah M. Stone and Abraham Stone, *A Marriage Manual: A Practical Guide-Book to Sex and Marriage* (New York: Simon & Schuster, 1935), 138–39.

47. Alan F. Guttmacher, John O. Haman, and John MacLeod, "The Use of Donors for Artificial Insemination: A Survey of Current Practices," *Fertility and Sterility* 1 (1950): 266.

48. Rohleder, *Test Tube Babies,* 173.

49. Kara W. Swanson, "Adultery by Doctor: Artificial Insemination, 1890–1945," *Chicago-Kent Law Review* 87 (2012): 612–13.

50. Abner I. Weisman, *Spermatozoa and Sterility: A Clinical Manual* (New York: Paul B. Hoeber, 1941), 171–72; and Abner I. Weisman, "The Selection of Donors for Use in Artificial Insemination," *Western Journal of Surgery, Obstetrics and Gynecology* 50 (Mar. 1942): 142–44.

51. Weisman, "Selection of Donors," 143.

52. Frances I. Seymour and Alfred Koerner, "Medicolegal Aspect of Artificial Insemination," *Journal of the American Medical Association* 107 (Nov. 7, 1936): 1533.

53. Walter E. Duka and Alan H. DeChenery, *From the Beginning: A History of the American Fertility Society* (Birmingham, AL: American Fertility Society, 1994), 176; and A. M. C. M. Schellen, *Artificial Insemination in the Human,* translated by M. E. Hollander (New York: Elsevier, 1957), 125.

54. Fred A. Simmons, "Cervix Uteri in Sterile Matings," in *The Problem of Fertility: Proceedings of the Conference of Fertility, held under the auspices of the National Committee on Maternal Health,* edited by Earl T. Engle (Princeton, NJ: Princeton University Press, 1946), 232; Wilfred J. Finegold, *Artificial Insemination,* 1st ed. (Springfield, IL: Charles C. Thomas, 1964), 36; and Seymour and Koerner, "Medicolegal Aspects," 1533.

55. Weisman, "Selection of Donors," 142–44.

56. Clintie Winfrey Kenney, "Artificial Insemination," *American Mercury* 66 (1948): 402–3.

57. Dickinson, "Artificial Impregnation," 147; Alan F. Guttmacher, "The Role of Artificial Insemination in the Treatment of Sterility," *Journal of the American Medical Association* 120 (Oct. 10, 1942): 443; Weisman, "Studies on Human Artificial Insemination," 127; Guttmacher et al., "The Use of Donors," 270; and Frances I. Seymour and Alfred Koerner, "Artificial Insemination: Present Status in the United States as Shown by a Recent Survey," *Journal of the American Medical Association* 116 (June 21, 1941): 2747.

58. Schellen, *Artificial Insemination,* 124–25.

59. Dickinson, "Artificial Impregnation," 144.

60. "Proxy Fathers," *Time,* Sept. 26, 1938, 28; Ed Neff, "Fathers Corps Is Formed to Aid Childless," *Washington Herald,* Sept. 13, 1938; Thomas R. Henry, "Gene Register Planned Here," *Washington Star,* Sept. 13, 1938; Memorandum dated Nov. 12, 1938, by David V. MacCauley, 1, Special Collections Research Center,

Georgetown University, Washington, DC. Cf. Daniels and Golden, "Procreative Compounds," 10–11; and Susan E. Lederer, *Flesh and Blood: Organ Transplantation and Blood Transfusion in Twentieth-Century America* (New York: Oxford University Press, 2008), 92.

61. Schellen, *Artificial Insemination,* 122; and Finegold, *Artificial Insemination,* 67.

62. Schellen, *Artificial Insemination,* 122; and Sanitary Code of the City of New York, as amended Feb. 10, 1948, Article 7, Section 112, 79–80.

63. Neff, "Fathers Corps."

64. Kevles, *In the Name of Eugenics,* 251–52.

65. R. T. Seashore, "Artificial Impregnation," *Minnesota Medicine* 21 (1938): 643.

66. Clair E. Folsome, "The Status of Artificial Insemination: A Critical Review," *American Journal of Obstetrics and Gynecology* 45 (June 1943): 923–24.

67. Seymour and Koerner, "Medicolegal Aspect," 1533.

68. Augustin Derby, "Family Relations and Persons," *Annual Survey of American Law* 1942 (1942): 773, 784; Susan Froelich Appleton, "Presuming Women: Revisiting the Presumption of Legitimacy in the Same-Sex Couples Era," *Boston University Law Review* 86 (2006): 231–33; and Naomi Cahn, *Test Tube Families: Why the Fertility Market Needs Legal Regulation* (New York: New York University Press, 2009), 74–75.

69. Derby, "Family Relations," 778; and Joanna L. Grossman and Lawrence M. Friedman, *Inside the Castle: Law and the Family in 20th Century America* (Princeton, NJ: Princeton University Press, 2011), 287–88.

70. Orford v. Orford, [1921] 49 O.L.R. 15; J. C. Schock, "The Legal Status of the Semi-Adopted," *Dickinson Law Review* 41 (1941–42): 275; and Sidney B. Schatkin, "Artificial Insemination and Illegitimacy," *New York Law Journal* 113 (1945): 2432.

71. Guttmacher, "The Role of Artificial Insemination," 445; and Alan F. Guttmacher, "A Physician's Credo for Artificial Insemination," *Western Journal of Surgery, Obstetrics and Gynecology* 50 (July 1942): 359.

72. Alan F. Guttmacher, "The Legitimacy of Artificial Insemination," *Human Fertility* 11 (1946): 17.

73. " 'Ghost' Fathers," 16.

74. Guttmacher, "A Physician's Credo," 358.

75. Kleegman, "Practical and Ethical Aspects," 114, 116; and Sophia J. Kleegman, "Therapeutic Donor Insemination," *Fertility and Sterility* 5 (1954): 20.

76. Schellen, *Artificial Insemination,* 121.

77. Guttmacher, "Physician's Credo," 358; and Alan Guttmacher, "Artificial Insemination: Genetic, Legal, and Ethical Implications: A Symposium," *Fertility and Sterility* 9 (1958–59): 368–75.

78. Schellen, *Artificial Insemination,* 153.

79. Ibid., 161–62; and Guttmacher et al., "Use of Donors," 267.

80. Dickinson, "Artificial Impregnation," 141.

81. "Editor's Foreword," to Enos J. Perry, ed., *The Artificial Insemination of Farm Animals*, 4th rev. ed. (New Brunswick, NJ: Rutgers University Press, 1968), vii.

82. Enos J. Perry, "Historical Background," in *The Artificial Insemination of Farm Animals*, edited by Enos J. Perry (New Brunswick, NJ: Rutgers University Press, 1945), 6–7; and J. W. Bartlett, "Artificial Insemination of Dairy Cattle," in Engle, *Problem of Fertility*, 213.

83. Weisman, *Spermatozoa and Sterility*, 173.

84. Perry, "Editor's Foreword," viii.

85. B. J. Luyet and P. M. Gehenio, *Life and Death at Low Temperatures* (Normandy, MO: Biodynamica, 1940), 31–34, 220–21; R. G. Bunge and J. K. Sherman, "Fertilizing Capacity of Frozen Human Spermatozoa," *Nature* 172 (Oct. 24, 1953): 767; and C. Polge, A. V. Smith, and A. S. Parkes, "Revival of Spermatozoa after Vitrification and Dehydration at Low Temperatures," *Nature* 164 (Oct. 15, 1949): 666.

86. Perry, "Historical Background," 8–9.

87. "Death Held No Bar to Being a Father," *New York Times,* Aug. 15, 1951.

88. J. K. Sherman, "Freezing and Freeze-Drying of the Human Spermatozoa," *Fertility and Sterility* 5 (1954): 357–71; Bunge and Sherman, "Fertilizing Capacity of Frozen Human Spermatozoa," 767; Jerome K. Sherman, "Freezing and Freeze-Drying of Human Spermatozoa," Ph.D. dissertation, University of Iowa, 1954; and Jerome K. Sherman, personal communication, Aug. 19, 2011 (hereafter "Sherman Interview").

89. William C. Keettel et al., "Reports of Pregnancies in Infertile Couples," *Journal of the American Medical Association* 160 (Jan. 14, 1956): 104; May, *Barren in the Promised Land,* 43–44; and Marsh and Ronner, *Empty Cradle,* 183–89.

90. R. G. Bunge, W. C. Keettel, and J. K. Sherman, "Clinical Use of Frozen Semen," *Fertility and Sterility* 5 (1954): 520–29.

91. Bunge and Sherman, "Fertilizing Capacity."

92. J. K. Sherman and R. G. Bunge, "Observations on Preservation of Human Spermatozoa at Low Temperatures," *Proceedings of the Society of Experimental Biology and Medicine* 82 (1953): 688.

93. Raymond Bunge to Dr. N. Alcock, Feb. 24, 1953, Correspondence "A," 1950–63, Box 1, Papers of Raymond Bunge, RG 99.0002, University of Iowa Archives, University of Iowa Libraries, Iowa City, IA (hereafter "Bunge Papers").

94. Bill Toran, "Fatherhood after Death Has Now Been Proved Possible," *Cedar Rapids (IA) Gazette,* Apr. 9, 1954.

95. William L. Laurence, "Science in Review," *New York Times,* Nov. 29, 1959; H. J. Muller, *Out of the Night: A Biologist's View of the Future* (New York: Vanguard Press, 1935), 111; H. J. Muller, "Human Evolution by Voluntary Choice of Germ Plasm," *Science* 134 (Sept. 8, 1961): 643–49; and Daniels and Golden, 'Procreative Compounds," 13–14.

96. Jerome K. Sherman curriculum vitae, dated Feb. 22, 1996 (copy in author's possession); Steve Maravetz, "Baby-Making Breakthrough," *Iowa Alumni Quarterly* 51 (1998): 29; and S. J. Behrman and Y. Sawada, "Heterologous and Homologous Inseminations with Human Semen Frozen and Stored in a Liquid-nitrogen Refrigerator," *Fertility and Sterility* 17 (1966): 457–66.

97. Swanson, "The Birth of the Sperm Bank," 258–61, 267–69.

98. Thurston A. Shell, "Artificial Insemination—Legal and Related Problems," *University of Florida Law Review* 8 (1955): 315 (quoting personal letter from Senator Root to author).

99. Finegold, *Artificial Insemination,* 1st ed., 68.

100. "Test Tube Baby Claim Puzzles Law," *Washington Post and Times Herald,* Aug. 11, 1954; "Man in Paternity Suit Gets Right to Fight Back: Court Permits Counteraction Stating That Child Involved Is Test Tube Baby," *Los Angeles Times,* Feb. 1, 1956; "Woman Tells Judge Test Tube Act Not Adultery," *Chicago Daily Tribune,* Dec. 6, 1957; "Brooklyn Wife Loses; Husband Gets Divorce in Birth Donor Case," *New York Times,* Mar. 1, 1958; and "Grandparents Fight for Test-Tube Babies," *Los Angeles Times,* Mar. 11, 1960.

101. Complaint in Chancery for Divorce, Mary B. Doornbos v. George Doornbos, Superior Court of Cook County, Chancery, No. 54 S. 14981, Sept. 20, 1954.

102. Petition for Declaratory Decree, *Doornbos v. Doornbos,* Oct. 20, 1954.

103. Answer of Defendant to Petition of Plaintiff for Declaratory Decree, *Doornbos v. Doornbos,* Oct. 29, 1954.

104. "Hits Artificial Birth as Act of Adultery," *Chicago Tribune,* Oct. 30, 1954; " 'Test Tube' Baby Ruling," *New York Times,* Dec. 14, 1954; "Mother Wins Divorce," *New York Times,* Jan. 19, 1955; Robert Goldenstein, "Are Test-Tube Babies Legal?," *Independent Press Telegram* (Long Beach, CA), Jan. 9, 1955; and "Obituary: Gibson E. Gorman, Jurist in Chicago," *New York Times,* Jan. 8, 1956.

105. Declaratory Judgment, *Doornbos v. Doornbos,* Dec. 13, 1954.

106. Motion to Vacate, *Doornbos v. Doornbos,* Feb. 16, 1955.

107. Decree for Divorce, *Doornbos v. Doornbos,* Jan 21, 1955; and Doornbos v. Doornbos, 12 Ill. App. 2d 473, 139 N.E. 2d 844 (1956).

108. J. D. Ratcliff, "Artificial Insemination—Has It Made Happy Homes?," *Reader's Digest,* June 1955, 77–80 (reprinted from *Women's Home Companion,* Mar. 1955).

109. "Our Two Test Tube Babies," *Coronet,* Mar. 1956, 66–69.

110. Daniel Lang, "Artificial Insemination—Legitimate or Illegitimate?," *McCall's,* May 1955, 33, 60, 64.

111. Norma Lee Browning, "The Tragedy of Test Tube Babies," *Chicago Tribune,* Oct. 12, 1958.

112. Kleegman, "Practical and Ethical Aspects," 114–15.

113. Bunge to Sophia Kleegman, Feb. 21, 1962, Correspondence "K" 1952–62, Box 2, Bunge Papers.

114. Kleegman, "Practical and Ethical Aspects," 118.

115. John A. Osmundsen, "Deep-Cold Storage Is Successful in Artificial-Insemination Tests," *New York Times,* Sept. 5, 1963; "Frozen Sperm Gives Babies to 4 Women," *Los Angeles Times,* Sept. 8, 1963; and J. K. Sherman, "Improved Methods of Preservation of Human Spermatozoa by Freezing and Freeze-Drying," *Fertility and Sterility* 14 (1963): 49–64.

116. Lloyd Shepard, "Life in the Deep Freeze," *Parade Magazine,* July 19, 1964.

117. Ruth Winter, "Babies to Order," *Charleston (WV) Gazette,* Mar. 30, 1965, *Lima (OH) News,* Mar. 31, 1965, and elsewhere.

118. Finegold, *Artificial Insemination,* 1st ed., 111.

119. Wilfred J. Finegold, "Preface to the Second Edition," *Artificial Insemination,* 2d ed., (Springfield, IL: Charles C. Thomas, 1976).

120. Donald A. Goss, "Current Status of Artificial Insemination with Donor Semen," *American Journal of Obstetrics and Gynecology* 122 (1975): 246, 248.

121. J. K. Sherman, "Synopsis of the Use of Frozen Human Semen since 1964: State of the Art of Human Semen Banking," *Fertility and Sterility* 24 (1973): 399.

122. Swanson, "Birth of the Sperm Bank," 249, 271.

123. Peter Gorner, "Sperm Banks—Fatherhood on Ice," *Chicago Tribune,* Nov. 18, 1972; and John Lundquist, "Frozen Sperm Preserved in St. Paul," *Brainerd (MN) Daily Dispatch,* Aug. 25, 1971.

124. Paul R. Erlich, *The Population Bomb* (New York: Ballantine Books, 1968).

125. Boyce Rensberger, "Sperm Banks: From the Day of Deposit—A Lien on the Future," *New York Times,* Aug. 22, 1971; and Mark S. Frankel, *The Public Policy Dimensions of Artificial Insemination and Human-Semen Cryobanking,* Monograph No. 18 (Washington, DC: Program of Policy Studies in Science and Technology, George Washington University, 1973), 1n4.

126. Rudy Maxa, "The Sterilization of the American Male," *Washington Post,* Nov. 21, 1971; "First of 'Frozen Sperm Banks' Open," *Independent Press-Telegram* (Long Beach, CA), Dec. 16, 1971; and May, *Barren in the Promised Land,* 182–84, 199–201.

127. Boyce Rensberger, "2 Banks for Freezing Human Sperm Planned in Midtown, with Services Available to Public," *New York Times,* Aug. 18, 1971.

128. "Vasectomies Breed Banks," *Star News* (Pasadena, CA), Aug. 26–27, 1971; "First of 'Frozen Sperm Banks' Open"; "Parenthood by Remote Control," editorial, *Des Moines (IA) Register,* July 2, 1971; and "Sperm Bank Plan Ready," *Anderson (IN) Daily Bulletin,* Aug. 19, 1971.

129. "Frozen Sperm Preserved in St. Paul," *Brainerd (MN) Daily Dispatch,* Aug. 25, 1971.

130. Constance Holden, "Sperm Banks Multiply as Vasectomies Gain Popularity," *Science* 176 (Apr. 1972): 32.

131. "First of 'Frozen Sperm Banks' Open."

132. Frankel, *Public Policy Dimensions,* 10.

133. Michigan Sperm Bank, Division of International Cryogenics, Inc., "History of Frozen Semen," 3–5 (undated), Papers of Senator Connie Binsfeld, Archives of Michigan, Michigan Historical Center, Lansing, MI (hereafter Binsfeld Papers). For founding date, see http://www.internationalcryo.com/, last viewed Apr. 11, 2013.

134. Frankel, *Public Policy Dimensions,* 10; and Skip Ferderberg, "Sperm Bank Solves Many Infertility Problems," *Los Angeles Times,* Nov. 4, 1973.

135. Cappy Miles Rothman, "Clinical Aspects of Sperm Banking," letter to editor, *Urology* 14 (July 1979): 105.

136. Maravetz, "Baby-Making Breakthrough"; and Sherman Interview.

137. Rene Almeling, interview with CryoCorp Founder, 2–3 (copy in possession of the author), quoted in Almeling, *Sex Cells,* 31–32.

138. Dorothy Oliver, "Vasectomy Topic of Conference," *Chicago Herald,* Oct. 21, 1971.

139. "Frozen Sperm Preserved in St. Paul."

140. Finegold, *Artificial Insemination,* 1st ed., 34–35.

141. Howard Miller, "Fact Finder," *Fresno Bee,* Nov. 8, 1971; and Finegold, *Artificial Insemination,* 2d ed., 180, 184.

142. Edward T. Tyler, "The Clinical Use of Frozen Semen Banks," *Fertility and Sterility* 24 (Mar. 1973): 414.

143. Sherman, "Synopsis of the Use of Frozen Human Semen," 401; Frankel, *Public Policy Dimensions,* 5–6; and E. Steinberger, Luis J. Rodriguez-Rigau, and Keith D. Smith, "Comparison of Results of AID with Fresh and Frozen Semen," in *Human Artificial Insemination and Semen Preservation,* edited by Georges David and Wendel S. Price (New York: Plenum Press, 1980), 283–94.

144. Keettel et al., "Report of Pregnancies," 104.

145. K. D. Smith and Emil Steinberger, "Survival of Spermatozoa in a Human Sperm Bank," *Journal of the American Medical Association* 223 (Feb. 12, 1973): 774–77; and K. D. Smith, D. R. Stultz, and Emil Steinberger, "Effects of Long-Term Storage of Human Spermatozoa in Liquid Nitrogen," in *Aging Gametes,* edited by R. J. Blandan (Basel: Karger, 1975), 265–77.

146. Stephen D. Mumford, *Vasectomy Counseling* (San Francisco: San Francisco Press, 1977), 66.

147. Michigan Sperm Bank, "History of Frozen Semen," 5–6.

148. Frankel, *Public Policy Dimensions,* 7.

149. Richard D. Amelar and Lawrence Dubin, "Frozen Sperm—A Poor Form of Fertility Insurance," *Urology* 14 (July 1979): 53–54.

150. Finegold, *Artificial Insemination,* 2d ed., 104.

151. Letters to Edward Tyler, dated Oct. 13 and Oct. 20, 1953, Nov. 27, 1953, Box 2, Correspondence "T," 1953–65, Bunge Papers; Edward T. Tyler, "Clinical Use of

Frozen Sperm Banks," 24 (1973): 413; and Almeling, interview with CryoCorp Founder, 2.

152. Martin Curie-Cohen, Lesleigh Luttrell, and Sander Shapiro, "Current Practice of Artificial Insemination by Donor in the United States," *New England Journal of Medicine* 300 (Mar. 15, 1979): 586–87.

153. Stuart Bergman, Stuart Howards, and Warren Sanger, "Practical Aspects of Banking Patient's Semen for Future Artificial Insemination," *Urology* 13 (1979): 409.

154. Harlyn Aizley, *Buying Dad: One Woman's Search for the Perfect Sperm Donor* (Los Angeles: Alyson, 2003), title.

155. California Cryobank, prices as of January 2013, http://www.cryobank.com /Services/Pricing/, last viewed Apr. 8, 2013.

156. California Cryobank, http://www.spermbank.com/newdonors/index.cfm ?ID=4, last viewed Apr. 8, 2013; Almeling, interview with CryoCorp Founder, 10, quoted in Almeling, *Sex Cells*, 72; and Spar, *Baby Business*, 39.

157. Daniels and Golden, "Procreative Compounds," 6–8; Moore, *Sperm Counts*, 108–10; and Almeling, *Sex Cells*, 33–34.

158. Daniel Wikler and Norma J. Wikler, "Turkey-Baster Babies: The Demedi-calization of Artificial Insemination," *Milbank Quarterly* 69 (1991): 11.

159. Georgia Code Annotated, §43-34-42 (formerly 74–101.1).

160. Georgia Code Annotated, §19-7-21 (formerly 74–101.1).

161. Uniform Laws Annotated, Uniform Act on Parentage (1973), Section 5A.

162. Lori Andrews, *New Conceptions: A Consumer's Guide to the Newest Infertility Treatments, Including In Vitro Fertilization, Artificial Insemination, and Surrogate Motherhood* (New York: St. Martin's Press, 1984), 191–92, 300–301.

163. Rene Almeling, interview with Gametes, Inc. founder, 2 (copy in possession of author), quoted in Almeling, *Sex Cells*, 31.

164. G. J. Stewart et al., "Transmission of Human T-Cell Lymphotropic Virus Type III (HTLV III) by Artificial Insemination by Donor," *Lancet*, Sept. 14, 1985, 581–84.

165. U.S. Congress, Office of Technology Assessment, *Artificial Insemination Practice in the United States: Summary of a 1987 Survey—Background Paper*, OTA-BP-BA-48 (Washington, DC: U.S. Government Printing Office, 1988), 10.

166. American Fertility Society, "Revised New Guidelines for the Use of Semen-Donor Insemination," *Fertility and Sterility* 49 (1988): 211.

167. Almeling, *Sex Cells*, 49; and Daniels and Golden, "Procreative Compounds," 16.

168. May, *Barren in the Promised Land*, 153–58; and Resolve, www.resolve.org, last viewed June 10, 2009.

169. Frankel, *Public Policy Dimensions*, 12–13.

170. Finegold, *Artificial Insemination*, 1st ed., 31.

171. Boston Women's Health Book Collective, *Our Bodies, Ourselves: A Book by and for Women* (New York: Simon and Schuster, 1973), 94–96; and Susan Robinson

and H. F. Pizer, *Having a Baby without a Man: The Woman's Guide to Alternative Insemination* (New York: Simon and Schuster, 1985), 15–16.

172. Susan Stern, "Lesbian Insemination," *CoEvolution Quarterly,* Summer 1980, 108–17.

173. Sarah and Mary Anonymous, *Woman Controlled Conception* (San Francisco: Womanshare Books, 1979).

174. Boston Women's Health Book Collective, *The New Our Bodies, Ourselves: A Book by and for Women* (New York: Simon & Schuster, 1984), 318–19.

175. Julie A. Waltz, *Artificial Insemination and the Unmarried Woman: Legal Rights and Responsibilities* (Aiken, SC: Opportunity Press, 1987), 3.

176. Wikler and Wikler, "Turkey-Baster Babies," 18–20; and Laura Mamo, *Queering Reproduction: Achieving Pregnancy in the Age of Technosemen* (Durham, NC: Duke University Press, 2007), 44–47.

177. Robinson and Pizer, *Having a Baby without a Man,* 16, 118–20, 110–11, 140–48, 150–62.

178. "First Test-Tube Baby," *Time,* July 31, 1978, 58–69.

179. Marsh and Ronner, *Empty Cradle,* 237–41.

180. Spar, *Baby Business,* 2–3, 28–29.

181. Wikler and Wikler, "Turkey-Baster Babies," 13–16; and Swanson, "'Adultery by Doctor,'" 127.

182. Andrews, *New Conceptions,* title.

183. U.S. Congress, Office of Technology Assessment, *Artificial Insemination Practice in the United States,* 11.

184. Ibid.

185. Curie-Cohen, Luttrell, and Shapiro, "Current Practice," 586.

186. Almeling, interview with Gametes, Inc. founder, 9, quoted in Almeling, *Sex Cells,* 32.

187. Andrews, *New Conceptions,* 175.

188. Memorandum from Nancy Shafer, Office of Majority Counsel, Senate, State of Michigan, to Senator Connie Binsfeld regarding interview with Mary Ann Brown (dated Feb. 27, 1990), 3, Binsfeld Papers.

189. "Sperm Bank for Geniuses: Artificial Insemination, Ethics and Genetics," flyer advertising Symposium, Sept. 23, 1982, New York City, copy in Box 185, Folder 2, MSC 552, Papers of Joshua Lederberg, History of Medicine Division, National Library of Medicine Archives, Bethesda, MD; David Plotz, *The Genius Factory: The Curious History of the Nobel Prize Sperm Bank* (New York: Random House, 2005), 3–5, 46, 74–75 and generally; and Tober, "Semen as Gift," 147–48.

190. Almeling, interview with Gametes, Inc. founder, 9–10, quoted in Almeling, *Sex Cells,* 33. See also Daniels and Golden, "Procreative Compounds," 14.

191. Memorandum from Nancy Shafer, Office of the Majority Counsel, State of Michigan, to Senator Connie Binsfeld regarding interview with Dr. Allen Menge (dated Feb. 8, 1990), Binsfeld Papers.

192. Almeling, interview with Gametes, Inc. founder, 10, quoted in Almeling, *Sex Cells*, 33.

193. Daniels, *Exposing Men*, 91.

194. See, for example, California Cryobank online catalogue: http://www .cryobank.com/Search.aspx, last viewed Feb. 23, 2013.

195. California Cryobank, http://www.cryobank.com/Services/Pricing/, last viewed Apr. 8, 2013; and Spar, *Baby Business*, 37, 39.

196. Moore, *Sperm Counts*, 106; Lisa Jean Moore and Matthew Schmidt, "On the Construction of Male Differences: Marketing Variations in Technosemen," *Men and Masculinities* 1 (1999): 339; and Tober, "Semen as Gift," 339.

197. http://www.spermbank.com/newdonors/index.cfm?ID=1, last viewed Oct. 10, 2013.

198. Daniels and Golden, "Procreative Compounds," 19; and Almeling, *Sex Cells*, 54–55.

199. Daniels and Golden, "Procreative Compounds," 17.

200. Tober, "Semen as Gift," 151; and Aizley, *Buying Dad*, 27.

201. Spar, *Baby Business*, 4.

202. M. L. P. van der Hoorn et al., "Clinical and Immunologic Aspects of Egg Donation Pregnancies: A Systematic Review," *Human Reproduction Update* 16 (2010): 704–12; and Almeling, *Sex Cells*, 64–68, 89–98.

203. Almeling, *Sex Cells*, 69–70, 120.

204. Ibid., 127–33. See also Ken R. Daniels and Gillian M. Lewis, "Donor Insemination: The Gifting and Selling in Semen," *Social Science of Medicine* 42 (1996): 1521; and Monica Konrad, "Ova Donation and Symbols of Substance: Some Variations on the Theme of Sex, Gender and the Partible Body," *Journal of the Royal Anthropological Institute* 4 (1998): 643.

205. Center for Human Reproduction, http://www.centerforhumanreprod.com /egg_donation.html., last viewed Nov. 14, 2013.

206. Almeling, *Sex Cells*, 168–74.

207. Lederer, *Flesh and Blood*, 83.

208. Herbert G. Harlan, "This Business of Selling Blood," *Hygeia*, May 1929, 470.

209. B. Raymond Hoobler, "An Experiment in the Collection of Human Milk for Hospital and Dispensary Uses," *Archives of Pediatrics* 31 (1914): 171–73.

210. Spar, *Baby Business*, 42–43.

211. American Society for Reproductive Medicine Ethics Committee, "Financial Incentives in Recruitment of AR Egg Providers," *Fertility and Sterility* 82, Supp. 1 (2004): S240–S244 (issued by committee in 2000); and American Society for Reproductive Medicine Ethics Committee, "Financial Compensation of Oocyte Donors," *Fertility and Sterility* 88 (2007): 305.

212. Almeling, *Sex Cells*, 77–78, 128–29.

CONCLUSION

Epigraph: Craigslist, http://sacramento.craigslist.org/bab/4181893111.html, last viewed Nov. 14, 2013.

1. For example, Liz Kowalczyk, "Vt. Woman Burned with Lye Gets Face Transplant," *Boston Globe,* Feb. 28, 2013; Daniel Woolls, "Hospital Claims First Full-Face Transplant," *Boston Globe,* Apr. 24, 2010; and Dan Nephin, "Patient in Nation's First Double Hand Transplant Recovering Well," *Boston Globe,* May 9, 2009.

2. Jennifer M. Vagel, "Putting the 'Product' in Reproduction: The Viability of Products Liability Action for Genetically Defective Sperm," *Pepperdine Law Review* 38 (2010–11): 1175, 1219–21.

3. 42 U.S.C. §274e(a)(Dec. 21, 2007), first enacted as Pub L. 98-507, Title III, §301, Oct. 19, 1984.

4. Kimberly D. Krawiec, "Altruism and Intermediation in the Market for Babies," *Washington & Lee Law Review* 66 (2009): 203; Linda C. Fentiman, "Marketing Mothers' Milk: The Commodification of Breastfeeding and the New Markets for Breast Milk and Infant Formula," *Nevada Law Review* 10 (2009): 29, 32; Official Compilation of Codes, Rules and Regulations of the State of New York, Title 10 (Health), Part 52, Subpart 52-9 (effective Feb. 24, 2007); and Cal. Health & Safety Codes §§1635–1635.2, 1639–1641.1.

5. Bridget Crawford, "Our Bodies, Our (Tax) Selves," *Virginia Tax Review* 31 (2011–12): 695, 703–5; and Stephen Pemberton, *The Bleeding Disease: Hemophilia and the Unintended Consequences of Medical Progress* (Baltimore: Johns Hopkins University Press 2011), 169–72.

6. Human Milk Banking Association of America, https://www.hmbana.org/milk-bank-locations, last viewed Apr. 3, 2013; Milkshare, http://milkshare.forumotion.com/, last viewed Apr. 3, 2013; Eats on Feets, http://www.eatsonfeets.org/, last viewed July 13, 2013; and Human Milk for Human Babies, http://hm4hb.net/, last viewed July 13, 2013.

7. Only the Breast, http://www.onlythebreast.com/, last viewed July 13, 2013.

8. Judy Dutton, "Liquid Gold: The Booming Market for Breast Milk," *Wired,* May 17, 2011, http://www.wired.com/magazine/2011/05/ff_milk/all/; and Jenny Lang, Frugal Guru, http://frugalguruguide.com/how-to-make-money-selling-breastmilk/, posted June 20, 2013, last viewed Nov. 14, 2013.

9. "Wet Nurse in Eastern PA," posted Sept. 14, 2010, Milkshare, http://milkshare.forumotion.com/t1747-wet-nurse-in-eastern-pa, last viewed Apr. 4, 2013; and "Wanted: Babysitter/Wet Nurse in DFW," posted Feb. 25, 2012, Milkshare, http://milkshare.forumotion.com/t4503-wanted-babysitter-wet-nurse-in-dfw, last viewed Apr. 4, 2013.

10. "What to Do with Leftover Frozen Sperm?," Mothering, Feb. 14, 2010, http://www.mothering.com/community/t/1195190/what-to-do-with-leftover-frozen -sperm, last viewed Mar. 14, 2013.

11. Known Donor Registry, http://knowndonorregistry.com/; Amber D. Abbasi, "The Curious Case of Trent Arsenault: Questioning FDA Regulatory Authority over Private Sperm Donation," unpublished manuscript, Aug. 9, 2012, electronic copy available at http://papers.ssrn.com/sol3/papers.cfm?abstract _id=2129437; Harlyn Aizley, *Buying Dad: One Woman's Search for the Perfect Sperm Donor* (Los Angeles: Alyson, 2003), 9–13; and Laura Mamo, *Queering Reproduction: Achieving Pregnancy in the Age of Technosemen* (Durham, NC: Duke University Press, 2007), 97–110.

12. "Sickle Cell Sufferer Seeks Kidney Donor," My Central Jersey, Mar. 14, 2013, http://www.mycentraljersey.com/article/20130317/NJOPINION0202 /303170005/Sickle-cell-sufferer-seeks-kidney-donor, last viewed Apr. 4, 2013; "Emanu-El Family Seeks Kidney Donor for Son," J Weekly, Mar. 21, 2013, http:// www.jweekly.com/article/full/68085/emanu-el-family-seeks-kidney-donor-for-son/, last viewed Apr. 4, 2013; and Nancy Scheper-Hughes, "Commodity Fetishism in Organs Trafficking," *Body and Society* 7 (2001): 31.

13. Alexander Chang et al., "Identifying Potential Kidney Donors Using Social Networking Web Sites," *Clinical Transplantation* 27 (2013): E320–26.

14. Living Donors Online, http://www.livingdonorsonline.org/index.htm, last viewed Nov. 14, 2013.

15. For example, Martha M. Ertman and Joan C. Williams, "Introduction: Freedom, Equality, and the Many Futures of Commodification," 1; Joan Williams and Viviana Zelizer, "To Commodify or Not to Commodify: That Is Not the Question," 693, both in *Rethinking Commodification: Cases and Readings in Law and Culture,* edited by Martha M. Ertman and Joan C. Williams (New York: New York University Press, 2005); Margaret Jane Radin, *Contested Commodities: The Trouble with Trade in Sex, Children, Body Parts and Other Things* (Cambridge, MA: Harvard University Press, 1996); Martha M. Ertman, "What's Wrong with a Parenthood Market? A New and Improved Theory of Commodification," *North Carolina Law Review* 82 (2003): 1; and Anne-Marie Farrell, *The Politics of Blood: Ethics, Innovation and the Regulation of Risk* (New York: Cambridge University Press, 2012).

16. Bertram M. Bernheim, *Adventure in Blood Transfusion* (New York: Smith & Durrell, 1942), 86, 165.

17. Michele Goodwin, "Formalism and the Legal Status of Body Parts," *University of Chicago Law Forum* 2006 (2006): 317; and Crawford, "Our Bodies," 695. There are exceptions to this legal trend, including, for example, Hecht v. Superior Court, 20 Cal. Rptr. 2d 275, 275 (Ct. App. 1993); and Kurchner v. State Farm Fire & Casualty Co., 858 So. 2d 1220, 1221 (Fla. Dist. Ct. App. 2003).

18. Moore v. Regents of the University of California, 51 Cal.3d 120 (1990).

19. The court did find that the patient might be able to make a claim for damages against his doctor for violation of his right to informed consent. *Moore,* 51 Cal.3d at 132–33.

20. Crawford, "Our Bodies," 709–10.

21. Scheper-Hughes, "Commodity Fetishism," 34, 42–52.

22. Madhavi Sunder and Margaret Jane Radin, "Foreword: The Subject and Object of Commodification," in Ertman and Williams, *Rethinking Commodification,* 1.

23. Leon E. Mermod and Hazel Bond, "The Blood Bank of Hawaii," *Proceedings of Blood Bank Institute,* Dallas, TX, Nov. 17–19, 1948, 30; and Bernice Hemphill, *The Mother of Blood Banking: Irwin Memorial Blood Bank and the American Association of Blood Banks, 1944–1994,* interviews by Germaine LaBerge (Berkeley: Regional Oral History Office, Bancroft Library, University of California, 1998), title.

24. Hemphill, *Mother of Blood Banking,* 69.

25. Mark A. Levine et al. for the Ethical Force Program, "Improving Access to Health Care: A Consensus Ethical Framework to Guide Proposals for Reform," *Hastings Center Report,* Sept.–Oct. 2007, 15–16; and National Federation of Independent Business v. Sebelius, 132 S.Ct. 2566 (2012) (ruling on constitutionality of the Affordable Care Act).

26. Michele Goodwin, *Black Markets: The Supply and Demand of Body Parts* (New York: Cambridge University Press, 2006), 6–7 and throughout; and Arthur L. Caplan, "Obtaining and Allocating Organs for Transplantation," in *Human Organ Transplantation: Societal, Medical-Legal, Regulatory, and Reimbursement Issues,* edited by Dale H. Cowan, Jo Ann Kantorowitz, Jay Moskowitz, and Peter H. Rheinstein (Chicago: Health Administration Press, 1987), 5–17.

27. Clark C. Havighurst, "Trafficking in Human Blood: Titmuss (1970) and Products Liability," *Law and Contemporary Problems,* Summer 2009: 7; Clark C. Havighurst, "Legal Responses to the Problem of Poor-Quality Blood," in *Blood Policy: Issues and Alternatives,* edited by David B. Johnson (Washington, DC: American Enterprise Institute for Public Policy Research, 1977), 21; Reuben A. Kessel, "Transfused Blood, Serum Hepatitis, and the Coase Theorem," *Journal of Law and Economics* 17 (1974): 265; Douglas Starr, *Blood: An Epic History of Medicine and Commerce* (1998; New York: Perennial, 2002), 231–49, 260–65; Thomas H. Murray, "A Poisoned Gift: AIDS and Blood," in *A Disease of Society: Cultural and Institutional Responses to AIDS,* edited by Dorothy Nelkin, David P. Willis, and Scott V. Parris (Cambridge, UK: Cambridge University Press, 1991), 216–40; and Susan Resnik, *Blood Saga: Hemophilia, AIDS, and the Survival of a Community* (Berkeley: University of California Press, 1999), 113–36.

28. B. Raymond Hoobler, "An Experiment in the Collection of Human Milk for Hospital and Dispensary Uses," *Archives of Pediatrics* 31 (1914): 172–73.

29. E. H. L. Corwin, "Community Control of Professional Blood Donors," *New York State Journal of Medicine* 35 (1935): 319; and Bernheim, *Adventure in Blood Transfusion*, 76–78, 86.

30. Herbert A. Perkins, *Irwin Memorial Blood Bank: Transfusion AIDS and the Safety of the National Blood Supply*, vol. 5: *The AIDS Epidemic in San Francisco: The Medical Response, 1981–1984*, interviews by Sally Smith Hughes (Berkeley: Regional Oral History Office, Bancroft Library, University of California, 1997), 86–91.

31. Rene Almeling, *Sex Cells: The Medical Market in Eggs and Sperm* (Berkeley: University of California Press, 2011), 103–8.

32. Kieran J. Healy, *Last Best Gifts: Altruism and the Market for Human Blood and Organs* (Chicago: University of Chicago Press, 2006); and Almeling, *Sex Cells*.

33. State v. Shack, 58 N.J. 297, 303 (1971), quoted in Joseph W. Singer, *Property Law: Rules, Policies and Practices*, 4th ed. (New York: Aspen, 2006), xi.

Acknowledgments

In order for this book to exist as a commodity that can be traded in markets and found on library shelves, I relied on many generous gifts from family, friends, colleagues, and strangers.

Tackling the history of banking the body across twentieth-century America from the perspective of law and medicine would not have been possible without the pioneering work of scholars both legal and historical. Insightful and carefully researched books and articles about human milk, blood, semen, and tissues by historians of medicine Janet Golden, Susan Lederer, Margaret Marsh, Wanda Ronner, and Jacqueline Wolf provided a foundation for my thinking about body product banking. At meetings of the American Association for the History of Medicine and elsewhere, their generous support and encouragement through the years I worked on this project are much appreciated. My intellectual debts in the legal academy are too numerous to mention, but for the gifts of their scholarship I would like to particularly thank Gregory Alexander, who has thought deeply about the dialectical nature of property in the history of American law and society; Margaret Jane Radin, who theorized contested commodities in philosophy and law; Joseph Singer, who provided guidance from the printed page as I taught first-year property using his casebook; and Martha Ertman and Joan Williams, whose edited volume on commodification so productively combined disciplinary approaches to the topic.

For their careful and wise guidance in early stages of this project, I thank Allan Brandt, Nancy Cott, and Steven Shapin, each of whom read drafts and pushed me to consider the big picture. I also received crucial early support and suggestions about how to write history, how to write a book, and how to survive academia from

Ellen Bales, Mario Biagioli, Jen Clarke, Clare Keefe Coleman, Katja Guenther, Ben Hurlbut, Hannah Landecker, Deborah Levine, Daniel Margocsy, John Matthew, Everett Mendelsohn, Amber Musser, Sharrona Pearl, Chitra Ramalingam, Bill Rankin, Charles Rosenberg, Sarah Tracy, Elly Truitt, Conevery Bolton Valencius, Alex Wellerstein, Christine Wenc, and Nasser Zakariya. For reading chapters and/ or the entire manuscript in the later stages of the project, I am grateful to Rene Almeling, Justin Barr, Allan Brandt, Rashmi Dyal-Chand, Daniel Medwed, Charles Rosenberg, Judith Swanson, and Steven Wilf.

Throughout the years I researched this topic, I taxed the resources of many libraries and librarians. Thank you to the staff at Widener Library and the Schlesinger Library at Harvard University and to the research librarians at the Harvard Law School, Drexel University School of Law, and Northeastern University School of Law. I am deeply appreciative to all the staff at Northeastern's law library, who were always cheerful and helpful with my endless requests, and I want to particularly thank Lydia Lafionatis, Scott Akehurst-Moore, and Warren Yee for the many miracles they accomplished on my behalf. I relied on assistance from archivists across the United States, including several who graciously searched their collections and pulled documents for me when I was unable to visit in person. My thanks to the Evanston History Center, Evanston, Illinois; Special Collections Research Center, Georgetown University, Washington, D.C.; the California Historical Society, San Francisco; the California State Archives, Sacramento; the Michigan State Archives, Lansing; Mayo Clinic Historical Unit, Rochester, Minnesota; Center for the History of Medicine, Countway Library, Harvard Medical School, Boston; the University of Chicago Archives; University of Iowa Archives, Iowa City; the Historical Research Center, University of Arkansas for Medical Sciences, Little Rock; the National Library of Medicine, Bethesda, Maryland; and the Tufts New England Medical Center Archives, Tufts University Hirsh Health Sciences Library, Boston.

This project was enhanced by the generosity of individuals who shared materials with me not yet archived. Lois D. W. Arnold took time from a busy workday to share her extensive collection relating to milk banking in the late twentieth-century United States. Laraine Lockhart Borman gave me access to the early scrapbooks of the Mothers' Milk Bank Colorado. Rene Almeling shared her interviews with sperm bank founders. Dr. Jerome K. Sherman interrupted a vacation to share his memories of his early discoveries in freezing human sperm and of his long career in sperm banking, as well as documents from his collection.

I had the pleasure of working on this project at multiple institutions, at each of which I found stimulating colleagues and supportive administrators. At Harvard University, I would like to thank the faculty, graduate students, and staff of the History of Science Department, the participants in the history of women, gender, and sexuality workshop at the Center for the Humanities, as well as Terry Fisher, Morton Horwitz, Jed Shugerman, my fellow fellows, and the other legal historians at Harvard Law School, where I spent a year in residence as the Berger-Howe Legal History Fellow. At Drexel University, I would like to thank Dean Roger Dennis for research support and my colleagues at the School of Law, as well as Rose Corrigan and Amy Slaton, for many productive conversations. At Northeastern University School of Law, Deans Emily Spieler and Jeremy Paul each supported my research with funds and encouragement, and my work benefited from interactions with my terrific colleagues. At Northeastern I also received help from student researchers Kenneth Parker, Julianna Malogolowkin, and Leah Porter, and I had the great good fortune to have the assistance of Rick Doyon in all administrative matters. Rick daily provided gifts of his time, talent, and humor. In addition to research support from Harvard University Graduate School of Arts and Sciences, Drexel University School of Law, and Northeastern School of Law, I benefited from grants from the National Science Foundation, the Mellon Foundation, and the State Historical Society of Iowa.

I was able to hone my ideas about body commodification with students in my bioproperty seminar at Drexel and Northeastern. Over the years I wrestled with aspects of this project, I also benefited from the comments and questions from audiences at History of Science Society; Society for the History of Technology; American Association of the History of Medicine; the Berkshire Conference of Women Historians; the History of Science Department at Harvard University; the program in the history of science and medicine at Yale University; the history departments at the New Jersey Institute of Technology, Santa Clara University, and Worcester Polytechnic Institute; the Third International Congress on Donor Human Milk Banking; the Center for Nanotechnology, University of California–Santa Barbara; Feminist Legal Theory Collaborative Research Network conferences; legal history workshops at University of Virginia School of Law, Boston University School of Law, and Chicago-Kent Institute for Law; the Business History Conference; and the Epidemiology Conference, Department of Neonatology, Beth Israel Deaconess Hospital. My scholarship has also benefited from my participation in the Bodies/Embodiment Working Group, a joint discussion group of Northeastern University and Uppsala University.

This book is yet another production of the Independent Women Scholars Salon, which I thank for bringing me into its community of stimulating and supportive writers. The membership of IWSS during the gestation of this book—Lara Freidenfelds, Joy Harvey, Susan Lanzoni, Rachael Rosner, Conevery Bolton Valencius, and Nadine Weidman—have given me gifts without number of encouragement, practical advice, rewritten sentences, critical questions, good food, and good cheer. Every author should be so lucky as to have a group of independent women scholars at her back. Thank you again and again.

For her sharp pencil and clear thinking, my thanks to Joyce Seltzer, editor at Harvard University Press, and thanks also to assistant editor Brian Distelberg, whose calm organization kept me moving forward from book proposal to book.

I am fortunate in being able to thank my mother, Judith Swanson, and my father, James Swanson, for their unswerving support and sacrifice every step of the way. Thank you for setting me on the path of obsessive reading, library visits, and love of scholarship that ultimately led to this book. During the years I worked on this project, I received from both my parents and from my stepfather, John Mazzitello, the gifts of companionship, car rides, and meals as I traveled on book research. Mom, the first blood banker I ever met, also stepped in with moving assistance and an editor's eye at crucial moments. Thank you, Mom, Dad, and John. For countless hours of child care and wonderful meals, I also thank my mother-in-law, Vivian Taylor, who always believed the book would be finished.

I thank my beloved daughters, Lucy and Clarissa, for their tolerance of my travels and of my endless work on body banking. More than that, I thank them for the joy they bring me every day and for the never-ending reasons they provide to leave my desk and the library. A household of two professors, two daughters, one dog, and one hedgehog requires a lot of juggling, and I am grateful I married someone who has been a practiced juggler for years. To Wati, my fellow circus master, chauffeur, cook, and bottle washer—thank you for each and every day you have been by my side. The book would not have gotten finished without you—and the journey would have been a lot less fun.

Index